How the Financial Crisis and Great Recession Affected Higher Education

**A National Bureau
of Economic Research
Conference Report**

How the Financial Crisis and Great Recession Affected Higher Education

Edited by **Jeffrey R. Brown and Caroline M. Hoxby**

The University of Chicago Press

Chicago and London

Jeffrey R. Brown is the William G. Karnes Professor of Finance at the University of Illinois at Urbana-Champaign and a research associate of the National Bureau of Economic Research. Caroline M. Hoxby is the Scott and Donya Bommer Professor in Economics at Stanford University, a senior fellow of the Hoover Institution, and a research associate and director of the Economics of Education Program of the National Bureau of Economic Research.

The University of Chicago Press, Chicago 60637
The University of Chicago Press, Ltd., London
© 2015 by the National Bureau of Economic Research
All rights reserved. Published 2015.
Printed in the United States of America

24 23 22 21 20 19 18 17 16 15   1 2 3 4 5

ISBN-13: 978-0-226-20183-2   (cloth)
ISBN-13: 978-0-226-20197-9   (e-book)
DOI: 10.7208/chicago/9780226201979.001.0001

Library of Congress Cataloging-in-Publication Data

How the financial crisis and great recession affected higher education /
    edited by Jeffrey R. Brown and Caroline M. Hoxby.
        pages cm—(A National Bureau of Economic Research
    Conference report)
        ISBN 978-0-226-20183-2 (cloth : alk. paper)—ISBN 978-0-226-
    20197-9 (e-book) 1. Education, Higher—United States—Finance.
    2. Education and state—United States. 3. Global Financial Crisis,
    2008–2009. I. Brown, Jeffrey R. (Jeffrey Robert), 1968– II. Hoxby,
    Caroline Minter. III. Series: National Bureau of Economic Research
    conference report.
        LB2342.H574 2015
        379.1'180973—dc23
                                                          2014008637

♾ This paper meets the requirements of ANSI/NISO Z39.48-1992
(Permanence of Paper).

Relation of the Directors to the
Work and Publications of the
National Bureau of Economic Research

1. The object of the NBER is to ascertain and present to the economics profession, and to the public more generally, important economic facts and their interpretation in a scientific manner without policy recommendations. The Board of Directors is charged with the responsibility of ensuring that the work of the NBER is carried on in strict conformity with this object.

2. The President shall establish an internal review process to ensure that book manuscripts proposed for publication DO NOT contain policy recommendations. This shall apply both to the proceedings of conferences and to manuscripts by a single author or by one or more co-authors but shall not apply to authors of comments at NBER conferences who are not NBER affiliates.

3. No book manuscript reporting research shall be published by the NBER until the President has sent to each member of the Board a notice that a manuscript is recommended for publication and that in the President's opinion it is suitable for publication in accordance with the above principles of the NBER. Such notification will include a table of contents and an abstract or summary of the manuscript's content, a list of contributors if applicable, and a response form for use by Directors who desire a copy of the manuscript for review. Each manuscript shall contain a summary drawing attention to the nature and treatment of the problem studied and the main conclusions reached.

4. No volume shall be published until forty-five days have elapsed from the above notification of intention to publish it. During this period a copy shall be sent to any Director requesting it, and if any Director objects to publication on the grounds that the manuscript contains policy recommendations, the objection will be presented to the author(s) or editor(s). In case of dispute, all members of the Board shall be notified, and the President shall appoint an ad hoc committee of the Board to decide the matter; thirty days additional shall be granted for this purpose.

5. The President shall present annually to the Board a report describing the internal manuscript review process, any objections made by Directors before publication or by anyone after publication, any disputes about such matters, and how they were handled.

6. Publications of the NBER issued for informational purposes concerning the work of the Bureau, or issued to inform the public of the activities at the Bureau, including but not limited to the NBER Digest and Reporter, shall be consistent with the object stated in paragraph 1. They shall contain a specific disclaimer noting that they have not passed through the review procedures required in this resolution. The Executive Committee of the Board is charged with the review of all such publications from time to time.

7. NBER working papers and manuscripts distributed on the Bureau's web site are not deemed to be publications for the purpose of this resolution, but they shall be consistent with the object stated in paragraph 1. Working papers shall contain a specific disclaimer noting that they have not passed through the review procedures required in this resolution. The NBER's web site shall contain a similar disclaimer. The President shall establish an internal review process to ensure that the working papers and the web site do not contain policy recommendations, and shall report annually to the Board on this process and any concerns raised in connection with it.

8. Unless otherwise determined by the Board or exempted by the terms of paragraphs 6 and 7, a copy of this resolution shall be printed in each NBER publication as described in paragraph 2 above.

Contents

Preface

In the several years leading up to the financial crisis, there were moments when the finances of American postsecondary institutions seemed almost *too* good. The well-endowed institutions enjoyed high rates of return on their investments. The earnings allowed them to renovate their campuses, pursue costly scientific projects (like the human genome project), and offer increasingly generous financial aid. One of the editors of this volume (Hoxby) even recalls university leaders openly worrying about whether the large endowment returns could be spent as quickly as institutions were constrained to spend them.

Of course, everything was not rosy. Less well-endowed institutions worried about the widening gap between their resources and those of the richest institutions. Some colleges and universities that appeared to be doing well financially had actually committed themselves to a great deal of debt to finance building projects. Families often drew down their home equity to finance their children's college education—a procedure that would cause grave difficulties if house prices were to fall. Funding from the National Institutes of Health was in decline, causing much worry among universities that had invested heavily in medical research centers.

Nevertheless, the sky was sufficiently bright that the financial crisis and recession came as a shock to American higher education. The shock brought to the surface many economic, especially financial, issues in higher education. We believe that the surfacing of these issues created a unique opportunity to bring together economists who study finance and economists who study higher education. James Poterba, president of the NBER, was especially prescient in seeing the chances for great collaborations and intellectual arbitrage. We are especially glad to report that not only did this volume bring together economists who might otherwise speak infrequently but it brought economists and practitioners together.

After putting our ideas together, we approached the Spencer Foundation for support and obtained not only funding crucial to the project but also the astute advice of its president, Michael McPherson. We are immensely grateful for the Spencer Foundation being not just a funder but a true intellectual partner in this and many other research "enterprises" in the economics of education.

The NBER is fortunate in having very strong researchers both in finance and in higher education, so we had no difficulty turning our vision for the volume into a reality. Many conversations lay behind the chapters, with the most formative occurring at an authors' preconference held early in 2012. Several months later, we enlarged the discussion at a second conference that included higher education leaders and endowment managers. We describe the highly productive conversations that occurred there in the introduction to this volume. The second conference created relationships between university leaders and NBER researchers that have only grown since. We believe that these relationships will both accelerate and "ground" the NBER's studies of higher education for years to come.

We are grateful to all those who participated in the second conference. More than anything, they brought refreshing doses of reality and constructive criticism with them. We are immensely grateful for their insights, and we can personally vouch that they improved our own contributions to this book. We gratefully acknowledge the discussants: Lawrence Bacow, president emeritus of Tufts University; Nancy Cantor, chancellor of Rutgers University-Newark; John Etchemendy, provost of Stanford University; Scott Evans, senior advisor, TIAA-CREF; John Griswold, executive director of the Commonfund Institute; Stanley Ikenberry, former president of the University of Illinois, and professor and senior scientist at the Center for the Study of Higher Education at Pennsylvania State University; Mike Knetter, president and chief executive officer of the University of Wisconsin Foundation; Jane Mendillo, president and chief executive officer of Harvard Management Company; Morton Schapiro, president of Northwestern University; and Scott Wise, president and chief investment officer of Covariance Capital Management. For their lively insights that improved one or more chapters, we also thank Seth Alexander (MIT), Linda Bell (Haverford), Charles Clotfelter (Duke), Ronald Ehrenberg (Cornell), Alan Garber (Harvard), Susan Hockfield (MIT), Chris Kaiser (MIT), Kirk Kolenbrander (MIT), Tim Nguyen (University of Connecticut), Morton Schapiro (Northwestern), Michael Smith (Harvard), Luis Viceira (Harvard), and Burton Weisbrod (Northwestern).

We gratefully recognize the NBER working group in higher education which was, for many years, splendidly led by Charles Clotfelter before becoming part of the NBER's Economics of Education Program in 2009.

The discussions and research collaborations among the members of this group transformed the economics of higher education from something of a sleepy backwater to a booming area of research that employs vast administrative data sets and frontier methods. Finally, we, the editors, thank our stars every day for the great NBER leadership, publications staff, conference staff, and other staff who make the NBER an incredibly productive place to start and scientifically advance any discussion.

Introduction

Jeffrey R. Brown and Caroline M. Hoxby

Economists often find research opportunities in times of crises. Although no one would propose to have a financial crisis and major recession to learn about universities, a period of crisis provides a valuable window into their conduct. In a time of unanticipated scarcity, an institution's objectives, constraints, and incentives come into high relief. This opportunity to learn general lessons about universities is the key reason why we chose to study how the financial crisis and Great Recession affected higher education. Of course, we were also greatly interested in discovering what actually occurred during and after the Great Recession as universities dealt with the events occurring in the financial markets and the economy more generally.

The economic disruption of this period came as a shock to many universities, especially coming after a long period of economic prosperity and steady endowment growth. The scale and nature of the changes varied greatly among universities, depending on the size of their endowments, how their endowments were invested, their area of the county, whether they were dependent on state government appropriations, and their reliance on various federal agencies' grants and contracts. The shocks were often unexpected, sharp, and variant among universities. The timing was also due to events beyond the universities' control, such as the collapse of Lehman Brothers, losses at AIG, and other events that led to substantial disruption of financial

Jeffrey R. Brown is the William G. Karnes Professor of Finance at the University of Illinois at Urbana-Champaign and a research associate of the National Bureau of Economic Research. Caroline M. Hoxby is the Scott and Donya Bommer Professor in Economics at Stanford University, a senior fellow of the Hoover Institution, and a research associate and director of the Economics of Education Program of the National Bureau of Economic Research.

For acknowledgments, sources of research support, and disclosure of the authors' material financial relationships, if any, please see http://www.nber.org/chapters/c12855.ack.

markets. Although these circumstances are troubling for universities, they are ideal for economic analysis: the period created the exogenous variation that is necessary for econometric identification.

In addition to being an ideal time for economists to analyze universities, it is also a good time for universities' leaders—past and present, financial and academic—to assess the state of higher education. Crises tend to make people reflective, if for no other reason than that they often must make active decisions (e.g., to end a program) and cannot simply stick with the status quo. It can also be easier to be candid when it is self-evident that things are not going well—as when some endowments fall by a third or when some campuses are riven by protests about tuition increases.

In short, the goals of "How the Financial Crisis and Great Recession Affected Higher Education" were threefold: (a) to improve our understanding of the economics of higher education, (b) to show factually how higher education changed during a period of great economic stress, and (c) to stimulate conversations between economists and university leaders. We believe that these conversations, once begun, will enrich economic analysis and sharpen researchers' and university leaders' thinking.

An Important Discussion of University Endowments

"How the Financial Crisis and Great Recession Affected Higher Education" began with several studies of university endowments. This was followed by a discussion of endowments led by Jane Mendillo (president and CEO, Harvard Management Company), Scott Wise (Covariance Capital), and John Griswold (Commonfund Institute). The studies and discussion were truly remarkable because there emerged a convergence of facts, thought, and ideas for the future. After briefly summarizing each paper, we then describe the themes on which the discussion converged.

Key Findings from the Chapters on Endowment Management

Caroline M. Hoxby, in "Endowment Management Based on a Positive Model of the University," began by noting the absence of a satisfactory model of why endowments exist and what function they should play. She observed that this was not merely her conclusion but also that of two of the most influential papers on the topic: Hansmann (1990) and Merton (1993). She then proposed a positive model of the university as a social venture capitalist in intellectual capital (embodied in students and research). A primary problem for the university-as-venture-capitalist is getting the alumni and societies that have benefitted from its investments to repay some share of their returns so that there is funding for future generations of students and research. Endowments, her chapter argues, help to solve this problem because they allow an alumnus or philanthropist who is "paying back" to commit the university to its social venture capitalist role.

According to Hoxby's model, the university has, at any time, two portfolios: an intellectual capital portfolio (students, research, similar projects) and a financial portfolio (the endowment). Like any good venture capitalist who funds projects from his financial portfolio, in this model the university should manage these two portfolios in a fully coordinated fashion with the goal of maximizing the university's ultimate contribution to society. This implies, for instance, that risks in the intellectual capital portfolio should be offset in the financial portfolio and vice versa. The liquidity of the financial side should be managed with an eye to the adjustment costs of projects on the intellectual capital side. A period of unusually good (poor) investments opportunities on one side should cause the university to draw funds from (give funds to) the other side.

Keith C. Brown and Cristian Ioan Tiu, in "The Interaction of Spending Policies, Asset Allocation Strategies, and Investment Performance at University Endowment Funds," closely examine the management of more than 800 university endowments from 2003 to 2011. They focus on what explains universities' spending policies and whether those policies are truly rules or merely "meant to be broken." Noting that many models of endowment management predict that the permanent portion of the spending policy should be highly stable, they find that most universities' policies are anything but stable. Half of the endowments revised their rules at least once over this time period and about a quarter of them changed their spending "rules" *each* year. (It should be noted that Hoxby's model does not imply that spending policies should be highly stable, so it is a potential—though so far untested—explanation for actual endowment management.)

While Brown and Tiu do not attempt to determine whether universities are better able to fulfill their overall objectives if they stick to their spending policies, they do convincingly demonstrate that there is no difference in benchmark-adjusted performance between institutions that did and did not stick to their spending rules.

William M. Goetzmann and Sharon Oster, in "Competition among University Endowments," take note of two phenomena: the fierce competition among elite private universities for undergraduates and the recent shift of endowment portfolios toward alternative investments such as hedge funds. They speculate that these phenomena are causally related—although which is the "chicken" and which the "egg" they leave as a matter of speculation. That is, they hypothesize that as universities compete more fiercely for undergraduates, they fear falling behind on endowment returns per student because high returns allow the university to enrich the undergraduate experience. Alternatively, it could be that some universities moved into alternative investments for exogenous reasons, made high returns, and then forced their near competitors (for undergraduates) to follow them into alternative investments, in a bid to keep up.

Goetzmann and Oster test their hypothesis using an overlap-in-applications metric that captures competition for undergraduates. They show that when a school's endowment performance falls behind that of its closest competitor, the endowment tends to change its investment policy in a manner consistent with the goal of catching up to that rival. An implication of such behavior, regardless of how it began, is that endowment managers are pressed to take risks in search of high returns, potentially at the expense of future generations of students.

David Chambers, Elroy Dimson, and Justin Foo, in "Keynes, King's, and Endowment Asset Management," consider another period in which colleges—or at least one college—used alternative investments and thereby caught up to its rival. The college in question was King's College of Cambridge University and the rival was Trinity College of the same university. Perhaps most interestingly, the endowment manager was John Maynard Keynes and the alternative investments at the time were equities (as opposed to agricultural real estate, the traditional portfolio for a Cambridge or Oxford college).

Chambers, Dimson, and Foo argue that Keynes's move into equities was an innovation "at least as radical" as the recent move into illiquid assets by universities like Yale and Harvard. After a number of rough years in which Keynes's portfolio earned poor returns, he shifted to a stock-picking model that allowed King's to earn risk premia through tilting the portfolio toward value and smaller-capitalization stocks. By the time of Keynes's death, King's endowment had drawn even with Trinity, the richest of the colleges.

Themes that Emerged from the Discussion of Endowment Management

The panelists (Jane Mendillo, Scott Wise, and John Griswold) brought several themes to the surface which, perhaps surprisingly for any discussion about universities or among economists, received wide agreement in the discussion that followed. From most to least important, these themes were as follows.

1. A university can be viewed as having two management teams: its financial or endowment management team, and those who manage intellectual investments like students and research. There are substantial gains to communication between these two sides of the university about future investments, returns on existing investments, risks, diversification, expected cash flows, and, importantly, adjustment costs. While the managers on each side may thoroughly understand the other side in *some* universities, most discussants viewed such understanding as the exception rather than the rule.

Both sides received some blame in this regard, but universities' nonendowment managers received a bit more. This is because, unlike the endowment managers, they hesitate to quantify many of their investments, risks, adjustment costs, and cash flows. They may be good at describing certain current and near-term future costs, but they are often vague about adjustment costs. Moreover, they are often very reluctant to put numbers on the *benefits* of their activities—benefits that flow through alumni donations, tuition, research grants, and philanthropic dollars. Of course, such benefits are difficult to quantify but they still have qualities like risk, diversification, and correlations with macroevents that can be described. Financial managers need more information if they are to understand how much of the university's intellectual investments will be lost if the endowment fails to provide a steady flow of cash.

Moreover, although endowment managers can describe their portfolios along numerous dimensions (risk, liquidity, diversification, horizons, and so on), they often hesitate to do so because they are dealing with university leaders who have very little training in finance. Some investment managers opt out of communicating much about their portfolios because they fear well-intentioned but misguided interference based on a leader's limited understanding of finance. The consequence is that neither side really understands the investments of the other side.

2. When a university regards its endowment as *part* of its portfolio, not a separate portfolio, this has numerous implications. For instance, during times when the endowment is earning high returns, university leaders might closely examine the marginal intellectual investments they are making and ensure that they have high expected returns as well. Discussants indicated that the opposite behavior seems to dominate in practice: during periods of high endowment returns, university leaders often seem to regard the endowment as a "slush fund" that permits them to make low-return investments on the intellectual side.

Another example is that endowment managers can be aware of a university's intellectual investments being disproportionately focused in a few industries (finance, high technology, biotechnology, and so on) or a specific area (often the city or region surrounding the university). Nearly all finance models suggest that such narrowness ought to be offset by diversification in the remaining (endowment) portfolio. Discussants argued that, often, it is not. In fact, for reasons of proximity or because alumni sit on their boards, endowment managers frequently disproportionately invest in the *same* industries and geography in which the university is already disproportionately invested.

A final implication concerns the liquidity of the endowment portfolio. When the university's total portfolio is the unit of analysis, not only the liquidity of financial investments, but also the adjustment costs of intellectual investments must be considered. Several participants used financial aid to illustrate this point. In the years from 2000 to 2007, many universities very publicly and forcefully committed themselves to financial aid policies that were intended to increase the economic diversity of their student bodies. These policies could not be changed in the short term—both because the university had made commitments to students who had already been admitted and because backing away from these policies would generate massive losses of reputation. In other words, these policies greatly increased the adjustment costs associated with any attempt to increase tuition revenue. They *predictably* cause the universities to spend more on financial aid during any financial crisis or recession—since families have lower wealth and incomes and the policies are formulas based on wealth and income. Endowment managers seem not to have been advised, when these policies were undertaken, that they should respond by modifying their portfolios to create additional cash during financial and economic downturns. This was despite the fact that the implications of the financial aid policies were not at all difficult to quantify for any given change in US wealth and gross domestic product (GDP).

3. Many endowment managers and university leaders, such as presidents, have contracts that reward them for endowment growth (often relative to a small group of peer institutions) regardless of its implications for the university as a whole. Such contracts may lead them to take undue risks or keep money in the endowment even when the university is most in need of cash for its core intellectual activities. Indeed, in separate work, Brown, Dimmock, Kang, and Weisbenner (2010) show that universities respond asymmetrically to shocks to their endowments.[1] They save endowment returns during periods of high returns (apparently as a precaution against periods of low returns) but then cut spending during periods of low returns (making it unclear why they were saving in the first place). The same authors demonstrate that university leaders' endowment decisions are sensitive to the size of the endowment on the day they were appointed—suggesting that they do not wish to have the endowment fall below an artificial target.

In the discussion, there was widespread interest in more sophisticated contracts that might align managers' and leaders' incentives more closely with the objectives of the university. After all, an endowment portfolio does not have a single moment (average return on investment), but many moments that can be built into a contract.

4. Owing to the long period from the mid-1980s to 2007 when some university endowments earned spectacular returns on investments in nontraditional assets, some university leaders and trustees have come to expect such returns as a matter of routine. Discussants agreed that such expectations are now unrealistic because so many sophisticated investors with long horizons (e.g., sovereign wealth funds) now also invest in nontraditional assets. Illiquidity premia are falling and hedge funds are becoming more correlated with the S&P 500.

Looking Ahead

Each financial crisis causes university and endowment leaders to engage in some self-examination. For instance, the bursting of the "tech bubble" in

---

1. Brown et al. (2010).

2000 caused some universities to alter their investment policies. However, it is unclear whether most universities took away larger lessons: it is much easier to plan for the last crisis than for future ones. Participants were optimistic that, through forums such as the NBER's conference, greater analytic firepower could be focused on endowment management and more could be learned from the recent financial crisis and recession than from previous events.

How Universities, Their Donors, and State Governments Responded to the Financial Crisis and Recession

The second half of "How the Financial Crisis and Great Recession Affected Higher Education" focused on how universities, their donors, and state governments responded to the financial crisis and recession. Researchers also examined how universities reacted to federal stimulus spending that was intended to counteract the recession. The papers were followed by discussions led by Mike Knetter (president, University of Wisconsin Foundation), Lawrence Bacow (president emeritus, Tufts University), Nancy Cantor (chancellor and president, Syracuse University), Stanley Ikenberry (president emeritus, University of Illinois), John Etchemendy (provost, Stanford University), and Scott Evans (senior advisor at TIAA CREF).

The discussions in this part of the conference revealed substantial stresses on universities. These "fault lines" apparently existed before the financial crisis and recession, but these economic tremors opened the fault lines and made the stresses more obvious for all to see. We describe these stresses after a brief summary of each paper.

Key Finding from the Chapters on Universities', Donors', and State Governments' Responses to the Financial Crisis and Recession

Jeffrey R. Brown, Stephen G. Dimmock, and Scott Weisbenner, in "The Supply of and Demand for Charitable Donations to Higher Education," investigate how donations to universities change when their economic circumstances change. Using panel data from 1997 to 2009, they employ university fixed effects to eliminate the relatively constant characteristics of each school and to focus on the *fluctuations* in each school's circumstances. They also take on the difficult task of separating changes in the supply of donations from changes in the demand for donations.

Using incomes and house values in the state where the university is located as shocks to the *supply* of potential donations, Brown, Dimmock, and Weisbenner find that donations to universities decrease when their alumni and other local donors (businesses, philanthropies) have reduced financial capacity to make gifts, such as during the Great Recession. Interestingly, it is capital donations that are most sensitive to the economic well-being of the donor base. Using large negative endowment shocks to identify a university's *demand* for donations, the authors find that donations—but especially donations earmarked for current use—increase when a school is short on cash. In short, while the scale of donations over the long run may be a function of a school's fundamental characteristics and activities, the timing and nature of the donations responds to current economic circumstances. There is substantial evidence that universities attempt to smooth their cash flow from donations by shifting between capital and current-use gifts.

Sarah E. Turner, in "The Impact of the Financial Crisis and Faculty Labor Markets," examines one margin along which universities can cut costs during times when budgets are tight: faculty salaries. Interestingly, it is not at all obvious that this is a sensible margin on which to cut since student demand for higher education is often *countercyclical*. That is, enrollments usually rise at postsecondary institutions during recessions. Thus, even without cuts to the number of faculty or to their real salaries, the instructional work per dollar spent on faculty tends to rise during recessions.

Turner finds that institutions differed in their responses to the financial crisis and recession. Public institutions suffered more from the long-lived depression of state government budgets than from the relatively short-lived financial crisis. Thus, they have reduced faculty hiring and real earnings for several years in succession. Well-endowed private institutions, which suffered sharp but ultimately short-lived shocks to their endowments, tended to freeze faculty hiring and salaries for two or three years. Their hiring recovered by 2010/11, and some private institutions even benefitted from the economic downturn by "poaching" desirable faculty from the still-struggling public institutions.

Turner finds little evidence that institutions used the crisis to eliminate their oldest faculty (e.g., through early retirement or similar inducements), thereby allowing them to continue hiring new, young faculty. More generally, she concludes that the financial crisis and Great Recession have widened the differences between private and public institutions and between the experiences of older and younger faculty. It is worth noting that not only Turner but also Brown, Dimmock, Kang, and Weisbenner (2010) find evidence that suggests that faculty, not administrators, bear the brunt of payroll cuts during times when universities are in fiscal stress.

In "The Financial Crisis and College Enrollment: How Have Students and Their Families Responded?" Bridget Terry Long begins with the observation that previous recessions have caused college enrollment to *increase*. This is apparently because the opportunity costs are a very important part—for most students, the dominant part—of the total cost of attending college. That is, during a period when the labor market is buoyant and young people can obtain jobs, the cost of foregone wages greatly exceeds the tuition and fees associated with college—except for a small number of affluent, high-aptitude students who attend expensive colleges and pay full tuition. If, during a recession, the wages or jobs available to young people fall, their opportunity cost may drop—possibly dramatically.

However, we do not *necessarily* expect college enrollment to rise during recessions. Family incomes and wealth (especially housing wealth) may fall, reducing students' ability to pay tuition and fees. State governments, faced with falling tax revenues and rising demands for social insurance often reduce appropriations to public colleges and universities. The universities may raise tuition and fees in response, just at the time when students are least able to pay it.

Long studies the response to the Great Recession using a detrended difference-in-differences approach. She allows each college enrollment and households' college-related expenditure to be on a separate trend before the Great Recession. She then estimates the change from that trend for states that had either a light or a heavy experience of the recession. A state is judged to have a heavy experience if its unemployment rate rose disproportionately or its house prices fell disproportionately. She shows that the Great Recession, like previous recessions, increased college enrollment. However, in a change from previous recessions, Long finds that students paid distinctly *higher* tuition during the Great Recession.

Why might students have paid unusually high tuition during the Great Recession, especially relative to previous recessions? Eric Bettinger and Betsy Williams, in "Federal and State Financial Aid during the Great Recession," show that federal financial aid may be a cause. The growth in expenditure for the federal Pell grant was 134 percent over just three years, an enormous and unprecedented increase.

Bettinger and Williams describe state governments in "a perfect storm" in which they saw federal funds, and the Pell grant in particular, as their rescuer. Specifically, they study whether states decreased state financial aid when they saw their students receiving increased federal financial aid. They find that about 50 percent of states did this. Their fascinating case study of Ohio shows that, for many Ohio students, every extra dollar of federal aid caused them to lose a dollar of state aid.

Bettinger and Williams show that states did not offset federal aid prior to 1990: indeed, states previously complemented increases in federal aid. Since 1990, however, states have greatly expanded the generosity and coverage of their Medicaid programs. Whereas Medicaid accounted for only a small share of state budgets in the last major recession of 1981–1983, by 2007 it accounted for a massive share of most states' budgets. Since Medicaid payments automatically rise when family incomes fall, states may have cut higher education spending disproportionately to keep Medicaid funded. Moreover, during the boom years of the 1990s and the first decade of the twenty-first century, most states systematically underfunded their public employees' pension systems. Mandatory pension payouts rose just when their tax revenue fell—again, force putting pressure on higher education spending. Finally, most states' spending on public primary and secondary education is now governed by state supreme court decisions, making it harder to cut that spending than to cut higher education spending.

A massive increase in Pell grant spending was part of the federal stimulus package that was intended to prop up demand and thereby pull the economy out of recession. However, the stimulus affected higher education not just through financial aid, but also through spending on research, which grew by about 20 percent in just two years. In "Did the Fiscal Stimulus Work for the Universities?" Michael F. Dinerstein, Caroline M. Hoxby, Jonathan Meer, and Pablo Villanueva examine how public and private institutions responded to the large, stimulus-driven increases in their revenue from federal sources. They focus on research universities because they received the vast majority of stimulus-driven research revenues and a substantial share of stimulus-driven aid revenues. Because the amount of stimulus revenue that a university received might be endogenous to its circumstances in the recession, the authors' instrument for each university's receipts with what it would have received if its share of each federal agency's spending remained the same, but each agency's spending went up by the percentage that it actually did.[2] Since some agencies' spending increased much more than others', different universities experienced very different stimulus-driven windfalls.

Dinerstein, Hoxby, Meer, and Villanueva show that private and public universities responded quite differently to stimulus windfalls. Private universities appear to have used the windfall revenue much like they would use a dollar of unrestricted revenue. That is, they implicitly held back some research funds that they would have spent and instead spent the federal money. The held-back funds could then be used to keep tuition from rising, limit unusually high payouts from the endowment, and so on. This is a partial flypaper effect: some, but not all, of the money "stuck where it landed." Economic analysis predicts that a partial flypaper effect will be the result if an institution is trying to spend new revenue optimally, but is constrained somewhat by the restrictions associated with the revenue.

The authors find that public universities reacted to stimulus windfalls in a very different and extremely interesting manner. They appear to have used the funds as the basis of a renegotiation with their state legislatures—with the result that they gave up revenues from state appropriations but gained autonomy over their spending, the right to raise tuition, and the right to admit more out-of-state students (who pay much higher tuition and have higher scores than in-state students). It is as though they said to their legislatures, "We know that you are short on cash and would like to reduce our appropriation. Because we currently have the capacity to bring in revenue from sources such as federal research funds, we will not protest much about the reduced appropriations *if* you give us the power to spend our budget more as we like, allow us to raise tuition (since our institutions are in excess

2. This is a shift-share or Bartik instrument. See Bartik (1991).

demand), and allow us to admit more 'paying,' high-aptitude students from out-of-state."

Themes That Emerged from the Discussion of Universities', Donors', and State Governments' Responses to the Financial Crisis and Recession

No one who heard the panel discussions would conclude that the life of a university leader is easy. Some key points, many of which emphasized the stresses facing universities, were as follows:

1. There was some debate about whether the financial crisis and recession should be considered an opportunity for "creative destruction" or just plain destruction. Creative destruction is the idea that, in times of fiscal or other stress, organizations make hard decisions that ultimately raise their productivity. The discussants agreed that most universities needed some creative destruction of programs that were obsolete, "white elephant" construction projects, some unproductive faculty members, outdated administrative units, frills for students that did not actually improve their college experience, and so on. Discussants were less agreed about whether such creative destruction was practicable. Private university leaders tended to think that it was very difficult owing to tradition, faculty governance, and alumni and donor preferences. However, they usually agreed that *some* of what had been eliminated during the recession was productivity enhancing. Public university leaders tended toward the view that destruction was occurring without much of it being productive. They argued that, in responding to the crisis, public universities were even more constrained than private ones. For instance, leaders might be able to see how their staff ought to be restructured and reduced, but they were forced to shrink payroll through furlough days rather than differentially reducing more days for less productive faculty and staff.

2. A theme that recurred throughout the discussion was that public and private universities seem less and less alike—owing to their differences in governance, constraints, and sources of revenue. Private universities are concerned about financial market returns because they rely on endowment- and donor-based revenues. Private university leaders also emphasized how difficult it was for them to maintain their precrisis commitments to financial aid in the face of declining family income. Public universities were more focused on the degree to which they could and should raise tuition, enroll out-of-state students, and induce appropriate faculty and staff retirements. It is stressful for them to know that—without having the same autonomy—they have to compete with private universities for students, faculty, and research funding. Public universities also face a somewhat different crisis than the private ones faced. Private universities, especially highly endowed ones, were sharply struck by the financial crisis, but recovery from that crisis has been fairly quick as asset markets recovered their value. In contrast, public universities' finances are more driven by the recession, with its consequences

for state tax revenues, family incomes, and pressures on appropriations. The period of slow growth in incomes continues and may last for several more years.

The notion that public and private universities face fundamentally distinct pressures fits neatly with the evidence. For instance, Bettinger and Williams find that many *public* universities' student aid fell as federal aid increased. There is no indication that something similar occurred at private universities. Turner suggests that private universities "poached" top faculty from public universities during the recession. Dinerstein, Hoxby, Meer, and Villanueva find that public and private universities responded to stimulus windfalls very differently.

3. Several discussants emphasized that, even within the private sector, there are widening differences between universities that rely on endowment returns and those that have such small endowments that their returns are hardly relevant. Even though endowment returns may never return to the heady rates of the 1990s and 2001–2006, a university leader ultimately has more discretion over endowment revenue than revenue from tuition. After all, a decision to raise the endowment payout rate involves fewer people and less public scrutiny than a decision to raise tuition.

Moreover, as made clear by Brown, Dimmock, and Weisbenner, universities that rely on gifts have ways to smooth their cash flow that are probably not available to institutions that rely almost entirely on tuition revenue.

4. There was widespread agreement that, at present, universities face headwinds. They are a popular "punching bag" for politicians and journalists, who often do not differentiate among institutions with excellent student and research outcomes and institutions with poor ones. Universities are increasingly called upon to demonstrate that their costs are justified by correspondingly high returns, but measuring the total social returns is very difficult. All institutions receive blame for the student debt crisis even though the vast majority of the defaulters attended nonselective institutions, especially nonselective for-profit schools.

Nearly all postsecondary leaders are excited about the potential of online education, but they do not yet see the financial model in which online education is compatible with on-campus education that is rich in student-faculty contacts and faculty research. They worry that online education may destroy the viability of in-person education much as online media have eliminated much of the traditional media like newspapers. While online media may be a reasonable substitute for traditional media, most discussants believed that substantial human capital would be lost if in-person education were largely destroyed by online education.

While the researchers did not claim that they could remedy the aforementioned problems, there was general optimism that research could help higher education to focus on its actual problems. For instance, the researchers suggested that they might be able to remedy the problem of measuring returns to the education at many institutions by examining data on earnings, occupations, and a variety of other life outcomes. This may not be possible immediately—owing to the need for government data that are not currently available—but it is something that can be tackled. Reasonably accurate measure of returns would at least focus scrutiny on the institutions where returns are low. Student debt would similarly benefit from research that focuses policy and scrutiny on those students and institutions that are most involved. The immediate (partial equilibrium) effects of online education can be analyzed rigorously with randomized control trials. The (general equilibrium) effects of online education on the market for higher education can be modeled rigorously, much in the same way economists would model entry in other markets. Such modeling may not produce precise predictions, but it would almost certainly focus attention on key parameters such as the employers' rewards for skills acquired online versus in person.

Looking Ahead

In short, there was a general sense that more economic research was needed on an array of issues in higher education. It appears that university leaders are both able and eager to digest such research, especially if it is designed to be relevant to them. We believe that the research is most likely to be relevant and digested if conversations among economists and university leaders, like the ones at the NBER conference associated with this volume, continue.

References

Bartik, Timothy. 1991. "The Effects of Metropolitan Job Growth on the Size Distribution of Family Income." Upjohn Working Paper no. 91-06. Kalamazoo, MI, W. E. Upjohn Institute for Employment Research.

Brown, Jeffrey, Stephen Dimmock, Jun-Koo Kang, and Scott Weisbenner. 2010. "How University Endowments Respond to Financial Shocks: Evidence and Implications." NBER Working Paper no. 15861, Cambridge, MA.

Hansmann, Henry. 1990. "Why do Universities Have Endowments?" *Journal of Legal Studies* 19 (1): 3–42.

Merton, Robert. 1993. "Optimal Investment Strategies for University Endowment Funds." In *Studies of Supply and Demand in Higher Education*, edited by Charles T. Clotfelter and Michael Rothschild. Chicago: University of Chicago Press.

1

Endowment Management Based on a Positive Model of the University

Caroline M. Hoxby

1.1 Introduction

In this chapter, I propose a positive model of the university in which many apparently peculiar features of universities—such as endowments and tuition subsidies—are generated by the internal logic of the model. The model proposes a specific objective function for universities and demonstrates how it is enforced. That is, the objective function leads to actions that reinforce the initial selection of the objective function. The model offers important predictions for the decisions that universities should make on many fronts if they are behaving in accordance with it. In this chapter, I focus on the implications for financial decisions, especially universities' endowment spending rules and portfolio allocations. The model is designed to explain America's great private research universities and very selective liberal arts colleges and—with modest adaptations—institutions that are partly

Caroline M. Hoxby is the Scott and Donya Bommer Professor in Economics at Stanford University, a senior fellow of the Hoover Institution, and a research associate and director of the Economics of Education Program of the National Bureau of Economic Research.

I am grateful to many people with whom I have had discussions that helped me refine ideas on this topic. I am similarly grateful to people who have written previously on this and related topics. These include William Bowen, Jeffrey Brown, Henry Hansmann, and Robert Merton. Eric Bettinger, Keith Brown, David Chambers, Stephen Dimmock, Elroy Dimson, William Goeztmann, Bridget Long, Sharon Oster, Cristian Tiu, Sarah Turner, and Scott Weisbenner gave me extremely helpful comments on an early outline of this chapter. This chapter draws very substantially on my 2011 Clarendon Lecture in Economics entitled "The Complex and Increasingly Global Market for Elite Higher Education," which is rewritten in the form of two chapters in the Clarendon Lectures monograph *The Role of Markets in Education* (Oxford University Press [OUP], under contract). I am grateful for the support of the OUP, especially Adam Swallow. I am solely responsible for the content of this chapter. For acknowledgments, sources of research support, and disclosure of the author's material financial relationships, if any, please see http://www.nber.org/chapters/c12856.ack.

controlled by the state such as America's and Britain's great public research universities. The model is designed to explain them precisely because many people find them hardest to explain, even enigmatic. An ancillary benefit of the model is that it provides a justification for the existence of all of the aforesaid institutions by assigning them a unique role in the creation of intellectual capital. A simpler version of the model could explain most other colleges and universities, and this is a topic to which I return briefly.

A very brief intuition into the model, laid out in section 1.3, is as follows. Each university maximizes its contribution to society's intellectual capital by making two types of investments: (a) investments in advanced human capital embodied in people and (b) investments in new knowledge embodied in research. These investments have peculiar properties that make them unlikely to be financed by conventional means. In making these investments, universities play a role that closely parallels that of a venture capitalist. They invest not only money, but also expertise and infrastructure. The university gets what is essentially an equity stake in its intellectual capital investments. Collecting these (equity-type) returns is a key difficulty for universities, and it is in overcoming this difficulty that universities (a) generate an endowment, not merely gifts and grants for current use; and (b) reinforce the initial choice of their objective function so that the model is, as a logical matter, closed.

This chapter draws heavily upon Hoxby (forthcoming) in that the model of the university is the same. However, those chapters present empirical evidence that justifies how the model characterizes universities. They also explain how universities evolved over decades into the institutions that they are modeled as being. In this chapter, I present the model without much empirical justification and without history. Hoxby also examines the implications of the model for universities' policies on tuition, admissions, and a variety of other outcomes. In this chapter, I touch on these policies briefly and focus on the implications for endowment management.

The papers to which this study is most closely related are Hansmann (1990) and Merton (1993). The Hansmann paper is a masterful review of many explanations of why universities have endowments and what each justification implies for endowment management. He carefully analyzes and rejects both the intergenerational equity model of Tobin (1974) and extensions of the intergenerational equity model that presume that there will be an increasing cost of education for succeeding generations. The latter type of model produces spending rules along the lines of the Stanford Rule (Merhling, Goldstein, and Sedlacek 2005). Hansmann also analyzes several partial explanations for endowments and their management rules— for instance, programming models—such as Grinold, Hopkins, and Massy (1978)—which do not maximize an objective function that values education and research but merely assess whether a rule can attain a metric such as maintaining a certain ratio of expenses to endowment. Hansmann even carefully assesses casual explanations for endowments such as the character and incentives of people who serve as university trustees.

Following his review—which I do not imitate in this chapter, partly because his review is so masterful and partly for reasons of length—Hansmann concludes:

> The argument that has been offered most frequently in recent years to explain the accumulation of endowments—that they are a means to inter-generational equity—is unpersuasive. More compelling reasons to accumulate endowments are that they serve as a financial buffer against periods of financial adversity, that they help to insure the long-run survival of the institution's reputational capital, that they protect the institution's intellectual freedom, and that they assist in passing on values prized by the present generation. It is not clear, however, that these are today the reasons why endowments are accumulated. Nor is it clear that the sizes of existing endowments, and the ways in which they are managed, are well chosen to serve these goals. In particular, prevailing endowment spending rules seem inconsistent with most of these objectives. We cannot say, from the arguments and evidence surveyed here, that the endowments of the major private universities today are either too big or too small. It does appear, however, that surprisingly little thought has been devoted to the purposes for which endowments are maintained and that, as a consequence, their rate of accumulation and the pattern of spending from their income have been managed without much attention to the ultimate objectives of the institutions that hold them. (1990, 39–40)

In other words, Hansmann concludes that there is not a satisfying, positive model of universities in which endowments play a logical and necessary role. He does not himself propose one.

In many ways, Merton takes off where Hansmann ends. Indeed, his paper begins with part of the above quotation from Hansmann. Merton's key contributions are (a) to focus attention on the nonendowment sources of cash flow for universities (tuition, gifts, and so on), and (b) to solve the problem of how to manage an endowment given these nonendowment sources of cash flow and flows of expenses. Merton treats the cash flow and expenses as exogenous because "that abstraction does not significantly alter the optimal portfolio allocations." Merton's article is a great contribution that is not only useful to the broad scholarly community, but that is specifically helpful to this study because it allows me to focus on questions that he leaves unresolved.[1]

I focus on what the university's objective is; why that objective generates sources of cash flow like gifts, tuition, and grants; why endowments exist;

---

1. I believe that this is a fair characterization of Merton's paper because he writes, "The course taken here is to address this question in the middle range: it does not attempt to specify . . . the objective function for the university, but it does derive optimal investment and expenditure for [the] endowment in a context which takes account of overall university objectives and the availability of other sources of revenue besides endowment" (1993, 212).

and how the endowment and cash flows are interdependent. Essentially, my model sets up the structural version of the university's investment problem. For each problem there exists a reduced-form version that can be written strictly in terms of cash flows. This reduced-form problem is solved in Merton's paper—except for some issues that I take up later.

In addition to the closely related papers by Hansmann and Merton, there is a rich but less related literature on the management of endowment portfolios (the types of securities in which they should invest) and on spending rules (the amount of the annual return on the endowment that should be spent rather than saved in the endowment).[2] Many of these papers provide important estimates of elasticities or other parameters—for instance, the sacrifice in average returns and decrease in risk that universities experience when they invest more of their portfolio in bonds. Or, to take another example, Brown, Dimmock, and Weisbenner (chapter 5, this volume) estimate the response of donations to the rate of return on the endowment. However, as noted by both Hansmann and Merton, this rich array of papers tend to take no stand on why endowments exist or the purpose they serve and instead rely—explicitly or implicitly—on a rule of thumb such as needing to maintain a perpetual level flow of expected real income. Thus, the body of papers referenced in this paragraph, although terribly useful given an objective function and reduced-form rules based on it, are logically posterior to this chapter.

This chapter contrasts with the small existing literature that does propose objective functions for universities—most notably prestige.[3] These papers strike me as unsatisfactory in that prestige is a fundamentally incomplete explanation. The authors never demonstrate why institutions should compete on the particular metrics of prestige—endowments and admissions thresholds—that the authors choose. They never explain why endowments or admissions thresholds exist in the first place so that they *could* be grounds for prestige competitions. Indeed, saying that universities compete for prestige seems merely to be conceding that there is no positive model of universities, with the result that universities must necessarily be said to pursue essentially superficial goals that happen to have predictive power.

The structure of the remainder of the chapter is as follows. In section 1.2, I review the venture capital problem because it clarifies important features of the university's investment problem. In section 1.3, I lay out a positive model of the university. Section 1.4 presents a less abstract, more down-

2. See, for example, the Advisory Committee on Endowment Management (1969); Black (1976); Donaldson, Lufkin, and Jenrette (1969); Ennis and Williamson (1976); Eisner (1974); Grinold, Hopkins, and Massy (1978); Litvack, Malkiel, and Quandt (1974); Malkiel and Firstenberg (1976); Tobin (1974); and Williamson (1975). More recent papers include Blume (2009); Brown et al. (2010); Brown, Dimmock, and Weisbenner (chapter 5, this volume); Brown, Garlappi, and Tiu (2010); Dimmock (2012); Lerner, Schoar, and Wang (2008); and Campbell (2012).
3. This literature is best exemplified by Ehrenberg (2000). A related but different and incomplete explanation is the ever-increasing demand for elite higher education (see Clotfelter 1996).

to-earth portrait of a university than is described by the model. In section 1.5, I describe the implications of the model for endowment spending and portfolio allocation. This is where Merton (1993) plays an important role. Finally, in section 1.6, I conclude by explaining what the model has to say about some questions that commonly arise.

1.2 The Venture Capital Problem

It may appear to be a digression to review the venture capital problem and how it is solved before moving to universities. However, it is efficient to conduct this review because it is easier to see the structure of the problem when it is presented in its more abstract form, without all of the details that often confound analysis of universities. Although economists who work on the venture capital problem usually lay it out in a fairly different way from the presentation here, the fundamental problem and aspects of the solution I present draw heavily upon this literature.[4]

1.2.1 Problematic Investment Projects

There exists a set of investment projects with the following characteristics:

- They are brought forward by a person (or persons) whose unique capacities are necessary for the success of the project. For instance, this person could be someone who has the idea for an invention. Hereafter, I call this person the "agent."[5]
- To be successful, the project requires assets—usually described as expertise and infrastructure—whose building or adjustment costs are convex in the per-period increase in their amount or diversity. This is just to say that it is expensive to build the relevant assets very quickly, especially if one does not already have a foundation of closely related assets. For instance, the project may require expertise in finance, marketing, the law, certain engineering, or some other body of knowledge. The infrastructure required may be the plant and equipment necessary to construct and test a prototype of the invention. What is important is that the project requires assets that have costs that are convex in the way described. Hereafter, I use the phrase "convex adjustment costs" to refer to such costs.
- Unless an assessor has expertise in areas related to the agent's unique capacity, his estimates of the potential profitability of the project will be extremely imprecise.

---

4. I rely particularly on Repullo and Suarez's (2004) elegant exposition. Other helpful papers include: Bergemann and Hege (1998), Berglof (1994), Casamatta (2003), Gompers (1995), Gorman and Sahlman (1989), Kaplan and Strömberg (2001, 2003), Sahlman (1990), and Trester (1998).

5. He is typically called the entrepreneur in the venture capital literature, but this conveys a false sense that the project is routinely a start-up business.

- The project is risky. This almost goes without saying since (a) it depends on the existence of the agent who could, say, be killed in an accident; and (b) something about the project must be advanced if only an expert can assess its potential profitability.

These conditions generate a problem. The agent cannot get financing for the project from a bank or raise money in some other conventional way because (a) the bank or other conventional financier has insufficient expertise to assess the project and cannot build this expertise without incurring prohibitive costs, and (b) the agent's costs of building the expertise and infrastructure himself are prohibitive. Even if the agent were able to get financing from a bank, he might substantially underfinance the project because he is risk averse and his investment would entail a great deal of undiversified risk.

1.2.2 The Potential for a Venture Capital Solution

Venture capitalists are a potential solution to this problem. They are modeled as people who have a pool of financial capital to invest and who have already built expertise and infrastructure in areas relevant to certain types of projects. A venture capitalist invests not only money but also expertise and infrastructure. Using his expertise, he selects projects whose expected rate of return exceeds a threshold based on the opportunity costs for his financial capital, expertise, and infrastructure. In return for making an investment, the venture capitalist gets what is essentially an equity position in the project (more on this below).

The venture capital problem exists precisely because the costs of building expertise and infrastructure are convex as described. This has a few implications. First, a venture capitalist's portfolio is necessarily limited in its breadth and size by the cost of building diverse expertise and infrastructure. His portfolio may contain many projects and be much more diversified than any one of these projects, but it will be far less diverse than, say, a market index fund. Second, the venture capitalist will want to finance a stream of projects over a number of years—not finance a single generation of projects and then get out of the business. This is because the costs of building expertise and infrastructure are convex in the speed of doing it. Thus, the venture capitalist's investments in expertise and infrastructure are more likely to pay off if he builds them gradually and employs them for several generations of projects. Third, the venture capitalist has strong incentives to maintain his expertise and infrastructure, as opposed to letting them depreciate. He will fear situations in which his returns from projects are insufficient to support maintenance-type investments in his expertise and infrastructure. For instance, a venture capitalist who was short on current income might lose his experts to other employers. If much of this were to occur, his ability to continue his venture capital business would be in doubt. Thus, venture capitalists may wish to have a smoother stream of investments than an investor in financial markets. Fourth, the cost structure implies that projects will crowd one another out at the margin. That is, two projects may have similar potential profitability and might each pass the venture capitalist's threshold if each could use his existing stock of expertise and infrastructure. However, neither project might justify the venture capitalist's quickly building enough new expertise and infrastructure to accommodate it. The potential for crowding out means that venture capitalists will acquire a good deal of information about an agent before making an offer to him.

The venture capital solution to the investment problem contains a two-sided moral hazard: the agent must make an effort and contribute his unique capacity but the venture capitalist must also contribute his expertise and infrastructure. This moral hazard has two important implications. First, the problems caused by moral hazard decrease as the project's potential profitability rises: both parties will be glad to make an effort when they realize that they are in a situation with vast potential profits. Thus, the optimal contract concentrates the returns to the venture capitalist in the best states of the world. For instance, a contract might specify that the venture capitalist receives no share of the returns if the profits are below some threshold, a certain share if the profits are in some intermediate range, and a higher share if profits are in a high range. Second, owing to the moral hazard, the optimal contract will make the agent fund some share of the project if he can. This is because the agent's moral hazard shrinks as he himself invests more: he will lose his own stake if he makes no effort. Thus, within a relevant range, the venture capitalist is willing to invest more when the agent invests more, and the entire project can be more optimally financed and managed.

A final thing worth mentioning is that venture capitalists can bring "outside money" to projects to improve their solution. That is, the venture capitalist may find himself in situations where he has sufficient expertise and infrastructure for a project but insufficient funds. In such cases, he may be able to get external financing for the project that the agent could never get on his own because (a) the venture capitalist is known to have the expertise to assess the project, and (b) the credibility of the venture capitalist's announced assessment is increased by his investing his own expertise, infrastructure, and money.

Summing up, an investment project of the type described is more likely to be optimally funded—that is, solved by venture capital—when:

- the expertise and infrastructure required are such that a venture capitalist can pay for the cost of building and maintaining them by earning returns on a sufficiently large and diverse portfolio of (somewhat related) projects;
- the venture capitalist does not so discount the future that he is unwilling to use his expertise and infrastructure over multiple generations of projects;

- the expected returns to the project are sufficient to clear the threshold set by a venture capitalist's opportunity costs of financial capital, expertise, and infrastructure; and
- reasonably optimal contracts are possible. These will entail the venture capitalist taking a sufficiently small equity share that the agent's moral hazard problem is not crippling. The agent will typically make some contribution (even if it is only his time and effort), and the venture capitalist will typically hold a nonlinear equity position in the project.

1.3 The University's Problem

In this section, I create a convenient fiction, the "founder," to embody the people whose assets and actions have shaped what universities have become. While actual universities have often developed what they do and how they finance it through a combination of vision, trial, muddle, competition, and imitation, the founder is blessed with extremely clear vision, rational expectations, and well-defined objectives. Obviously, the founder is not meant to be taken literally, but he makes it easier to lay out a positive model of the university because he is the prime mover and has an abstract understanding of the problem he is trying to solve. It is by no means necessary for actual university leaders to have been so concerted or to articulate similarly abstract models of their universities—just as it is not necessary for actual corporate leaders to manage or speak about their firms in highly abstract ways.[6]

The founder's goal is to use his initial capital, acquired through some exogenous means, to make the maximum contribution to society's intellectual capital, each unit of which he values at its social (private plus public) return. It is important that the founder wants to add intellectual capital, not merely fund intellectual capital that society would readily create in his absence. For instance, if a person's optimal education is such that he could finance it on his own using conventional means, that person is not of interest to the founder. In practice, this puts aside a good share of human capital investments that earn private returns, are not terribly risky, do not require

---

6. Although the founder is probably best thought of as an abstract person or persons, there are people who have founded universities recently enough for us to observe their motives and actions: Leland and Jane Stanford (founders of Stanford University); Andrew Carnegie and Richard and Andrew Mellon (founders of the two parts of what is now Carnegie-Mellon University); Peter and Hannah Widener (founders of Widener University); John D. Rockefeller (founder of Rockefeller University); and so on. All of these people took funds that they had earned in enterprises that were privately profitable—railroads, steel, chemicals, shipping, oil—and dedicated them to society's good by founding a university. Their first moves were hiring faculty from other universities, accumulating libraries, building laboratories, and otherwise creating expertise and infrastructure. Of course, great private universities like Harvard and Yale also had founders, but they are sufficiently "historical" for their motives to be less easily characterized. This is not to say that these universities do not fit the model, but that explaining them requires a more historical approach.

great expertise for a loan officer to assess, and do not require highly expert instructors or infrastructure with convex adjustment costs.

Rather, the founder takes as his problem some part of the market for intellectual capital that will be missing without his intervention. This is parallel to the venture capitalist taking on some set of investments that will not occur if they are constrained to use conventional financing. Advanced intellectual capital has properties that make investments in it likely to be missing or undersized.

1.3.1 The Peculiar Properties of Advanced Intellectual Capital

I define intellectual capital as knowledge that generates welfare for society in any way—private earnings, private nonmonetary benefits, public benefits, and so on. Intellectual capital takes one of two forms: human capital and research, which I differentiate for clarity, as follows. Human capital is knowledge that is stored in a person's brain and that cannot be used without his making complementary effort. Human capital need not be new knowledge: a engineer who knows how to solve a certain well-understood type of problem has human capital. Research is a contribution to the stock of world knowledge that can be embodied in some form—a publication, for instance—that it is independent of any particular person. This is not to say that research generates returns without some person's effort. A publication that contains new knowledge does not generate returns unless someone interprets and employs it.

Creating advanced intellectual capital generally requires three factors: human capital, research, and infrastructure. It is hard to get to the frontier of knowledge without benefitting from previous knowledge in the form of research and/or the human capital of instructors, who help people learn how to interpret research for themselves and who transfer the knowledge in their own brains. It is hard to conduct research without infrastructure such as laboratories in which experiments are conducted, libraries in which research is stored, or classrooms in which people with human capital instruct others. Moreover, these three factors—human capital, research, and infrastructure—interact in complex ways so that, for instance, there is little point in building a laboratory without the right complement of researchers to go in it. The result of all this is that it is hard to build the capacity to create advanced intellectual capital "from scratch." Building this capacity has costs that are convex in the per-period increase in amount and in diversity.

Even if they have access to the same human capital, research, and infrastructure, people vary in their capacity to store human capital, generate research, and earn returns on knowledge to which they have access. To store, create, or use advanced intellectual capital, a person may need to be intelligent, have original ideas, or have the will to exercise human capital or develop research into useful products. For convenience, I call this array of capacities "aptitude" and note that there is ample evidence that the distribution of it has a long right-hand tail.[7] Thus, a person who has 99th percentile aptitude may generate returns that are an order of magnitude greater for a given investment in intellectual capital than a person with 90th percentile aptitude.

Estimating where a person is in the long right-hand tail of aptitude is a costly exercise. It generally requires the person's own time or effort, the time and effort of an assessor who himself has high aptitude, and the use of infrastructure. Furthermore, even a good estimate of aptitude is only an estimate: we expect aptitude to be revealed over much of a person's adult life. For instance, whether a person's contributions to knowledge are worthy of a Nobel Prize or only a solid academic post is something usually revealed after midlife. Similarly, whether a person will use his knowledge to create a Fortune 500 company or to conduct a very successful but largely unremarkable career is usually revealed slowly.

Because aptitude varies and is revealed slowly, an individual should be risk averse when making human capital investments in himself. If the person knows that his aptitude is at least fairly high, then the risk of such investments is heightened by the long right-hand tail of aptitude, the fact that his optimal investment may be very large relative to average income, and the fact that completely unrelated risks (a debilitating accident, for instance) may destroy his ability to exercise the advanced intellectual capital in which he has invested.

The prohibition of slavery or, more prosaically, forced labor has the consequence that people cannot easily take equity positions in one another's advanced intellectual capital and thereby share risk. Similarly, even if a bank wished to invest in a portfolio of advanced intellectual capital (presumably by financing many persons' education and research), its inability to take equity positions would cause it to underinvest greatly: it could not earn more on persons whose returns happened to be very high than it could earn on persons whose returns were only moderate. A bank or person who attempted to hold a diverse, advanced intellectual capital portfolio would also find it challenging to acquire the expertise to assess each person's aptitude well.

Finally, it is hard to keep intellectual capital—especially research—fully private. It tends to get revealed in the process of being used. Thus, a good share of the returns to intellectual capital accrue to society, not to the people who produce them. The returns to human capital are typically far more private but still not fully private because colleagues of a person with advanced human capital typically acquire some of his knowledge through spillovers.[8]

---

7. "Aptitude" is *not* the same as IQ or any other narrow definition of ability. It includes forms of motivation, management and leadership skills, interpersonal skills, linguistic and rhetorical abilities, political skills, luck, and so on.

8. Of course, some individuals may have human capital that they use mainly for private returns and may also produce research that earns mainly public returns. A physician who does both clinical and research work would be an obvious example.

1.3.2 The Founder's Problem

If he is to maximize his contribution to society's intellectual capital, the founder must invest in such a way that he deals with the peculiar properties of advanced intellectual capital, as described above. In particular, he cannot add much to society's intellectual capital all by himself. He needs people who can store and exercise human capital. He also needs people who can create new knowledge. He needs the expertise to assess which people have the highest aptitude. He needs to combine the people with expertise and infrastructure. His expertise and infrastructure assets must be sufficient in breadth and scale to support a portfolio of intellectual capital investments with some diversity in risks and opportunities. Since the costs of building expertise and infrastructure are convex in the per-period increase in amount and diversity, he will want to keep his investments going for some time, not make a one-off investment in intellectual capital and then get out of the activity.

In all these ways, the founder is in a position parallel to the venture capitalist. We can give a name to his two types of projects: (a) students, people who have the capacity to store and use human capital as alumni; and (b) researchers, people who have the capacity to invent new knowledge. (To be clear, the founder of a university would have hundreds or thousands of projects, not two projects called students and researchers.) High-aptitude students are parallel to agents with projects because, like them, they have a unique capacity (aptitude) to acquire and exercise human capital that the founder cannot do without. Even the most able student requires instruction and infrastructure, and his human capital pays out over a long career in which his aptitude to generate social returns with it is slowly revealed. Even if they are able to capture all of the returns to their human capital (none are public), high-aptitude students should be risk averse about making very large investments in their own human capital and will find it hard to get external financing for such investments without being vetted by an expert. Research projects are also parallel to agents except that their problem is aggravated by the more public nature of research. A researcher has a unique capacity to invent knowledge. He typically requires an array of infrastructure and other experts to do so. The social benefits of the knowledge he creates are likely to be revealed slowly and he will probably find it hard to capture more than small share of them. Thus, he will underinvest and be risk averse if asked to make large investments by himself. Getting external financing will be stymied by others' lack of ability to assess his ideas and by their (often justified) conviction that most of the returns will be public, not private.

1.3.3 The Founder's Solution

Since the problem is parallel to the venture capitalist's, the founder's solution should logically also be parallel. In particular, he would like to be in a situation where:

- He can build a foundation of experts and infrastructure useful for making investments in intellectual capital. This is a university.
- He can use the experts to assess which students and researchers have the greatest expected social returns to investments in their intellectual capital. His threshold rate of (social) return should be based on the opportunity costs associated with his funds and the infrastructure and expertise he has built. His threshold is embodied in a university's admissions and hiring standards.
- He can invest money, expertise, and infrastructure in researchers and students who meet his threshold. His investment is the "tuition subsidy" or difference between the cost of a student's education and what he actually pays for it—as much as 80 percent on average in the case of very high aptitude students (Hoxby 2009).
- He can demand that students who benefit from his investment contribute whatever they are able to invest in their own human capital to reduce the moral hazard problem. This contribution is tuition, which is often need-based for high-aptitude students.[9]
- He can ensure that his experts and infrastructure will be employed over sufficient cohorts of students and researchers to justify their costs.

It is on the final point that the founder runs into difficulties that the venture capitalist does not have. The venture capitalist can expect to earn enough on one generation of projects to finance the next, thereby keeping his stock of expertise and infrastructure employed long enough to make it worthwhile to have built them. The founder cannot write explicit contracts with his students in which he takes equity stakes in their earnings since such contracts would entail illegal forms of forced labor. Also, unlike the venture capitalist who is concerned with purely private returns, the founder cannot write contracts in which he gets an equity stake in public returns to research or human capital.

This is where the founder's solution is, depending on how one thinks about it, clever or fortuitous. It is also where endowments become necessary.

Students

Consider what the founder would like to do with his students. He would like to convince them that it is their social and moral obligation to give the university the equivalent of what the venture capitalist would require from them. This is the amount that will maximize the intellectual returns generated by his initial capital. Because some of the students' returns will presumably be social, the obligation on them can be multifaceted. Those who earn private returns on their human capital can be asked for gifts in

---

9. Because much research earns only public returns, there is no obvious parallel for a researcher's contribution to reduce moral hazard—unless his research is likely to generate private returns from, say, a patent.

the form of money. Others could be asked for gifts in the form of expertise. Others could be asked to use their political influence to ensure that the university is treated well by the government. And so on. The founder will not couch their obligation as an obligation to provide him with returns so as to maximize the impact of his initial capital. He will instead couch it as an obligation to provide for the next generation of students as they were provided for themselves.

There are a variety of "soft" ways in which the founder could hope to convince students that this is their obligation. The university could use exhortation and inculcation. It could develop loyalty by creating athletic teams, clubs, traditions, songs, events, and special apparel. It is my belief that many of these soft methods work because the founder himself and the people whom he recruits to run the university *truly* believe in the obligation and take a *true* interest and pleasure in providing for the next generation.

Nevertheless, it will be easier to convince a student of his obligation if, when he donates, he knows that the university has tied its own hands in such a way that the gift will be worth much less if it is not actually used to invest in the human capital of future generations. This is why endowments make sense. Even if it has no restrictions other than that the principal must be preserved in perpetuity and spent for university activities (broadly construed), much of the value of a gift to the endowment is in the future. Therefore, a university that receives a gift as endowment has a greater incentive to exist, as a university, in the future. It is less likely to so exist if it uses its funds in some manner that does not generate solid returns to intellectual capital.

To see this, consider a university that, starting with some cohort of students, begins to instruct students in vacuous material that will not be valued by employers or society. Even if these students and their equally vacuously educated successors feel an obligation to donate a share of their earnings to the university, their donations will be small because they do not have valuable human capital. The university will become increasingly unable to maintain its infrastructure and expertise—losing experts to competing institutions, for instance. Eventually, the university will find it hard to attract students because its infrastructure and expertise are so depreciated, and at this point it will fold. The larger the share of its (prevacuity) gifts in the form of endowment, the faster the university will fold and more value it must sacrifice when it folds.[10] In short, by moving much of the value of a gift into the future, an endowment gives a university's leaders an immediate incentive to engage in investments that can sustain the university. These are

10. There are numerous colleges in the United States that have arguably suffered precisely the fate described. There are examples in which the curriculum truly became vacuous. However, a more common problem is curriculum not having kept pace with changes in what employers and the rest of society valued.

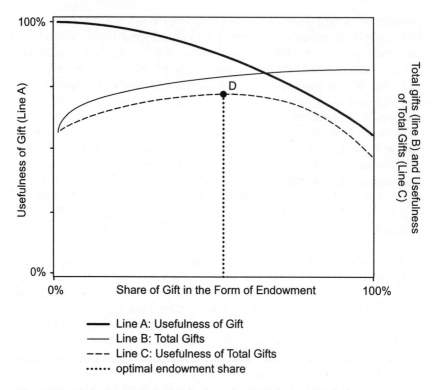

— Line A: Usefulness of Gift
— Line B: Total Gifts
– – – Line C: Usefulness of Total Gifts
•••••• optimal endowment share

Fig. 1.1 Heuristic diagram of university's preferred endowment share

necessarily investments in intellectual capital that are *valued*, socially if not privately. (Below, I consider how a university might sustain investment in intellectual capital that earns only public returns.)

A simple figure (figure 1.1) illustrates the point that the university will accept gifts in the form of endowment up a point. Line A shows how the usefulness—for the purpose of maximizing the contribution to intellectual capital—of a dollar of gift falls the larger the share of it that arrives in the form of endowment. This line necessarily slopes down simply because the timing of the use of the endowment is relatively inflexible. It will slope more steeply if there are additional restrictions on how the endowment is used. Line B shows how total gifts increase as the share of gift dollars going into the endowment rise. The logic of the shape of this line is described in the previous paragraph, but it is not clear whether it merely flattens or actually falls as the endowment share gets close to 100 percent. This is not important for line C, which is the product of lines A and B: the usefulness of total gifts for contributing to intellectual capital. Line C peaks at a point like D, and this point determines the share of gifts that the university accepts in the form of endowments.

Researchers

Now consider researchers, the returns on whose intellectual capital are more likely to be public, not private. Of course, the university can explicitly contract with researchers who are likely to generate private returns using university-derived expertise or infrastructure. For instance, the university can share in patents. In such cases, the university should solve the problem no differently than a venture capitalist would. In addition, the university can oblige its researchers to devote part of their effort to instruction so that they produce human capital in students, like any other input at the university. In this case, we are back to the problem of students, with that problem's solution of obligations and implicit contracts. Indeed, the optimal ratio of researchers' instructional-to-research time depends on the next part of the founder's solution.

This is the interesting problem of maximizing the university's ability to generate research that earns only public returns. The founder could simply sink his investment into a few generations of research, but these investments would quickly peter out because the purely public returns to this research would not generate university funds for new ones. The solution is a semiimplicit/semiexplicit contract—this time with external funders—that is made more credible by the endowment.

The founder is not the only entity interested in knowledge that is a public good. There are other philanthropists who wish similarly to maximize their contribution to intellectual capital but who lack the wherewithal (or, perhaps more realistically, the timing) to build the expertise and infrastructure that would allow them to invest efficiently in intellectual capital. There are also philanthropists who wish only to contribute to intellectual capital in a narrow area and who therefore could not support expertise and infrastructure assets on an efficient scale. Finally, there is the government, which—to the extent that it maximizes social welfare—should internalize many of the public returns to research as though they were private.

To maximize his contribution to research that generates only public returns, the founder can use his initial funds to build expertise and infrastructure assets and to sponsor some first generation of research as a demonstration. He can then seek outside philanthropic and government funds to support research that can use the university's existing infrastructure and expertise or that only requires the university to build infrastructure and expertise in a cost-efficient way—that is, gradually and in a manner related to existing infrastructure and expertise. This is exactly parallel to the venture capitalist's problem. Recall, however, that the venture capitalist could credibly vouch for a project because he would have his own contract with the agent and would also stand to lose if his equity share were worthless. It is not so easy for a university to credibly vouch for research that is projected to earn purely public returns. Of course, the provisions of a grant can ensure that, as a formal matter, every dollar is spent as the funder intends, but an outside funder should have more confidence in the research if the founder, with his expertise, has also put his own investment at stake.

This is where it will help to encourage some share of gifts for research to be in the form of endowment. It will be easier to convince outside funders that their money will be used for the intended research if the university has tied its own hands by making some research gifts less useful if the university does not, in fact, build and maintain infrastructure and expertise in the area in question over a long period. That is, the benefit of having some gifts for research go to the endowment—as opposed to current use—is that the university thereby increases the total outside funds (including government funds) for research. This benefit must be traded-off against the costs of the restrictions imposed by the endowment rules.[11]

In short, maximizing his contribution to intellectual capital through research should cause the founder to solicit an optimal share of research-related gifts in the form of endowment. The implied figure would parallel to that for student gifts in form, although—of course—the parameters of the relevant curves would differ depending on the inferences outside funders draw from the university's restricting itself via the endowment.

1.4 A Portrait of the University

The university's problem, as presented in the previous section, is so abstract that it can be hard to see how it matches the universities that we know from our own experience. What would this university, which maximizes its contribution to society's intellectual capital by acting as a social venture capitalist, actually look like?

The instigating financial capital of the universities' founders—who undoubtedly would have been less prescient than the fictional founder—would be unimportant, having long ago been dwarfed or replaced by the gifts of former students complying with their implicit contracts. Some alumni gifts would go to endowment and some to current use. The ratio would be a (surely not explicit) function of the degree to which the endowment nature of gifts increased the amount of gifts. Alumni who earned little (perhaps because they worked in public service) would not give or would give in some nonmonetary form: time, expertise, and so on. Above some earnings threshold, alumni would tend to give a share of their lifetime returns that was either steady or increasing in the scale of those returns. Thus, if the distribution of lifetime returns among alumni had a long right-hand tail, so would the distribution of donations within a cohort. (Note the word *returns*, as opposed

11. Interestingly, this is an argument for tenure of researchers that is quite independent of other arguments for and against. If the university wants to increase the credibility of its commitment to research in some area, tenuring researchers in that area is an effective way to tie its own hands to supporting that area for some time.

to earnings or wealth. An alumnus who was born rich, for instance, might have modest returns on the investment that the university made in him, even if he had high earnings.)

Second, research would be supported by a few means. The university would have venture capital-like contracts with its researchers who use its assets to produce patentable or otherwise private return-generating research. Faculty time would often be split between instruction (human capital production) and research since the former activity would provide reliable returns through students. Finally, research that generated popular public goods would be supported by a combination of the university's assets (infrastructure and experts) and outside funders' money. Some gifts for research would be in the form of endowment, with the ratio again being dictated by the degree to which the endowment nature of funds increased the amount of outside funds.

The infrastructure and expertise of the university would continually, gradually drift from the areas that earned high social returns in the past to areas that were likely to earn them in the future. This would not necessarily be intentional. Rather, it would be an organic response to the project (student and research) opportunities that arose. For instance, the university might routinely accept grants that required it to add incrementally to infrastructure and experts, and the gradual piling up of these increments would slowly change the nature of these key university assets.

The higher the aptitude of the students at a university, the greater would be the investment in their education. Students would be asked to pay for part of the investment, according to their ability to do so, to reduce their moral hazard. Unless the highest-aptitude students were systematically much more able to pay than their slightly lower-aptitude peers (and so on down the aptitude spectrum), the universities that enrolled the highest-aptitude students would also subsidize the current cost of their education the most. These same universities would thus be most reliant on inculcating an sense of obligation to the next generation of students and on supporting the credibility of their implicit contracts through thoughtful use of the endowment.

A few caveats are in order here. First, it seems unlikely that a university could create a sense of loyalty or obligation if it invested substantially different amounts in different students. Thus, universities are likely to be fundamentally constrained in how heterogeneous their admissions can be.[12] Second, an alumnus's sense of obligation may be reduced if the next generation of students looks too dissimilar from his own cohort. Thus, the university may be constrained to alter the character of its student population gradually. Third, it may be easier to instill a sense of obligation in a

---

12. That is, a university might find two students who have the same rate of return on human capital investments but whose optimal size of investments differed substantially. If the university were constrained to make similar investments in all of its students, it could not admit both students even if both students could, in fact, benefit from the same university assets.

student if he is surrounded by a critical share of students who already have it. Thus, a university may find it difficult to move wholesale into new campuses at which none of the students already have the tradition of obligation. Fourth, nothing that has been said constrains a university to contribute intellectual capital through *both* human capital and research. Indeed, very selective liberal arts colleges fit the university model except that the research components do not apply.[13]

It is important to observe that the university modeled here might make investments in intellectual capital that simply do not get made in countries in which no one has solved the founder's problem in the founder's way. That is, there is no reason to think that every country will develop very selective private universities that make investments in human capital on the same per-person scale as America's top private universities do. If some mechanism that mimics the founder's solution does not arise, some intellectual capital investments will probably just not be made because conventional financing would not work. Of course, in theory, it would be possible for a government to mimic the founder's solution. However, governments have political constraints that private universities do not.

1.5 Implications for Endowment Management

It will be observed that the model implies that university endowments came into being for fairly simple reasons. If the object of the university is to maximize its contributions to intellectual capital, its social venture capital activities are its reason for existence. The endowment arises simply because returns must enter an investment pool before being reinvested and the university is able to make greater investments in intellectual capital if it accepts some returns (and some gifts to support research) in the form of endowment. Thus, the main thing that is true of the endowment is the obvious thing: it represents a series of commitments that the university has made to invest funds in a set of intellectual capital projects. Importantly, the endowment has no independent purpose or objective of its own. This is why it should *not* be possible to define an objective for the endowment that is independent of the other side of the university's portfolio—the social venture capital side.

1.5.1 The University's Investment Problem, the Basic Version

Consider a university that is deciding what to do with its available investment pool. This pool consists of all current-use funds, all endowment income, and other funds that the university could legally use, including various forms of decapitalization, and even borrowing. (In this subsection,

---

13. A handful of all-research universities appear to be sustainable (Rockefeller University, for instance), but they are narrowly focused. The fact that many universities combine human capital creation and research suggests that the activities enjoy substantial production synergies.

I ignore specific restrictions on the use of funds but will return to this problem.) The university's problem is fairly straightforward to describe, though not straightforward to solve in practice.

The university knows the current set of intellectual capital projects that it could pursue—that is, all of the students and research in which it could potentially invest in the current period. Let us suppose it has rational expectations about the intellectual capital projects that will arise in each future period. For each project, current or future, the university can assign probabilities to each possible scenario of expenses and returns. That is, the university can reduce each project to the market value and investment risk characteristics it would have if it were a traded asset: it has a certain expected return, variation around that expected return, and correlations between its return and those of other projects owing to exogenous events. For instance, some projects might be sensitive to the price of oil. Other projects might be sensitive to which party controls Congress.

Suppose, for a moment, that projects did not need to use the assets specific to the university—its infrastructure and expertise—that have the convex adjustment costs we have emphasized. That is, suppose that projects only required inputs (in addition to the student or researcher himself) that could be bought at a world market price. Then, the projects could be evaluated fairly independently. The university would compute the properties of each potential project as an asset and find the optimal path of current and future portfolios, knowing that funds would be available in each future period for projects in one of three ways: (a) there would be returns generated by the endowment principal, (b) there would be funds if some money currently in the investment pool (such as current endowment returns) were not invested in current intellectual capital projects but "saved" for future projects by being invested in financial markets, and (c) there would be returns from past intellectual capital projects or cash flow from outside funders who were committed to research projects. Then, the procedure for finding the optimal *financial market* portfolio would be what Merton outlines—except that his solution is framed quite differently because he does not think of projects/assets with expected investments flowing out and returns flowing in. He thinks of cash flows, including expenses, which he models as an exogenous, dynamic, stochastic process. However, for any given path of current and future intellectual capital projects, there is a reduced-form that can be expressed purely as cash flows. Thus, Merton's fundamental solution method carries over, although of course the solution would look different with cash flows that are more realistic than the processes he actually uses. Moreover, the insights he derives carry over as well, namely:

- The spending rate on the endowment falls out of the optimization process and depends on the social venture capital side of the portfolio. In fact, no rule that is independent of the intellectual capital side of the

portfolio makes sense. This excludes simple rules such as "4.5 percent of the last three years' rolling average of total endowment market value."
- The optimal portfolio allocation for the endowment will be such that the university's financial assets have risks and returns that offset those of the university's intellectual capital portfolio. For instance, if the university's intellectual capital is disproportionately in projects that depend on demand for computer software, its financial assets ought to diversify its total portfolio away from that industry.
- An important function of endowment investments is to hedge against unanticipated changes in the costs of university activities. For instance, a university might invest some of its financial portfolio in real estate near campus that could be used for faculty housing.[14]

1.5.2 Incorporating Restrictions on the Uses of Funds

In fact, a university's pool of available investment funds is not unrestricted as to uses. Sizeable parts of it are restricted, and returns and cash flows associated with current intellectual capital projects are often restricted as well. Flows from outside funders are often highly restricted, but alumni sometimes place restrictions on their gifts as well.

Thus, instead of solving a single investment problem as described above, in the model the university instead solves a series of investment problems, sequentially, as follows:

- Begin with the most restricted investment pools and the potential projects that qualify for them. Solve for the optimal current and future portfolio of these projects. Remove the projects that get funded from consideration. Remove the funds that are invested in these projects from the pool that could be invested in financial markets instead of the intellectual capital side of the portfolio.
- Proceed to the next most restricted investment pools and consider all of the remaining potential projects that qualify for them. Again, solve and then remove the relevant projects and funds from further consideration.
- Continue sequentially until the unrestricted investment pool is reached, at which time all remaining potential projects are considered. Solve the problem as described in the last section, noting that all investment pool funds that were not committed (that is, those from all of the restricted pools as well as those from the unrestricted pool, if any) should be invested in the financial market side of the portfolio to attain goals like diversification and cost hedging.

Although the sequential process may appear at first to be onerous, in fact it should reduce the scale of the problem at the final stages greatly because

---

14. This is an example drawn from Merton (1993).

the university will need to consider a smaller number of potential projects for unrestricted funds.

1.5.3 Adding Adjustment Costs to the University's Problem

Unfortunately, if we make the problem more realistic by allowing for convex costs of adjusting the university's expertise and infrastructure, the problem could go from being tractable (though certainly demanding) to intractable. I first describe the problem broadly, at which point it should appear intractable, and then discuss why it might be fairly tractable in practice.

Suppose that the university fully understands the costs of adjusting its expertise and infrastructure.[15] Then, when it considers every potential intellectual capital project, it must consider the costs of adjusting its expertise and infrastructure to serve the project. Those adjustment costs will, in turn, depend on which other projects are being implemented concurrently and which projects were done in the past. If we consider all of the ways in which projects' use of expertise and infrastructure could interact, the number of portfolios that we should consider would grow explosively large. That is, the state space would explode.

To make this concrete, suppose that the same faculty member can either engage in important instruction or lead an important research project. If the university considers the research project first, it might allocate her to that project and invest in it. It might then find that the instruction was a poor investment because it would require the university to hire someone else just like her, and the cost of making this hire might be very expensive. If the university had considered the same projects in the other order (instruction first, research second), it might have come to a different conclusion—for instance, investing in the instruction but not the research. Moreover, although the difference in these two decisions might seem small, they would not be because whichever project gets done would not only occupy the faculty member's time but would also absorb some other infrastructure and expertise—which would have domino effects on other projects. These other affected projects would affect yet more projects, and so on.

For another example, consider a university that foresees that some area of research that is not productive now will possibly be highly productive in twenty years—if the university has certain expertise and infrastructure by then. Then, the university must consider all of the possible paths:

- starting projects now that are unproductive but that build some infrastructure and expertise in the relevant areas. This will make related future projects more attractive, leading to more infrastructure and expertise being built;

---

15. Of course, it might not understand its adjustment costs fully, but allowing for this would merely add a layer of difficulty without adding clarity.

- starting projects at some intermediate time (ten years, say) and incurring greater adjustment costs then, in the hope that the ten-year-out projects are sufficiently productive to justify the costs, especially when the twenty-year-out projects' dependence on that infrastructure and expertise is considered; and
- waiting for twenty years to start the relevant projects and incurring massive adjustment costs then.

Each of these paths will have domino effects on other potential projects that overlap in time and use of the university's infrastructure and expertise.

Thus, with adjustment costs, the investment portfolios that should be considered would appear to be endless in number. I would argue, however, that the situation is not so dire because: (a) many of tomorrow's projects are extremely similar to today's projects so that the number of future contingencies is much smaller than it appears, and (b) although universities' per-period adjustment costs at the extensive margin are large and highly convex, its adjustment costs at intensive margins are small.

The first of these points is easy to see: next year's cohort of potential students is so much like this year's cohort of potential students that they are nearly interchangeable. Thus, it is *possible* that a biology course developed for this year's cohort of students (because it was a good investment in them) might be a bad investment for next year's cohort of students. However, possible is not likely. Similarly, a good share of the "new" research ideas that arise each year are, in fact, very closely related to the "old" research ideas that arose in the previous year.

The second of these points—extensive versus intensive margin adjustment costs—means that it is costly for universities to quickly acquire expertise and infrastructure that forces them to grow (in size or area of expertise), but not costly for universities to transform existing expertise and infrastructure among uses that are already in their project portfolios. For instance, if a university decided to double the size of its entering class overnight, this would entail tremendous adjustment costs owing to the need to build student housing, increase faculty, and so on very quickly. In contrast, if a university decided to stop admitting classes that were one-third humanities majors, one-third sciences, and one-third social sciences and start admitting classes that were two-thirds humanities, one-sixth sciences, and one-sixth social sciences, this would generate costs but they would not be nearly so dramatic. Some libraries, classrooms, housing, administrators, student support staff, and so on would flow fairly easily from, say, social science to humanities use. Thus, the university should treat as similar various project portfolios that have the same implications for the extensive margins of adjustment, even if they have different implications for the intensive margins of adjustment.

In short, including adjustment costs in the university's investment problem does make the problem more difficult, but perhaps not absolutely intractable. A practical person solving the university's investment problem might do well to focus only on the adjustment cost implications of (a) new projects that are very unlike existing projects, and (b) projects that involve building substantial expertise or infrastructure at the extensive margin.

1.6 Conclusions

The proposed, positive model of the university has implications for numerous questions, and many of the more abstract questions have already been addressed. For instance, section 1.5 described how the spending rule—which probably should be called a "function" rather than a "rule"—would arise in this model. It also described how optimal portfolio allocations should be determined by a university following this model—on both the intellectual capital and the financial capital side. But these answers, which include the insights first derived by Merton, are very abstract. It may therefore be useful to answer a few, less abstract but related questions.

In the context of the model, what would a university do if, for exogenous reasons, its financial market portfolio were temporarily earning a very high rate of return?

This is the circumstance in which a university thinks about keeping funds in the financial market portfolio that might, in an ordinary period, be invested in the intellectual capital side of the portfolio. The logic is that the university could make so much money on financial assets that reducing its current intellectual capital investments would make sense: it would be enabled, thereby, to increase future intellectual capital investments by so much that the university's total contribution to world intellectual capital would increase.

This logic is, indeed, what falls out of the model: current intellectual capital projects face a higher hurdle rate. *However*, the university's managers would take account of the fact that, if they restricted or reduced intellectual capital projects now, they would face even higher adjustment costs of implementing intellectual capital projects in the future, when the period of remarkable financial returns was over and they needed to start making intellectual capital investments at a higher rate than before.

A related question that often occurs to potential donors is whether they should donate now or later—because they believe that their *personal* rate of return will be high in the near future, relative to the university's. Of course, potential donors are not always correct that their personal rate of return will be higher than the university's. But, even if they are, potential donors probably do not take account of how they affect adjustment costs when they give in the future instead of now. In the context of the model, this is problematic. The model implies that universities would try to make potential donors internalize the adjustment costs they impose.

In the context of the model, what would a university do if, for exogenous reasons, considerable parts of its financial market portfolio were underwater and could not be liquidated except at very high cost?

This is another circumstance in which a university thinks about keeping funds in the financial market portfolio that might, in an ordinary period, be invested in the intellectual capital side of the portfolio. The logic is that it is very expensive, in terms of foregone future intellectual capital, to invest in intellectual capital because the cost of funds is the rate at which the institution can borrow.

This logic is, indeed, what falls out of the model: current intellectual capital projects would face a higher hurdle rate. Most obviously, the university might wish to shed expenses that are not associated with assets that have convex adjustment costs—certain staff who have fairly generic skills, for instance. *However*, the university's managers would again take account of the fact that, if they shed infrastructure or expertise, they might face high costs of reacquiring it in the future. In short, the model implies that universities will gain from developing a clear understanding of their adjustment costs, especially those that occur after downward adjustments in infrastructure and expertise (since these are not common).

In the context of the model, what would a university do if its financial market portfolio seemed always to be earning a substantially higher rate of return than its intellectual capital portfolio?

Because the universities do not actually attempt to compute the value of their intellectual capital projects as assets, it is quite possible that this question only appears to be common. Thus, one response to this question is that it should not be answered until the university has made the calculations to show that it is, in fact, a question.

However, assuming that it is a legitimate question, the model quite possibly implies "do nothing." In the model, the funds given to universities are there for the purpose of investing in intellectual capital, not running a financial business on the side. Thus, the only legitimate, alternative use of current-investment funds would be later investments in intellectual capital. It is possible that the intellectual capital side of the portfolio will always earn lower returns.

More specifically, the model implies that the university should assess its intellectual capital investments in a slightly different way, depending on whether they do or do not have related financial assets. Consider first the intellectual capital projects that should be related to financial market assets. For instance, if some firms are making tremendous profits, why are some of the university's alumni not leaders of or investors in these firms? If some inventors/entrepreneurs are making great profits, why does the university not have a stake in them, either through a patent or through having educated the inventors? Perhaps the university trains future managers and investors poorly. Perhaps the university's research in areas that generate private profits is not conducted well. Perhaps the university is not pursuing patents in which it has a legitimate stake. Perhaps the university is not succeeding in convincing its students of their obligation to the next generation.

Now consider the intellectual capital investments that have scarcely related or no financial assets. The lack of related financial assets is prima facie evidence that the returns are largely public. However, even these investments can be subdivided. For some, external funders are in as good a position as university experts to evaluate the social return to the project—curing a disease that affects a population of poor people, say. For other projects, external funders may lack the expertise to evaluate the social return to the project—for instance, moving the frontier in an abstruse area of math or deciphering a papyrus that contains a lost Greek tragedy. If external funders are not funding a public returns-producing project that they can evaluate, the model implies that the university ought to improve its communications with them or reconsider the public value of the project. However, if the only people expert enough to understand the project's public value are experts who dwell in universities, then the model suggests that the university can do no better than consulting its own understanding and that of experts at peer institutions.[16]

In the context of the model, what would a university do if its financial market portfolio seemed always to be growing as a share of its total (financial plus intellectual capital) portfolio?

Again, because universities do not actually attempt to compute the value of their intellectual capital projects as assets, it is quite possible that this question is wrongheaded. This is another argument for making the calculations, even if they are imperfect.

Assuming that the question is not wrongheaded, however, the model implies that the financial side would only grow persistently as a share of the total portfolio if (a) the returns on future intellectual capital projects were *substantially* higher than those of today's intellectual capital projects, and (b) adjustment costs were such that when those future days arrive, the cost of suddenly needing to provide infrastructure and expertise to them would not be exorbitant.

Since circumstances (a) and (b) probably do not often arise in conjunction, the model implies that a university should examine itself if its financial market portfolio's share of its total portfolio rises very persistently. It seems most likely that this would occur if the university were not solving its investment problem correctly according to the model.

1.6.1 Key Implications of the Model

A few key implications of the model should now be evident. First, it implies that an optimizing university would actively attempt to compute

---

16. In the long run, there may be returns to universities from educating more people to understand the public value of projects of the type in question.

the values in its intellectual capital portfolios. This may be difficult, but the best available estimates would be better than none for the purposes of university and endowment management. Second, it implies that an optimizing university would attempt to calculate its adjustment costs. Knowing these costs is important for making every investment decision, whether on the intellectual or financial portfolio side. Third, the model implies that an optimizing university's leaders (the president, provost, and so on) would be in close communication with its endowment managers, with the specific goal of exchanging information on the value of existing intellectual capital investments, on returns to prospective investments in intellectual capital, and on adjustment costs. These exchanges should generate spending rates on the endowment that depend on and routinely adjust to circumstances on the social venture capital side of the portfolio. Overall, the model implies that highly endowed universities can make greater contributions to world intellectual capital—arguably, contributions that no other entities can make—if they manage both sides of their portfolios in a rigorous and coordinated manner.

References

Advisory Committee on Endowment Management. 1969. *Managing Educational Endowments: Report to the Ford Foundation*. New York: Ford Foundation.
Bergemann, D., and U. Hege. 1998. "Venture Capital Financing, Moral Hazard and Learning." *Journal of Banking and Finance* 22:703–35.
Berglof, E. 1994. "A Control Theory of Venture Capital Finance." *Journal of Law, Economics, and Organization* 10:247–67.
Black, Fischer. 1976. "The Investment Policy Spectrum: Individuals, Endowment Funds and Pension Funds." *Financial Analysts Journal* 32 (1): 23–31.
Blume, Marshall E. 2009. "Institutional Spending Rules and Asset Allocation." Wharton Working Paper no. 01-09, University of Pennsylvania.
Brown, Jeffrey, Stephen Dimmock, Jun-Koo Kang, and Scott Weisbenner. 2010. "How University Endowments Respond to Financial Market Shocks: Evidence and Implications." NBER Working Paper no. 15861, Cambridge, MA.
Brown, Keith, Lorenzo Garlappi, and Cristian Tiu. 2010. "Asset Allocation and Portfolio Performance: Evidence from University Endowment Funds." *Journal of Financial Markets* 13:268–94.
Campbell, John. 2012. "Investing and Spending: The Twin Challenges of University Endowment Management." In *Forum Futures*, edited by Maureen Devlin. Washington, DC: American Council on Education.
Casamatta, C. 2003. "Financing and Advising: Optimal Financial Contracts with Venture Capitalists." *Journal of Finance* 58:2059–86.
Clotfelter, Charles. 1996. *Buying the Best*. Princeton, NJ: Princeton University Press.
Dimmock, Stephen. 2012. "Background Risk and University Endowment Funds." *Review of Economics and Statistics* 94 (3): 789–99.
Donaldson, Lufkin, and Jenrette, Inc. 1969. *Managing Endowment Capital*. New York: Donaldson, Lufkin, and Jenrette.

Ehrenberg, Ronald G. 2000. *Tuition Rising: Why College Costs So Much.* Cambridge, MA: Harvard University Press.

Eisner, Robert. 1974. "Endowment Income, Capital Gains and Inflation Accounting: Discussion." *American Economic Review* 64:438–41.

Ennis, Richard, and J. Peter Williamson. 1976. *Spending Policy for Educational Endowments.* Wilton, CT: The Common Fund.

Gompers, Paul A. 1995. "Optimal Investment, Monitoring, and the Staging of Venture Capital." *Journal of Finance* 50:1461–89.

Gorman, M., and W. A. Sahlman. 1989. "What do Venture Capitalists Do?" *Journal of Business Venturing* 5:77–90.

Grinold, Richard, David Hopkins, and William E. Massy. 1978. "A Model for Long-Range University Budget Planning under Uncertainty." *Bell Journal of Economics* 9:396.

Hansmann, Henry. 1990. "Why do Universities Have Endowments?" *Journal of Legal Studies* 19 (1): 3–42.

Hoxby, Caroline M. 2009. "The Changing Selectivity of American Colleges." *Journal of Economic Perspectives* 23 (4): 95–118.

———. Forthcoming. *The Role of Markets in Education.* The 2011 Clarendon Lectures in Economics, Oxford University Press.

Kaplan, S. N., and P. Strömberg. 2001. "Venture Capitalists as Principals: Contracting, Screening, and Monitoring." *American Economic Review Papers and Proceedings* 91:426–30.

———. 2003. "Financial Contracting Theory Meets the Real World: An Empirical Analysis of Venture Capital Contracts." *Review of Economic Studies* 70:281–315.

Lerner, Joshua, Antoinette Schoar, and Jialan Wang. 2008. "Secrets of the Academy: The Drivers of University Endowment Success." *Journal of Economic Perspectives* 22 (3): 207–22.

Litvack, James M., Burton G. Malkiel, and Richard E. Quandt. 1974. "A Plan for the Definition of Endowment Income." *American Economic Review* 64:433.

Malkiel, Burton G., and Paul Firstenberg. 1976. *Managing Risk in an Uncertain Era: An Analysis for Endowed Institutions.* Princeton, NJ: Princeton University.

Merhling, Perry, Paul Goldstein, and Verne Sedlacek. 2005. *Endowment Spending, Goals, Rates, and Rules.* Forum for the Future of Higher Education.

Merton, Robert C. 1993. "Optimal Investment Strategies for University Endowment Funds." In *Studies of Supply and Demand in Higher Education*, edited by Charles T. Clotfelter and Michael Rothschild. Chicago: University of Chicago Press.

Repullo, Rafael, and Javier Suarez. 2004. "Venture Capital Finance: A Security Design Approach." *Review of Finance* 8:75–108.

Sahlman, W. A. 1990. "The Structure and Governance of Venture-Capital Organizations." *Journal of Financial Economics* 27:473–521.

Tobin, James. 1974. "What Is Permanent Endowment Income?" *American Economic Review* 64:427.

Trester, J. J. 1998. "Venture Capital Contracting under Asymmetric Information." *Journal of Banking and Finance* 22:675–99.

Williamson, J. Peter. 1975. "Background Paper." In *Funds for the Future: Report of the Twentieth Century Fund Task Force on College and University Endowment Policy*, edited by Peter J. Williamson. New York: McGraw-Hill.

2

The Interaction of Spending Policies, Asset Allocation Strategies, and Investment Performance at University Endowment Funds

Keith C. Brown and Cristian Ioan Tiu

2.1 Introduction

Suppose that you are contemplating the launch of a new investment management firm. Before determining the myriad logistical details involved with staffing and running the business, you must first make a basic decision on the general approach to managing assets that the company will adopt. Consider two alternative schemes for organizing the business:

Approach 1: Develop a thorough understanding of what the clients expect to accomplish by investing their financial capital and then design an investment portfolio (i.e., asset allocation and security selection strategies) that represents the optimal solution to the clients' "problem"; or,

Approach 2: Design the specific elements of an investment portfolio (i.e., asset allocation and security selection strategies) and then market that port-

Keith C. Brown is the University Distinguished Teaching Professor and the Fayez Sarofim Fellow at the McCombs School of Business at the University of Texas at Austin. Cristian Ioan Tiu is associate professor of finance at the University of Buffalo.

This study has benefitted greatly from input provided by all of the participants at the NBER conference "How the Great Recession Affected Higher Education," in Cambridge, Massachusetts, September 2012. We are particularly grateful for the comments of Jeffrey Brown, Stephen Dimmock, Elroy Dimson, Thomas Gilbert, Will Goetzmann, Caroline Hoxby, Christopher Hrdlicka, and Scott Weisbenner. We would also like to express our appreciation to the following individuals connected to the endowment fund industry who have provided us with valuable resources as well as their comments: John Griswold and Bill Jarvis (Commonfund), Kenneth Redd (NACUBO), Uzi Yoeli and Bruce Zimmerman (UTIMCO), Andrea Reed and Scott Wise (Covariance Capital), Tim Nguyen (University of Connecticut Foundation), Ed Schneider (University at Buffalo Foundation), Chris Adkerson (Mercer), and Larry Tavares (TAP Inc.). Finally, we also thank Sergey Maslennikov and Woongsun Yoo for their research assistance. For acknowledgments, sources of research support, and disclosure of the authors' material financial relationships, if any, please see http://www.nber.org/chapters/c12857.ack.

folio to investors for whom it represents an appropriate solution to their financial problem.

While both organizational formats are used widely in practice (e.g., private wealth management firms exemplify approach 1; the mutual fund industry is typical of approach 2), the question remains as to which is the more conceptually valid method. For many investors, approach 1 represents the proper sequence of events in that it starts with an understanding of what the investor is trying to accomplish before proceeding to form a portfolio that represents the optimal ex ante solution to that problem. Conversely, although approach 2 suffers the potential criticism of reversing that order (i.e., forming the portfolio "solution" first), it is often the more cost-effective scheme, particularly for those investors with relatively small amounts of capital to manage.

For firms managing institutional assets (e.g., defined-benefit pension plans, endowment funds and foundations, sovereign wealth funds), resolving this question is critical if for no other reason than the amount of invested capital involved.[1] Defined-benefit pension plans and university endowments are particularly interesting to contrast in this respect because both types of institutions face reasonably well defined, if otherwise dissimilar, investment problems. For example, asset allocations in pension fund portfolios are often made in response to complex asset-liability management problems, with a broad array of client-specific (e.g., annual payout needs, workforce age) and firm- and industry-wide (e.g., plan-funded status, legal and regulatory restrictions) factors serving as constraints on the process. Further, this investment decision is complicated by the fact that defined-pension benefits are a legally binding obligation of the plan sponsor, which creates and manages the fund portfolio for the purpose of meeting those liabilities, but must also be prepared to cover the shortfall if fund income (or assets) proves to be insufficient. It is for this reason that Merton (2003) argues that the relevant investment risk in pension fund management is not that of the assets alone but rather the volatility of the surplus of fund assets over liabilities.

Endowment funds are even more intriguing entities because they simultaneously combine some of the salient characteristics of other institutional investors with several features that make them truly unique. Like pension funds, the conventional endowment portfolio—as typified by the building and operating funds at a college or university—must be managed with regard to a well-specified set of spending rules. However, as Garland (2005) notes, an important difference between endowment funds and pension plans is that

---

1. For instance, by the end of 2005, professional managers for three of the most prominent institutions—mutual funds, defined-benefit pension funds, and endowment funds and foundations—controlled $8.9 trillion, $4.7 trillion, and $1.3 trillion in assets, respectively. These assets under management statistics are for US-based institutions and come from the Investment Company Institute (mutual funds) and Standard & Poor's *Money Market Directory* (pension funds, endowments, and foundations).

trustees of endowment funds "expect to preserve their capital for a very long time; trustees of pension funds expect their capital to be consumed" (44).[2] In fact, endowment funds are among the only economic agents for which the assumption of an infinite investment horizon is *not* an approximation, making them especially well-suited laboratories for studying management practices under "textbook" conditions.[3]

Given this description, arguably the most significant conceptual challenge that any endowment fund must resolve is the tension that exists between the desire to increase the future wealth of the portfolio—and in so doing help to insure the long-term viability and autonomy of the institution it supports—and the need to provide spending capital for the current generation. Addressing this tension, which can be viewed as the primary investment problem that endowment funds confront, is the chief role of the *spending policy*, which is the formal statement that the educational institution's governing authority adopts to express its intentions. Despite its apparent importance, though, the topics of how endowment funds are organized and how they determine their spending policies have received remarkably little attention in the literature. Further, much of this research is quite dated; for example, Cain (1960) summarizes the details of a survey of 200 institutions of higher education regarding a variety of operational issues ranging from specific investment holdings to the use of outside advisors and the existence of income reserve accounts.[4]

Still, from what has been written, there are two important hypotheses about the way in which endowments should define and revise their spending policies that remain untested. The first hypothesis involves the relationship between the organization's spending and investment policies, and on this matter there are opposing predictions. One side of the argument is typified by Litvack, Malkiel, and Quandt (1974), who concentrate on the more narrow question of how endowment income should be defined so as "to make investment management independent of the spending decisions of the university" (433), which is consistent with organizational approach 1. Other studies reflecting this view include Tobin (1974) and Garland (2005). On the other hand, Dybvig (1999) argues that an endowment's choice of a spending rule should be linked to its asset allocation decision in an explicit and dynamic fashion, while Blume (2010) uses data simulations to conclude that a fund's spending and investment strategies are best determined jointly,

---

2. Swensen (2009) reinforces this point as follows: "Investing with a *time horizon measured in centuries* to support the educational and research mission of society's colleges and universities creates a challenge guaranteed to engage the emotions and intellect of fund fiduciaries" (3, emphasis added).

3. There is a well-developed literature addressing the problem of optimal portfolio choice over an infinite planning horizon under the conditions of income consumption; see, for example, Samuelson (1969), Merton (1971), and Bodily and White (1982).

4. Cejnek et al. (2012) provide an excellent review of the endowment fund literature, which encompasses a number of relevant topics including the determination of spending policies.

which would be more in line with approach 2. Gilbert and Hrdlicka (2012), who examine the issue of the intergenerational fairness of the spending rule decision, come to a similar conclusion.

The second untested hypothesis from the extant literature on endowment spending involves the identity and temporal stability of the permanent payout policy that a given institution adopts. That is, what is the optimal spending policy in the face of the endowment's specific circumstances and how frequently should that rule be adjusted? On this matter, the theoretical literature that exists is considerably less ambiguous. Specifically, Merton (1993) creates a formal model of an endowment fund as one of several tangible and intangible assets that a university possesses for the purpose of establishing the optimal spending and investment policies the fund should choose. In the context of the current discussion, he shows that (a) the optimal spending rule for any period t should be a constant proportion of the net worth of the fund in that same period, and that (b) the proportion of wealth expended is *not* stochastic given the underlying conditions of the model. Thus, absent a substantial change in the institution's circumstances (e.g., the educational and research activities in which it engages), the optimal rule by which any given endowment determines its annual expenditures *should not* vary over time. Woglom (2003), who expands Merton's conceptual framework to explore the Tobin (1974) notion of "intergenerational fairness" in more detail, produces a more complex optimal spending rule but one that remains nonstochastic given the endowment's intertemporal rate of substitution between current and future income needs.

In this study, we extend and test these lines of inquiry by providing a comprehensive examination of which endowment spending policies are used in practice as well as how frequently and why those mandates are revised over time. Starting with an overview of a typical endowment organizational structure, we consider the role that both the institution's spending and investment policies play in the portfolio management process. In particular, we describe an endowment's spending policy as consisting of two distinct elements: the *spending rules*, which represent the formal set of instructions used to determine the amount of capital that will be paid out of the endowment portfolio on an annual basis, and the *policy payout rate*, which is the particular percentage level used to convert the general spending rule into a specific dollar disbursement. Given the very long-term horizon of the sponsoring institution, as well as the relatively invariant nature of the present-versus-future trade-off that defines its investment problem, the underlying premise of our investigation is that the endowment spending policy should require modification on a very infrequent basis.

Our analysis is based on an examination of spending, asset allocation, and investment performance data for more than 800 public and private university endowment funds located mainly in North America. The primary database we utilize is constructed from the annual surveys of the organizational structure, spending and investment policies, and spending and investment practices that the National Association of College and University Business Officers (NACUBO) collects from its member institutions. Focusing of the survey years from 2003 to 2011, the period of time for which NACUBO collected information regarding spending rules and policy payout rates, we classify into one of seven broad categories the stated payout rules that every endowment fund adopted in each year. The frequency with which endowments adopt these seven spending rules is not uniform; in fact, the moving average rule, which sets the annual payout as a prespecified percentage of an average of past market values for the endowment portfolio, is used in roughly three-quarters of the cases. Further, we also document that there is a considerable degree of heterogeneity in spending rule adoption practices within the endowment sample. Generally speaking, we find significant differences in the formulas favored by funds with disparate payout needs and that larger funds are far less reliant on moving average rules than are smaller endowments.

One of the most surprising results in the study is that endowment funds modify their spending policies to a far greater extent than the investment problems faced by the sponsoring institution would seem to warrant. In particular, we show that while half of the funds in the sample maintained the same policy throughout the 2003–2011 period, the other half changed their permanent spending rules between one and eight times; the weighted mean frequency of endowments altering their spending policy in a given year was almost 25 percent. An analysis of the migration patterns in spending rule adoption practices showed that the various rule categories produced dramatically different likelihoods of being retained or changed from one year to the next; for example, moving average rules (and more complex hybrid formulas involving moving average rules) had markedly larger retention rates than did simpler rules, such as payout formulas based on percentage of the income the fund generated in the current year.

Extending this investigation, we consider the effect that the global financial market crisis that began in 2008 had on an endowment's propensity to adjust its spending policy. By focusing on behavior in the postrecession period (i.e., 2009–2011), our analysis documents two significant findings. First, despite the additional funding burdens caused by a substantial loss of market value in their asset portfolios, endowments actually showed an *increased* tendency to maintain their existing permanent policies following the economic downturn. Second, roughly one in three funds imposed some form of *temporary* incremental appropriations to supplement their permanent spending rules after 2008. The combination of these effects can be viewed as a rational marginal response to what was perceived as a temporary, albeit severe, perturbation in normal economic conditions.

We also examine the issue of what motivates an educational institution to alter its stated payout policy. Our investigation of the economic determinants of spending rule changes reveals that the larger the endowment is and the lower the return to its portfolio, the more likely it is to make a modification. Also, spending rule changes are significantly and negatively related to historical payout levels, but the percentage of the institution's budget that the fund is responsible for delivering is not a meaningful factor. Our lead-lag analysis of the relationship between spending rule changes and asset allocation adjustments reveals that it is the former that tends to precede the latter and that adjustments to both types of policy are strongly persistent over time. Finally, despite the fact that endowment funds produce strong benchmark-adjusted returns as a group, there is no detectable difference in the investment performance between institutions that either did or did not alter their spending rules. Overall, we conclude that the typical educational endowment has changed its permanent spending policy far more frequently than might be reasonably expected and that these adjustments are linked to, or interact with, characteristics of the funds themselves (e.g., level of assets under management, historical payout level) as well as various aspects of the investment practices of the institution (e.g., asset allocation patterns).

The remainder of the chapter is organized as follows. In the next section, we provide an overview of how, and by whom, endowment spending rules and investment practices are determined. Section 2.3 discusses the data we use in our empirical analysis and describes our endowment fund sample, including summary statistics on fund size, annual investment returns, annual payout rates, asset class allocations, and the spending rules that are used in practice. In section 2.4 we present a detailed analysis of the way spending policy adoption has evolved over time, while section 2.5 identifies several economic determinants of these policy modifications. Section 2.6 examines the interaction between an endowment's spending policy decision, its investment strategy, and the portfolio's investment performance. Section 2.7 concludes the study.

2.2 Spending and Investment at University Endowment Funds

2.2.1 Endowment Organization: A Brief Overview

Generally speaking, endowment funds are portfolios of assets invested in support of the short- and long-term mission of a particular institution. Within the context of this broad definition, Hansmann (1990) notes that endowments can have several specific purposes, from helping the institution remain financially solvent by providing a source of funding to offset current operating expenses to insuring its continued existence and economic independence into the foreseeable future to enhancing the reputational capital of the sponsoring institution.[5] As Kochard and Rittereiser (2008) discuss,

5. Hoxby (chapter 1, this volume) proposes a model of the university in which the institution's objective function is to maximize its contribution to the intellectual capital of society. Within this framework, she argues that both endowment funds and tuition subsidies arise naturally in support of that mission.

the presence of endowment funds can be traced back to fifteenth-century England, when wealthy donors provided churches and schools with financial gifts intended to support them in perpetuity. In the United States, university endowment investing ostensibly began in the mid-1600s with a real estate gift bestowed upon what is now Harvard University by several of its alumni.

For most of their existence, educational endowments have been managed under "prudent man" laws, which have historically been rooted in state trust statutes as opposed to federal law, and tended to focus on the disposition of individual holdings rather than the development of the entire portfolio.[6] As characterized by Sedlacek and Jarvis (2010), the management of university endowments began to gravitate toward the precepts of modern portfolio theory in the 1950s, culminating with the passage of the Uniform Management of Institutional Funds Act (UMIFA) in 1972, which standardized many of the rules regarding the way in which spending and investing could take place. In 2006, the UMIFA statutes were revised further with the Uniform Prudent Management of Institutional Funds Act (UPMIFA). Among other things, UPMIFA updates the old standards, particularly with regard to the level of flexibility the endowment's governing authority has to invest and spend assets, in the absence specific restrictions imposed by the original donor. Under UPMIFA, an institution is permitted to accumulate or spend as much of the endowment fund as the board deems appropriate, even to the point where the current value of the fund falls beneath the original level (i.e., the fund is "underwater").

Figure 2.1 provides a stylized view of the way in which a typical university endowment is organized. The two main economic actors involved in the process of deploying the fund's financial capital are the University/Endowment Board (i.e., "board"), which represents the governing authority ultimately responsible for the endowment's assets, and the Investment Committee/Firm (i.e., "staff"), to which falls the day-to-day responsibilities of designing and maintaining the actual investment portfolio. Broadly speaking, the primary functions of the board are twofold: (a) *create the policy statements* that define the investment problem faced by the university (i.e., the spending policy), as well as the way in which the endowment's financial assets should be invested to address this problem (i.e., the investment policy); and (b) monitor the staff's ongoing operations on a regular basis to *insure compliance* with those policies. By contrast, the staff—which may comprise anything from a single individual to representatives of a multiperson committee of the board (e.g., Yale Investments Office) to an entirely separate operating firm (e.g., University of Texas Investment Management Company)—is charged with the responsibility of managing the fund's assets in the most effective

---

6. Indeed, prudent man laws first came into existence with the *Harvard College v. Amory* case in 1830, which involved a dispute over how investments tied to the Harvard College endowment had been handled.

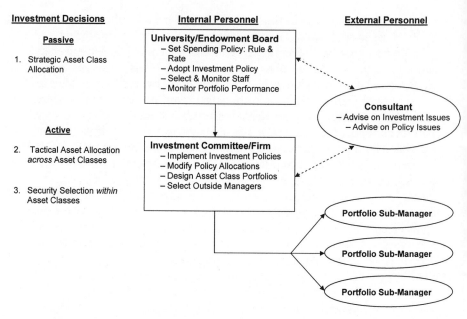

Fig. 2.1 Typical endowment fund organizational structure

Note: This exhibit illustrates the organizational structure of the typical educational endowment fund. The respective responsibilities of the university/endowment board (e.g., setting
spending and investment policy, monitoring investment performance) and the staff of the
investment committee/firm (e.g., designing portfolio strategy, selecting external investment
managers) are highlighted.

manner possible, within the context of the policy parameters set forth by the
board.[7] Thus, in the typical endowment there is a clear delineation between
those responsible for defining the investment problem and setting the broad
parameters for the investment solution and those who make those mandates
operational.[8]

---

7. In its annual survey of educational endowment practices, NACUBO reported that for
the 2010 fiscal year, the average number of full-time equivalent professional staff persons
employed by the 842 funds in their sample was just 1.5. However, the cross-sectional distribution of professional staffing levels is highly skewed; the mean number of full-time professionals
employed by endowments with assets of over $1 billion is 10.0 (see Walda and Griswold 2011).

8. Two additional economic actors are represented in the exhibit: consultants, who can provide guidance to either the board or the staff on a variety of topics, and portfolio submanagers, who the staff may select to manage part or all of the endowment's assets. This "external
manager" model (i.e., in which staff selects investment managers from outside the endowment
organization to construct asset class-specific security portfolios) is an increasingly popular
format in practice and the role of the consultant is often to advise the board or staff on which
submanagers to select. Walda and Griswold (2011) report that 80.0 percent of the endowments
surveyed in 2010 employed an external consultant and 85.0 percent of those endowments using
a consultant did so to advise them on the manager selection process.

2.2.2 Endowment Spending Policy

We begin by formally defining the spending policy adopted by a particular endowment as consisting of two distinct components: (a) a spending *rule*, and (b) a prespecified payout *rate*. The distinction between these two entities is that the spending rule defines the general procedure by which the payout amount will be determined, whereas the payout rate represents the specific percentage that is to be applied within the context of the spending rule. For example, during the 2007 fiscal year Texas Christian University determined their annual endowment payout using a "50/50 hybrid" approach in which the institution calculated a weighting consisting of (a) 50 percent of the dollar amount of the prior year's spending incremented by the Higher Education Price Index (HEPI) inflation index, and (b) 50 percent of an amount established by taking 5.0 percent of an average of the market values of the endowment portfolio over the previous four quarters, starting at the beginning of the current fiscal year. In this case, the *rule* used is actually a combination of two more fundamental rules (i.e., increase by percentage and moving average, as defined more formally below) while the *rates* specified are the HEPI inflation index for the increase by percentage rule and 5.0 percent for the moving average rule.[9] In the analysis that follows, it is important to recognize that an endowment fund can change its spending policy by altering either the rule it uses or the rate that is applied within that rule.

For our purposes, two endowments will initially be considered to have comparable spending policies if those policies are based on the same spending rule. That is, funds that adopt a moving average payout rule based on, say, annual portfolio valuations over the previous three years will be classified in the same way regardless of what specific policy spending rate each fund applies to their respective average asset values. There are seven broad categories of spending rules used in practice, which in turn represent aggregated versions of twenty more detailed subclasses.[10] While the appendix lists a more complete description of this spending rule taxonomy, the seven broad payout policy categories are given here as:

1. *Decide on an appropriate rate annually*: Determines the spending rate deemed appropriate on a yearly basis.

---

9. It is interesting to note that NACUBO reported that the *actual* payout rate for the Texas Christian University endowment fund for the 2007 fiscal year was 4.6 percent (expressed as a percentage of beginning-of-period fund assets). This indicates that there often can be a measurable difference between the ex ante policy payout rate and the ex post actual payout rate, particularly when moving average spending rules that combine several past asset values are used.

10. This spending rule classification system was created after a comprehensive analysis of the series of annual NACUBO surveys, which began collecting this information in 2003. It differs somewhat from other classification schemes (e.g., Lapovsky 2009; Blume 2010) primarily because the way in which NACUBO has reported spending rule data has evolved over time, particularly after Commonfund became involved in the reporting process in 2009. We provide a more complete discussion of the data acquisition process in section 2.3.

2. *Increase prior year's spending by a percentage*: Adjusts spending upward each year, using either a simple formula or one based on the inflation rate.

3. *Spend a percentage of a moving average of market values*: Determines annual payout as a percentage of an average of beginning-of-period market values over a prespecified series of past periods.

4. *Spend a percentage of current yield*: Spend a percentage of current income generated during the investment period.

5. *Spend a percentage of assets under management (AUM)*: Determines annual payout as a percentage the beginning-of-period fund assets for the current period.

6. *Hybrid rules*: Uses a simple formula to combine two or more different payout categories into a single spending rule.

7. *Other payout rules*: Uses a formula or approach that differs from those listed above or did not provide a complete set of information.

Thus, the TCU endowment fund from the previous example would be classified as following a hybrid rule (i.e., category 6), which itself is a combination of category 2 (i.e., increase prior spending by percentage) and category 3 (i.e., moving average).

At a broad level, these spending rule categories can be differentiated by the nature of the dollar payout amount they produce. Clearly, the decide annually rule is the most flexible in that it allows the board to determine the exact amount of payout it wants to extract from the portfolio each year. Of course, this maximizes the tension on the board in managing the trade-off between spending in the present versus preserving the endowment's value for future generations, particularly since UPMIFA removes the onus of making decisions that lead to an underwater fund. On the other hand, the increase by percentage rule makes the payout level exactly predictable and preserves the real spending level of the institution when the policy payout rate is tied to an inflation index. However, in years when asset values are falling, an increase by percentage rule will exacerbate the decline in the endowment portfolio's value. By contrast, a percentage of AUM rule adjusts the payout to changes in the portfolio's beginning-of-year value, which has the effect of making the dollar payout level extremely volatile in financial markets that are themselves volatile. Moving average rules attempt to mitigate this volatility by smoothing out the portfolio value to which the payout rate is tied, whereas percentage of yield rules are intended to set a payout that will not diminish the value of the endowment portfolio, which may be a factor that the board of a fund that is already underwater might need to take into account. Finally, hybrid rules, which often combine moving average and increase by percentage inflation rules, seek a middle ground between predictable dollar payout and the preservation of the endowment's market value.

2.2.3 Endowment Investment Policy

Beyond setting the organization's spending policy, figure 2.1 also highlights the role that the endowment fund's board plays in determining the direction of its investment operation. As summarized in the endowment's investment policy statement, the primary function of the board in this regard is two-fold: (a) to select the permissible asset classes that define the endowment's allowable investable universe; and (b) to specify the target investment levels (i.e., weights) for each of these asset classes. Collectively, these two decisions represent the fund's *strategic* asset allocation policy, which is widely acknowledged to be the single most important decision that an organization makes to increase the value of its investment portfolio over time; see, for example, Brinson, Hood, and Beebower (1986) and Ibbotson and Kaplan (2000). Further, Acharya and Dimson (2007) note that most endowment funds use a strategic allocation approach to arrive at their policy portfolios due largely to the long-term nature of the investment problem they face.[11]

Of course, a crucial aspect underlying the board's strategic allocation judgment is the perceived level of risk tolerance characterizing the organization. Like mutual funds, endowment fund assets are most often managed without a "safety net," such as that provided for pension plans by the plan sponsor's balance sheet or the Pension Benefit Guarantee Corporation. In this sense, endowment funds are often regarded as having risk tolerance similar to that of a tax-exempt wealthy individual investor, although Black (1976) argues that endowment funds generally require less diversification in their asset portfolios than do otherwise comparable individuals. However, this appears to be a notion that has fallen out of favor, as the so-called *endowment model* approach to investing prevalent today is grounded on the principle that a wide variety of both traditional (e.g., public fixed-income and equity securities) and nontraditional (e.g., hedge funds, private equity) asset classes should form the investable universe (see Leibowitz, Bova, and Hammond 2010). Finally, endowment funds generally face the widest variety of investment restrictions, most of which are institution-specific since there is comparatively little regulation in this industry.[12] This suggests that, as an institutional class, endowment funds might have considerable range in their investment policies and thus represent a setting in which the manipulation of allocation strategies might be able to add substantial value to portfolio performance.

11. Typically, investment policy statements contain two additional features that are the responsibility of the board: (a) the permissible *tactical* ranges for the extent to which asset class-level investments can differ from their strategic target weights; and (b) the portfolios or indexes that represent the *benchmarks* for each asset class (e.g., the S&P 500 index for US public equity), which are used primarily for measuring the performance of the managed portfolio.

12. In fact, Hill (2006) implies that the largest and least restricted endowment funds essentially operate as hedge funds in their pursuit of superior risk-adjusted returns, an observation borne out by the recent experience at the Harvard Management Company.

Given the strategic allocation policy set by the board, figure 2.1 shows that the responsibility for designing and maintaining the actual endowment portfolio falls to the staff. A baseline (or *passive*) approach for this process would be to mimic the strategic allocation policy by investing in the permissible asset classes at exactly their target weights and replicating the contents of the benchmark indexes as closely as possible; this is what Leibowitz (2005) terms "beta grazing." Within the context of the investment policy, the staff can also usually engage in *active* portfolio management (i.e., "alpha seeking") in either of two ways: (a) *tactical asset allocation*, in which deviations from strategic asset class weights are selected; and (b) *security selection*, in which asset class-level security portfolios that differ from those in the respective benchmarks are held.[13] In their analysis of the relationship between asset allocation and investment performance for university endowment funds, Brown, Garlappi, and Tiu (2010) find that while strategic policy portfolios are remarkably similar across their sample, actively managed endowments are able to generate significantly larger alphas than passively managed ones, largely through the staff's use of its security selection skills. Indeed, Swensen (2009) argues that the ability to make high-quality active management decisions is the most important factor that distinguishes two otherwise similar investors. Thus, both board and staff appear to play an important role in the development and execution of an endowment's investment policy.

2.3 Data and Descriptive Statistics

2.3.1 Data Description

The primary source of information for the spending and investment practices of educational endowment funds comes from a database maintained by the National Association of College and University Business Officers (NACUBO), a service and advocacy organization formed in 1962 to represent college, university, and higher education service providers throughout the United States, Canada, and Puerto Rico. Since 1984, NACUBO has surveyed its members on topics ranging from asset allocation and investment performance to endowment expenditures and other fund flows to organizational design and governance issues and then publishes a summary of that information in its annual *Study of Endowments*.[14] Arguably, this survey represents the most comprehensive published source of data on college and

13. In addition to tactical range restrictions or restrictions on which securities can or cannot be held (e.g., no tobacco stocks), investment policy statements can also specify risk-control measures at the aggregate portfolio level, such as tracking error limits.

14. Since 2009, Commonfund has administered the survey process and jointly authored the studies with NACUBO. Before the current arrangement, other NACUBO partners involved in producing the annual surveys included TIAA-CREF (2000–2008) and Cambridge Associates (1988 to 1999); the NACUBO Investment Committee generated the surveys prior to 1988.

university endowments anywhere in the world. Although the underlying data are self-reported by the member institutions, the study is free of survivorship bias as any college that could eventually have gone bankrupt but participated in the survey in the early years is retained in the database (see Brown et al. 1992). Indeed, the large cross section of colleges represented in the survey suggests that there is little self-selection bias. Furthermore, the study does not backfill data; that is, a college can only fill out the survey for the current year and not for previous years in which no information was originally provided.

For the analysis that follows, we have obtained access to the survey data for fiscal years from 1984 to 2011.[15] For the purpose of our study, easily the richest part of the NACUBO database involves endowment investment practices. Specifically, information for some data items—such as the AUM for a particular fund, the annual investment return (net of fees) that it produced—is available from the inception of the surveys in 1984. However, while aggregated sample-wide data on asset allocation patterns are available from 1984, *fund-specific* asset allocation data (i.e., where it is possible to match each endowment with its actual asset class investment weights during the investment period) was only obtainable starting with the 1989 survey. Given the number of partners involved in producing the annual surveys for NACUBO, it is not surprising that the asset class definitions have been modified three times during the 1989–2011 sample period, most recently in 2009 with Commonfund's administration of the surveys. To maintain consistency with the most recent reporting standards, we adopt the following ten different asset classes: US public equity, non-US public equity, fixed income, real estate, hedge funds, venture capital, private equity, natural resources, cash, and other assets. All of the asset allocation data dating to 1989 has been adjusted, where necessary, to correspond to these asset class definitions.[16]

Unfortunately, information on spending practices in the endowment sample does not extend as far back as does the investment data. The NACUBO began reporting the actual annual payout rate associated with a fund in 1994. This actual payout rate statistic is calculated as the total dollar amount of the payment from the endowment to the institution during a given fiscal year as a percentage of market value (i.e., AUM) of the portfolio at the *beginning* of the fiscal year. More specific information regarding the spending policy—both spending rule and policy rate—for every fund did not appear until the 2003 survey, meaning that we are able to trace the evo-

15. To match the academic calendar, the fiscal year for an endowment typically ends on June 30. So, the NACUBO survey for 2011 covers the period from July 1, 2010, through June 30, 2011.

16. For example, from 2001 to 2008, NACUBO reported twelve asset class categories by accounting for fixed income in two subcategories (i.e., United States and non-United States) and similarly listing real estate in its public (i.e., REITS) and private forms.

lution of this aspect of the endowment management process (as well as the link between spending and investment practices) over the 2003–2011 period. Further, the categories defining the spending rule classifications were modified once during this time frame (i.e., when Commonfund got involved in the effort in 2009). Consequently, the seven spending rule categories listed in the previous section were defined with sufficient breadth to allow for the proper placement of all twenty of the subcategories used throughout the nine years for which these data were reported, as indicated in the appendix. Finally, recognize that not every endowment self-reported spending policy data in each year for which they participated in the survey in other ways (e.g., reported asset allocation and investment performance results). As explained in more detail below, we assume the conservative posture that such omissions, when they occur, indicate that the endowment *did not* change its spending policy from the last reporting date.

2.3.2 Endowment Summary Statistics: Fund Size, Returns, and Payout Rates

Table 2.1 provides a broad overview of the number and size, investment performance, and spending practices for our sample of endowment funds. Specifically, the display reports on a yearly basis summary statistics for three different variables: (a) assets under management (AUM), measured as the market value of the total assets held in a fund as of the end of the respective reporting year; (b) the overall investment return, reported net of all relevant fees; and (c) the payout rate, which is defined as the actual dollar-level of spending during the year in question expressed as a percentage of the beginning-of-period AUM of the fund. For all three of these statistics the table lists the mean, median, minimum, and maximum values and standard deviations for each of the annual cross sections.

The first thing to note from table 2.1 is that the number of institutions surveyed by NACUBO quadrupled (i.e., from 200 to 803) from 1984 to 2011 and that there was a roughly sixteenfold increase in the aggregate level of assets managed in the industry (i.e., from $25.4 billion to $408.0 billion) during that time. By contrast, the level of AUM for both the mean and median endowment increased only fourfold over the sample period—from $127.0 million to $508.1 million, on average—which represents a relatively modest compound annual growth rate in net-of-payout assets of 5.3 percent, especially given that none of the amounts listed have been adjusted for inflation. However, the remaining AUM data reported in the exhibit indicate that focusing on the behavior of the average endowment may provide a poor representation of the entire universe. For example, the difference between the largest and smallest funds reported annually (e.g., $31.7 billion versus $0.6 million in 2011) shows the tremendous cross-sectional heterogeneity in the sample and suggests that endowments of different sizes may face very different asset management problems.

Table 2.1 Summary statistics of the NACUBO/Commonfund endowment fund universe

year	N. obs.	AUM ($ millions)						Return					Payout				
		Total	Mean	Median	Std.	Min	Max	Mean	Median	Std.	Min	Max	Mean	Median	Std.	Min	Max
2011	803	407,997.44	508.09	91.70	1,902.36	0.57	31,728.08	18.58	19.70	5.44	-4.19	31.75	4.49	4.68	3.31	0.00	85.00
2010	821	346,140.68	421.61	74.14	1,596.50	0.43	27,223.22	11.53	12.00	3.86	-5.76	36.20	4.43	4.86	2.05	0.00	16.60
2009	817	306,403.51	375.03	68.18	1,455.25	0.60	25,662.06	-17.79	-18.80	6.60	-39.96	15.90	4.23	4.50	1.98	0.00	25.20
2008	698	303,705.38	447.94	93.20	1,823.32	0.60	36,556.28	-3.08	-3.35	3.97	-22.60	12.10	4.59	4.50	2.34	0.00	45.60
2007	678	304,482.12	463.44	97.65	1,784.91	0.57	34,634.91	17.38	17.60	3.58	2.90	62.20	4.59	4.50	1.92	0.00	36.90
2006	731	283,020.67	387.17	79.80	1,451.24	0.49	28,915.71	10.61	10.80	3.38	-0.20	20.50	4.66	4.60	1.32	0.00	15.50
2005	711	249,275.94	351.59	75.41	1,291.35	1.26	25,473.72	9.16	9.00	3.29	-11.40	22.20	4.79	4.85	1.40	0.24	17.10
2004	707	228,466.66	323.61	69.75	1,136.52	1.92	22,143.65	15.02	15.70	4.41	-0.60	32.10	4.89	5.00	1.62	0.00	18.40
2003	667	196,111.70	294.02	71.65	1,001.70	0.32	18,849.49	2.70	2.60	3.68	-14.70	28.10	5.22	5.00	1.50	0.10	22.00
2002	534	176,545.39	337.56	91.25	1,053.05	0.16	17,169.76	-5.96	-6.20	4.23	-19.80	10.10	5.21	5.00	1.53	0.30	22.00
2001	572	218,185.98	390.31	105.65	1,167.41	1.15	17,950.84	-3.26	-3.60	6.30	-26.90	24.80	5.17	5.00	1.43	0.30	14.20
2000	507	222,928.50	461.55	119.96	1,371.55	6.19	18,844.34	12.69	10.70	10.10	-12.20	58.80	4.97	5.00	1.40	0.10	13.30
1999	468	181,781.61	409.42	130.24	1,083.10	7.19	14,256.00	10.90	10.50	5.25	-15.80	60.95	4.83	5.00	1.24	0.10	13.00
1998	445	159,620.93	371.21	113.08	991.42	5.17	13,019.74	18.05	18.00	3.97	3.70	31.80	4.69	4.70	1.21	0.30	14.70
1997	456	145,122.97	328.33	98.37	858.05	5.78	10,919.67	20.10	19.90	4.44	6.80	46.90	4.80	4.60	1.77	0.30	24.00
1996	406	112,603.94	281.51	81.15	737.70	3.65	8,811.78	17.26	17.20	4.02	0.80	39.00	4.84	4.80	1.29	0.10	12.80
1995	423	99,416.70	235.58	71.59	600.03	0.07	7,045.86	15.08	14.80	4.16	0.50	37.90	4.95	5.00	1.47	0.10	15.00
1994	375	70,354.31	189.12	61.23	406.58	0.47	3,529.00	3.29	3.20	4.27	-13.00	43.00	5.24	5.00	1.75	1.80	18.20
1993	393	76,838.21	196.52	60.51	469.59	1.46	5,778.26	13.13	13.30	4.30	-2.80	36.30	n.a.	n.a.	n.a.	n.a.	n.a.
1992	317	62,236.12	196.95	54.22	534.68	1.73	5,315.47	13.40	13.00	8.82	1.10	143.00	n.a.	n.a.	n.a.	n.a.	n.a.
1991	326	56,023.55	172.91	52.03	439.20	3.39	5,118.12	7.24	7.10	4.90	-14.40	53.00	n.a.	n.a.	n.a.	n.a.	n.a.
1990	298	51,420.16	174.31	58.89	410.97	2.01	4,653.23	10.02	9.55	6.01	-10.30	75.00	n.a.	n.a.	n.a.	n.a.	n.a.
1989	279	45,481.16	165.39	56.74	392.35	1.87	4,478.98	14.64	13.40	13.46	-6.20	163.00	n.a.	n.a.	n.a.	n.a.	n.a.
1988	262	49,467.06	157.04	47.64	381.40	1.65	4,155.78	1.26	0.70	4.78	-14.70	17.40	n.a.	n.a.	n.a.	n.a.	n.a.
1987	276	45,222.98	152.78	46.38	360.68	1.54	4,018.27	13.63	13.82	5.69	-6.88	31.89	n.a.	n.a.	n.a.	n.a.	n.a.
1986	258	39,317.86	150.64	46.29	354.88	1.10	3,435.01	27.17	27.16	6.72	5.24	52.46	n.a.	n.a.	n.a.	n.a.	n.a.
1985	280	31,511.82	112.54	31.19	295.30	1.02	2,927.20	25.61	25.95	6.96	1.25	52.12	n.a.	n.a.	n.a.	n.a.	n.a.
1984	200	25,399.06	127.00	40.12	289.12	0.97	2,486.30	-1.40	-2.24	15.12	-17.00	209.00	n.a.	n.a.	n.a.	n.a.	n.a.

Source: The exhibit presents annual data summarizing various aspects of the college and university endowment funds contained in the NACUBO/Commonfund sample over the period from July 1, 1983, to June 30, 2011.

Notes: In addition to listing the number of funds included in each yearly survey and the aggregate market value of those portfolios, the display reports cross-sectional mean, median, standard deviation, minimum, and maximum statistics for (a) the fiscal-year end market value for the endowment portfolio (assets under management, or AUM); (b) net-of-expense portfolio return (Return), expressed as a percentage of beginning-of-period AUM; and (c) the actual payout to the sponsoring institution (Payout), expressed as a percentage of beginning-of-period AUM. Data are available for AUM and Return for the 1984–2011 fiscal years; Payout data are reported for the 1994–2011 fiscal years.

There are two other ways in which the reported statistics for fund investment performance and payouts suggest that the endowment universe is extremely varied. First, while the annual distributions of the overall fund returns do not appear to be highly skewed (e.g., there is not a large discrepancy between the mean and median returns reported for most years), the difference between the best and worst performing funds is considerable.[17] For instance, while the mean fund returned 9.2 percent in 2005, the minimum and maximum returns for the 711 participating endowments were −11.4 percent and 22.2 percent, respectively. The indicative range of performance for this particular year was by no means abnormally large; if anything, it is less pronounced than the most dramatic years in the sample (e.g., 1989, 2000, 2007–2009). While there are several factors that might explain these different investment outcomes, such as portfolio risk levels or manager-specific skills, they nevertheless underscore our earlier point regarding the diversity of the objectives, constraints, and characteristics that represent these institutions.

The final way in which college endowments can be differentiated with these data is by the amount of their annual spending needs. The last five columns in the exhibit summarize the annual distributions of the actual dollar expenditures (as a percent of AUM) paid out by the funds. The average annual value for this payout rate is about 4.8 percent, which did not appear to change much from one year to the next during the sample period. However, this relative constancy in the average value masks a considerable degree of cross-sectional variation in actual payouts rates, where the spread of values in a given year ranges from 0 to 85.0 percent. Further, as indicated by both the cross-sectional standard deviations and difference between the minimum and maximum values, the sample-wide variation in payout rates appears to have increased substantially after 2008. In fact, this highly variable pattern of endowment spending over time is consistent with that reported by Nettleton (1987) for the pre-1985 period. In the present context, the important point to consider is that fund spending policies *may* be linked to the risk tolerance of the endowment and, as a consequence, should be related to the allocation decision and ultimate investment performance, as suggested by Dybvig (1999).[18]

2.3.3 Endowment Summary Statistics: Asset Allocation

Table 2.2 lists the actual percentage allocations by the endowment fund universe to each of the ten NACUBO asset classes in use as of the 2011 sur-

17. The return data shown in table 2.1 are net of fund expenses, but they are not adjusted for risk. A more thorough analysis of the nature and sources of risk-adjusted performance across a comparable sample of endowment funds can be found in Brown and Tiu (2010).

18. In an interesting extension of this point, Dimmock (forthcoming) conducted a cross-sectional analysis of endowment fund allocation patterns during the year 2003 and concluded that factors such as the riskiness of a university's nonfinancial income, cost structure, and credit constraints can also affect its investment decision making and performance.

Table 2.2   Asset allocation statistics for the NACUBO/Commonfund endowment fund universe

	US Eq.	Non-US Eq.	Fixed income	Real estate	Cash	Other	Hedge funds	VC	PE	Nat. res.	AUM ($ mil.)	No. of obs.
2011	31.7	17.0	19.3	3.4	3.6	2.3	12.6	1.3	5.3	3.5	508.1	803
2010	31.7	15.3	22.0	3.2	3.9	2.2	12.5	1.1	5.0	3.0	421.6	821
2009	32.9	14.7	21.9	3.6	5.7	1.8	11.6	1.2	4.3	2.3	375.0	817
2008	34.5	17.1	18.9	4.3	3.7	1.5	13.3	1.1	3.4	2.3	447.9	698
2007	40.0	17.4	17.9	3.5	3.5	1.4	11.2	1.0	2.4	1.6	463.4	678
2006	42.3	15.3	20.0	3.5	3.4	1.4	9.7	0.9	2.0	1.5	387.2	731
2005	45.7	12.7	21.4	3.2	3.4	1.4	8.9	0.8	1.6	1.0	351.6	711
2004	48.7	11.0	21.9	2.8	3.6	1.6	7.5	0.8	1.4	0.6	323.6	707
2003	47.4	9.7	25.7	2.8	3.9	1.6	6.3	0.8	1.4	0.4	294.0	667
2002	46.4	10.1	27.0	2.6	4.0	1.6	5.6	1.0	1.2	0.4	337.6	534
2001	49.5	10.0	25.0	2.1	4.0	5.9	0.6	1.5	1.0	0.4	390.3	572
2000	50.7	11.6	23.3	2.0	4.0	4.0	0.7	2.4	1.0	0.3	461.5	507
1999	53.9	10.6	23.8	1.9	3.9	0.6	3.1	1.3	0.7	0.2	409.4	468
1998	53.1	10.9	25.5	3.4	2.3	0.6	1.6	0.9	0.5	1.2	371.2	445
1997	52.5	11.1	25.7	2.0	4.6	0.5	2.2	0.8	0.3	0.2	328.3	456
1996	51.8	9.4	27.7	2.0	5.4	0.7	1.9	0.8	0.3	0.2	281.5	406
1995	47.0	7.9	29.9	2.1	6.5	3.9	1.6	0.7	0.2	0.3	235.6	423
1994	46.3	7.4	31.8	1.9	7.3	2.8	1.5	0.7	0.2	0.3	189.1	375
1993	48.3	4.2	34.8	1.6	7.3	2.0	0.7	0.2	0.6	0.3	196.5	393
1992	48.1	3.0	35.8	2.4	9.4	0.0	0.4	0.6	0.2	0.2	196.9	317
1991	47.6	2.3	35.8	2.8	10.2	0.0	0.3	0.6	0.2	0.2	172.9	326
1990	47.5	2.3	35.6	2.9	10.3	0.0	0.3	0.6	0.2	0.2	174.3	298
1989	47.0	1.7	31.7	3.0	12.8	2.9	0.0	0.6	0.2	0.1	165.4	279

Source: The table reports annual means of the actual asset allocations maintained by the university endowment funds contained in the NACUBO/Commonfund database over the period from July 1, 1988, to June 30, 2011.

Notes: Cross-sectional mean allocation levels (expressed as a percentage of beginning-of-period AUM) are listed for the following asset class definitions: US public equity (US Eq.), non-US public equity (non-US Eq.), fixed income, real estate, cash, other assets (Other), hedge funds, venture capital (VC), private equity (PE), and natural resources (Nat. res.). The last two columns report the cross-sectional mean AUM and number of endowments contained in each yearly survey, respectively.

vey date: US public equity, non-US public equity, fixed income, real estate, hedge funds, venture capital, private equity, natural resources, cash, and other assets. The figures reported represent the equally weighted average annual values of the percentage of AUM allocated to a particular asset class using all of the participating funds in a given year starting in 1989. Viewed over time, there are several trends in these data that imply important shifts in the way endowment fund managers have approached the asset allocation process. First, the percentage invested in public equities (i.e., US equities and non-US equities) has changed substantially over time, while remaining well below the level advocated by Thaler and Williamson (1994). Interestingly, this allocation both started and ended the sample period at just under 50 percent, but maintained a level of 55 percent to 65 percent for the years between 1996 and 2007. Further, the composition of this allocation has changed dramatically over the entire period, with non-US equities experiencing a substantial increase (e.g., from 1.7 percent in 1989 to 17.0 percent in 2011) while US equities declined significantly (e.g., from 47.0 percent to 31.7 percent). Allocations to the traditional fixed-income categories also declined dramatically during the sample period, from around 31.7 percent at the beginning of the sample period to just 19.3 percent in 2011.

It is the alternative asset classes—typically defined by endowment funds to include hedge funds, nonpublic equity positions (both venture capital and private equity [i.e., buyout] investments), real estate, and natural resources— that benefitted the most from the decreased allocation to traditional fixed-income products. Some of these allocation gains were modest, such as the increases from 0.6 percent to 1.3 percent for venture capital investments or from 3.0 percent to 3.4 percent in real estate.[19] Clearly, then, the biggest beneficiary of the increased pattern of "alternatives" investing occurred in the hedge fund category, which represented just under 13.0 percent of the AUM of the average endowment fund by 2011, placing them in size just below the average dollar investment in non-US equity securities. Given that the first hedge fund allocation did not show up in the data until 1990, this represents a truly significant shift in the investment approach adopted by endowment managers. To underscore this point, we also computed a more complete cross-sectional analysis of the annual asset allocation samples, including the median, maximum, and minimum values as well as the standard deviation of the distribution. Although not reported in table 2.2, these additional statistics are nevertheless useful in understanding the diversity in the investment commitment to hedge funds across the endowment universe.

19. Recall that beginning in 2009, NACUBO collapsed two real estate asset classes—public (i.e., REITS) and private—into a single category, moving the REIT allocation to US public equity. Consequently, to insure comparability with the reported allocation data from 1989 to 2008, we have added (subtracted) 1.20 percent to the real estate (US public equity) asset class for the years 2009 to 2011. This percentage represents the average REIT allocation for the five-year period ending in 2008.

For instance, in 2005, the minimum allocation was 0.0 percent while the maximum allocation was 82.1 percent! Clearly, different endowments have very different strategies concerning alternative assets.

A significant factor related to these different asset allocation patterns is the size of the endowment fund. Simply put, larger funds invest assets in a very different fashion than do smaller funds. This phenomenon is illustrated in figure 2.2, which provides snapshots of endowment investments at different points of time and for funds of different size. To generate these comparisons, we separated the fund sample into quartiles based on beginning-of-period AUM for each year in the sample period. We then calculated mean asset allocation percentages for each quartile as an equally weighted average within the subsample, rebalancing those stratifications on a yearly basis. Further, for comparative ease, we consolidated the asset classes into four broader categories: public equity (US and non-US), fixed income, alternatives (real estate, hedge funds, venture capital and private equity, natural resources), and cash and other assets. Panel A of the display compares these aggregated allocation percentages across AUM quartiles at the beginning and end of the sample period, while panel B compares how those allocation patterns evolved over time for the largest (Q4) and smallest (Q1) size quartiles.[20]

As both panels of the exhibit help make clear, while there were significant differences *across asset classes*, there were relatively small differences in asset allocations patterns *across endowments* of different size at the beginning of the sample period (e.g., investments in alternatives in 1989 were 3.9 percent and 6.5 percent for quartiles Q1 and Q4, respectively). However, this situation changed dramatically by 2011, when alternatives investing for the largest fund quartile rose to 45.0 percent while the alternatives allocation for the smallest funds remained relatively low at 9.6 percent. To finance this increased allocation to alternatives, the average Q4 endowment reduced its allocation to both public equity (50.7 percent in 1989 to 37.6 percent in 2011) and fixed income (29.5 percent to 12.2 percent). Conversely, the smallest endowments actually increased their public equity investments over this period (44.9 percent in 1989 to 56.2 percent in 2011) primarily by reducing their cash allocation, whereas their fixed-income allocation remained relatively stable (32.2 percent to 26.3 percent). Thus, it is reasonable to conclude that the overall trend toward an increased allocation to alternatives at the expense of public equity and fixed income we noted earlier is predominantly the result of actions taken by the managers of the largest endowments.

20. To conserve space, figure 2.2 compares asset allocations for the various subsamples of the endowment universe for just two years: 1989 and 2011. It should be noted that data for the omitted years do not change our conclusions about how endowment allocation patterns have changed over time; we have produced a complete set of annual findings for the entire 1989–2011 sample period and these results are available upon request.

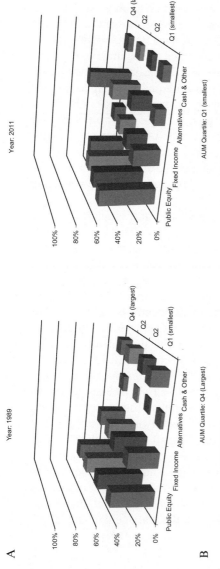

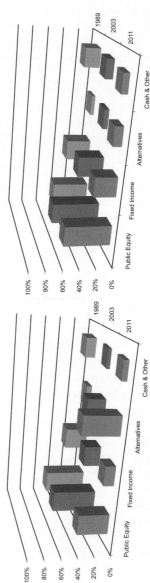

Fig. 2.2 Comparative asset allocation patterns over time and endowment fund size

Note: This figure illustrates how mean asset class allocation percentages for the endowment fund sample have changed over time and for portfolios of different size. The ten asset classes reported in the NACUBO/Commonfund surveys are aggregated into the following four categories: public equity (US and non-US), fixed income, alternatives (hedge funds, venture capital, private equity, real estate, and natural resources), and cash and other assets. Panel A lists asset allocation statistics for funds in different AUM quartiles (largest [Q4] to smallest [Q1]) for two different years (1989 and 2011). Panel B lists asset allocation statistics across time (1989, 2003, and 2011) for two different fund size quartiles (Q4 and Q1).

2.3.4 Endowment Summary Statistics: Spending Rules

As discussed above, the annual NACUBO surveys have included details of the spending rules used by their sample of educational endowments since the 2003 fiscal year. For each yearly report between 2003 and 2011, we analyzed the stated rule for every available fund and placed it into one of the twenty specific subcategories—which, in turn, led to its placement into one of the seven broader categories—described in the appendix. Table 2.3 summarizes these classifications, reporting for each year the following statistics: total number of sample endowments; percentage frequency of rule use; mean (median) actual payout, as a percentage of AUM; mean (median) AUM; mean (median) annual investment return; and mean (median) standard deviation of the policy (i.e., benchmark) portfolio corresponding to funds in that spending rule class.[21] Further, starting with the fiscal year 2009, the spending rule portion of the NACUBO survey was expanded to include additional information regarding the relationship between endowment payout amounts and the institution's budget, as well as the funding status of the portfolio. Consequently, for the years 2009–2011, we also report summary statistics for mean (median) payout as percentage of budget; the mean number of endowments that impose a special spending appropriation (i.e., temporary expenditures in addition to the stated permanent policy); and the percentage of funds that are "underwater" (i.e., has a current market value that is less than its original level).

Perhaps the most intriguing finding shown in the display is the sizeable fraction of endowment funds that base their spending policies on some form of a moving average of past portfolio values, which is intended to smooth out year-to-year variations in the dollar level of the portfolio payout. Looking at each of the annual samples, the fraction of funds using a moving average rule ranges from a low of about two-thirds (65.4 percent in 2010) to three-quarters (75.6 percent in 2008). By contrast, the second most frequently used spending rule—the decide annually category—is also the most flexible in the payout amount it allows from one period to the next and accounts for as much as 10.6 percent of funds in 2011 and as few as 4.9 percent in 2008.[22] The remaining categories—increase by percentage,

21. More precisely, this volatility statistic was calculated as follows: First, for each fund in a given survey year and rule class, we observed their asset allocation weights. Second, using time-series return data for the benchmark indexes associated with each asset class (which are described in detail in section 2.6), we calculate a sample asset class variance-covariance matrix. Finally, a policy standard deviation statistic was then calculated for each fund as the square root of the product of its investment weights and the variance-covariance matrix; the exhibit lists the mean (median) of these values within each rule category.

22. To underscore this "smoothing versus flexibility" comparison, notice that in 2009 (i.e., the fiscal year incorporating the financial market decline of late 2008, 36.1 percent of the endowments using the decide annually rule were underwater, compared to just 22.1 percent using moving average rules. By 2011, the economic recovery that took place during the preceding two years had reduced the frequency of underwater funds in these two categories to be virtually the same (i.e., 5.5 percent and 4.9percent, respectively).

Table 2.3   Descriptive statistics for endowment fund spending policy rules

	Decide annually	Increase by pct.	Moving average	Pct. of yield	Pct. of AUM	Hybrid rule	Other rule
2011 *n* = 804							
Use (%)	10.6	4.7	66.0	3.5	3.4	6.2	5.7
Payout (%)	4.2 (4.5)	5.2 (5.1)	4.5 (4.6)	4.2 (4.3)	4.1 (4.1)	4.8 (5.0)	4.0 (4.5)
Size ($ millions)	756.9 (75.5)	1750.8 (514.7)	326.8 (80.2)	268.1 (69.9)	642.3 (68.1)	1143.3 (186.7)	984.5 (79.4)
Ret. (%)	18.3 (20.0)	19.4 (19.6)	18.6 (19.7)	18.1 (19.9)	16.2 (18.3)	19.8 (19.6)	19.6 (20.5)
Vol. (%)	9.9 (9.7)	10.0 (9.9)	9.8 (9.8)	9.9 (10.3)	9.3 (9.2)	10.4 (10.1)	10.2 (10.2)
Budget (%)	13.4 (6.6)	17.0 (12.3)	8.3 (3.0)	7.6 (2.4)	2.8 (0.9)	18.2 (9.4)	11.1 (3.1)
Appropriations (%)	20.4	24.4	17.6	18.8	13.3	25.9	29.4
Underwater (%)	5.5	6.1	4.9	6.3	5.2	4.5	5.3
2010 *n* = 822							
Use (%)	9.4	3.7	65.4	3.3	3.5	5.4	9.4
Payout (%)	4.2 (4.0)	5.1 (5.4)	4.5 (4.9)	3.7 (3.8)	3.4 (3.4)	4.9 (5.0)	4.0 (4.5)
Size ($ millions)	546.7 (60.5)	1270.2 (346.6)	269.5 (67.9)	161.1 (29.3)	80.3 (32.7)	1005.7 (200.0)	804.1 (78.7)
Ret. (%)	11.7 (11.9)	11.6 (12.1)	11.5 (12.0)	11.5 (12.4)	11.6 (12.0)	12.5 (12.6)	11.9 (12.1)
Vol. (%)	9.3 (9.3)	9.5 (9.9)	9.4 (9.4)	9.4 (9.7)	9.4 (9.5)	9.9 (9.7)	9.4 (9.4)
Budget (%)	12.1 (2.9)	18.4 (14.1)	9.1 (3.2)	4.2 (0.7)	11.4 (1.0)	24.2 (16.2)	13.7 (4.7)
Appropriations (%)	24.1	17.6	19.1	6.7	15.6	31.9	22.6
Underwater (%)	16.3	13.1	13.3	12.9	14.7	15.9	13.0
2009 *n* = 818							
Use (%)	8.4	3.5	66.7	3.8	3.7	5.6	8.2
Payout (%)	4.1 (4.0)	4.6 (4.7)	4.3 (4.5)	4.1 (4.2)	4.2 (4.8)	4.6 (4.5)	4.0 (4.6)
Size ($ millions)	574.1 (36.0)	1282.2 (448.0)	263.9 (63.9)	203.5 (58.0)	86.7 (44.3)	866.7 (140.8)	819.9 (92.0)
Ret. (%)	−16.5 (−17.6)	−19.9 (−20.1)	−18.0 (−19.0)	−16.4 (−17.3)	−16.3 (−17.8)	−18.7 (−18.8)	−17.7 (−18.3)
Vol. (%)	9.3 (9.8)	9.8 (9.7)	9.4 (9.5)	9.1 (9.5)	9.5 (9.6)	9.9 (9.9)	9.2 (9.5)
Budget (%)	14.6 (2.4)	20.1 (14.8)	11.6 (4.3)	10.2 (3.0)	11.0 (0.8)	24.2 (13.2)	14.7 (6.0)
Appropriations (%)	28.2	34.5	18.1	21.2	3.0	27.7	19.7
Underwater (%)	36.1	12.1	22.1	28.1	20.4	22.5	21.5
2008 *n* = 775							
Use (%)	4.9	3.2	75.6	1.8	3.9	8.8	1.9
Payout (%)	5.0 (4.1)	4.5 (4.3)	4.6 (4.5)	2.8 (3.1)	4.3 (5.0)	5.1 (4.5)	3.9 (4.0)
Size ($ millions) (%)	1726.0 (46.8)	615.7 (398.7)	322.7 (85.9)	61.1 (18.8)	69.1 (36.6)	957.1 (190.3)	320.5 (186.3)
Ret. (%)	−3.1 (−3.5)	−1.0 (−0.9)	−3.3 (−3.5)	−5.0 (−4.8)	−2.7 (−3.9)	−1.6 (−1.7)	−2.6 (−5.0)
Vol. (%)	10.0 (9.8)	9.7 (9.9)	9.9 (10.0)	10.1 (9.6)	9.6 (9.6)	9.8 (9.8)	9.7 (9.6)
2007 *n* = 747							
Use (%)	5.1	3.3	73.2	2.7	5.1	4.7	6.0
Payout (%)	4.5 (4.3)	4.6 (4.6)	4.6 (4.5)	4.1 (4.5)	4.3 (4.5)	4.9 (4.5)	4.1 (4.3)
Size ($ millions) (%)	1977.3 (70.1)	920.0 (544.6)	341.8 (91.7)	175.3 (28.5)	432.0 (55.8)	1659.8 (409.3)	301.8 (191.4)

	(1)	(2)	(3)	(4)	(5)	(6)	(7)
Ret. (%)	18.3 (17.7)	20.0 (19.3)	17.3 (17.5)	15.8 (17.4)	16.3 (17.0)	19.6 (19.3)	17.5 (17.1)
Vol. (%)	10.2 (10.4)	10.3 (10.0)	10.5 (10.5)	11.0 (10.7)	10.2 (10.6)	10.4 (10.4)	10.2 (10.4)
2006 *n* = 746							
Use (%)	5.8	2.8	71.3	2.7	5.4	4.5	7.5
Payout (%)	4.8 (4.3)	4.8 (4.9)	4.6 (4.6)	4.3 (4.3)	4.4 (4.5)	5.2 (4.8)	4.3 (4.5)
Size ($ millions) (%)	1364.3 (69.0)	691.7 (463.1)	305.6 (81.2)	196.1 (38.7)	361.0 (51.6)	1287.2 (255.1)	211.9 (88.0)
Ret. (%)	10.1 (10.2)	12.5 (12.2)	10.7 (10.9)	8.8 (9.3)	10.0 (10.4)	12.5 (13.2)	10.3 (9.7)
Vol. (%)	10.2 (10.1)	10.4 (10.4)	10.5 (10.6)	9.4 (10.3)	10.2 (10.3)	10.2 (10.2)	10.4 (10.5)
2005 *n* = 735							
Use (%)	9.4	8.4	66.8	10.6	4.4	0.3	0.1
Payout (%)	4.7 (4.8)	4.6 (4.5)	4.8 (5.0)	4.5 (4.7)	4.8 (5.0)	4.8 (4.8)	5.3 (5.3)
Size ($ millions) (%)	370.9 (99.9)	582.6 (156.5)	325.1 (66.1)	558.4 (78.1)	308.8 (93.0)	276.0 (276.0)	189.3 (189.3)
Ret. (%)	9.4 (9.0)	10.0 (9.8)	8.9 (8.8)	9.3 (9.5)	10.3 (10.2)	11.1 (11.1)	14.0 (14.0)
Vol. (%)	10.5 (10.3)	10.6 (10.5)	10.4 (10.5)	10.1 (10.3)	10.7 (10.6)	10.6 (10.6)	11.0 (11.0)
2004 *n* = 710							
Use (%)	9.5	3.6	70.3	5.5	5.5	2.8	2.8
Payout (%)	4.9 (5.0)	5.2 (5.3)	5.0 (5.0)	4.6 (5.0)	4.0 (4.3)	5.3 (5.3)	3.9 (4.5)
Size ($ millions) (%)	814.6 (65.0)	440.3 (322.4)	239.6 (62.5)	310.7 (80.1)	253.8 (50.2)	1561.2 (359.7)	228.9 (131.4)
Ret. (%)	14.7 (15.6)	16.2 (16.6)	15.1 (15.7)	14.2 (15.8)	13.4 (13.5)	15.6 (17.0)	14.7 (15.9)
Vol. (%)	10.6 (10.5)	10.5 (10.6)	10.6 (10.7)	10.1 (10.3)	10.0 (10.2)	10.3 (10.2)	10.8 (10.8)
2003 *n* = 676							
Use (%)	7.0	2.2	74.3	6.6	6.7	3.1	0.0
Payout (%)	5.6 (5.0)	5.1 (5.0)	5.3 (5.0)	4.6 (4.8)	4.8 (5.0)	5.4 (5.2)	
Size ($ millions) (%)	871.6 (39.2)	873.8 (517.0)	236.9 (75.0)	242.5 (58.5)	245.6 (55.7)	1364.4 (423.4)	
Ret. (%)	3.0 (3.2)	2.6 (2.8)	2.5 (2.5)	3.4 (4.0)	3.2 (3.0)	3.2 (3.2)	
Vol. (%)	9.7 (9.9)	10.5 (10.5)	10.3 (10.4)	10.0 (10.3)	9.3 (9.5)	9.6 (9.6)	

Notes: This exhibit summarizes several characteristics of the university endowment sample by the spending rule the fund employs. Fiscal year data are reported for the period July 1, 2002, to June 30, 2011, for the following spending rule categories, as defined in the appendix: decide annually, increase by percentage, moving average, percentage of yield, hybrid rule, and other rule. Cross-sectional mean (median) statistics are reported for: (a) frequency of rule use (Use), as a percentage of total endowments reporting in a given survey year; (b) actual payout (Payout), as a percentage of beginning-of-period AUM; (c) beginning-of-period AUM (Size); (d) annual investment return (Ret.), as a percentage of beginning-of-period AUM; (e) cross-sectional standard deviation of the policy (i.e., benchmark) portfolio for the rule category (Vol.). Data are also reported for the period from July 1, 2008, to June 30, 2011, for three additional variables: (a) the percentage of the sponsoring institution's annual budget that the actual endowment payout represents (Budget); (b) the percentage of funds in a rule category that employ special spending appropriations (Appropriations); and (c) the percentage of funds in a rule category that have current AUM less than initial AUM (Underwater).

percentage of yield, percentage of AUM, and hybrid—are roughly equally distributed, with each accounting for 3.5 to 5.5 percent, on average, over the nine years for which these data have been collected.

Of course, an interesting question implicit in these reported frequencies is what motivates a given endowment to select one spending rule over another? Table 2.3 provides some useful indications of how funds differ by spending rule choice. In particular, notice that in each of the yearly cross sections there is considerable variation in the average percentage payout generated by the various rules (e.g., 3.4 to 5.1 percent in 2010, 4.6 to 5.6 percent in 2003). Generally speaking, it appears that the increase by percentage and hybrid rules are associated with the largest average payout percentage, while the percentage of yield rule produces the smallest payout. Further, judging from the data reported over the most recent three years in the sample, it also appears that those endowments responsible for producing a larger percentage of the institution's budget select a hybrid or increase by percentage rule (e.g., 2011 mean payout-as-percentage-of-budget statistics of 18.2 percent and 17.0 percent, respectively), whereas endowments with payouts that are a significantly smaller percentage of their institution's budgets seem to gravitate toward moving average or percentage of yield rules (e.g., 8.3 percent and 7.6 percent, respectively, in 2011). Given that funds using hybrid rules need to produce more of the institution's total budget, it is not surprising to see that these endowments also tend to have special appropriation frequencies that are among the highest for any rule class (e.g., 25.9 percent and 31.9 percent in 2011 and 2010, respectively).

These summary statistics also contain an indication that an endowment's spending rule and its investment performance may be connected, albeit it in a surprising fashion. From the mean policy volatility statistics reported for each of the spending rule categories in the nine annual cross sections, it is apparent that endowment funds seem to target similar levels of benchmark risk exposure regardless of what other differences they might have. This fact, which was first noted by Brown, Garlappi, and Tiu (2010), can best be seen by the remarkably narrow ranges for the volatility measures in any given year (e.g., 9.3 percent to 9.9 percent in 2010, 9.6 percent to 10.1 percent in 2008). On the other hand, while these comparable "risk budgets" sometimes lead to a similarly narrow range of realized investment returns (e.g., mean annual returns of 11.5 percent to 12.5 percent in 2010), the dispersion in actual investment performance often varied far more widely across spending rule groups than differences in the policy risk levels would imply (e.g., −5.0 percent to −1.0 percent in 2008).

Given the relative importance of the moving average spending rule in practice, table 2.4 provides an additional breakdown of this classification by the various valuation frequencies and time horizons that define it. The display lists summaries for fiscal years 2009, 2010, and 2011, the three annual samples for which Commonfund collected these more detailed data in the

Table 2.4   Descriptive statistics for endowment funds employing a moving average spending rule

		Monthly freq.	Quarterly freq.	Annual freq.	Years T $0 \leq T < 3$	Years T $3 \leq T < 5$	Years T $5 \leq T < 7$	Years T $7 \leq T \leq 10$
2011	Use (%)	2.0	39.9	34.7	1.8	78.3	18.8	1.1
$n = 611$	Payout (%)	4.7 (4.7)	4.7 (5.0)	4.3 (4.6)	4.9 (4.6)	4.5 (4.7)	4.5 (4.5)	4.6 (4.1)
	Size ($ millions)	506.5 (229.5)	306.1 (84.1)	352.7 (77.5)	87.1 (65.0)	296.1 (79.1)	394.4 (94.1)	1723.7 (303.3)
	Ret. (%)	19.3 (18.6)	18.6 (19.8)	18.5 (19.6)	15.3 (18.4)	18.2 (19.6)	19.8 (20.3)	22.3 (24.0)
	Vol. (%)	10.0 (10.5)	9.9 (9.8)	9.7 (9.8)	10.0 (10.4)	9.7 (9.7)	10.0 (10.1)	10.7 (10.6)
	Budget (%)	5.8 (3.3)	8.1 (3.7)	7.6 (2.6)	15.0 (2.4)	7.1 (3.0)	12.0 (3.7)	5.4 (4.8)
	Appropriations (%)	12.5	18.8	17.0	18.2	16.8	19.8	50.0
	Underwater (%)	4.3	5.1	4.3	13.7	5.0	3.5	16.9
2010	Use (%)	1.3	36.4	37.8	1.9	82.8	14.0	1.3
$n = 620$	Payout (%)	4.9 (4.8)	4.8 (5.0)	4.3 (4.8)	5.4 (5.4)	4.5 (4.9)	4.3 (4.8)	5.6 (5.7)
	Size ($ millions)	290.0 (168.7)	284.1 (74.1)	260.2 (64.1)	167.6 (67.6)	235.9 (66.8)	392.4 (121.9)	1409.2 (456.3)
	Ret. (%)	11.2 (12.0)	11.7 (12.3)	11.4 (11.8)	10.9 (11.2)	11.4 (12.0)	12.1 (12.1)	12.8 (12.7)
	Vol. (%)	9.3 (9.9)	9.5 (9.4)	9.4 (9.4)	8.7 (8.8)	9.4 (9.4)	9.8 (9.6)	11.3 (11.7)
	Budget (%)	13.6 (2.2)	9.3 (4.0)	8.2 (2.3)	5.6 (2.6)	8.7 (3.2)	12.2 (2.6)	4.0 (2.8)
	Appropriations (%)	0.0	21.8	17.9	16.7	18.1	21.8	71.4
	Underwater (%)	13.5	14.2	12.3	12.7	13.3	13.2	27.5
2009	Use (%)	2.0	33.5	39.2	2.4	84.7	11.9	1.0
$n = 610$	Payout (%)	4.5 (4.6)	4.5 (4.8)	4.1 (4.4)	5.2 (5.0)	4.3 (4.5)	4.2 (4.4)	4.3 (4.2)
	Size ($ millions)	625.4 (224.9)	247.4 (71.8)	265.1 (56.6)	486.0 (69.5)	226.6 (62.7)	434.0 (115.7)	1039.4 (54.9)
	Ret. (%)	−17.6 (−18.3)	−18.5 (−19.1)	−17.6 (−18.9)	−18.2 (−17.9)	−17.7 (−18.9)	−19.3 (−19.5)	−28.2 (−29.7)
	Vol. (%)	9.4 (9.7)	9.4 (9.5)	9.4 (9.5)	9.7 (10.2)	9.4 (9.4)	9.7 (9.7)	12.4 (12.3)
	Budget (%)	19.0 (6.2)	11.9 (4.8)	11.1 (3.6)	11.7 (9.0)	11.2 (4.0)	15.0 (4.5)	6.2 (3.2)
	Appropriations (%)	6.3	19.9	17.2	26.7	17.2	25.4	0.0
	Underwater (%)	33.5	22.4	21.2	32.0	22.5	16.7	56.1

Notes: This exhibit summarizes several characteristics for university endowment funds that reported using a moving average spending rule in a given annual survey. Fiscal year data are reported for the period July 1, 2008, to June 30, 2011, for the following cross-sectional mean (median) statistics: (a) frequency of rule use (Use), as a percentage of total endowments reporting in a given survey year; (b) actual payout (Payout), as a percentage of beginning-of-period AUM; (c) beginning-of-period AUM (Size); (d) annual investment return (Ret.), as a percentage of beginning-of-period AUM; (e) cross-sectional standard deviation of the policy (i.e., benchmark) portfolio for the rule category (Vol.); (f) the percentage of the sponsoring institution's annual budget that the actual endowment payout represents (Budget); (g) the percentage of funds in a rule category that employ special spending appropriations (Appropriations); and (h) the percentage of funds in a rule category that have current AUM less than initial AUM (Underwater).

NACUBO surveys. The three frequency columns show that the vast majority of moving average rules in use are based on either quarterly or annual measures of past AUM values. Further, these two measurement frequencies are used in roughly comparable amounts, although there appears to have been a slight shift toward the quarterly averaging process (i.e., 33.5 percent to 39.9 percent usage from 2009 to 2011) and away from annual averaging. Beyond that, as indicated by the four time-horizon columns, averaging the AUM base over a period between three to five years is easily the most popular single choice in all three cross sections, despite the fact that five- to seven-year averaging became more prevalent over the period (i.e., 11.9 percent usage in 2009, 18.8 percent in 2011).

Finally, as with the asset allocation patterns discussed above, endowment size is also apparently a factor in determining the spending rule that is selected. For example, from table 2.3, the mean AUM for funds in the hybrid rule category in 2011 is $1,143.3 million, compared to $756.9 million and $326.8 million mean portfolio values in the decide annually and moving average categories, respectively. To get a better sense of these size dynamics, we also calculated spending rule frequencies by fund-size quartile, from the smallest (Q1) to the largest (Q4), for each of the nine annual samples. Panel A of figure 2.3 illustrates these interquartile distributions at the two yearly end points of the sample while panel B shows the rules used in quartiles Q4 and Q1 for three different years. In 2003, it is apparent that the smallest endowments used moving average rules to a lesser extent than larger funds, in favor of a relatively bigger use of decide annually and percentage of AUM rules. However, by 2011, use of a pure moving average policy in the Q4 quartile had declined dramatically to the point that those funds had the lowest comparative frequency, with an increased use of hybrid rules providing the offset. On the other hand, the use of moving average rules by Q1 funds remained much steadier over the same time frame. Thus, as with asset allocation changes over time, variations in spending rule use also appear to be driven primarily by the largest endowments in the sample, a topic we explore in more detail in the analysis that comes next.

2.4 The Evolution of Spending Policies over Time

Having just established some important cross-sectional differences in spending rule adoption practices, it is also useful to consider the issue of how a given endowment fund's spending policy has changed (if at all) over time. In one sense, this is a more interesting question to address since, given the prediction of Merton (1993) in the context of the relatively static nature of the investment problem that most educational institutions face, it is not clear that there is *any* reason to expect an endowment to modify the fundamental way in which it views its spending mandate from one year to the next. On the other hand, recent research suggests that endowments do face

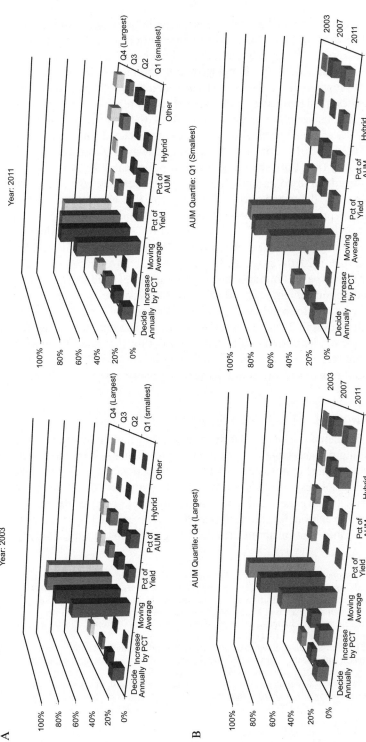

Fig. 2.3 Comparative spending rule patterns over time and endowment fund size

Note: This figure illustrates how spending rule adoption frequencies for the endowment fund sample have changed over time and for portfolios of different sizes. Using the seven categories defined in the appendix, panel A lists spending rule frequencies for funds in different AUM quartiles (largest [Q4] to smallest [Q1]) for two different years (2003 and 2011). Panel B lists spending rule frequencies across time (2003, 2007, and 2011) for two different fund size quartiles (Q4 and Q1).

changing circumstances in the form of unexpectedly adverse economic conditions (see Brown et al. 2010) or competition for resources with peer institutions (see Goetzmann and Oster [chapter 3, this volume], and Lerner, Schoar, and Wang [2008]) that necessitate changing their spending policies on an occasional basis. However, there appears to be little in the way of a priori justification for a widespread frequency of changes to the nature of these statements.[23]

To analyze this issue, we examine how all of the endowment funds in the NACUBO sample specified their spending policies during every year between 2003 and 2011. Formally, for each endowment E, we examine its spending policy (i.e., both spending rule and policy rate) for every year T that it reported survey data and characterize its spending rule according to the taxonomy described earlier. Endowment E is considered to have changed its spending policy if at least one of two conditions occur: (a) the spending rule it uses in year $T + 1$ falls into a different category than its spending rule in year T (e.g., a switch from a decide annually rule in 2009 to a hybrid rule in 2010); or (b) a change from year T to year $T + 1$ in the designated policy payout rate specified within the same spending rule (e.g., a switch from a commitment to spend 4.0 percent of a twelve-quarter moving average of past portfolio values in 2005 to 5.0 percent of a similar moving average calculation in 2006). Notice that while an adjustment in either the spending rule or the designated rate applied within that rule is regarded as policy change, a modification in the former is considered to be a more extreme alteration of the way in which the endowment's investment problem is viewed.[24]

2.4.1 Tabulating Spending Policy Changes on a Yearly Basis

Table 2.5 documents at a broad level the extent to which endowments alter their spending policies from one year to the next. Panel A summarizes the frequency of change to any aspect of the spending policy (i.e., rule or rate) while panel B isolates just those endowments that altered the nature of the spending rule to the extent that it switched categories in consecutive years. To interpret the exhibit, for the fiscal year 2009, there were 842 endowments that reported information about their spending policy in the annual survey.

23. In this discussion, it is important to keep in mind the distinction between permanent spending needs, as defined by Tobin (1974), and temporary needs that might be driven by changing macroeconomic or institution-specific factors. As documented in table 2.3, roughly one in three endowments exercised its capacity to make special appropriations as necessary, which mitigates the need to change their formal spending policies to accommodate temporary changes in circumstances.

24. With this definition, an endowment that altered its spending rule from a three-year moving average based on an annual observation frequency to a five-year moving average based on a quarterly observation frequency *would not* be viewed as having made a policy change, assuming it also kept its designated payout rate the same. In this regard, the procedure we use for identifying spending policy changes that occurred in the sample is conservatively biased.

Table 2.5   **Changes in endowment spending policy and spending rule adoption**

Year T	Obs. at T	Reported at $T+1$	Maintained at $T+1$	Changed at $T+1$	Not reported at $T+1$	Pct. changing
			A. Policy changes			
2010	850	782	519	263	68	30.94
2009	842	749	463	286	93	33.97
2008	864	675	514	161	189	18.63
2007	833	698	545	153	135	18.37
2006	816	683	610	73	133	8.95
2005	818	680	382	298	138	36.43
2004	755	661	392	269	94	35.63
2003	744	607	504	103	137	13.84
			B. Rule changes			
2010	850	782	663	119	68	14.00
2009	842	749	618	131	93	15.56
2008	864	675	514	161	189	18.63
2007	833	698	613	85	135	10.20
2006	816	683	652	31	133	3.80
2005	818	680	382	298	138	36.43
2004	755	661	392	269	94	35.63
2003	744	607	504	103	137	13.84

Notes: This exhibit reports statistics summarizing how university endowment funds altered their spending policies (i.e., spending rule or stated policy payout rate, in panel A) or just their spending rules (in panel B) over the period July 1, 2002, to June 30, 2011. Listed for each fiscal year T are: (a) the number of reporting funds in year T; (b) the number of those funds also reporting in year $T+1$; (c) the number of year $T+1$ reporting funds that maintained their year T spending mandate; (d) the number of year $T+1$ reporting funds that changed their year T spending mandate; (e) the number of year T funds not reporting in year $T+1$; and (f) the ratio of funds that changed their year T spending mandate in year $T+1$ and the total number of year T funds.

Of those, 749 also reported the details of their spending policy in the 2010 NACUBO survey, meaning that 93 endowments that reported spending data in 2009 did not report in the following year.[25] Of those 749 endowments from the 2009 survey that also reported in the 2010 survey, 463 maintained their spending policies from one year to the next whereas 286 of those funds altered either their spending rule or their policy rate (panel A). Consistent with our convention of treating nonreporting endowments as ones that did not modify their policies, we list the frequency of spending policy change as 33.97 percent (= 286/842). Panel B then shows that of the 286 endowments that changed some aspect of their spending policies from 2009 to 2010, 131

25. An endowment might be listed at "not reported at $T+1$" either because it chose not to report data for that particular item (but otherwise participated in the survey) or because it dropped out of the survey altogether. To be conservative, in our calculations of the frequency of endowments that change their spending policy, we treat a nonreporting fund as one that did not change any aspect of its previous policy.

of them actually altered their spending rule in a way that caused a change in classification. This is represented in the last column as a rule frequency change of 15.56 percent (= 131/842).[26]

The clear and surprising implication from the findings in table 2.5 is that endowment funds adjust their spending policies far more often than might be reasonably expected given the long-term nature of their investment mandates. Specifically, the data in panel A show that annual frequencies with which either spending rules or policy payout rates (or both) are changed range from 8.95 percent (2006) to 36.43 percent (2005). The weighted mean (as a percentage of reporting funds) for these annual change frequencies is 24.62 percent, meaning that, on average, one in four of the endowments in the sample altered its spending policy each year. Further, as summarized by panel B, the percentage of endowments changing their actual spending rule—the most extreme policy adjustment they could make—in a given year ranged from 3.80 percent to 36.43 percent, with a weighted mean annual change frequency of 18.35 percent.[27]

Although theory (i.e., Merton 1993; Woglom 2003) predicts that the expected number of spending policy changes in a given survey year is zero, it is difficult to say whether these change frequency patterns can be considered extremely abnormal absent more information of how the investment problem faced by the sponsoring institutions might have changed. Nevertheless, testing the observed frequencies against two different prospective null hypotheses is instructive. First, assuming that 5.0 percent of the endowments will modify their spending mandates in a given year (i.e., a 1-in-20 event), the Pearson chi-squared statistics testing the goodness of fit between the observed and forecasted distributions for the spending policy and spending rule change samples are 6,350.46 and 3,843.25, respectively. Both of these statistics are statistically significant with p-values of less than 0.0001, indicating that endowments make adjustments far more frequently than might occur on a random basis if the true proportion of expected changes was zero. Beyond that, the respective chi-squared statistics testing whether the observed annual change frequencies equal the weighted mean frequencies (i.e., 24.62 percent for spending policy, 18.35 percent for spending rules only) are 269.45 and 413.38, which are also statistically reliable at better than a 0.0001 level. Thus, it is also the case that the spending policy changes shown in table 2.5 vary significantly from one another on a year-to-year basis.

Finally, as a supplement to this analysis of how frequently spending policies changed annually, it is also useful to consider the total number of times

26. Of course, both of these change frequencies would be larger if based on just those funds from the 2009 survey that also reported data in 2010; 38.18 percent (= 286/749) and 17.49 percent (= 131/749) for policy and rule changes, respectively.

27. Prior to the 2006 survey, NACUBO did not report separate data for policy payout rates. So, for 2003–2005, the change frequencies for the total spending policy are based solely on changes to the reported spending rules.

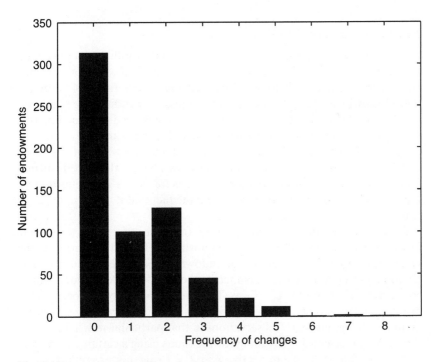

Fig. 2.4 Frequency of spending rule changes

Note: This figure shows the frequency of spending rule changes for the endowments in the NACUBO/Commonfund sample over the period July 1, 2002, to June 30, 2011. For each endowment that reports sufficient spending policy data for at least two consecutive annual surveys, we calculate the number of times the endowment changes the spending rules it adopted for each fiscal year from 2003 to 2010. The figure depicts the histogram of the number of rule changes.

during the 2003–2011 sample period that each endowment altered its stated spending rule. To tabulate this information, we focused on the 628 funds that reported their rules continuously over the entire set of nine surveys for which spending data were collected. As before, a fund was considered to have made a modification if the spending rules it reported in year T and year $T + 1$ fall into different categories, so that the maximum number of changes that could be observed for any endowment E is eight. Figure 2.4 presents a histogram of these statistics. Exactly half (i.e., 314 of 628) of the funds did not adjust their spending rule at all during this interval, meaning that exactly half of the funds did make at least one formal adjustment. In fact, more endowments made two changes to their stated rule (129) than those that made only one modification (101). Further, 13.38 percent (84 of 628) changed this aspect of their spending policy three or more times and one endowment altered its spending rule in *every one* of the available surveys!

2.4.2 Spending Rule Migration Patterns

Given this unexpectedly large number of annual spending policy changes, a natural question to ask is which mandates are most likely to be abandoned and which are most likely to be subsequently adopted? Table 2.6 addresses this issue by focusing on the more narrow topic of spending rule migration trends. Specifically, for every endowment E, we observed the spending rule it adopted for both year T as well as in the following year $T + 1$. Then, for each year T spending rule classification, we tabulated which of the seven categories the same fund fit into in the next year. Notice that by this sorting process, we account for all possible outcomes for how a given endowment E can modify its spending rule, including the fact that it might not change it at all.

Panel A reports these annual transition frequencies for all of the sample funds over the entire 2003–2011 time horizon. The first column lists the seven spending rule categories that endowments adopted in year T. The remaining seven columns then summarize the spending rule category, a given endowment E fit into in year $T + 1$. The data in the table have been scaled by dividing the number of raw observations in a particular cell by the total number of original year T observations in that particular row. Thus, all of the entries represent the percentage of the funds using a certain rule at year T that now fall under the respective year $T + 1$ rule. For example, the first row of panel A in table 2.6 corresponds to those endowments that adopted the decide annually rule in year T. Of those, 47.72 percent remained in the decide annually rule (i.e., did not change) during the following year, while 39.82 percent of those endowments switched their spending policy to a moving average rule. By construction, each of the rows in the display sums to 100.00 percent.[28]

Arguably the most interesting aspect of the reported findings is that the various spending rules have dramatically different likelihoods of being retained from one survey year to the next. The diagonal elements of the matrix (starting from the top left cell) indicate the percentage of a particular spending rule category that *did not* change (i.e., was retained) in the following period. Clearly, with 88.12 percent and 79.85 percent retention, respectively, the moving average and hybrid rule categories are the only ones that have a better than three-in-four chance of remaining in place in consecutive years and are therefore the only rules whose adoption appears to be stable. Conversely, the retention rate for percentage of yield rules is just 35.74 percent, meaning that approximately two out of three funds that adopted that mandate in year T formally altered their spending policies within the next twelve months.

28. Notice also that this exhibit is constructed so that each endowment is likely to appear multiple times since a comparison of rules in place for year T and year $T + 1$ produces up to eight observations per fund over the nine-year time frame for which spending rule data were available. Of course, any fund that changed spending policies will see its data represented in different rows.

It is also useful to consider which spending rules are the most likely to be adopted, once an endowment decides to modify its current policy. This information can be inferred by looking down the last seven columns displayed in panel A. Given the previous findings, it is not surprising that moving average rules appear to be the most popular destination to which the other six spending rules migrate; for instance, in addition to the 39.82 percent change from the decide annually rules noted above, moving average rules are also adopted by 36.55 percent of funds changing from percentage of yield rules, by 35.25 percent of funds altering other rules, and by 34.29 percent of funds altering percentage of AUM rules. By inspection, no other single rule category even comes close to matching this migration pattern. In contrast, hybrid rules, which was the only category besides moving average rules that was able to retain more than three-quarters of its adopters in a given year, was not able to attract as much as 4.00 percent of the annual migration from the other spending rules. This suggests that hybrid rules represent a highly fund-specific form of spending policy that is likely to be stable once adopted, but unlikely to be the destination for the typical endowment seeking to alter its payout rules.

The last two panels in table 2.6 extend this analysis by focusing on the behavior in different subdivisions of the sample. Panel B reproduces the spending rule migration patterns just described for two different sample periods straddling the global economic downturn that began in the fall of 2008: (a) 2003–2008, and (b) 2009–2011.[29] Panel C then reproduces these findings over the entire sample period for funds in the largest (Q4) and smallest (Q1) AUM quartiles as of a particular year T. The most striking feature of these transition matrices before and after the 2008 financial market downturn is the marked increase in the probability that endowments retain their previous spending rules. As shown in diagonal entries in the upper and lower portions of panel B, all seven of the rule categories show higher retention frequencies in the 2009–2011 subperiod than they did in 2003–2008 time frame. For some of these rule classes (e.g., increase by percentage, 48.39 percent to 80.85 percent; percentage of yield, 30.35 percent to 58.33 percent), the change in retention frequency is quite dramatic. On the surface, this appears to be a curious outcome; the findings of Brown et al. (2010), in fact, would suggest that adverse economic environments might induce *more* policy adjustments than fewer. However, one explanation for this increased reluctance for endowments to alter their spending rules in the two years following the market downturn is that, as a result of steep declines in AUM, the gap between the required spending dollars and projected dollars using *any* rule was so extreme that any adjustment to the permanent

---

29. Recall the convention in the educational endowment industry to designate fiscal years that end on June 30. Thus, the 2009 fiscal year began on July 1, 2008 (i.e., before the putative start of the crisis), and ended on June 30, 2009.

Table 2.6   Endowment fund spending rule transition matrices

A. Entire sample

	Decide annually at $T+1$	Increase by pct. at $T+1$	Moving average at $T+1$	Pct. of yield at $T+1$	Pct. of AUM at $T+1$	Hybrid rule at $T+1$	Other rule at $T+1$
Decide annually at T	47.72	1.82	39.82	1.82	5.17	0.30	3.34
Increase by pct. at T	3.96	55.94	30.69	1.98	1.98	1.49	3.96
Moving average at T	2.55	1.43	88.12	2.24	1.68	1.09	2.89
Pct. of yield at T	8.43	3.61	36.55	35.74	4.02	2.01	9.64
Pct. of AUM at T	4.90	2.45	34.29	2.86	48.98	1.22	5.31
Hybrid rule at T	2.24	0.75	8.21	5.97	0.00	79.85	2.99
Other at T	2.30	2.68	35.25	4.21	3.07	3.83	48.66

B. Before and after the economic crisis

Rule changes, 2009–2011

	Decide annually at $T+1$	Increase by pct. at $T+1$	Moving average at $T+1$	Pct. of yield at $T+1$	Pct. of AUM at $T+1$	Hybrid rule at $T+1$	Other rule at $T+1$
Decide annually at T	58.33	1.67	25.00	0.00	8.33	0.00	6.67
Increase by pct. at T	4.26	80.85	6.38	0.00	0.00	2.13	6.38
Moving average at T	1.02	0.47	91.81	1.49	0.37	1.02	3.81
Pct. of yield at T	0.00	0.00	29.17	58.33	2.08	0.00	10.42
Pct. of AUM at T	0.00	1.89	13.21	1.89	64.15	3.77	15.09
Hybrid rule at T	3.33	1.11	5.56	0.00	0.00	85.56	4.44
Other at T	3.16	3.80	29.11	3.16	3.16	5.06	52.53

Rule changes, 2003–2008

	Decide annually at $T+1$	Increase by pct. at $T+1$	Moving average at $T+1$	Pct. of yield at $T+1$	Pct. of AUM at $T+1$	Hybrid rule at $T+1$	Other rule at $T+1$
Decide annually at T	45.35	1.86	43.12	2.23	4.46	0.37	2.60
Increase by pct. at T	3.87	48.39	38.06	2.58	2.58	1.29	3.23
Moving average at T	3.09	1.78	86.81	2.50	2.14	1.12	2.57
Pct. of yield at T	10.45	4.48	38.31	30.35	4.48	2.49	9.45
Pct. of AUM at T	6.25	2.60	40.10	3.13	44.79	0.52	2.60
Hybrid rule at T	0.00	0.00	13.64	18.18	0.00	68.18	0.00
Other at T	0.97	0.97	44.66	5.83	2.91	1.94	42.72

C. Large (Q4) versus small (Q1) endowments

Large funds-q1 of AUM

	Decide annually	Increase by pct.	Moving average	Pct. of yield	Pct. of AUM	Hybrid rule	Other
Decide annually at T	78.57	0.00	14.29	0.00	0.00	0.00	7.14
Increase by pct. at T	3.23	51.08	34.95	2.15	2.69	2.15	3.76
Moving average at T	2.99	1.78	87.06	2.70	2.42	0.71	2.35
Pct. of yield at T	0.00	0.00	80.00	0.00	0.00	0.00	20.00
Pct. of AUM at T	0.00	20.00	20.00	0.00	40.00	20.00	0.00
Hybrid rule at T	0.00	0.00	0.00	0.00	0.00	97.62	2.38
Other at T	1.89	7.55	28.30	0.00	0.00	3.77	58.49

Small funds-q1 of AUM

	Decide annually	Increase by pct.	Moving average	Pct. of yield	Pct. of AUM	Hybrid rule	Other
Decide annually at T	50.00	0.00	25.00	0.00	15.00	0.00	10.00
Increase by pct. at T	50.00	50.00	0.00	0.00	0.00	0.00	0.00
Moving average at T	1.24	0.00	91.32	1.65	0.83	1.24	3.72
Pct. of yield at T	0.00	0.00	23.53	52.94	5.88	0.00	17.65
Pct. of AUM at T	0.00	0.00	5.00	0.00	70.00	5.00	20.00
Hybrid rule at T	8.70	0.00	39.13	0.00	0.00	47.83	4.35
Other at T	2.38	0.00	30.95	9.52	4.76	2.38	50.00

Notes: This table summarizes endowment fund spending rule migration patterns between year T and year $T + 1$ over the period July 1, 2002, to June 30, 2011. For endowments adopting a given spending rule in year T, each row lists which rule those funds subsequently adopted in year $T + 1$. The frequencies are expressed as the percentage of the year T funds in a given spending rule that fall into each year $T + 1$ category; by construction, the listed values in each row sum to 100 percent and the diagonal elements represent the percentage of funds that maintained their spending rule from one year to the next. Panel A reports the transition matrix calculated over the entire endowment universe, panel B separates the sample in the before-economic crisis (2003–2008) and after-economic crisis (2009–2011) periods, and panel C presents transition matrices for funds in the largest (Q4) and smallest (Q1) AUM size quartiles over the entire sample period.

policy guidelines would not have solved the problem. Instead, many endowments relied on temporary measures to close this spending gap; for instance, the summary statistics in table 2.3 show that about one out of every three endowments invoked special appropriations in the 2009, 2010, and 2011 fiscal years. Thus, consistent with the notion that the spending rule policy statement represents a vision of the long-term investment problem faced by the institution, boards tend to respond to extreme events of a temporary nature with solutions that are similarly short lived.

The transition matrices for the largest and smallest fund size quartiles shown in panel C of table 2.6 also indicate significant cross-sectional differences in the way endowments with disparate AUM levels alter their spending policies. While the values reported for the various cells appear to be more erratic than those shown in panel B, due to the small frequencies associated the sample quartiles, they nevertheless indicate some similarities and disparities. First, the retention rate for moving average rules was extremely high for both large (87.06 percent) and small (91.22 percent) endowments and the migration *into* this rule category (i.e., the data in the respective columns) occurred for both size quartiles with about the same frequency. Conversely, the retention rate in the large funds for hybrid rules was virtually 100.00 percent, indicating that the biggest endowments adopting this spending policy category essentially never change. For small endowments, however, the loyalty to hybrid rules was far more suspect (47.83 percent retention), meaning that more Q1 endowments switched away from hybrid rules than kept them from one year to the next. For these funds, it was almost as probable (39.13 percent) that they would modify the spending rule by changing to a simpler moving average formula—which is likely to have been one of the rule categories combined in the hybrid approach—than retain the previous combination rule. Finally, notice that *no* small funds switched to an increase by percentage rule—and only 50.00 percent of previous adopters retained that policy—over the entire sample period and that no large funds retained an exclusive reliance on a percentage of yield rule.

2.5 The Determinants of Spending Rule Changes

The preceding results leave little doubt that, collectively, university endowment funds alter their formal spending policies far more frequently than might be expected. However, beyond some suggestions from the reported data that patterns in these rule and payout rate changes are linked to some cross-sectional and temporal differences in the sample, it is not clear what the determinants of spending policy modifications actually are. In this section, we address that question by examining the formal links between a measure summarizing these changes and several variables observable in advance of a period in which an endowment either did or did not adjust its spending rules.

2.5.1 Defining Potential Determinants

In the statistical analysis that follows, we begin by defining the dependent variable ($POLCHG_{T+1}$) as an indicator variable assuming the value of 1 if endowment E changed its stated spending rule between the survey years T and $T + 1$, and 0 otherwise. Accordingly, each of the potential explanatory factors that we consider is observable as of year T. The following discussion describes these regressors, including how each of them is defined, as well as the direction of the predicted influence they have on $POLCHG$.

The findings discussed in section 2.3.4 revealed a potential connection between an endowment's spending policy decision and the nature of the returns produced by its investment portfolio. Although the ranges in the mean levels of portfolio return and policy volatility reported in table 2.3 for the seven spending rule categories were fairly narrow, it is nevertheless a reasonable conjecture that both the amount and stability of the change in the fund's market value could influence the institution's decision to alter its payout formula. We therefore define as potential determinants the endowment portfolio's year T investment return (RET_T) and policy portfolio volatility level (VOL_T), as described earlier. The relationship between $POLCHG$ and VOL should be positive: the less predictable the portfolio's asset value is, the more likely the endowment might have to alter its spending plan. Conversely, positive investment returns in a given fiscal year should make it less likely that the endowment will need to adjust its long-term policy, leading to a negative predicted relationship between RET and $PLCHG$.[30]

Two other variables that were shown earlier to be connected to an endowment's choice of spending policy are the level of its actual payout and the size of its investment portfolio. The year T values of these factors—which we label as $PAYOUT_T$ and $LOGAUM_T$, respectively—are also included as potential determinants in the analysis reported below. As shown in table 2.3, funds with higher (lower) payout rates were more likely to use increase by percentage or hybrid (percentage of yield) rules over the sample period. Thus, the relationship between $PAYOUT$ and $POLCHG$ is likely to be negative in that funds with higher required payouts are likely to have already adopted the rules that best serve that purpose. On the other hand, it is not clear what impact the market value of the endowment portfolio, which for scaling purposes is expressed here as the natural logarithm of the fund's AUM, might have on $POLCHG$. The data summarized in figure 2.2 show that the largest funds have been far more willing and able to adjust their asset allocations than smaller endowments, which might suggest that they are also

---

30. The negative forecasted connection between RET and $POLCHG$ might be better seen from the other direction. That is, negative portfolio returns might cause a spending policy change—perhaps in addition to the special appropriations discussed earlier—because the income generated by the portfolio, as well as the fund's reduced AUM level, is not sufficient to generate the required expenditures under the old policy.

less likely to need to adjust their spending policy definition in changing economic environments, implying a negative relationship. However, as indicated by figure 2.3, it is also the case that large endowments appear to change their spending rules more frequently, perhaps because their organizational mobility permits making quick adjustments to all of their various operating policies.

It is possible that spending rule changes are also linked to the specific nature of an endowment's asset allocation decision. In particular, it was also shown in section 2.3.3 that endowments vary considerably in the use of alternative assets and these investments are especially critical to determining both the absolute and risk-adjusted returns that an institutionally managed portfolio produces (see Lerner, Schoar, and Wongsunwai 2007; Brown, Garlappi, and Tiu 2010). Thus, as described earlier, we define $ALTINV_T$ as the percentage of an endowment's year T portfolio that is invested in the hedge fund, private equity, real estate, and natural resources asset classes. The effect of $ALTINV$ on $POLCHG$ could go in either direction; the fact that larger allocations to alternatives might produce higher returns could generate the negative correlation hypothesized above for RET, but the greater degree of illiquidity associated with the alternative asset classes could create less investment policy flexibility, which in turn could lead to a higher likelihood of modifications to the spending policy.

Returns to the investment portfolio are not the only way that an endowment can fund its spending needs. Educational institutions routinely receive donations from a variety of public and private supporters that can either be used to increase the size of the current portfolio or be earmarked for direct expenditure (see Brown, Dimmock, and Weisbenner 2012). In either case, we posit that larger levels of these supplemental contributions would make it less likely that an endowment would have to modify its spending rule to meet its budgetary needs, implying a negative relationship between year T donations (labeled as $DONATE_T$) and future $POLCHG$. The NACUBO database does not contain observations on donations directly, but these contributions can be inferred for a given fund by taking the difference between the portfolio's value at the end and beginning of the period, adjusted for the returns earned during the period, plus the payout amount. That is, expressed as a percentage of assets, we have

(1) $DONATE_T = [AUM_{T+1} - AUM_T X(1 + RET_T)] / AUM_T$

$+ PAYOUT_T,$

where the AUM levels are expressed as beginning-of-period asset values.

Finally, the descriptive data in table 2.3 also strongly indicated that both the percentage of the institution's overall budget that the endowment was responsible for delivering as well as its ability to make special payout appropriations were linked to the choice of permanent spending rule. We therefore allow for the possibility that the year T value of the budget variable (defined earlier as the actual payout in year T divided by the school's budget over the same period and labeled here as $PCTBDGT_T$) and a variable indicating whether a special appropriation was made in year T (labeled as $APPROP_T$) help to explain future $POLCHG$. We posit a positive relationship between $PCTBDGT$ and $POLCHG$ if, ceteris paribus, a fund obligated to deliver a bigger proportion of the university's spending needs must stand ready to alter its payout rules to do so in changing economic conditions. Conversely, consistent with the results in table 2.6, the use of temporary appropriations should make formal spending rule changes less likely, leading to a negative relationship between $APPROP$ and $POLCHG$. A challenge to testing either of these hypotheses, however, is that NACUBO only reports data for $PCTBDGT$ and $APPROP$ beginning with their 2009 survey, leaving only three yearly observations.

2.5.2 Statistical Analysis

Given the dichotomous nature of our spending rule change dependent variable, we examined the statistical relationship between $POLCHG$ and the various prospective determinants using a series of probit regression models that represent variations of the following functional form:

$$(2) \qquad Z_{T+1} = f \begin{pmatrix} RET_T, PAYOUT_T, LOGAUM_T, \\ ALTINV_T, DONATE_T, VOL_T \end{pmatrix} + \epsilon_{T+1},$$

where Z_{T+1} represents an unobservable, continuously distributed index variable related to $POLCHG_{T+1}$. Because of the well-known statistical challenges inherent in working with panel data (e.g., a time series of cross-sectional observations), we estimate equation (2) as a linear model using three different approaches: (a) a full-panel data regression with year fixed effects only; (b) a full-panel data regression with both year and fund fixed effects; and (c) the multistage approach of Fama and MacBeth (1973), wherein separate cross-sectional versions of equation (2) are estimated for each of the survey years and then the estimated coefficients from each of the annual cross sections are averaged for all of the relevant explanatory variables. Further, we also include in the estimation process various additional terms to account for the interaction between regressors (e.g., RET_T x $PAYOUT_T$) and indicator variables to assess behavior in the posteconomic crash environment (e.g., RET_T x D_T , where D_T equals 1 if $T = 2009$, 2010, or 2011 and 0 otherwise).

Table 2.7 lists the calculated coefficients for each of the hypothesized determinants for endowment spending rule changes, along with the associated t-statistics in parentheses, and the R-squared values for each regression. To begin with, panel A reports findings for the three forms of the probit model using all of the available data (i.e., an unconditional specification of $POLCHG$ where each endowment from every annual survey is included whether the spending policy was changed or not and without any addi-

Table 2.7   The determinants of spending rule changes

	Panel, year fixed effects		Panel, year/fund fixed effects		Fama-MacBeth	
A. All rule changes						
Constant	229.78	(10.71)	228.86	(10.65)	−1.85	(−4.08)
RET	−1.32	(−2.12)	−1.31	(−2.10)	−1.18	(−0.30)
PAYOUT	−8.74	(−5.51)	−8.73	(−5.50)	−4.57	(−0.79)
LOGAUM	0.08	(4.78)	0.07	(4.24)	0.10	(5.79)
ALTINV	−0.19	(−1.31)	−0.17	(−1.19)	−0.40	(−2.77)
DONATE	0.06	(0.93)	0.06	(0.98)	0.04	(0.16)
VOL	−0.55	(−0.44)	−0.56	(−0.44)	0.15	(0.10)
RET x *PAYOUT*	31.09	(2.67)	31.14	(2.67)	56.61	(0.79)
RET x *D*(2009–2011)	−1.01	(−2.42)	−1.03	(−2.46)		
Total obs.	5,627		5,627		5,627	
Obs. (*POLCHG* = 1)	948		948		948	
R-squared	5.42%		5.54%		2.67%	
B. Rule changes resulting in higher payouts						
Constant	197.80	(6.63)	197.14	(6.60)	−2.06	(−2.67)
RET	−1.32	(−1.69)	−1.31	(−1.68)	0.55	(0.17)
PAYOUT	−20.01	(−9.40)	−20.04	(−9.41)	−21.85	(−2.77)
LOGAUM	0.05	(2.15)	0.05	(1.97)	0.06	(1.62)
ALTINV	0.60	(3.06)	0.61	(3.10)	0.24	(0.75)
DONATE	0.10	(1.34)	0.10	(1.36)	−0.39	(−1.39)
VOL	3.81	(2.09)	3.80	(2.08)	3.52	(1.73)
RET x *PAYOUT*	−7.08	(−0.48)	−7.10	(−0.48)	24.30	(0.33)
RET x *D*(2009–2011)	0.40	(0.70)	0.39	(0.68)		
Total obs.	5,627		5,627		5,627	
Obs. (*POLCHG* = 1)	317		317		317	
R-squared	3.28%		3.30%		4.13%	
C1. Rule change by budget contribution: Highest quartile						
Constant	163.58	(4.07)	167.50	(4.15)	−2.35	(−2.01)
RET	−1.30	(−1.03)	−1.17	(−0.93)	−6.26	(−0.82)
PAYOUT	−7.40	(−2.42)	−7.27	(−2.37)	−13.94	(−0.78)
LOGAUM	0.07	(2.00)	0.06	(1.58)	0.12	(2.51)
ALTINV	−0.37	(−1.38)	−0.26	(−0.98)	−0.37	(−1.43)
DONATE	−0.18	(−0.77)	−0.17	(−0.72)	−0.62	(−0.65)
VOL	2.61	(0.96)	2.33	(0.86)	6.62	(1.52)
RET x *PAYOUT*	25.65	(1.11)	23.57	(1.02)	165.64	(1.16)
RET x *D*(2009–2011)	−0.88	(−1.16)	−0.90	(−1.20)		
Total obs.	1,425		1,425		1,425	
Obs. (*POLCHG* = 1)	294		294		294	
R-squared	4.40%		4.81%		6.74%	
C2. Rule change by budget contribution: Lowest quartile						
Constant	272.04	(5.28)	272.12	(5.27)	−2.32	(−2.24)
RET	0.36	(0.29)	0.38	(0.31)	−13.12	(−0.53)
PAYOUT	−8.05	(−2.67)	−8.14	(−2.71)	−18.06	(−0.46)
LOGAUM	0.05	(1.12)	0.04	(0.88)	0.22	(1.59)
ALTINV	−0.14	(−0.32)	−0.14	(−0.33)	1.09	(1.00)
DONATE	0.27	(0.98)	0.27	(1.00)	1.86	(0.92)

(*continued*)

Table 2.7   (continued)

	Panel, year fixed effects		Panel, year/fund fixed effects		Fama-MacBeth	
VOL	−3.82	(−1.59)	−3.85	(−1.61)	−21.25	(−1.10)
RET x PAYOUT	−0.16	(−0.01)	−0.26	(−0.01)	405.98	(0.53)
RET x D(2009–2011)	−2.06	(−1.94)	−2.08	(−1.95)		
Total obs.		985		985		985
Obs. (POLCHG = 1)		192		192		192
R-squared		8.56%		8.64%		12.29%
D1. All rule changes, no appropriations						
Constant	254.74	(9.13)	254.69	(9.12)	−1.71	(−2.85)
RET	−0.85	(−1.02)	−0.84	(−1.02)	−3.60	(−0.51)
PAYOUT	−8.23	(−3.76)	−8.23	(−3.75)	−0.31	(−0.04)
LOGAUM	0.07	(3.12)	0.07	(3.04)	0.11	(4.12)
ALTINV	−0.14	(−0.74)	−0.14	(−0.73)	−0.39	(−1.12)
DONATE	0.08	(1.08)	0.08	(1.08)	0.01	(0.02)
VOL	−3.35	(−2.07)	−3.34	(−2.07)	−2.44	(−1.03)
RET x PAYOUT	26.24	(1.68)	26.22	(1.67)	102.36	(0.86)
RET x D(2009–2011)	−1.07	(−1.98)	−1.08	(−1.98)		
Total obs.		3,434		3,434		3,434
Obs. (POLCHG = 1)		559		559		559
R-squared		5.91%		5.91%		3.96%
D2. All rule changes, uses appropriations						
Constant	305.67	(3.67)	311.83	(3.72)	0.33	(0.27)
RET	−0.65	(−0.24)	−0.44	(−0.16)	−29.97	(−0.82)
PAYOUT	−9.63	(−1.40)	−9.77	(−1.40)	−14.81	(−0.77)
LOGAUM	0.05	(0.66)	0.05	(0.62)	0.07	(0.82)
ALTINV	−0.34	(−0.62)	−0.32	(−0.57)	−0.53	(−0.74)
DONATE	−0.89	(−0.78)	−0.94	(−0.82)	−3.08	(−1.06)
VOL	−5.82	(−1.13)	−4.57	(−0.87)	−12.24	(−2.60)
RET x PAYOUT	25.53	(0.51)	20.03	(0.40)	448.52	(0.78)
RET x D(2009–2011)	−0.81	(−0.52)	−0.68	(−0.43)		
Total obs.		380		380		380
Obs. (POLCHG = 1)		70		70		70
R-squared		8.53%		9.28%		12.27%

Notes: This table reports regression results examining the determinants of endowment spending rule changes over the period July 1, 2002, to June 30, 2011. The primary dependent variable (*POLCHG*) is an indicator variable assuming a value of 1 if an endowment changed its spending rule in year $T + 1$, 0 otherwise. The base set of potential explanatory factors (observable at year T) includes portfolio net-of-fee return (*RET*), actual percentage payout (*PAYOUT*), logarithm of fund size (*LOGAUM*), percentage of portfolio invested in alternative assets (*ALTINV*), external contributions to the endowment (*DONATE*), and risk level of the policy-level investment portfolio (*VOL*). Three different forms of the probit regression in equation (2) are specified: (a) panel data with year fixed effects, (b) panel data with year and fund fixed effects, and (c) Fama-MacBeth. Panel A lists findings for the full sample using all rule changes. Panel B modifies the spending rule change definition to focus on just those changes that also resulted in a higher subsequent payout. Panel C reports results for the endowment sample quartiles with the highest (C1) and lowest (C2) average payout-as-percentage-of budget (*PCTBDGT*) statistics. Panel D reports results for endowment subsamples that either did not (D1) or did (D2) use special payout appropriation measures. The *t*-statistics are listed parenthetically next to the respective coefficient estimates.

tional restrictions). Panel B then presents a modified analysis by focusing on just those rule changes that subsequently resulted in a larger payout from the endowment portfolio. Panel C reestimates the unrestricted model from panel A for two nonoverlapping subsets of the endowment fund sample determined by the relative amount of an institution's budget that the payout represented over the 2009–2011 fiscal years. Specifically, panel C reports separate sets of estimated coefficients from equation (2) for funds that fall in the highest and lowest $PCTBDGT$ quartiles in the sample.[31] Finally, panel D reports regression estimates for two nonoverlapping subsets of the endowment fund sample according to whether the sponsoring institution either did or did not invoke a special spending appropriation in year T.

Looking first at the two fixed effects (FE) panel data regressions for the entire sample (panel A), the most statistically meaningful determinants of spending rule changes are $LOGAUM$, $PAYOUT$, and RET. In particular, the strong positive relationship between fund size and $POLCHG$ suggests that it is the largest endowments that are the most likely to alter their spending policies, a finding consistent with the notion that the greater degree of organizational flexibility that they possess permits a greater ability to make adjustments to all aspects of their operations. The t-statistics for the reported coefficients (i.e., 4.78 for the year FE parameter of 0.08, 4.24 for the year/fund FE parameter of 0.07) indicate that this relationship is highly tractable even after controlling for the possibility of variables omitted from the analysis, both across time and between endowments. Beyond that, the Fama-MacBeth coefficient for $LOGAUM$ is also statistically reliable, which is especially notable given that this t-statistic (i.e., 5.79) is based on averaging parameter estimates from eight annual cross sections.[32]

The two other significant relationships documented in panel A involve the level of the endowment's actual payout and the return to its investment portfolio. As predicted in section 2.5.1, the coefficients for both the $PAYOUT$ and RET variables are negative, implying that funds that have produced smaller past payout levels and generated smaller investment returns are more likely to adjust the spending rules in the future. The coefficients for $PAYOUT$ from the two FE models are particularly strong (e.g., a t-statistic of 5.51 for the year FE parameter of -8.74), but the statistical significance

31. As discussed earlier, data for the percentage of an institution's budget supplied by the annual payout from its endowment portfolio have only been available since the 2009 survey year. We make the implicit assumption with our analysis in panel C that the $PCTBDGT$ variable for a given fund is stable across time *on a relative basis*, meaning that the set of endowments with the greatest (least) budget responsibility does not change in a material way from one year to another.

32. Since the specification in equation (2) is a probit equation, it is also useful to provide an economic interpretation for the estimated coefficients. For instance, the $LOGAUM$ parameter of 0.07 for the year/fund FE model corresponds to an increase in the probability of altering the spending policy of 0.15 percent for each incremental $10 million in the size of the endowment's portfolio. For perspective, recall from the sample overview in table 2.1 that the AUM for the average endowment in 2011 was $508.09 million.

of this variable is attenuated somewhat in the more severe conditions of the Fama-MacBeth model, although the sign of the coefficient does not change. The same pattern holds for the relationship between *POLCHG* and *RET* as well, with the additional observation that the negative effect becomes even stronger starting with the 2009 fiscal year ($RET_{2009-2011}$), emphasizing the effect that the financial market crisis had on running a university endowment fund. It is also interesting to note that the interaction between return and payout variables (RET_T x $PAYOUT_T$) is also a significant determinant of *POLCHG*, but in a way that mitigates the two separate effects just described. Specifically, funds with lower past returns *and* lower past payouts are *less* likely to change their spending rules more frequently, a finding that is difficult to explain beyond the possibility that these funds may also face more organizational barriers to affecting operating changes of any kind.

There are two other findings in involving these probit regressions for the entire unrestricted sample worth noting. First, endowment funds with a larger allocation to alternative assets tend to be less likely to modify their spending policies, as indicated by the consistently negative parameter values on *ALTINV*. Surprisingly, this relationship becomes more significant in the Fama-MacBeth regression than in either of the FE specifications. Since, as noted before, funds with larger alternative asset investments often produce higher risk-adjusted returns, this outcome suggests that there may be additional aspects of investment performance beyond nominal portfolios returns (i.e., *RET*) that are important in explaining the tendency to adjust formal spending mandates. Second, the effects that both the benchmark-level risk of the fund (*VOL*) or its external contributions from donors (*DONATE*) had on *POLCHG* were negligible. The former is not necessarily unexpected given the finding of Brown, Garlappi, and Tiu (2010) that endowments tend to target similar policy volatilities. However, it is surprising that the impact that supplemental contributions to the fund have on the decision to adjust spending policy is extremely unreliable as well as of the wrong sign.

Panel B of table 2.7 reexamines these relationships after altering the *POLCHG* variable by assigning a value of 1 only to those observations for which (a) the spending rule was changed at year $T + 1$, *and* (b) $PAYOUT_{T+1}$ exceeds $PAYOUT_T$.[33] Presumably, this modification allows us to focus on those endowments whose express intention in changing their long-term spending mandate was to increase the future payout level of the fund. While the main findings from panel A continue to hold (e.g., large endowments with smaller past payout levels and lower past returns are more likely to change their rules), these new findings indicate some interesting differences. Most notably, the relationship between *PAYOUT* and *POLCHG* becomes much more

---

33. By this construction, spending rule changes that *did not* result in an increased payout level are assigned a value of 0, so that the total number of observations in the sample does not change, but the number of observations for which *POLCHG* takes the value of 1 is reduced. These frequencies are listed in the exhibit for each set of regression output.

strongly negative than before, even becoming statistically significant in the Fama-MacBeth specification. This does indeed suggest that the experience of low past payout rates is a major factor driving an institution to seek a more accommodating set of rules. Further, there is also evidence that, for these specific funds, investing to a greater extent in alternative assets makes changing their policies *more* likely, which is consistent with the argument that increased illiquidity in the investment portfolio makes that dimension of the board's decision making less flexible. Interestingly, it is also the case that the portfolio's volatility level now matters, with the significant positive coefficient for *VOL* predicted in section 2.5.1 obtaining. Finally, the interaction term between *PAYOUT* and *RET* and the indicator variable highlighting returns in the postcrisis period are no longer statistically reliable.

The results contained in panel C restore the original definition of *POLCHG* (i.e., assigns a value of 1 for *any* spending rule adjustment), but divides the endowment sample into two subgroups representing the largest and smallest quartiles ranked by the average value of the *PCTBDGT* variable over the 2009–2011 period. The display lists a full set of probit regression findings for each of these sample divisions.[34] The surprising result from a comparison of panel C1 (High *PCTBDGT*) and panel C2 (Low *PCTBDGT*) is that this variable appears to make virtually no difference to the fundamental relationships between *POLCHG* and its underlying determinants. For both sample divisions, the only variable that shows both the predicted sign and consistent statistical significance is *PAYOUT*, although *LOGAUM* does appear to be a stronger explanatory factor in the high *PCTBDGT* subsample. Portfolio returns in year *T* are not statistically reliable for either budget quartile, whether viewed over the entire sample period or just in the postcrisis years.

One possible explanation for *PCTBDGT*'s lack of influence is that, if an educational institution has the ability to extract incremental payouts from its endowment portfolio on a temporary basis, it may not need to change its permanent spending rules with any greater or lesser frequency regardless of how much of the budget the fund must cover. Thus, it could be the case that the presence of special appropriation measures mitigates the influence of budget percentage constraints. The final panel of table 2.7 reports spending rule determinant regression output for those funds that either did not (panel D1) or did (panel D2) make use of a special payout appropriation during the last three years of the sample period for which these data were reported. The results support the notion that it is the set of endowments that *do not*—perhaps *cannot*—use temporary appropriations that changes its permanent spending rules in a more predictable manner, as indicated by the

---

34. To get a better sense of the range across the entire sample in the percentage of an institution's budget that the endowment fund is responsible for producing, the values of the three-year average *PCTBDGT* variable falling at the 75th and 25th percentiles are 13.2 percent and 1.0 percent, respectively.

sign and statistical reliability of the *PAYOUT* and *LOGAUM* determinants. Neither of these variables are statistically significant for the uses appropriations subsample in panel D2, an outcome consistent with the spending rule transition results in section 2.4.2 that showed endowments using special payouts were more likely to retain their permanent policies from one year to the next.

2.6 The Interaction between Spending Policy, Asset Allocation, and Investment Performance

The findings reported so far support three stylized conclusions. First, the governing authorities of university endowment funds have changed both their spending policies and investment strategies (i.e., asset allocation weights) quite often over the past several years. Second, at least with respect to spending policy changes, these modifications appear to occur too frequently to be consistent with hypothesized behavior given the relatively invariant nature of the institution's long-term investment problem. Third, patterns in spending rule changes are significantly related to certain characteristics of the endowment's operations and the investment performance of the portfolio. In this section, we address two additional questions that involve the interaction between the endowment's spending policy decision and both its ex ante investment policy decision and the ex post policy-adjusted portfolio performance.

2.6.1 The Relationship between Changes in Spending Rules and Investment Policy

As the introductory discussion in section 2.1 suggests, a strong argument (e.g., Litvack, Malkiel, and Quandt 1974) can be made that the most compelling way to organize an investment management operation begins with a clear definition of the institution's investment problem and then designs a portfolio strategy that represents the "optimal" solution. In the context of university endowments, such a sequence of events clearly implies that the development of the endowment's spending policy should both precede and inform the development of its investment policy. However, it is also plausible (e.g., Dybvig 1999) that spending and investment policies are best determined simultaneously. From the preceding analysis on the frequency and determinants of spending policy adjustments, it is not altogether clear which (if either) of these predictions is true.

To establish more precisely the nature of the interaction between spending rule changes and asset allocation changes for our endowment fund sample, we begin by defining a measure that captures the essence of how endowment E's investment strategy evolves from year $T - 1$ to year T. Specifically, for each fund, we create an index of the change in the allocation weights (i.e., $AACHG_T^E$) by summing the absolute values of the differences in the actual investment levels for each of the ten asset classes representing the investable universe for the NACUBO sample during consecutive years:

(3) $$AACHG_T^E = \sum_{i=1}^{10} |w_{i,T}^E - w_{i,T-1}^E|.$$

Notice that, by construction, higher levels of $AACHG$ indicate a greater adjustment in the endowment's asset class investment strategy, due to either a change in its policy-level strategic allocation weights or a tactical rotation permitted within the existing policy.[35]

To see whether spending rule changes are more likely to precede or follow asset allocation changes, we use a vector autoregression (VAR) process to estimate the structural relationship between the two variables. Specifically, we estimate the VAR(1) model using: (a) $POLCHG_{T+1}$ and $AACHG_T$; and (b) $POLCHG_T$ and $AACHG_{T+1}$. Our null hypothesis is that the second form of the model (i.e., spending changes leading asset allocation changes) should provide the stronger results. The specific forms of the two panel data regression equations comprising the VAR system are:

(4) $POLCHG(T + 1) = a_1 + b_{11}POLCHG(T) + b_{12}AACHG(T)$

$$+ c_{11}LOGAUM(T) + c_{12}PAYOUT(T) + e_{1,T+1},$$

and

(5) $AACHG(T + 1) = a_2 + b_{21}POLCHG(T) + b_{22}AACHG(T)$

$$+ c_{21}LOGAUM(T) + c_{22}PAYOUT(T) + e_{2,T+1}.$$

Given their significance in earlier findings, we include $LOGAUM$ and $PAYOUT$ as control variables in the estimation of equations (4) and (5).

Table 2.8 tabulates these results, which contain two substantive findings. First, from equation (4), it is apparent that $POLCHG_{T+1}$ is significantly and positively related to $POLCHG_T$ (i.e., estimated coefficient of 0.2550 with a t-statistic of 23.93) but its relationship with $AACHG_T$ is not statistically reliable (i.e., t-statistic of -0.65). This supports the conclusion that spending rule changes are indeed persistent over time, at least for the half of the endowment sample that altered their policies at all. Further, it also highlights the fact that institutions *are not* adjusting their spending rules in response to previous changes in asset allocation strategies that may have produced less-than-desirable portfolio performance. This is consistent with a hypothesized view of the investment management process holding that the statement of the investment problem should not be determined by the myriad aspects of the investment decision-making process.

---

35. The measure in equation (3) is a straightforward variation of the class of statistical distance measures used elsewhere in the financial economic literature; see, for instance, Hansen and Jagannathan (1997).

Table 2.8   Spending rule changes and asset allocation changes

	POLCHG(T + 1)					AACHG(T + 1)				
	Const.	POLCHG(T)	AACHG(T)	LOGAUM(T)	PAYOUT(T)	Const.	POLCHG(T)	AACHG(T)	LOGAUM(T)	PAYOUT(T)
Coef.	−0.0330	0.2550	−0.0134	0.0119	−0.3121	0.1928	0.0165	0.2815	−0.0031	0.2325
t-stat	(−0.91)	(23.93)	(−0.65)	(3.95)	(−1.45)	(5.32)	(1.54)	(13.72)	(−1.02)	(1.08)
Obs.	4,101									

Notes: This table reports estimates of a panel data vector autoregression (VAR[1]) model for the relationship between changes in spending rules (*POLCHG*) and changes in asset allocation (*AACHG*) in the NACUBO/Commonfund endowment fund sample over the period from July 1, 2002, to June 30, 2011. The model, which includes controls for endowment fund size (LOGAUM) and past payout rate (*PAYOUT*), is estimated according to equations (4) and (5) as:

$$POLCHG(T + 1) = a_1 + b_1 POLCHG(T) + b_2 AACHG(T) + c_1 LOGAUM(T) + c_2 PAYOUT(T) + e_{1,T+1}$$

$$AACHG(T + 1) = a_2 + b_1 POLCHG(T) + b_2 AACHG(T) + c_1 LOGAUM(T) + c_2 PAYOUT(T) + e_{2,T+1}.$$

The *t*-statistics are listed parenthetically beneath the respective estimated coefficients.

The second main finding in table 2.8 involves the estimated coefficients for equation (5), which indicate that the relationship between $AACHG_{T+1}$ and $AACHG_T$ is also statistically significant (i.e., estimated coefficient of 0.2815 with a t-statistic of 13.72). This means that the typical endowment adjusts its asset allocation weights in a persistent manner over time, which can in turn be interpreted as suggesting that this dimension of its investment policy is not static. Further, $AACHG_{T+1}$ is positively correlated with $POLCHG_T$, although at a marginal level of statistical significance (i.e., estimated coefficient of 0.0165 with a t-statistic of 1.54). The implication of this finding is that future asset allocation changes *are* tied to past adjustments in spending rules, albeit with an attenuated level of strength. Specifically, an endowment that altered its payout rule in one year is *more likely* to modify its asset class-level investment strategy in the next year. This outcome implies that whatever it was that caused the fund to change its payout policy in the first place does indeed lead to a subsequent allocation adjustment in its portfolio construction.

2.6.2 Spending Rule Changes and Endowment Investment Performance

The findings in table 2.7 provide compelling evidence that the nominal level of an endowment fund's investment performance helps influence the institution's future spending policy decisions. It is not clear, though, whether endowments that change their spending rules perform appreciably better or worse than those that maintain stable payout mandates. A complication in addressing this issue is that a simple comparison of total portfolio returns between the two groups is not sufficient since we know that there is considerable variation in the asset allocation patterns—particularly for the alternative asset classes—across the sample and that these allocation differences are alone sufficient to produce substantial variation in measured returns. Therefore, we proxy endowment E's *active* return in year T ($ALPHA_T^E$) as the difference between its actual total return (R_T^E) and its associated policy benchmark return (R_T^B):

$$(6) \qquad ALPHA_T^E = R_T^E - R_T^B = R_T^E - \sum_{i=1}^{10} w_{i,T}^E R_{i,T}^B,$$

where w_i^E is the fund's allocation weight for the i-th asset class and R_i^B is the nominal return to the benchmark index representing the i-th asset class.[36]

36. Strictly speaking, the calculation in equation (6) measures the portion of the endowment's active return that is associated with the endowment portfolio manager's security selection skills. For *ALPHA* to include the contribution of both sources of active management skills (i.e., security selection and market timing), this calculation would need to be amended to include the set of strategic allocation weights from the endowment's investment policy statement (i.e., $[w_i^B]$). Unfortunately, the NACUBO/Commonfund database does not report these $[w_i^B]$ for many funds in any given annual survey or for any fund over the entire sample period. However, as Brown, Garlappi, and Tiu (2010) show, the portion of the endowment's true *ALPHA* generated by the manager's market timing skills is, on average, fairly negligible.

Table 2.9   **Spending rule changes and investment performance**

	EW		VW	
	ALPHA	R^B	ALPHA	R^B
No change	0.90	7.48	1.35	8.21
t-stat	(0.59)	—	(0.80)	—
Change	0.94	7.60	1.22	8.60
t-stat	(0.73)	—	(0.81)	—
Diff	−0.04	−0.12	0.14	−0.39
t-stat	(−0.32)	(−1.67)	(0.27)	(−1.67)

Notes: The table reports investment performance statistics for two non-overlapping subsamples of the NACUBO/Commonfund endowment sample over the period from July 1, 2002, to June 30, 2011, according to whether an institution either (a) did not change its spending rules (No change), or (b) did change its spending rules at least one time (Change). The display shows for each division of the sample average annual returns to the policy benchmark portfolio (R^B) and the benchmark-adjusted performance measure (*ALPHA*, as calculated by the formula in equation [6]). Differences in these return measures for the No change and Change subgroups are listed, along with the associated *t*-statistics. Separate sets of statistics are reported for equal-weighted (EW) and value-weighted (VW) portfolios of the respective endowment subsamples.

As in Brown and Tiu (2010), in the computation of equation (6) we use the following benchmark index definitions for each asset class: US public equity (CRSP value weighted), non-US public equity (MSCI World-Ex US), fixed income (Barclays Global Aggregate), real estate (NCREIF), hedge funds (HFRI Composite), venture capital (Cambridge Associates VC), private equity (Cambridge Associates PE), natural resources (GSCI), cash (thirty-day US T-bill), and other assets (not applicable).

We divide the overall endowment sample into two subgroups according to whether a fund did or did not alter its spending rules at least once during the 2003–2011 period. (Recall from figure 2.4 that each of these groups represent half of the overall sample.) Labeling these subsamples as the "no change" and "change" groups, respectively, we form both equal-weighted and market value-weighted portfolios of the endowments contained in each for the purpose of assessing investment performance. For the portfolios in each subgroup, we calculate the (a) average actual total return, (b) the average policy benchmark return associated with each fund, and (c) the average *ALPHA* statistic, as measured in equation (6). The focus of the analysis is then to see whether the difference in average benchmark-adjusted returns for the no change and change portfolios (i.e., [$AvgALPHA^{NC}$ − $AvgALPHA^C$] is equal to zero).

Table 2.9 lists the average *ALPHA* and policy benchmark (i.e., R^B) returns to the equal-weighted and value-weighted portfolios for both endowment subsamples, along with the difference in the *Avg ALPHA* calculations for each portfolio formation category. There are two primary conclusions to be drawn from these data. First, regardless of the institution's spending policy revision strategy, it appears that endowment fund managers are good investors. The reported average benchmark-adjusted returns are uniformly positive and, at about 100 basis points per annum, relatively large (e.g., 0.90 percent for the equal-weighted no change portfolio, 1.22 percent for the value-weighted change portfolio). While the high level of cross-sectional performance volatility within the subsamples renders these performance measures statistically insignificant (e.g., t-statistics of 0.59 and 0.81 for the two portfolios mentioned above), it nevertheless is the case that the average fund manager in each subgroup produced returns at least as good as his or her policy benchmark.

The second notable finding from the exhibit is that there is virtually no difference in the risk-adjusted investment performance statistics between those endowments that changed their spending policies with some frequency or those that maintained a single set of rules throughout the sample period. The reported values for $[AvgALPHA^{NC} - AvgALPHA^C]$—which is shown as "Diff" in the next-to-last row—are just –0.04 percent (EW) and 0.14 percent (VW), with respective t-statistics of –0.32 and 0.27. Interestingly, there is a marginally significant difference in policy benchmark returns between the two categories (i.e., –0.12 percent [EW] and –0.39 percent [VW]), which suggests that they may face slightly different initial risk budgets. However, once any such risk differentials are accounted for (even implicitly in the benchmark adjustment process), there is no indication that the frequency with which an institution revises its spending policy has any impact—either adverse or positive—on the returns its endowment portfolio produces.

2.7 Concluding Comments

The sponsors and asset managers associated with an endowment fund face an interesting intergenerational investment problem with at least two conflicting goals: they need to produce steady increases in the portfolio's market value to insure the security and long-term viability of the institution and future beneficiaries, but they also need to produce sufficient current income to sustain existing operations. The endowment's spending policy statement is the document in which the governing authority of the institution expresses its intentions as to how this tension should be resolved. Once the permanent spending policy is set, prudent decisions can then be made concerning the investment policies and strategies that should be followed. While there is a growing body of research focusing on endowment investment practices (e.g., Acharya and Dimson 2007; Brown, Garlappi, and Tiu 2010; Dimmock, forthcoming), there is a general dearth of analysis concerning the salient aspects of the spending policy decision, which is curious given its central role in the endowment management process.

In this study, we have addressed this perceived need by providing a comprehensive examination of the spending policy decisions made by over 800 university endowment funds during the period from 2003 to 2011. For each fund, during every year, we categorized the specific spending rule and policy payout rate it used and documented how frequently and why the sponsoring institution was motivated to change those mandates over time. While there is a considerable degree of variation within the sample, we showed that a sizable majority of endowments adopt a payout formula based on a percentage of a moving average of the portfolio's past values. However, the most surprising result in our analysis is that endowments altered their permanent spending policies far more often than what theory would predict given the nature of the investment problem they face; on average, 25 percent of the funds adjusted their policies in any given year, and half of the funds surveyed amended their stated rules at least once during the sample period. We also demonstrated that large endowments that had produced lower past returns and had lower actual payout levels were more likely to alter their long-term spending policies, but that funds with the ability to use special appropriations on a temporary basis were less likely to adjust their permanent rules, a tendency that became more pronounced in the aftermath of the global economic crisis of 2008. Further, we showed that payout rule changes are more likely to precede adjustments to the fund's asset allocation strategy than the other way around and that the tendency for institutions to alter both types of policy is strongly persistent over time. Finally, despite their disparate characteristic profiles, we found no difference in the benchmark-adjusted investment performance for portfolios of endowments that either did or did not alter their spending policies during the sample period.

The intriguing questions that remain to be addressed are whether changing the permanent spending policy too frequently represents suboptimal behavior on the part of the endowment's decision makers and, if so, what the economic cost of such actions might be? Those may well be questions that are not easily answered, particularly in the absence of specific information about the investment problem an institution faces and whether sufficient changes in its underlying circumstances took place to warrant a revision of its previous rules. From our analysis, we do know that any expenses associated with frequent payout policy revisions are not borne at the portfolio investment level. However, a diminution in risk-adjusted return performance is not the only possible cost that a fund might bear as a result of these changes—use of board and staff time, misaligned objectives for the institution, loss of confidence among sponsors and donors, for example—and, while challenging, quantifying these values might tell a very different story. An equally challenging effort would involve trying to define and measure the incremental benefits that accrue to institutions that make frequent changes to their permanent policy; if such revisions to the formal statement of its investment problem do not lead to asset allocation solutions that generate superior returns, what might the benefits of those changes be? Certainly, considering these issues is fruitful ground for future research.

Appendix

A Taxonomy of Spending Policy Rules

The statistical summary presented in table 2.3 classifies the spending rules used by our sample of college and university endowment funds into seven separate categories. Further, several of the seven broad categories can be meaningfully split into two or more subdivisions. These classifications are based on those used in practice as defined and collected by the National Association of College and University Business Officers (NACUBO) and the Commonfund; see Mehrling, Goldstein, and Sedlacek (2005), Sedlacek and Jarvis (2010), and Murray (2011) for more details.

Listed below are spending rule categories and subcategories used in this study, along with descriptions and, where applicable, the formulas used for determining endowment payouts.

1. *Decide on an appropriate rate annually.* Gives the governing authority complete discretion to determine the spending rate it deems appropriate on a yearly basis.

2. *Increase prior year's spending by a percentage.* Adjusts spending upward each year, using either a simple formula or one based on the inflation rate.

(a) *Increase prior year's spending by a prespecified percentage.* Determines the annual payout as the previous year's payout adjusted upward by a pre-specified rate.

(b) *Increase prior year's spending by the inflation rate.* Determines the annual payout as the previous year's payout adjusted for a prespecified inflation rate (I); that is, $(Payout)_t = (Payout)_{t-1} \times (1 + I)$.

(c) *Increase prior year's spending by a collared inflation rate.* Determines the annual payout as the previous year's payout adjusted for the actual inflation rate (e.g., CPI, HEPI) during the investment period, subject to prespecified minimum and maximum rate levels.

3. *Spend a percentage of a moving average of market values.* Determines annual payout as a percentage (P percent, which can be either fixed or variable) of an average of beginning-of-period market values over a prespecified series of past periods; that is, P percent x average $(AUM_0, AUM_{-1}, \ldots, AUM_{-N})$, where AUM_{-t} represents the fund's assets under management t periods in the past.

(a) *Spend a prespecified percentage of moving 12-quarter average of market values.* Uses a quarterly frequency over three years to calculate the moving average of fund AUM.

(b) *Spend a prespecified percentage of moving 3-year average of market values.* Uses an annual frequency over three years to calculate the moving average of fund AUM.

(c) *Spend a prespecified percentage of moving 20-quarter average of market values.* Uses a quarterly frequency over five years to calculate the moving average of fund AUM.

(d) *Spend a prespecified percentage of moving 5-year average of market values.* Uses an annual frequency over five years to calculate the moving average of fund AUM.

(e) *Spend a percentage of moving average of market values, other than 12 quarters/3 years or 20 quarters/5 years.* Uses a percentage-of-moving-average approach based on a different frequency (e.g., semiannual), number of periods (e.g., seven years), or percentage determination method (e.g., variable inflation rate) than those listed above.

4. *Spend a percentage of current yield.* Spend a percentage (Y percent, which can be either fixed or variable) of current income generated during the investment period; that is, Y percent x income.

(a) *Spend a prespecified percentage of current yield:* Spend a predetermined percentage (less than 100 percent) of current income generated during the investment period.

(b) *Spend all current yield.* Spend all current income generated during the investment period (Y percent = 100 percent).

(c) *Spend all dividends or earnings.* Spend all income generated during the investment period specifically through dividend payments or earnings.

(d) *Spend a percentage of current yield determined annually.* Spend a predetermined percentage (possibly 100 percent) of current income generated during the investment period, where the percentage spent is determining on a yearly basis.

5. *Spend a percentage of assets under management (AUM).* Determines annual payout as a percentage P percent of the beginning-of-period fund AUM for the current period; that is, P percent x AUM_0.

(a) *Spend a prespecified percentage of beginning-of-period AUM.* Specify a predetermined level for P percent.

(b) *Does not spend at all.* The endowment does not make distributions in current year; this can be interpreted as setting a prespecified percentage spending rate of zero.

6. *Hybrid rules.* Uses a simple formula to combine two or more payout categories into a single spending rule.

(a) *Yale rule.* A weighted average calculated as X percent of prior year's spending, adjusted for inflation, and $(1 - X)$ percent of a prespecified payout rate multiplied by beginning-of-period endowment AUM (i.e., combination of categories 2 and 5). The value for X was fixed at 80 percent throughout the sample period.

(b) *Stanford rule.* A variation of the preceding rule based on a different smoothing proportion using $X = 60$ percent.

(c) *Other combinations.* Combines two or more payout categories other than those listed above.

7. *Other payout rules*:

(a) *Rules not otherwise classified*. Uses a formula or approach that differs from those listed above (e.g., increases spending by a prespecified fixed percentage unless a political or economic contingency event occurs, in which case the governing authority uses its discretion in setting the payout amount).

(b) *Insufficient information*. Endowment did not provide a complete set of information that allowed for the classification of its spending policy.

References

Acharya, Shanta, and Elroy Dimson. 2007. *Endowment Asset Management*. New York: Oxford University Press.

Black, Fischer. 1976. "The Investment Policy Spectrum: Individuals, Endowment Funds, and Pension Funds." *Financial Analysts Journal* 32:23–31.

Blume, Marshall E. 2010. "Endowment Spending in Volatile Markets: What Should Fiduciaries Do?" *Review of Quantitative Finance and Accounting* 35:163–78.

Bodily, Samuel L., and Chelsea C. White. 1982. "Optimal Consumption and Portfolio Strategies in a Discrete-Time Model with Summary-Dependent Preferences." *Journal of Financial and Quantitative Analysis* 17:1–14.

Brinson, Gary P., L. Randolph Hood, and Gilbert L. Beebower. 1986. "Determinants of Portfolio Performance." *Financial Analysts Journal* 42:39–48.

Brown, Jeffrey R., Stephen G. Dimmock, Jun-Koo Kang, and Scott Weisbenner. 2010. "How University Endowments Respond to Financial Market Shocks: Evidence and Implications." NBER Working Paper no. 15861, Cambridge, MA.

Brown, Jeffrey R., Stephen G. Dimmock, and Scott Weisbenner. 2012. "The Supply and Demand for Charitable Donations to Higher Education." NBER Working Paper no. 18389, Cambridge, MA.

Brown, Keith C., Lorenzo Garlappi, and Cristian Tiu. 2010. "Asset Allocation and Portfolio Performance: Evidence from University Endowment Funds." *Journal of Financial Markets* 13:268–94.

Brown, Keith C., and Cristian Tiu. 2010. "Do Endowment Funds Select the Optimal Mix of Active and Passive Risks?" *Journal of Investment Management* 8:62–86.

Brown, Stephen J., William Goetzmann, Roger G. Ibbotson, and Steven A. Ross. 1992. "Survivorship Bias in Performance Studies." *Review of Financial Studies* 5:553–80.

Cain, J. Harvey. 1960. "Recent Trends in Endowment." *Review of Economics and Statistics* 42:242–44.

Cejnek, Georg, Richard Franz, Otto Randl, and Neal Stoughton. 2012. "A Survey of University Endowment Management Research." Working Paper, Research Institute for Capital Markets, Vienna.

Dimmock, Stephen G. Forthcoming. "Portfolio Choice, Background Risk, and University Endowment Funds." *Review of Economics and Statistics*.

Dybvig, Philip H. 1999. "Using Asset Allocation to Protect Spending." *Financial Analysts Journal* 55:49–62.

Fama, Eugene F., and James D. MacBeth. 1973. "Risk, Return, and Equilibrium: Empirical Tests." *Journal of Political Economy* 81:606–36.

Garland, James P. 2005. "Long-Duration Trusts and Endowments." *Journal of Portfolio Management* 31:44–54.

Gilbert, Thomas, and Christopher Hrdlicka. 2012. "Fairness and Risk-Sharing across Generations: An Application to University and Non-Profit Endowments." Working Paper, University of Washington.

Hansen, Lars Peter, and Ravi Jagannathan. 1997. "Assessing Specification Errors in Stochastic Discount Factor Models." *Journal of Finance* 52:557–90.

Hansmann, Henry. 1990. "Why Do Universities Have Endowments?" *Journal of Legal Studies* 19:3–42.

Hill, Joanne M. 2006. "Alpha as a Net Zero-Sum Game." *Journal of Portfolio Management* 32:24–32.

Ibbotson, Roger G., and Paul D. Kaplan. 2000. "Does Asset Allocation Policy Explain 40, 90, or 100 Percent of Performance?" *Financial Analysts Journal* 56:26–33.

Kochard, Lawrence E., and Cathleen M. Rittereiser. 2008. *Foundation & Endowment Investing*. Hoboken, NJ: John Wiley & Sons.

Lapovsky, Lucie. 2009. *Endowment Spending: External Perceptions and Internal Practices*. Wilton, CT: Commonfund Institute.

Leibowitz, Martin L. 2005. "Alpha Hunters and Beta Grazers." *Financial Analysts Journal* 61:32–39.

Leibowitz, Martin L., Anthony Bova, and P. Brett Hammond. 2010. *The Endowment Model of Investing: Return, Risk, and Diversification*. Hoboken, NJ: John Wiley & Sons.

Lerner, Josh, Antoinette Schoar, and Jialan Wang. 2008. "Secrets of the Academy: The Drivers of University Endowment Success." *Journal of Economic Perspectives* 22:207–22.

Lerner, Josh, A. Schoar, and W. Wongsunwai. 2007. "Smart Institutions, Foolish Choices: The Limited Partner Performance Puzzle." *Journal of Finance* 42: 731–64.

Litvack, James M., Burton G. Malkiel, and Richard E. Quandt. 1974. "A Plan for the Definition of Endowment Income." *American Economic Review* 64: 433–37.

Mehrling, Perry, Paul Goldstein, and Verne Sedlacek. 2005. "Endowment Spending: Goals, Rates, and Rules." In *Forum for the Future of Higher Education*. Washington, DC: Educause.

Merton, Robert C. 1971. "Optimum Consumption and Portfolio Rules in a Continuous-Time Model." *Journal of Economic Theory* 3:373–413.

———. 1993. "Optimal Investment Strategies for University Endowment Funds." In *Studies of Supply and Demand in Higher Education*, edited by Charles T. Clotfelter and Michael Rothschild. Chicago: University of Chicago Press.

———. 2003. "Thoughts on the Future: Theory and Practice in Investment Management." *Financial Analysts Journal* 59:17–23.

Murray, Steve. 2011. "Non-Profit Spending rules." Working Paper, Russell Investments. http://www.russell.com/us/institutional-investors/research/non-profit-spending-rules.page.

Nettleton, Minot B. 1987. "The Impact of Spending Rules on Endowments." In *The Challenges of Investing for Endowment Funds*, edited by Cathryn E. Kittell. Institute of Chartered Financial Analysts and Dow Jones-Irwin.

Samuelson, Paul A. 1969. "Lifetime Portfolio Selection by Dynamic Stochastic Programming." *Review of Economics and Statistics* 51:239–46.

Sedlacek, Verne O., and William F. Jarvis. 2010. *Endowment Spending: Building a Stronger Policy Framework*. Wilton, CT: Commonfund Institute.

Swensen, David F. 2009. *Pioneering Portfolio Management: An Unconventional Approach to Institutional Investment*, 2nd ed. New York: Free Press.

Thaler, Richard H., and J. Peter Williamson. 1994. "College and University Endowment Funds." *Journal of Portfolio Management* 21:27–37.
Tobin, James. 1974. "What Is Permanent Endowment Income?" *American Economic Review* 64:427–32.
Walda, John D., and John S. Griswold. 2011. *Nacubo-Commonfund Study of Endowments*. Washington, DC: National Association of College and University Business Officers.
Woglom, Geoffrey. 2003. "Endowment Spending Rates, Intergenerational Equity and the Sources of Capital Gains." *Economics of Education Review* 22:591–601.

3

Competition among University Endowments

William N. Goetzmann and Sharon Oster

3.1 Introduction

Why did so many American universities find themselves with such troubling liquidity issues during the Great Recession of 2008 and 2009 when their endowments suffered large declines? With endowments in the billions of dollars, and what had long been touted as conservative spending policies, many observers outside the academy were surprised by how difficult the financial crisis was for universities like Harvard, Yale, and Stanford. Within the academy, many have talked about the role played by the change in asset allocation policies that occurred in the last several decades, particularly in the increased use of alternative investments. For example, Lerner, Schoar, and Wang (2007) show that this change in asset allocation increased the skewness in endowment size, paradoxically leading the now-much-richer universities to rely more heavily on endowment returns to fund operations. At the same time, the increased reliance on relatively illiquid, alternative investments by many universities exacerbated difficulties in adjusting to the market downturn, at least in the short run.

Our chapter focuses on the process by which universities decide to change their asset allocation policies. We are particularly interested in the deci-

William N. Goetzmann is the Edwin J. Beinecke Professor of Finance and Management Studies and the director of the International Center for Finance at the Yale School of Management and a research associate of the National Bureau of Economic Research. Sharon Oster is the Frederic D. Wolfe Professor of Management and Entrepreneurship at the Yale School of Management.

We thank John Griswold, Minhua Wan, and Larry Itavares for their help and advice. We thank Commonfund and NACUBO for providing data for research. We thank the Yale, Harvard, and Princeton endowment offices for providing data. All errors are the responsibility of the authors. For acknowledgments, sources of research support, and disclosure of the authors' material financial relationships, if any, please see http://www.nber.org/chapters/c12858.ack.

sions leading to the adoption of alternative investments. We will argue and provide some evidence in favor of the proposition that competition in the product market of universities, particularly in the competition for quality students, influenced patterns of diffusion of innovation in asset allocation. We argue that the dynamic patterns that we see in asset allocations in university endowments are consistent with an arms race model of universities, in which the competitive pressures in the "real" part of the university business (research and teaching) drive an imitative diffusion of endowment policies across schools in similar submarkets.

Using data on prospective applicant comparison behavior to identify clusters of competitive universities, we find evidence that schools competing in the same markets for students follow similar asset allocation policies over time, even when we hold endowment size and other school characteristics constant. We further find that when a school's endowment return lags relative to its immediate rival, it systematically changes its asset allocation. Thus, in a very real sense, the competitive environment of US education may have contributed to their exposure to illiquid asset classes such as private equity during the period leading up to the Great Recession and left them with a sudden shortage of cash when the recession hit.

Section 3.2 of this chapter provides some historical background on asset allocation by universities in the United States, and sketches our theory of the link between product market competition and asset allocation choices. Section 3.3 describes the data we use to provide evidence for our theory, section 3.4 describes our results, and section 3.5 discusses the implications.

3.2 Some History and a Theory

University endowments have long been at the forefront of innovative investment. For example, Goetzmann, Griswold, and Tseng (2010) document a strategic shift in university endowments toward equities in the 1920s and 1930s, despite the financial crisis at the time. This shift proved beneficial in the long run, but caused observers to question its wisdom in the short run.

Prior to the 1980s virtually all universities and colleges restricted themselves to domestic equities, bonds, and cash. Even at Harvard and Yale, the two innovators in asset allocation policy, the share of endowment devoted to these traditional classes was dominant in 1985. Our first three figures capture the central and dramatic changes in the portfolios of the Harvard, Yale, and Princeton endowments over the last twenty-five years.[1] Figure 3.1 shows the decrease in allocation to US publicly traded equities by the three endowments over the period from 1985 to 2011. The Yale and Princeton stock holdings decreased from over 60 percent to less than 10 percent in the

1. We thank the endowment offices of Harvard, Yale, and Princeton for the data for these figures.

time period. Harvard's stock holdings dropped from 40 percent to about 10 percent at the end of the period. Yale and Princeton's shift from public equities appears to be partially explained by substitution into private equity. Figure 3.2 shows a dramatic rise in Yale and Princeton's private equity allocation from below 5 percent to over 30 percent. The speed with which interest in the new asset classes grew and the movement away from both domestic equities, and more dramatically bonds, is striking. We note in particular that at the time of earlier substantial recessions in 1980–1981 and then later in the early 1990s, the asset allocations of the major research universities were much less vulnerable, with much more reliance on fixed income and much less private equity. Figure 3.3 shows a sequential adoption of new investment "technology" over the 1990s. From 1990 to 1998, first Yale then Princeton then Harvard began to invest in hedge funds—that is, marketable alternatives. These investments reached a peak in the early twenty-first century and have since tapered to about a 20 percent allocation. While some of the recent shifts from marketable alternatives and publicly traded equities may have been driven by liquidity needs around the financial crisis (and conversely the difficulty in liquidating private equity positions at that time), the broad trends are clear. In 1985, all three institutions were heavily invested in domestic equity and fixed income. Harvard had 69 percent of its endowment invested in domestic equities and bonds, while Princeton had 85 percent and Yale 78 percent. None of the three institutions had any investment in absolute returns and all were relatively light on private equity, with Harvard leading at 7 percent, Yale at 3 percent, and Princeton at 2 percent. These strategies virtually reversed themselves over the twenty-five-year period.

The similarities in the diffusion of the new asset allocation strategies of Harvard, Yale, and Princeton are even more striking when mapped against the strategies of the rest of the universe of colleges. In the NACUBO[2] database, as late as 2000 the average university endowment was still invested more than 50 percent in domestic equities, with under 2 percent in private equity and hedge funds (Brown, Garlappi, and Tiu 2010). Figure 3.4 compares the time trend of domestic equity investments for Harvard, Yale, and Princeton with the general NACUBO population of schools from 1989 to 2005.

The similarities in the rate of adoption of the new financial models by Harvard, Yale, and Princeton could, of course, be attributed to a number of factors. In all industries, there are early and late adopters of innovations, and we know that early adopters differ systematically from later adopters. On the firm level, early adopters tend to be those firms with the most to gain from an innovation and firms with the requisite complementary assets.

2. NACUBO, the National Association of College and University Business Officers, has maintained an annual survey of its members for a number of years; this has been managed by the Commonfund since 2009 and combined with the Commonfund's own survey of college and university endowment offices. The Commonfund is a nonprofit investment management firm serving primarily endowments and foundations.

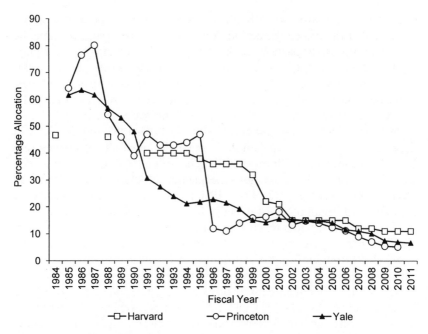

Fig. 3.1 Allocation to US publicly listed equities by Yale, Harvard, and Princeton endowments, 1990–2011

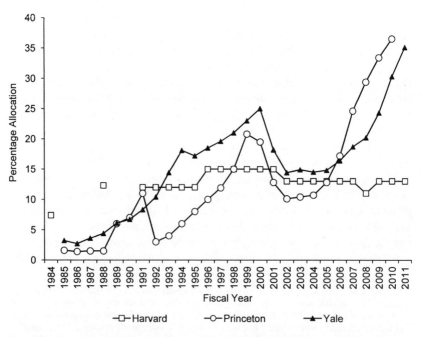

Fig. 3.2 Allocation to private equity by Yale, Harvard, and Princeton endowments, 1990–2011

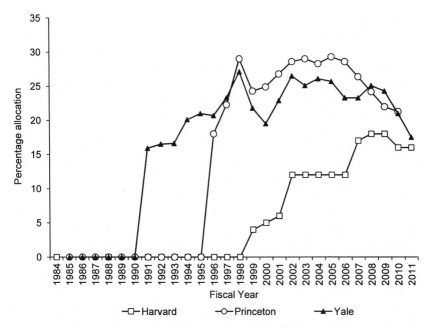

Fig. 3.3 Allocation to marketable alternatives by Yale, Harvard, and Princeton endowments, 1990–2011

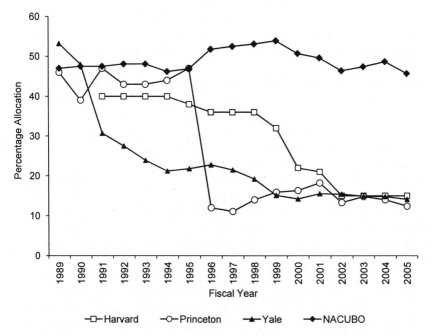

Fig. 3.4 Allocation to US publicly listed equities by Yale, Harvard, Princeton, and NACUBO, 1989–2005

Early adopters also tend to cluster geographically or belong to the same trade organizations, which facilitates transmission of new ideas (Griliches 1957; Oster 1982). For example, Harvard, Yale, and Princeton were all large endowments, all located in the East, and all part of the Ivy League. Surely, these commonalities facilitated the diffusion of innovation across the three.

But there is another feature of Harvard, Yale, and Princeton that we believe plays a fundamental role in their common adoption of endowment strategies: the strong competition among the three in their product market. References to H-Y-P as the goal of many elite high school scholars are common; close rankings of the three are also evidenced in more sophisticated revealed-preference rankings (Avery et al. 2004). We argue that this product line competition also affects investment decisions.

To understand why product market competition might influence the diffusion of investment strategies, we need to think about the role of endowments for universities more broadly. The classic argument in favor of an endowment beyond that required to accommodate cash flow swings is to create intergenerational equity across students, by creating a perpetual flow of real income to support university activities (e.g., Litvak, Malkiel, and Quant 1974; Tobin 1974). Sometimes this goal is referred to as "preserving purchasing power" from a gift (Swensen 2000, 35).

Some have interpreted this mandate as requiring that spending rules and investment returns be managed to maintain the real value of the endowment spending using, for example, the Higher Education Price Index (HEPI) to measure changes in the costs of inputs used by universities.

We would argue that the objective of intergenerational equity is more complicated than simply maintaining a level real value of resources. In producing a superb education, two key ingredients are faculty and students. Student quality is especially important: better students attract better faculty, peer effects are important in improving educational outcomes, and quality of student on the incoming side is clearly highly correlated with student outcomes. (For evidence on the importance of peer effects see Epple, Newlon, and Romano [2002] and Burke and Sass [2008]). It is for this reason that various measures of student quality and student admissions choices play such a large role in the many college rating systems. *U.S. News & World Report*, for example, weights SAT scores 15 percent in devising their college ranking and adds another 25 percent weight for another, more subjective measure of student quality. Notice, however, that while changes in competition for faculty will arguably show up (at least on average) in the Higher Education Price Index, competition for students will typically not be reflected in the price index. Schools compete for students via increasing resources available to them such as scholarships, housing, and athletic facilities (Hoxby [2009] describes this process). They thus bid up the number of inputs needed to produce good students rather than the price of those inputs. Perhaps more importantly, the competition for students occurs in very narrow markets.

Colleges ranked among the top ten schools rarely compete for students with schools ranked 100 rungs below them. As we describe later in this chapter, there is reason to think that the narrow competition for students within quality bands of schools may have increased over time. With local competition for a key input like students, preserving intergenerational equity requires that universities keep up with their proximate rivals and not just maintain the real value of their assets, as they might do in a case in which their inputs were widely traded. If Yale wants to produce as good an education in 2020 as it did in 2010 it needs to preserve its competitive position vis-à-vis the other narrow set of colleges with which it competes for students. If the real value of Harvard's endowment doubles in the next ten years, and Yale's remains flat, Yale will no longer be able to compete for the same quality of students that it attracted earlier.

A goal of producing the same level of service over time, in a market in which groups of universities compete for scarce resources, creates a linkage across those universities in both asset allocation decisions and spending rules. We will observe a form of arms race in which universities focus on ensuring adequate resources for tomorrow's battlefield. There are, as a result, strong competitive pressures that may encourage adoption of similar policies within competitive submarkets. This is the hypothesis we will explore in this chapter.

3.2.1 Related Research: Keeping Up with the Joneses

Economic research has not addressed competitive endowment behavior to any large extent, but it has intensely examined competitive household investment behavior. Much of this work has focused on the effects of the utility for relative wealth on asset price dynamics in an equilibrium setting (e.g., Abel 1990; Gali 1994; Chan and Kogan 2002). Generally called "keeping up with the Joneses" (KUJ) or "catching up with the Joneses," this research has been used to explain the equity risk premium, as well as labor and consumption dynamics. Gali (1994), for example, shows that when consumption demand is positively related to average consumption, the equity premium falls. Bakshi and Chen (1996) examine a model in which relative wealth determines status and show it leads to excess market volatility. Ravina (2005) empirically identifies KUJ behavior in consumption through credit cards. These asset-pricing results may be tangentially relevant to the endowment universe in asset markets with limited capacity, but this question is not the focus of the current chapter.

Most relevant for our study, however, are papers by DeMarzo, Kaniel, and Kremer (2005, 2008). They analyze how investors respond to local economic factors. In a KUJ setting, when a subset of investors (the Joneses) within a community takes a large position in a particular security for hedging reasons—or even irrational reasons—this can induce herding by others concerned with keeping up with them. This setting leads to underdiversification, increased investment in risky assets, and may lead to asset market bubbles. They argue that a diversified portfolio becomes a community asset—inducing positive externalities for competitors. In this case, the innovators in the endowment universe characterized by KUJ preferences can have positive or negative externalities. If they become more diversified—or choose a strategy that is superior in meeting the long-term goals of a university, then this has a positive spillover to their competitors. On the other hand, if the innovator picks a strategy that is optimal for himself, but is not replicable or not optimal for imitators, this can have negative external consequences. For example, if the leader invests in an asset class—such as venture capital—with limited capacity, this may generate increased demand for this specific asset and drive up the price, or lead imitators to invest in lesser-quality venture funds.

Also related to our work is the investment funds tournament literature (e.g., Chevalier and Ellison 1997; Sirri and Tufano 1998; Brown, Goetzmann, and Park 2001; Brown, Harlow, and Starks 1996). These papers study the behavior of investment managers in a competitive setting in which capital flows reward positive performance. Chevalier and Ellison (1997) and Sirri and Tufano (1998) document asymmetric rewards to performance, which implies option-like compensation that can induce risk taking to stretch for high returns. Brown, Harlow, and Starks (1996) and Brown, Goetzmann, and Park (2001) focus on risk taking by mutual fund managers and hedge fund managers. The former shows increased risk taking by funds that lag their peers after the first half of the year. The latter shows that positive performance relative to peers in the hedge fund industry is associated with reduced risk taking in subsequent periods, consistent with preserving relative performance.

University endowments differ considerably from households and managed funds, but the studies cited above offer useful frames for understanding the effects of competition in the endowment market. Endowments are a bit like mutual funds and hedge funds because their managers operate within a labor market in which track record (and survival) are important determinants of employment and compensation. Endowments are also a bit like households in that they are confronted with a savings and investment problem conditional on a set of mission objectives. These mission objectives may include a dimension of relative consumption—or even relative wealth.

3.2.2 Strategic Competition among Universities

There is considerable research on the competition among universities. Epple, Romano, and Sieg (2003, 2006), for example, find that competition among universities generates a rigorous quality hierarchy in which a few select schools have market power. These researchers abstract away from the role of the university endowment as either a metric for market power or a determinant of it. Other research examines trends in student preferences for universities consistent with increasing mobility. Hoxby (2009) finds "the elasticity of a student's preference for a college with respect to its proximity to that student's home has fallen substantially over time and there has been a corresponding increase in the elasticity of each student's preference for a college with respect to its resources and peers" (96). This, in turn, may have intensified the competition among "national" universities. In the mid-1950s, 20 percent of the Yale undergraduate population came from Connecticut.[3] By 2011, much of that specialization had gone by the wayside: in 2011, only 6 percent of the Yale student body was from Connecticut, fewer than those who came from outside US borders. At the elite colleges, the diminishing role of family connections also serves to increase competition across schools. In the mid-1950s, 25 percent of the enrollees at Yale were the sons of Yale fathers.[4] By 2011, this number had fallen to 10 percent (and, of course, included daughters of Yale mothers and fathers). This increased competition naturally increased the importance of maintaining financial parity to enable selective colleges to maintain their ability to attract high-quality students in what has become an international marketplace.

Scholars have also recognized the effects of competition in the market for professors. In the humanities, Shumway (1997) has derided the "star" system as a threat to merit-based evaluation of research in literary studies. Volkwein and Sweitzer (2006) report that full-time professor salaries are positively correlated to prestige rankings of universities and colleges. Bastedo and Bowman (2011) find that published rankings of colleges influence future revenues. The clear implication is that a larger endowment makes possible higher faculty salaries, enhanced prestige, and in turn this may generate future economic benefits as well.

If there is an arms race in university endowment management, born of increased competition for key inputs, we should expect to see a higher degree of similarity of investment strategies for schools that most directly compete. The data we looked at for Harvard, Yale, and Princeton is suggestive, but we turn now to describe the broader data we will use to explore this hypothesis.

3.3 The Data

We are interested in exploring the similarities in asset allocation patterns among colleges that compete most directly with one another in the product market, here defined as the market for students. We thus need data on asset allocations by schools and by narrow categories as well as data on the levels of competition among schools.

3.3.1 Asset Allocation

In describing the endowment assets and investment policies of universities and colleges we relied on the annual NACUBO-Commonfund Study

---

3. See the Yale Office of Institutional Research (OIR) website at http://oir.yale.edu/.
4. Ibid.

of Endowments. The survey covers 1,033 funds associated with 1,261 universities or colleges for the July to June fiscal years 2006–2011. It collects comparative data on endowment investment policies and practices across the participating universe of US colleges and university endowments. The data are self-reported by university endowment offices and not always complete for each year, although the annual rate of compliance is very high. As necessary, we adjust our empirical analysis for competing universities (for example, some state institutions) that have a common endowment. With these and other data-driven exclusions, 947 universities remain in our sample.

Much of our analysis focuses on the types of assets held by university funds. The NACUBO-Commonfund sample classifies assets into domestic equities, fixed income, international equities, alternative strategies, and cash/other. Each category is broken down further. For our analysis, we are especially interested in the subgroups within the alternative asset category: private equity, real estate, venture capital, energy and natural resources, marketable alternatives (i.e., hedge funds), and distressed debt. As we have already seen in the data on Harvard, Yale, and Princeton, the major change in endowments since 1985 was the movement into alternatives. These alternative assets have three features of interest. First, most of these alternative asset categories are actively managed so that a necessary component of the value proposition of the investment involves access to skillful managers. When top managers have limited capacity, they may not be able to accommodate both innovators and followers. Second, alternative assets are generally less liquid than other asset categories. Indeed, one of David Swensen's key insights is that part of the returns to alternative assets comes from the "liquidity premium," that is, compensation for holding illiquid, nonmarketable assets. The common notion, at least until 2008, was that endowments were patient investors who could "harvest" the liquidity premium that shorter-term investors must avoid. Finally, alternative assets were thought to be attractive because they were uncorrelated with the stock and bond markets, and thus played a role in reducing portfolio volatility.

The NACUBO data provides, for each responding college, both the percent investments in each asset class and the return achieved for that class, if available. These data allow us to benchmark the endowments' self-reported performance by asset class. In addition, for some years, funds are asked whether their marketable alternative investments underperformed, met expectations, or exceeded expectations.

We are particularly interested in tracing the diffusion of allocation strategies across schools that compete. Part of this analysis will involve looking at how closely allocations match at various points in time. But we also have more direct data on planned changes by endowment managers that we will exploit in our empirical work. A key survey question we rely on for our analysis is whether the fund is considering changing "its approach to con-

	Domestic Equities	Fixed Income	International Equities	Alternatives
2006	45.534	19.9669	13.5706	17.703
2007	42.3251	17.7306	15.8226	18.941
2008	37.9991	18.8349	15.1108	23.848
2009	33.5849	21.6286	14.269	23.024
2010	32.3573	21.7605	14.7836	24.976
2011	32.4115	18.975	16.463	26.368

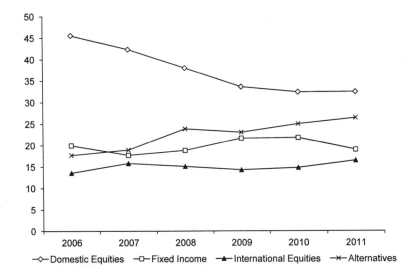

Fig. 3.5 Change in asset allocation over time

structing the asset allocation" of the portfolio and, if so, the nature of the contemplated change. Thus we are potentially able to connect the decisions to change investment strategy to the behavior of competitive rivals.

The key data set we use from the survey is a time-series, cross-section panel of individual endowment asset allocations. Figure 3.5 shows the aggregate allocation of university assets in the sample to major asset classes: domestic equities, fixed income, international equities, and alternatives. The shift from domestic equities to alternative assets is clearly evident, though as we see, it happened later in the general population than it did in the HYP sample. This shift away from domestic equities by colleges is well documented. Lerner, Schoar, and Wang (2007), using data beginning in 1992, find a dramatic doubling of the share of the average endowment invested in alternatives from 9 percent in 1993 to 18 percent in 2005.

	large funds	medium funds	small funds
2006	30.347	16.532	6.361
2007	31.296	17.206	5.644
2008	37.877	21.024	7.094
2009	40.98	22.406	10.35
2010	43.235	23.587	10.559
2011	43.186	23.655	10.328

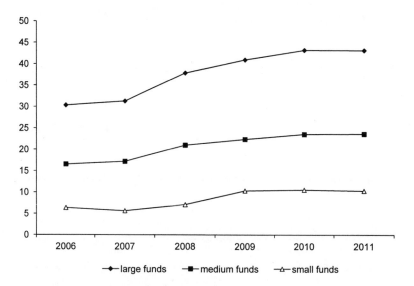

Fig. 3.6 Change in alternatives over time

As we suggested earlier, there are a number of features of colleges that are correlated with asset allocations. Size of endowment clearly affects asset allocations; the substitution toward alternative investments is even more dramatic for larger endowments, which moves from 30 percent allocation in 2006 to 43 percent in 2011. Clearly, larger funds have capabilities different from smaller ones. Differences in the investment strategies of the small and large funds are evident in figure 3.6. There is also some regional variation in portfolios. Figure 3.7 separates endowments by the first-digit zip code regions and shows the greater exposure of the New England and Mid-Atlantic areas to alternative assets. The regional pattern we see is consistent with other regional diffusion models, given the fact that the move to alternatives began, as we saw earlier, at Harvard, Yale, and Princeton, all located in the mid-Atlantic and New England areas.

First Zip	avg_MktAlt (%)	avg_VC (%)	avg_PE (%)	avg_TotalAlt (%)
0 New England	14.437	1.335	6.872	27.747
1 NY-PA	12.631	1.176	5.333	23.610
2 Mid-Atlantic	15.365	1.680	5.561	30.267
3 South East	9.808	0.694	4.451	19.706
4 Michigan - KY	10.380	1.301	5.504	21.143
5 MT to WI	8.396	0.813	4.961	17.853
6 Mid West	7.667	1.008	5.431	18.084
7 TX & Oil	10.537	0.781	5.797	22.754
8 Rockies	10.501	0.440	4.948	20.276
9 West Coast	9.657	1.404	5.571	22.196

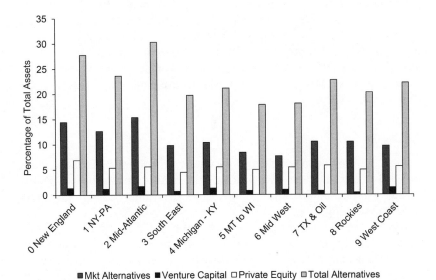

■ Mkt Alternatives ■ Venture Capital □ Private Equity ▨ Total Alternatives

Fig. 3.7 Regional distribution of the use of alternative assets (percentage of total assets)

3.3.2 Data on School Competition

Universities compete in many markets from the labor market to the market for government grants. For our work, a key market is the market for students. We are interested in finding a measure of the degree of head-to-head competition among colleges for students.

The search process for information about colleges for students and their families has, like much else, transitioned to the web. There are a few major websites that aggregate useful information about universities and also provide software tools for building portfolios of schools for potential consideration. For our measure of competition, we rely on one of these sites: Cappex.com.

Cappex claims to have nearly three million student users and it covers roughly 3,000 colleges and aggregates basic information about the school and the application process. On the Cappex web page for each college, there is a section entitled "students also considered," which includes the names of ten other schools visited by other users who visited that particular college page. These other schools appear to be ranked in order of frequency of visit from one school to the next. In other words, students who considered school X also considered these ten other schools. In effect, we are able to observe comparison shopping by college students browsing schools.[5]

Table 3.1 provides a sampling of the pairings we found in this exercise along with data on the relative ranking of the colleges using the revealed preference rankings found by Avery et al. (2004). In the table we have provided information on the top ten browsing pairs for five schools in the sample; in the empirical work we aggregate these ten competitors as our measure of school competition. The pairings seem broadly sensible. Thus for Yale, we see Harvard and Princeton appear, while for the San Francisco Conservatory of Music we find the Manhattan School of Music and the New England Conservatory of Music.

3.4 Results

Table 3.2 provides some descriptive data on the sample of college funds we used in our analysis. Two-thirds of the institutions in the sample are private schools and the mean endowment size is almost $500 million with a substantial range.

Table 3.3 reports the results of regressions explaining allocation to alternative assets. In panel A, the dependent variable is the percent of a university's endowment invested in alternatives at the end of the fiscal year. In column (1) we report results from a pooled sample, using year dummies. In the remaining columns, we break the data out year by year, allowing coefficients to vary over the years. The results are qualitatively similar, so we will focus on the pooled regression. Panel B presents the same analysis for the percent of endowment invested in marketable alternatives (i.e., hedge funds).[6]

Not surprisingly, the results indicate that larger schools, both in terms of number of students and size of the endowment, have, on average, higher shares of their endowments in alternatives. For marketable alternatives,

---

5. Our data was downloaded in mid-December 2011.
6. For comparison, we also use the single-closest school on the list as the nearest competitor. The results are slightly stronger in that specification.

Table 3.1 A sample of pairings from Cappex

	Yale University (2) *	University of Michigan-Ann Arbor (42) *	Arizona State University (80) *	San Francisco Conservatory of Music	Boston Architectural College
Competitor 1	Harvard University	Michigan State University	University of Arizona	Manhattan School of Music	Southern California Institute of Architecture
Competitor 2	Princeton University	Northwestern University	Northern Arizona University	The New England Conservatory of Music	Wentworth Institute of Technology
Competitor 3	Stanford University	University of Chicago	San Diego State University	The Curtis Institute of Music	Pratt Institute
Competitor 4	Brown University	University of Illinois at Urbana-Champaign	University of Southern California	Berklee College of Music	Rhode Island School of Design
Competitor 5	Columbia University	University of Pennsylvania	University of California-Los Angeles	Cleveland Institute of Music	Syracuse University
Competitor 6	Cornell University	Cornell University	University of Oregon	Longy School of Music	Lawrence Technological University
Competitor 7	Duke University	New York University	Stanford University	The Boston Conservatory	Massachusetts College of Art and Design
Competitor 8	University of Pennsylvania	Stanford University	University of Colorado-Boulder	The Juilliard School	California College of the Arts-CCA
Competitor 9	Dartmouth College	Purdue University	University of Nevada-Las Vegas	VanderCook College of Music	Northeastern University
Competitor 10	New York University	Duke University	University of California-Berkeley	Puerto Rico Conservatory of Music	Drexel University

* Ranking source: Avery et al. (2004).

Table 3.2   **Summary statistics of college funds**

	2006–2011	2006	2007	2008	2009	2010	2011
Number of observations	4070	557	549	461	838	845	820
Percentage of private schools	64.50	64.99	66.30	65.29	63.60	63.79	64.15
College endowments (mean, million)	463.60	480.38	581.72	526.56	364.44	408.13	496.22
Number of students (mean)	10254	—	—	—	9,996.99	10,058.99	10,732.18
Percentage in Northeast area	40.02	38.60	39.53	40.78	39.62	40.36	40.98
Richness	0.095	0.106	0.130	0.127	0.073	0.078	0.092

Notes: Richness = college endowments/number of students, as "number of students" is not available in 2006–2009 and it does not vary much over time. The average number of students of each college is used to calculate richness. The Northeast area includes New England, New York, Pennsylvania, and the mid-Atlantic.

every one hundred million dollar increase in endowment size increases the percent of assets invested in marketable alternatives by 2.2 percent. A comparable increase in asset size increases the percent in all alternatives by 12 percent. Every thousand students, another measure of school size, increases the share in marketable alternatives by 1.3 percent and all alternatives by 1.9 percent. Smaller endowments, those below $25 million, have a natural disadvantage in investing in marketable alternative funds since they may not meet the definition of a qualified institutional investor. In addition, hedge funds face a limit on the number of investors they can serve and this rationing process favors large investors. Larger schools have both the financial resources and the staff to consider alternative investments, although the scale of their investment offices may reflect the complexities of investing in alternative assets. Schools located in the New England or mid-Atlantic regions have, on average 3.5 percent more of their endowments invested in marketable alternatives, all else equal, and 3.8 percent in all alternatives. The regression also suggests that richer schools, measured by endowment per student, invest more in alternative assets, perhaps reflecting a higher taste for risk or a belief in their ability to carry illiquid assets.

The key variable in the regression from our point of view is the nearest competitor. Again, this variable measures the percent of alternative investments or marketable alternatives held by a school's ten nearest competitors. As we see, the variable is positive and highly significant both in explaining marketable alternatives and all alternative investments. In the pooled sample in column (1), a 1 percent increase in a rival's allocation to marketable alternatives increases own allocation to this asset class by .43 percent and all alternatives by .64 percent. Coefficients are roughly equivalent and all are significant across the six years in our sample.

We take these results to be consistent with our model of strategic asset allocation. Within school pairings, constructed to reflect competition among schools in the product market, we observe—holding constant size, richness, and location—very similar patterns of investments in alternatives.

In 2009, the NACUBO-Commonfund survey began asking endowment managers whether they were considering a change in their asset allocations and, if so, what change was being contemplated. Almost 25 percent of the sample reported in any given year were considering an allocation change. This in itself is interesting and is consistent with the transition of the endowment population observed over our longer period of study. In table 3.4, we estimate a log-linear regression, asking whether a manager's interest in changing plans is related to an endowment's own lagged performance and that of its nearest competitors. The results suggest that high-lagged own returns decrease the likelihood of wanted to change asset allocations, while good performance by an index of nearest competitors are associated with an increased likelihood of change.

Table 3.3   Factors associated with allocation to alternative assets

Variable	Pooled sample	2006	2007	2008	2009	2010	2011
	A. Dependent variable: Percent of endowment invested in alternatives						
Intercept	0.167	3.097	2.359	4.546	0.241	-1.203	-3.391
	(0.17)	(1.85)	(1.30)	(2.00)	(0.15)	(-0.66)	(-1.82)
Nearest competitors_Alternatives	0.645	0.540	0.578	0.482	0.653	0.670	0.748
	(27.41)	(8.60)	(8.97)	(7.29)	(12.81)	(12.43)	(14.02)
Total assets (hundred million)	0.120	0.083	0.066	0.224	0.191	0.151	0.110
	(7.01)	(2.35)	(2.18)	(3.93)	(3.89)	(3.17)	(2.83)
Avg_students (thousand)	0.194	0.147	0.164	0.218	0.135	0.220	0.246
	(6.00)	(1.86)	(1.99)	(2.26)	(1.89)	(2.95)	(3.38)
School richness	5.188	5.579	4.659	4.311	5.919	6.626	5.253
	(6.93)	(3.40)	(3.37)	(2.58)	(2.68)	(2.94)	(2.76)
Region dummy	3.835	4.145	4.068	5.398	2.794	4.073	3.221
	(6.71)	(2.91)	(2.81)	(3.17)	(2.20)	(3.09)	(2.55)
Year dummy	Yes						—
Number of obs.	3,452	410	413	373	754	764	738
R-square	0.3269	0.3054	0.3192	0.3193	0.3220	0.3128	0.3530

B. Dependent variable: Percent of endowment invested in marketable alternatives

Intercept	2.511	2.922	1.555	3.122	0.997	2.751	3.690
	(3.93)	(2.70)	(1.21)	(2.26)	(0.92)	(2.29)	(2.80)
Nearest competitors_Mkt alternatives	0.433	0.344	0.485	0.421	0.557	0.402	0.351
	(13.21)	(4.42)	(5.39)	(4.88)	(7.69)	(5.34)	(4.20)
Total assets (hundred million)	0.022	0.020	-0.018	0.062	0.018	0.048	0.034
	(1.90)	(0.77)	(-0.82)	(1.61)	(0.55)	(1.57)	(1.30)
Avg_students (thousand)	0.133	0.086	0.164	0.104	0.117	0.148	0.156
	(5.96)	(1.46)	(2.71)	(1.56)	(2.41)	(2.96)	(3.10)
School richness	3.616	3.891	3.663	2.842	4.094	3.905	3.255
	(7.11)	(3.23)	(3.66)	(2.49)	(2.78)	(2.63)	(2.53)
Region dummy	3.464	3.840	4.142	4.566	2.432	3.615	3.183
	(8.63)	(3.51)	(3.86)	(3.76)	(2.76)	(4.09)	(3.59)
Year dummy	Yes	—	—	—	—	—	—
Number of obs.	3,452	410	413	373	754	764	738
R-square	0.1371	0.1601	0.1811	0.1885	0.1445	0.1179	0.0897

Notes: If fund in Northeast (New England, New York, Pennsylvania, or mid-Atlantic), then region = 1; otherwise, region = 0. The T-statistics are in parentheses.

Table 3.4 Is an expressed consideration to change allocation policy related to endowment performance and the performance of nearest competitors?

	One-year return		Three-year return		
Intercept	-1.200***	-1.157***	-1.108***	-1.152***	-1.602***
	(0.054)	(0.064)	(0.056)	(0.061)	(0.100)
Own return ($t-1$)	-0.016	—	0.032***	-0.032*	—
	(0.004)		(0.008)	(0.017)	
Nearest competitors: Return ($t-1$)	0.0006	—	—	0.085***	—
	(0.013)			(0.019)	
Own return ($t-2$)	—	-0.010	—	—	-0.027
		(0.015)			(0.023)
Nearest competitors: Return ($t-2$)	—	0.040**	—	—	0.087***
		(0.015)			(0.024)
Number of obs.	2,032	1,454	1,754	1,548	1,208
Likelihood ratio	19.09	61.19	14.80	36.98	45.08

Notes: $C_t = \alpha + \beta_1 r_{t-1}^o + \beta_2 r_{t-1}^{nc} + \beta_3 r_{t-2}^o + \beta_4 r_{t-2}^{nc} + e_t$, where c takes on the value 1 if a desire to change is expressed in a given year. $C_t = 1$ if fund considers to change asset allocation; otherwise, (no and uncertain) $C_t = 0$. Standard errors are in parentheses.

***Significant at the 1 percent level.

**Significant at the 5 percent level.

*Significant at the 10 percent level.

Table 3.5   **Conditional policy change**

Frequency percent	Yes	No	Uncertain	Growth	Risk
	A. Three-year return				
Loser	210	475	75	0.673	0.817
	27.63	62.50	9.87		
Winner	213	592	66	0.623	0.722
	24.45	67.97	7.58		
Total	423	1067	141	*Pr* = 0.3701	*Pr* = 0.0415
	25.94	65.42	8.65		
	B. Five-year return				
Loser	214	522	74	0.658	0.812
	26.42	64.44	9.14		
Winner	169	439	57	0.632	0.713
	25.19	65.97	8.85		
Total	383	961	131	*Pr* = 0.6583	*Pr* = 0.0453
	25.97	65.15	8.88		

Notes: For panel A, test of the independence of decision to consider an asset allocation change: yes/no: $Pr > t = 0.0734$; test of the difference in proportion for conditional response to considering a change toward growth-oriented assets: growth: $Pr > t = 0.3701$; test of the difference in proportion for conditional response to considering a change toward risk/hedge-oriented assets risk: $Pr > t = 0.0415$. For panel B, test of the independence of decision to consider an asset allocation change: yes/no: $Pr > t = 0.6052$; test of the difference in proportion for conditional response to considering a change toward growth-oriented assets: growth: $Pr > t = 0.6583$; test of the difference in proportion for conditional response to considering a change toward risk/hedge-oriented assets risk: $Pr > t = 0.0453$.

Table 3.5 further explores the type of change contemplated by endowments. Ideally, we are interested in whether superior performance by a rival drives an endowment more into alternatives. The survey data provides some interesting evidence in this regard. Table 3.5 examines comparative performance to the set of nearest competitors at three-year and five-year horizons. Winners are defined as those funds that beat their competitors over that time interval. Counts and proportions are reported, and test of the independence of rows and columns are also reported.

Consistent with the evidence in table 3.4, we find that, over the three-year horizon, the propensity to change is related to whether or not the fund is a winner or loser relative to competitors. This is positive, although the *p*-value is 7 percent, and over the five-year horizon, we do not reject the null. The focus of this table, however, is the further detail provided by endowments about the TYPE of change being contemplated. At both three- and five-year return horizons, losers contemplating a change were significantly more likely to seek assets in the risk/hedge category as opposed to the growth category. Unfortunately, the NACUBO classifications are not a perfect match for our interests. Choices for contemplated changes are: growth assets, defined as domestic and international equities, private equities, and so forth; risk reduction, defined as long/short, hedged equities, fixed income; inflation protection, defined as real assets (e.g., real estate, oil and gas, timberland, and TIPS); opportunistic investment (undefined); liquidity(undefined); and other. We use only the growth assets and risk reduction categories. Hedge funds are included in the risk reduction category along with fixed income. While it is generally true that hedge fund returns have lower standard deviations than equities, the common reasons to invest in them is to capture risk-adjusted returns (alpha) based on proprietary trading techniques. This makes hedge funds quite different from fixed income, with which they are lumped. With this caveat we can interpret the significant preference by losers for the risk reduction category provisionally as a tendency to move toward marketable alternatives as opposed to private equity, although it is also possible that it reflects a tendency to increase bonds. Note, however, that it is not the result of a movement toward more liquidity engendered by the 2008–2009 crisis—this would presumably fall into the liquidity category.

Table 3.6 follows up on the reported desire to change asset allocation. We take responses to the question about intent to change allocation and see whether the endowments in fact change their percentage allocation in the following year. The table treats the increase in percentage allocation each asset class in a separate regression, using the indicator variables for intent to change or uncertain about a change as explanatory variables. We also include a dummy for year 2011, to address secular changes in endowment preferences for certain asset classes. Since this question has only been asked for two years and we are using a one-year forward lag as the dependent variable, we only have two years of annual panel data.

The time dummy in the regression is significant in each case and indicates two things. First, it likely partly reflects change in the market value of each asset class—in years when the stock market goes up, it will be positive. Second, it also likely reflects industry-wide rebalancing toward certain asset classes. For example, although domestic equities increased in market value in fiscal year 2011, the coefficient on intent to change is negative, indicating that, controlling for market growth, endowments intending to change withdrew funds from domestic equities in the following year.

The coefficient on marketable alternatives is strongly positive, while the 2011 dummy is negative—the overall industry trend and/or the performance of hedge funds in 2011 may have been down, but for those endowments reporting an intent to change policy, they followed through by increasing their exposure to hedge funds. The same is true for international equities (which would include emerging market stocks), but interestingly it is not true for private equity and venture capital. This is consistent with the evidence we saw in the previous table—that, conditional on intent to change, the risk reduction category was significant for losers but not the growth assets category.

Finally, we use the data to explore whether the documented pattern of competitive response that has led endowments toward greater allocation to

Table 3.6   Do funds contemplating a change in asset allocation actually follow through the next year?

	Domestic_equities	Fixed_income	International_equities	Marketable_alternatives	PE	VC
Intercept	-0.257	0.127	0.414	0.439	-0.0154	-0.017
	(-0.80)	(0.46)	(2.21)	(1.39)	(-0.10)	(-0.29)
FY2011	1.595	-2.835	0.923	-1.029	0.458	0.194
	(4.18)	(-8.69)	(4.15)	(-2.75)	(2.54)	(2.86)
C=intent	-2.731	0.499	0.508	1.565	0.175	-0.014
	(-6.41)	(1.37)	(2.04)	(3.74)	(0.87)	(-0.18)
U=uncertain	-1.149	-0.295	0.266	0.567	-0.589	-0.044
	(-1.72)	(-0.52)	(0.68)	(0.87)	(-1.87)	(-0.37)
No. obs.	1,580	1,580	1,580	1,580	1,580	1,580
R-square	0.0391	0.0484	0.0126	0.0147	0.0076	0.0054

Notes: $\Delta Assets_t = \alpha + \beta_1 d_{2011} + \beta_2 r_{t-1}^{nc} + \beta_3 C_{t-1} + \beta_4 U_{t-1} + e_t$. T-statistics in parentheses. C = intent to change; U = uncertain. Intent = 1 if yes; Q4E1 = 0 otherwise; U = uncertain = 1 if uncertain; Q4E9 = 0 otherwise. Intent data is available only in years 2009, 2010, and 2011, so only one year dummy is included in the regression.

marketable alternatives has differential effects for large versus small institutions. Table 3.7 reports the results of regressions explaining the reported returns within each asset class. The explanatory variables include a benchmark index for that asset category in the observation year (for example, the domestic equities benchmark is the S&P 500), the size and richness of the endowment at the beginning of the year, and a dummy for the Northeast region. Focusing in the marketable alternatives, we see that the benchmark explains performance well, but that certain factors add or detract. Taking the average values for endowment size ($463 million) and richness (.095), the estimated model indicates that these add about .30, or 30 basis points per year to the return to marketable alternatives. The Northeast dummy adds 57 basis points. Thus a school of average size and average richness situated in the Northeast would likely have a return that exceeds the benchmark (0.868–0.696 = .182), which suggests that the hedge fund allocation has matched or exceeded industry performance. For less rich, smaller schools outside the Northeast this is likely not the case. Given the standard errors about the coefficient in the marketable alternative regression, however, this calculation is only a gross estimate: while the intercept is significantly negative, the other coefficients (besides the intercept) are not. Among the other regressions, the overall alternatives portfolio (constructed with reported asset weights) gives similar results, although the richness factor approaches standard significance levels. Performance from domestic equities, by contrast, does not vary at all by asset size, school richness, or region. Interestingly, though somewhat outside the scope of this chapter, we find that international equity performance also varies with endowment size, school richness, and region, suggesting that this asset class, like alternatives, requires more endowment management skill to pay off. This may give one some pause when we remember the small uptick in the general trend toward international equities in figure 3.5, and a significant loading on intent to change for the international equities regression in table 3.6.

3.5 Discussion

Our empirical results demonstrate a few things. First, we show that the college endowment allocations to alternative assets—and more specifically to marketable alternatives, is associated with the allocation policies of their near competitors and single-closest competitor. This is true even in controlling for regional effects, size, and richness. Second, we show that the decision by college endowments to change their asset allocations is not independent of the relative performance compared to rivals. In particular, prior one- and two-year past returns of rivals are positively associated with an intent to change allocation. We find that, conditional upon an intent to change, losing funds (i.e., those that underperformed rivals) more frequently indicated a choice for a category that includes hedge funds compared to winners who

Table 3.7   **Explaining asset class returns**

			Dependent: Return (%)		
	Marketable alternatives	Alternatives	Domestic equities	Fixed income	International equities
Intercept	−0.696	−2.047	0.678	0.703	3.486
	(−2.67)	(−4.77)	(3.64)	(2.64)	(14.57)
Benchmark index	0.863	0.792	0.970	0.961	0.984
	(54.94)	(45.23)	(146.11)	(25.85)	(129.17)
Total assets (thousand million)	0.319	0.162	0.027	0.157	0.806
	(1.65)	(0.34)	(0.22)	(1.07)	(3.22)
Richness	1.599	4.296	−0.208	0.625	2.913
	(1.62)	(1.95)	(−0.34)	(0.88)	(2.72)
Northeast region	0.569	0.887	−0.004	−0.074	0.516
	(1.61)	(1.43)	(−0.02)	(−0.33)	(1.49)
Number of obs.	1,651	1,313	2,675	2,481	2,234
R-square	0.65	0.61	0.89	0.21	0.88

Note: The *T*-statistics are in parentheses.

intended to change. This difference is not true for the asset category that includes private equity and venture capital. We find that the announced intent to change allocation is significantly related to a subsequent reduction in domestic equities and an increase in international equities and marketable alternatives.

These results are consistent with the hypothesis that the relative performance of a university's competitors' endowments influences its asset allocation policy and the decision to change it. The general direction of the change is also consistent with the trends set by HYP—toward marketable alternatives—that is, hedge funds.

The welfare effects of this allocation shift are unclear. The implication of DeMarzo, Kaniel, and Kremer (2005, 2008) is that keeping up with the Joneses can create positive externalities if, indeed, the action is welfare improving. After all, that is what new technology is all about. Is the shift to alternative investments a benefit to the universities who respond to competitive pressure by reallocating? The answer is not straightforward. There is considerable literature on the returns to hedge funds. Brown, Goetzmann, and Ibbotson (1999) find that hedge funds delivered positive risk-adjusted returns over the period 1989 to 1995. Ibbotson and Chen (2005) and Stulz (2007), in a review article, finds that this basic result holds true over a longer sample period. Perhaps the competition among university endowments has led to greater diversification, less exposure to market risk, and the utilization of manager skill. Unfortunately, time is needed to fully assess the benefits of a new technology. Our analysis of the relative benefits of small and less rich funds moving to marketable alternatives is constrained to recent years. With this qualification, we find some evidence that the benefits to the allocation shift are differential.

If the returns to marketable alternatives continue as they have historically, then the competition will have been a good thing. If, on the other hand, markets are efficient—or at least access to managers who can take advantage of inefficiencies for the benefit of clients is limited—then this shift may have long-term costs. One lesson of the Great Recession is that allocation into less liquid alternatives such as private equity increases endowment exposure to emergency demands on cash. While this may be a source of higher expected returns for investors with a long horizon, the shock of 2008 has likely caused a recalibration of institutional sensitivity to financial crises.

References

Abel, Andrew B. 1990. "Asset Prices under Habit Formation and Catching up with the Joneses." *The American Economic Review* 80 (2): 38–42. Papers and Proceedings of the Hundred and Second Annual Meeting of the American Economic Association.

Avery, Christopher, Mark Glickman, Caroline Hoxby, and Andrew Metrick. 2004. "A Revealed Preference Ranking of US Colleges and Universities." NBER Working Paper no. 10803, Cambridge, MA.

Bakshi, Gurdip S., and Zhiwu Chen. 1996. "The Spirit of Capitalism and Stock-Market Prices." *American Economic Review* 86 (1): 133–57.

Bastedo, Michael N., and Nicholas A. Bowman. 2011. "College Rankings as an Interorganizational Dependency: Establishing the Foundation for Strategic and Institutional Accounts." *Research in Higher Education* 52 (1): 3–23.

Brown, Keith, Lorenzo Garlappi, and Cristian Tiu. 2010. "Asset Allocation and Portfolio Performance: Evidence from University Endowment Funds." *Journal of Financial Markets* 1:268–94.

Brown, Keith, W. V. Harlow, and L. T. Starks. 1996. "Of Tournaments and Temptations: An Analysis of Managerial Incentives in the Mutual Fund Industry." *Journal of Finance* 51:85–110.

Brown, Stephen J., William N. Goetzmann, and Roger G. Ibbotson. 1999. "Offshore Hedge Funds: Survival and Performance, 1989–95." *Journal of Business* 72 (1): 91–117.

Brown, Stephen J., William N. Goetzmann, and James Park. 2001. "Careers and Survival: Competition and Risk in the Hedge Fund and CTA Industry." *Journal of Finance* 56 (5): 1869–86.

Burke, Mary, and Tim Sass. 2008. "Classroom Peer Effects and Student Achievement." Working Paper no. 08-5, Federal Reserve Bank of Boston.

Chan, Yeung Lewis, and Leonid Kogan. 2002. "Catching Up with the Joneses: Heterogeneous Preferences and the Dynamics of Asset Prices." *Journal of Political Economy* 110 (6): 1255–85.

Chevalier, Judith A., and Glenn D. Ellison. 1997. "Risk Taking by Mutual Funds as a Response to Incentives." *Journal of Political Economy* 105 (6): 1167–200.

DeMarzo, Peter M., Ron Kaniel, and Ilan Kremer. 2005. "Diversification as a Public Good: Community Effects in Portfolio Choice." *Journal of Finance* 59 (4): 1677–716.

———. 2008. "Relative Wealth Concerns and Financial Bubbles." *Review of Financial Studies* 21 (1): 19–50.

Epple, Dennis, Elizabeth Newlon, and Richard Romano. 2002. "Ability Tracking, School Competition and Distribution of Educational Benefits." *Journal of Public Economics* 83:1–48.

Epple, Dennis, Richard Romano, and Holger Sieg. 2003. "Peer Effects, Financial Aid and Selection of Students into Colleges and Universities: An Empirical Analysis." *Journal of Applied Econometrics* Special Issue: Empirical Analysis of Social Interactions 18 (5): 501–25.

———. 2006. "Admission, Tuition, and Financial Aid Policies in the Market for Higher Education." *Econometrica* 74 (4): 885–928.

Galí, Jordi. 1994. "Keeping up with the Joneses: Consumption Externalities, Portfolio Choice, and Asset Prices." *Journal of Money, Credit and Banking* 26 (1): 1–8.

Goetzmann, William N., John Griswold, and Yung-Fang (Ayung) Tseng. 2010. "Educational Endowments in Crises." *Journal of Portfolio Management* 36 (4): 112–23.

Griliches, Zvi. 1957. "Hybrid Corn: An Exploration of the Economics of Technological Change." *Econometrica* 25 (4): 501–22.

Hoxby, Caroline. 2009. "The Changing Selectivity of American Colleges." *Journal of Economic Perspectives* 23:95–118.

Ibbotson, Roger G., and Peng Chen. 2005. "Sources of Hedge Fund Returns: Alphas, Betas, and Costs." Working Paper no. 05-17, Yale International Center for Finance, Yale University.

Lerner, Josh, Antoinette Schoar, and Jialan Wang. 2007. "Secrets of the Academy: The Drivers of University Endowment Performance." Harvard Business School of Finance, Working Paper no. 07-066, Harvard University.

Litvak, J., Burton Malkiel, and Richard Quandt. 1974. "A Plan for the Definition of Endowment Income." *American Economics Review* 64:433–37.

Oster, Sharon. 1982. "The Diffusion of Innovation among Steel Firms." *Bell Journal of Economics* 13 (1): 45–56.

Ravina, Enrichetta. 2005. "Habit Persistence and Keeping Up with the Joneses: Evidence from Micro Data." NYU Working Paper no. FIN 05-046, New York University, November.

Shumway, David R. 1997. "The Star System in Literary Studies." *PMLA* Special Topic: The Teaching of Literature 112 (1): 85–100.

Sirri, Erik R., and Peter Tufano. 1998. "Costly Search and Mutual Fund Flows." *Journal of Finance* 53 (5): 1589–1622.

Stulz, René. 2007. "Hedge Funds: Past, Present, and Future." *Journal of Economic Perspectives* 21 (2): 175–94.

Swensen, David. 2000. *Pioneering Portfolio Management.* New York: Free Press.

Tobin, James. 1974. "What is Permanent Endowment Income?" *American Economic Review* 64:427–32.

Volkwein, J. Fredericks, and Kyle V. Sweitzer. 2006. "Institutional Prestige and Reputation among Research Universities and Liberal Arts Colleges." *Research in Higher Education* 47 (2): 129–48.

Keynes, King's, and Endowment Asset Management

David Chambers, Elroy Dimson, and Justin Foo

4.1 Introduction

John Maynard Keynes's experiences managing his Cambridge College endowment illustrate several lessons still relevant to endowments and foundations today. Keynes himself, when looking back over his investment career in the late 1930s, spoke of the need to understand the illiquidity risk attached to an alternative asset such as real estate and of the benefits to recognizing the extent of an organization's investment skills and resources in tailoring investment policy.

Most pertinent to the subject of this volume, Keynes's investment experiences during the Great Depression of the 1930s are relevant to modern-day investors during the Great Recession. He had to discover for himself the difficulty of making profits from market timing when the stock market crashed in 1929. Thereafter, his self-proclaimed switch to a more careful buy-and-hold

David Chambers is reader in finance at Cambridge Judge Business School. Elroy Dimson is chairman of the Centre for Endowment Asset Management at Cambridge Judge Business School and emeritus professor of finance at London Business School. Justin Foo is a CERF postdoctoral fellow at Cambridge Judge Business School.

We wish to acknowledge the support of the King's College Cambridge first bursar and assistant bursar, Keith Carne and Simon Billington, and the archivist, Patricia McGuire. Valued comments were received from Jeffrey Brown, Keith Brown, Caroline Hoxby, James Poterba, and other participants at the NBER preconference "The Great Recession and Higher Education." We thank Paul Marsh, Peter Scott, Mike Staunton, and James Wyatt for data and ideas. This chapter was prepared while David Chambers held a Keynes Fellowship and a CERF Fellowship at Cambridge University and a Thomas McCraw Fellowship at Harvard Business School, Elroy Dimson held a Leverhulme Trust Emeritus Fellowship, and Justin Foo held a CERF Postdoctoral Fellowship and was supported by the Cambridge Commonwealth Trust. We are also grateful to the Robert Brown Memorial Trust for providing financial support. For acknowledgments, sources of research support, and disclosure of the authors' material financial relationships, if any, please see http://www.nber.org/chapters/c12860.ack.

stock-picking approach in the early 1930s allowed him to maintain his commitment to equities when the market fell sharply once more in 1937–1938. In so doing, he provides an excellent example of the natural advantages that accrue to such long-horizon investors as university endowments in being able to behave in a contrarian manner during economic and financial market downturns.

King's, one of the thirty-one Cambridge Colleges, was founded in 1441 by King Henry VI and lavishly endowed with agricultural real estate that stretched the length and breadth of England. Famous Kingsmen other than John Maynard Keynes include Sir Francis Walsingham, secretary of state and organizer of Queen Elizabeth I's spy service; Sir Robert Walpole, prime minister; Alan Turing, the father of modern computing; and the novelists E. M. Forster and Salman Rushdie.

For centuries, their agricultural estates formed the bulk of the endowment assets of the oldest Colleges and King's was no exception. When Keynes became involved in the management of King's endowment just after World War I, he immediately undertook a substantial reallocation of the portfolio away from real estate into the new asset class, equities. At the time, other institutional investors remained reluctant to follow suit and it was not until after Keynes's death that they began to follow his example. Oxford and Cambridge ("Oxbridge") Colleges have a natural concern for preserving their wealth for future generations (Tobin 1974) and are the ultimate long-horizon investors. Keynes spotted an opportunity for such patient, long-term investors to make a substantial allocation to equities, an innovation at least as radical as the commitment to alternative assets in the late twentieth century by Yale and Harvard. He selected an asset mix for King's consistent with the implications of standard models of consumption and portfolio choice that were to appear many decades later, as described, for example, by Campbell and Viceira (2002). Keynes can justly be regarded as among the first institutional equity investors.

This chapter describes why Keynes held strong views about equities and how he changed his investment approach to the benefit of lower transaction costs. We also highlight how King's benefitted from earning an emerging risk premium on UK equities despite the economic turbulence of the 1930s, as well as additional risk premia obtained through tilting the portfolio toward both value and smaller-capitalization stocks.

His investment strategy benefitted the endowment considerably, to the extent that upon his death King's had at least drawn level with Trinity, the richest of the Cambridge Colleges. In the post-Keynes era, the endowment has had a more checkered history, illustrating the challenges in trying to emulate Keynes's unconventional investment approach.

The chapter begins with a summary of Keynes's various investing roles in section 4.2. Section 4.3 describes our data, followed by a discussion of endowment asset management before Keynes in section 4.4. We then review Keynes's management of the endowment in section 4.5 and how investment policy evolved after Keynes in section 4.6. Finally, we discuss Keynes's legacy in section 4.7 and section 4.8 concludes.

4.2 Keynes's Investing Life

While still a Cambridge student, Keynes had written in 1905 to his friend, Lytton Strachey, saying that:

I want to manage a railway or organise a Trust, or at least swindle the investing public; it is so easy and fascinating to master the principles of these things. (Moggridge 1992, 95)

Here was a young man supremely confident in his abilities. It was therefore no surprise that he remained extremely active throughout his life investing in stocks, bonds, currencies, and commodities.[1] He was, in effect, similar to a modern global macro hedge fund manager.

Just after World War I, Keynes began trading currencies both for himself and on behalf of the Syndicate, an investment pool he formed with the City financier Oswald Toynbee (O. T.) Falk, whom he had met at the British Treasury. Keynes was one of the first traders to exploit the development of the forward currency markets and pursued a fundamentals-based trading strategy (Accominotti and Chambers 2014).

Keynes also traded, largely on his own account, a wide variety of commodities—cotton (Cristiano and Naldi 2012), tin (Cavalli and Cristiano 2012), and wheat (Fantacci, Marcuzzo, and Sanfilippo 2010; Foresti and Sanfilippo 2012). Overall, his record trading in commodities was rather mixed and marked by periods of large gains and losses.

In addition to his considerable personal investment activity, Keynes was involved with a number of investment institutions. He was appointed director of the National Mutual Life Insurance Company, one of the City's oldest institutions, in 1919, becoming its chairman in 1921. Following persistent disagreements over investment policy, he resigned in 1938. Keynes's experience at a smaller family-run insurer, the Provincial Insurance Company, was altogether more fruitful. As a director from 1923 until his death in 1946, Keynes successfully persuaded Francis Scott, the managing director, of the advantages of investing in equities and frequently recommended shares that were also held in his personal account (Moggridge 1983, 51).

Three other funds, the A. D. Investment Trust, the P. R. Finance Company, and the Independent Investment Company, were cofounded with O. T. Falk in the early 1920s. The latter two had checkered histories. The P. R. Finance Company was eventually liquidated in 1935. Similarly, the Independent Investment Company lost nearly all its capital by the early 1930s and management subsequently passed into other hands (Davenport 1975, 227).

Above all, however, Keynes had his longest association with the King's College endowment—the primary focus of our study. This was the insti-

---

1. See, for example, Moggridge (1983), Pierce (1993), and Kent (2012) for a commentary on Keynes's investing activities.

tution that was closest to his heart and where he enjoyed full investment discretion.

4.3 Data

Annual investment reports of the King's endowment are kept in the King's College Archive for each financial year ended in August from 1921 up to the present, with only occasional years missing. College income, including spending from the endowment, are taken from the annual *Abstract of Receipts* printed in the *Cambridge University Reporter* from 1882 to 2000 and thereafter from the College Accounts published on the King's College website. Data applying to the period of Keynes's management of the endowment, 1921–1946, are described in detail in Chambers, Dimson, and Foo (forthcoming).

There is no published valuation of King's real estate holdings until 1966, the only disclosures regarding real estate investment being the rents received. For the preceding period, we draw on Wilkinson's (1980, 85) £1.0 million estimate of the 1919 value of real estate holdings, and then track the major disposals over the following years to 1927. Subsequent to this date, we assume the College real estate portfolio fluctuated in line with the real estate price appreciation index of Scott (1996),[2] such that the valuation converges on the figure of £1.2 million for 1966 as stated in the *Report of the Inspectors of Accounts* (King's College Archive, KCGB/4/1/1/23/19).

For benchmark purposes we employ the 100 Share UK equity index series estimated by Dimson, Marsh, and Staunton (2002, 2014), which is representative of the sectoral composition of the broad market and includes natural resource stocks as well as commercial and industrial companies. We use both the main version of the 100 Share index, which is market capitalization weighted, and the equally weighted index estimated in Dimson, Marsh, and Staunton (2002). Our UK government bond and cash indexes are, respectively, the total return on UK Consols and UK Treasury bill returns (Dimson, Marsh, and Staunton 2002, 2014). For real estate returns from 1973 onward, we utilize the Investment Property Databank (IPD) UK Annual Index.

4.4 King's before Keynes

Henry VI lavished the College with an endowment of thirty-six manorial estates and eight appropriated rectories by 1453 (Saltmarsh 1958, 3,7). Despite the expropriation of a substantial part of the original endowment during the reign of Edward IV, which halved its annual income, King's ben-

---

2. The price change of commercial buildings (pence per square foot) is used for the period 1939 to 1946 when the Scott index is unavailable.

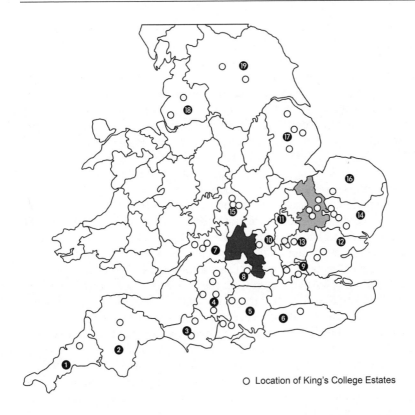

O Location of King's College Estates

❶ Cornwall	❺ Hampshire	❾ Middlesex	⓭ Hertfordshire	⓱ Lincolnshire
❷ Devon	❻ Sussex	❿ Buckinghamshire	⓮ Suffolk	⓲ Lancashire
❸ Dorset	❼ Gloucestershire	⓫ Bedfordshire	⓯ Warwickshire	⓳ Yorkshire
❹ Wiltshire	❽ Berkshire	⓬ Essex	⓰ Norfolk	

Fig. 4.1 King's real estate portfolio at its foundation

Note: This map indicates the approximate location of King's estates endowed by Henry VI as described in Saltmarsh (1958, 9, 10). Cambridgeshire is shown in light gray and Oxfordshire is shown in dark gray.

efitted from the support of Henry VII and VIII and remained the richest College in Cambridge for a century until the foundation of Trinity in 1546.

Its agricultural land holdings stretched right across England, embracing real estate in more than twenty counties (figure 4.1). The bursar's job was to manage these estates by approving new leases, renewing old ones, selling its timber, and appointing stewards and gamekeepers, among other things. Although added to through gifts, bequests, and purchases, there were few major changes to King's real estate portfolio over the next four centuries

(Saltmarsh 1958, 12). Until the late 1850s the Oxford and Cambridge Colleges were prohibited by their statutes from selling land (Dunbabin 1975, 631). Even after that, there were no significant disposals of real estate until the intervention of Keynes in 1920.

King's investment policy focused exclusively on real estate for four centuries up to the mid-nineteenth century. On the whole, this investment policy was rewarding. The English Agricultural Revolution led to an eightfold rise in agricultural rents between 1700 and 1850 (Turner, Beckett, and Afton 1997, 207, table 10.1) compared to a fivefold increase in agricultural output. While we lack reliable agricultural returns data for this long span of history, the rise in rents is indicative of the success of this investment policy.

However, King's, along with other Colleges, did suffer a considerable setback in the last quarter of the nineteenth century with the onset of the Agricultural Depression in Britain. The revolution in land and sea transportation opened up new agricultural lands in North America, Australia, and Argentina, and brought sharp falls in agricultural prices. As a result, English agricultural rents fell 30 percent from the mid-1870s to the mid-1890s and reverted back to the levels of sixty years earlier (Turner, Beckett, and Afton 1997, 150). During the same two decades, King's real estate income declined by 20 percent. This slightly better performance was most probably due to its ability to switch from long-standing "beneficial leases" charging considerably below-market rents to so-called "rack-rents," which now reflected the market (Dunbabin 1975, 633). Although King's real estate income subsequently recovered, by 1913 it had still not returned to the level on the eve of the Agricultural Depression.

Prior to the College first disclosing a market valuation of its real estate holdings in 1966, we can gauge the almost complete reliance on real estate from analyzing the sources of College income (table 4.1). In 1882, the first year that the College published its accounts, its real estate holdings yielded an income of £36,400 compared to an income of only £1,600 from its security portfolio. A combination of inertia in investment policy and College statutes that constrained disposal of originally endowed real estate explains the very small allocation to financial securities, principally British government bonds.

Toward the end of the nineteenth century, Oxbridge Colleges found themselves free to reinvest some of the proceeds from the sale of estates into financial securities (Neild 2008, 87). As a result, King's small security portfolio grew to include Indian government bonds (guaranteed by the British government) and British railway bonds in the 1880s, and then British municipal government bonds and Colonial government bonds in the 1890s. These bonds were deemed "first class" and representative of those "safe" securities drawn from a list of approved "Trustee Securities." This list comprises securities in which trustees, in the absence of a trust deed conferring more liberal powers of investment, were authorized first by the courts and then by the Trustee Acts of 1893 and 1900 to invest trust money. The list of

Table 4.1 King's College income

	1910	1920	1930	1940	1950	1960	1970	1980	1990	2000	2010
Total income £'000	36	52	81	93	219	313	572	2,218	5,582	7,712	13,033
	(%)	(%)	(%)	(%)	(%)	(%)	(%)	(%)	(%)	(%)	(%)
Property income	85	71	50	46	41	32	29	31	30	13	13
Securities income	7	14	12	24	34	38	36	26	35	28	22
Academic fees	2	10	8	7	5	6	7	15	11	15	17
Residence, catering, etc.	7	5	26	23	20	22	28	27	22	33	34
Donations	0	0	4	1	0	2	0	1	1	11	14
	100	100	100	100	100	100	100	100	100	100	100

Note: Income figures for 1910 to 2000 are taken from the *King's College Abstract of Receipts* published in the *Cambridge University Reporter* and for 2010 from the King's College Accounts. Total income is expressed in nominal prices.

permitted securities was a very narrow one and most notably precluded any investment in equities.

In summary, King's endowment remained undiversified with an almost total reliance on real estate up to World War I. The interest income produced by its security portfolio, despite having doubled over the previous forty years, was still only one-tenth of its real estate income, leaving King's unable to avoid the substantial negative shock to its income from the Agricultural Depression.

4.5 King's during Keynes's Time

Keynes was elected to a fellowship and appointed an Inspector of the Accounts in 1909, followed by his election in 1912 to the Council, the governing body of King's College. He took an immediate interest in reforming the investment practices of King's with the inspectors unprecedentedly recommending a change in the policy of placing cash surpluses on deposit. However, the then bursars were unmoved and this policy remained in place until just after World War I when he was appointed Second Bursar and had primary responsibility for investments. In 1924 he was appointed First Bursar and was entrusted with full discretion over investment policy until his death in 1946. His College fellows gave him a free hand in managing the endowment, and there seems little doubt that within the College his investment policy went unchallenged. Indeed, his annual "Chancellor of the Exchequer" speech became a not-to-be-missed fixture in the College calendar.

Chambers, Dimson, and Foo (forthcoming) document in considerable detail Keynes's investment approach and his trading record on behalf of King's. While Keynes's investment performance was not as stellar as previously thought, nonetheless the authors estimate that the King's Discretionary Portfolio generated over the quarter century to 1946 an annualized return of 16.0 percent compared to 10.4 percent, 6.8 percent, and 7.1 percent for the UK equity market, the Restricted Portfolio, and UK government bonds, respectively. Notwithstanding the higher volatility from allocating to equities, the Sharpe ratio of the Discretionary Portfolio at 0.73 exceeded that of the Restricted Portfolio at 0.57. Finally, the Discretionary Portfolio generated a Jensen's alpha of 7.7 percent, with a very high tracking error relative to the UK equity index of 13.9 percent.[3] The time series tracking error for contemporary US university endowment funds averaged 3.4 percent over the period 2002–2007, according to Brown et al. (2014). Indeed, the tracking error of the 95th percentile fund in the latter study still only reached 6.3 percent.[4] The high-tracking error of Keynes's fund was in part attributable to his idiosyncratic stock selection, which we discuss further below.

---

3. Tracking error is a measure of risk calculated as the standard deviation of the difference between the portfolio and index returns.
4. We are grateful to Stephen Dimmock for providing this estimate.

Table 4.2   **Allocation to equities**

	1920–1929 (%)	1930–1939 (%)	1940–1946 (%)
A.			
King's Discretionary Portfolio	75	57	73
Harvard University	16	32	47
Princeton University	9	31	52
Yale University	24	57	52
B.			
Endowments with asset values:			
More than $15 million	17	25	43
Between $2 to $15 million	19	29	42
Less than $2 million	6	13	28

Source: For panel A, Foo (2014). Panel B provides equivalent figures for US educational endowments using data from Cain (1942) as quoted by Goetzmann, Griswold, and Tseng (2010).

Note: Panel A provides the allocation to equities of the King's College Discretionary Portfolio, and Harvard University, Princeton University, and Yale University endowments spanning the period when Keynes managed the King's College endowment. The Harvard, Princeton, and Yale allocations exclude real estate investments to provide a comparable basis against King's (see text for full description).

In the rest of this section, we draw on the main findings of Chambers, Dimson, and Foo (forthcoming) that are most relevant to a consideration of the long-run management of the King's endowment and of endowments in general.

4.5.1 The Shift into Equities

Keynes exerted his influence on investment policy as soon as he had been elected to College office by pushing for the disposal of one-third of the real estate portfolio between 1920 and 1927 (Wilkinson 1980, 85). At the same time, he persuaded King's to segregate a part of the real estate disposal proceeds into a Discretionary Portfolio, free to invest in equities and unaffected by the Trustee Act restrictions. Over the 1920s, the equity weighting of the Discretionary Portfolio averaged 75 percent, over the 1930s 57 percent, including an allocation to US common stocks, and over 1940–1946 73 percent (panel A, table 4.2). In contrast, the equity weighting of the remaining Restricted Portfolio, which was subject to the Trustee Acts, averaged only 1 percent across the period 1921–1946, and from 1933 onward there were no ordinary share holdings.

Other Oxbridge Colleges did not follow King's into equities during Keynes's time in office. The largest Cambridge Colleges, Trinity and St John's, only amended their statutes to permit equity investment after World War II (Moggridge 1992, 352; Neild 2008, 122). To the best of our knowledge, and in contrast to Oxford and Cambridge, the ability of US universities to invest in common stocks was not restricted by government legislation or university statute during this period. Panel A of table 4.2 provides a comparison between King's and three leading US endowments, Harvard, Princeton, and Yale. According to Foo (2014), Harvard's total exposure to equities was only 16 percent in the 1920s, doubling to 32 percent in the 1930s, and averaged 47 percent from 1940 to 1946. Princeton's allocation to equities was even lower at 9 percent over the 1920s but increased significantly to an average of 31 percent and 52 percent in the following two periods, respectively. Yale's exposure to equities was 24 percent, 57 percent, and 52 percent, respectively.[5] Although the largest US university endowments had committed more to common stocks relative to their smaller counterparts, this allocation on a historical cost-weighted basis remained below 10 percent in the 1920s and only rose above 20 percent in the late 1930s (Goetzmann, Griswold, and Tseng 2010). Their average total allocation to equities as a proportion of total assets excluding real estate is shown in panel B of table 2.

In a similar fashion, major UK institutional investors such as pension funds, investment trusts, and insurance companies largely eschewed equities in favor of fixed income securities in this period (Burton and Corner 1968; Hannah 1986; Baker and Collins 2003).

The impact of this switch from real estate into equities on King's asset allocation can be seen in figure 4.2. By 1946, the year of Keynes's death, the real estate weighting had declined from above 80 percent just before Keynes became bursar to below 50 percent compared to common stocks now representing over 30 percent and preferred stocks another 10 percent of the portfolio. Keynes moved his College from a centuries-long almost total reliance on UK real estate into a more diversified position with a substantial allocation to both UK and non-UK equities. We discuss the latter non-UK exposure in section 4.5.5.

What led Keynes to undertake such a dramatic shift in asset allocation? First, he believed the attractions of real estate were overstated. Hence, in 1938 he wrote a memorandum to the Estates Committee and reflected on his period in charge of managing the endowment. He stressed that the appearance of stability from investments that are not marked to market—in King's case, real estate—masked volatility in the underlying investment. However, equally importantly, Keynes wanted to put money into equities. He explained this enthusiasm for equities when reviewing Smith (1924), a US study of the attractions of investing in common stocks.

4.5.2 The Attractions of Equity Investing

In summarizing Smith's (1924) findings, Keynes championed the virtues of US common stocks as residual claims on industrial growth and foresaw

---

5. Asset allocation stated at book value, except for Harvard at market value from 1941 onward and Princeton from 1931 onward. Figures exclude real estate investments to provide a comparable basis against King's endowment. The weightings are qualitatively similar if real estate investments are included.

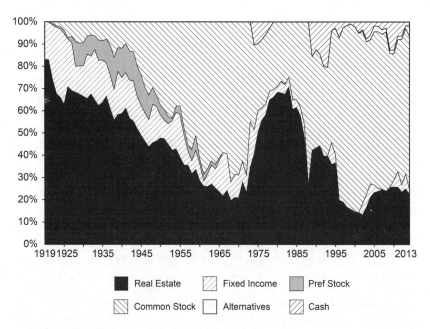

Fig. 4.2 King's endowment asset allocation, 1919–2013

Source: King's College, Cambridge.

Notes: This figure shows the proportion of the endowment held in real estate, fixed income, preferred stock, common stock, alternative investments, and cash. The value of real estate holdings is estimated at £1 million in 1919 according to Wilkinson (1980, 85) and major disposals are tracked over the following years to 1927. From 1928, the College real estate portfolio is assumed to have fluctuated in line with the real estate price appreciation index of Scott (1996) such that the valuation converges on the College valuation of £1.2 million in 1966. Cash is only consistently disclosed from 1988 onward. For the period 1973–1978, the initial cash position was disclosed at approximately £2 million, and we assume it was drawn down to fund the Blackfriars development over the following five years.

the same potential in UK ordinary shares as in US common stocks (Keynes 1925). He went on to list the attractions of equities as offering "an investment in real values" and an income premium over bonds.

During 1900–1920, when the annualized inflation rate was 5.6 percent, UK equities generated a negative annualized real return (–1.6 percent) and failed to substantiate Keynes's belief that they offered an investment in real values. However, they subsequently provided an annualized real return of +8.3 percent over the period 1921–1946, during which he moved King's into equities and Britain experienced deflation (–1.1 percent). UK equities continued to generate strong real returns (+7.9 percent) over the remainder of the century when annualized inflation ran at 6.1 percent.

Further, Keynes was proved correct in his belief that his investment policy would not have an adverse impact on endowment income (Chambers and Dimson 2013). In making such a large allocation to equities, the King's

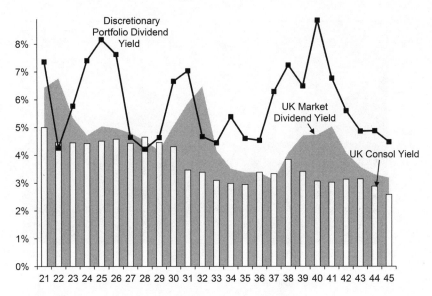

Fig. 4.3 King's Discretionary Portfolio dividend yield, 1921–1945

Source: (Chambers and Dimson 2013).

Note: The Discretionary Portfolio dividend yield is the total dividend income for the financial year ended in August divided by the market valuation of UK equities held in the Discretionary Portfolio. The UK market dividend yield is the dividend yield on the DMS 100 index. The UK Consol yield is the running yield on UK government perpetual bonds.

endowment did not give up anything in terms of income compared to the yields available on bonds (figure 4.3).[6] According to Chambers, Dimson, and Foo (forthcoming), the College's UK equity portfolio provided an average dividend yield of 6.0 percent during 1921–29, which was above the UK equity market dividend yield of 5.2 percent and income return of 4.6 percent on government bonds. In the 1930s, the dividend yield of the College's UK equity holdings averaged 5.9 percent, higher than the 4.4 percent dividend yield on the UK equity market and 3.4 percent income return from government bonds. Over 1940–1946, the College's UK equity holdings produced a dividend yield of 5.8 percent, again exceeding the 4.0 percent yield from UK equity markets and 3.0 percent income return from government bonds.

4.5.3 Change in Investment Approach

In the period up to the early 1930s, Keynes's approach is best characterised as top-down or market timing as he believed that he had the ability to

---

6. Data on property yields in this period are imperfectly documented. It is unclear as to whether appropriate maintenance costs have been deducted from income, and this obstructs making comparisons with dividend and bond yields.

time moves into and out of equities, bonds, and cash. In the 1938 memorandum to his investment committee, he reflected on this approach and confessed that:

> We have not proved able to take much advantage of a general systematic movement out of and into ordinary shares . . . at different phases of the trade cycle. (Moggridge 1983, 106)

Further, he also lamented the failure of this "credit-cycling" approach in an accompanying note to Richard Kahn, who was his student and subsequent colleague at King's, writing that:

> I have seen it tried by five different parties . . . over a period of nearly twenty years . . . I have not seen a single case of success." (Moggridge 1983, 100)

The archival evidence suggests that he had changed his investment approach by 1934. He appears to have abandoned the previous top-down approach in favor of a bottom-up, stock-picking approach as he explained in a 1934 letter to the chairman of Provincial Insurance:

> As time goes on, I get more and more convinced that the right method in investment is to put fairly large sums into enterprises which one thinks one knows something about . . . there are seldom more than two or three enterprises at any given time in which I personally feel myself entitled to put *full* confidence. (Moggridge 1983, 57)

Woods (2013) argues that Keynes's approach changed from being based on "speculation" to one founded on "enterprise," terms that Keynes himself used in chapter 12 of *The General Theory of Employment, Interest and Money* (Keynes 1936). Evidence of this shift in investment approach can be seen in the fact that he traded less in UK stocks, both ordinary and preference shares, in the Discretionary Portfolio (figure 4.4). Annual turnover dropped progressively through each decade and approached levels characteristic of a patient buy-and-hold investor.

To examine the impact of the change in investment approach, we undertake a Sharpe (1992) returns-based style analysis of the UK Discretionary Portfolio. Keynes invested in bonds and cash in addition to equities and therefore the time-varying exposure weights estimated by this method is preferable to a fixed-benchmark return. We estimate the style of the fund by regressing each month's portfolio return against five benchmark returns: UK equity index, UK government bond index, UK Treasury bill returns, oil price returns, and a tin-rubber price index. Oil and tin-rubber is included as Keynes invested in commodity-linked stocks but gold is excluded as the price of gold was fixed for most of this period. The estimation period uses a rolling forty-eight-month window centered on the estimation month, and we also impose a nonnegative weight restriction on all benchmarks as the portfolio did not have any short positions. We then calculate the monthly

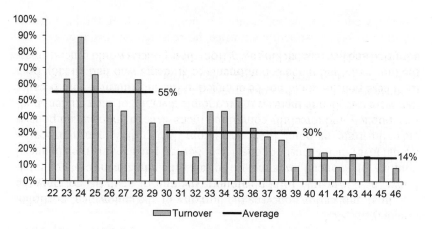

Fig. 4.4 King's UK equity portfolio turnover, 1922–1946
Source: Chambers, Dimson, and Foo (forthcoming).
Note: Turnover is defined as the average of purchases and sales divided by the average value of the UK equity portfolio, both ordinary and preference shares, held at the start and end of the financial year. The subperiod averages for the financial years 1922–1929, 1930–1939, and 1940–1946 are 55 percent, 30 percent, and 14 percent, respectively.

selection return as the portfolio return minus the style return estimated from the resulting weights above.

We follow Chambers, Dimson, and Foo (forthcoming) and partition the sample into two periods before and after the financial year ending August 1932. In the period up to August 1932, the average monthly selection return was 0.2 percent and not significantly different from zero. However, the monthly selection return increased to 0.7 percent in the period post-August 1932 (significant at the 1 percent level). For robustness, we also move the breakpoint to August 1931 and August 1933. In both cases, the prebreak average return is not significantly different from zero, whereas the postbreak average return is positive and statistically significant at the 1 percent level. This break in performance is consistent with other evidence documenting the improvement in his stock trading, particularly the improved timing of his purchases in the 1930s and 1940s compared to the 1920s (Chambers, Dimson, and Foo, forthcoming).

4.5.4 Tilting to Value and Size

King's income did not suffer by moving into stocks. As documented in section 4.5.2, the margin of the dividend yield on King's UK equity portfolio over the market yield increased to 1.5 percent in the 1930s and 1.8 percent in the 1940s versus 0.8 percent in the 1920s. This pattern reflects Keynes's shift to picking value stocks with above average dividend yields. Note that in all periods the average dividend yield for King's includes nondividend-paying securities. These holdings reflect Keynes's investing in so-called "recovery plays."

Since book values are unavailable on any consistent and reliable basis pre-1946, we use dividend yield as our measure of fundamental firm value. Dimson, Nagel, and Quigley (2003) show that classifying UK equities by dividend yield produces very similar value and growth portfolios to those based on classifying stocks by their market-to-book ratio. On this basis, by tilting his equity portfolio toward higher-yielding stocks, we credit Keynes with exploiting the existence of a value premium in stocks long before financial economists were to identify any such premium. In all three periods in the United Kingdom, 1900–1920, 1921–1946, and 1947–2013, high-yielding stocks have outperformed low-yielding stocks by 3.8 percent, 1.8 percent, and 3.1 percent, respectively.

In a similar way, although Keynes held some large stocks such as Union Corporation and Austin Motors, he generally tilted the King's equity portfolio toward small- and medium-sized stocks (Chambers and Dimson 2013). In so doing, he again identified in his investment actions the size premium available to patient long-term investors long before Banz (1981) and Fama and French (1992) ever uncovered its existence.

4.5.5 International Diversification

Keynes invested heavily in non-UK equities with substantial allocations to Asian tin-mining stocks in the 1920s and to South African gold stocks[7] and US stocks in the following decade (figure 4.5). The non-UK allocation reached 75 percent of the portfolio in the mid-1930s, a degree of international diversification that suggests Keynes exhibited a weaker level of home bias than that displayed by modern investors (see, e.g., French and Poterba 1991; Lewis 1999). Ahearne, Griever, and Warnock (2004) estimate that in the year 2000, foreign equities accounted for 12 percent of US investors' equities portfolios and only 1 percent two decades earlier. Again, King's and Keynes were not typical. Leading US endowments such as Harvard, Yale, and Princeton were almost completely invested in their domestic market during Keynes's time (Foo 2014).

4.6 King's Investment Policy after Keynes

4.6.1 Asset Allocation

The policy of switching the endowment into equities initiated by Keynes was continued after his death, and through a combination of performance and additional modest property disposals the equity weight doubled, reach-

---

7. These stocks were listed in London but their business operations were solely concentrated in Asia and South Africa, respectively.

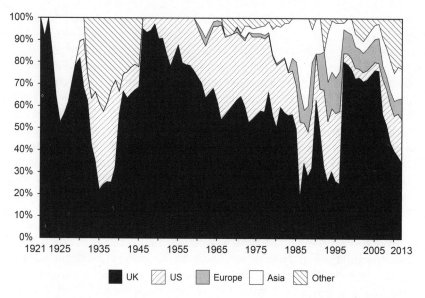

Fig. 4.5 King's UK equity portfolio by geographic region, 1921–2013

Source: King's College, Cambridge.

Notes: The regional allocation of the equity portfolio at market values is taken from King's investment reports and grouped into the United Kingdom, United States, Europe, Asia, and Other regions. In the 1930s and 1940s, Other is represented by Africa, and in the late twentieth and early twenty-first centuries by emerging markets and global equities.

ing a high point in 1968 of two-thirds of the endowment (figure 4.2). The real estate and fixed-income weightings correspondingly declined to 21 percent and 12 percent. By the late 1960s, King's endowment had surpassed St John's and quite probably overtaken the richest College, Trinity (Barter 1995). No doubt buoyed by their continued good fortune, disclosure in the investment reports regarding the composition and performance of the security portfolio during this period remained clear and informative.

In the late 1960s investment policy underwent a major reversal as the College reinvested in real estate, both commercial and industrial. The most significant decision taken in the early 1970s was to develop a piece of land, forming part of its original endowment, in Blackfriars on the edge of the city of London, in partnership with British Rail. The impact on the endowment's asset allocation was as dramatic as the decision taken by Keynes half a century earlier. The real estate weighting rose sharply from 23 percent in 1971 to exceed 70 percent in the early 1980s, 40 percentage points of which was accounted for by the Blackfriars project (figure 4.2). The rationale behind this change in investment strategy is not disclosed in the archival papers and remains unclear.

The higher real estate allocation initially benefitted endowment performance during the UK stock market crash of 1974. Indeed, King's was able to sell this project in 1986 for £10.5 million, having invested a total of £4.5

million. However, over the whole period from 1973 to 1986, UK equities still outperformed real estate by a substantial margin of 4.1 percent annually.

Following the disposal of their interest, King's continued to invest in real estate until, in 1995, the first formal investment policy was introduced and it was decided to dispose of all real estate other than that around Cambridge (see Barter 1995). The policy marked the return to a core reliance on equities with properties limited to those that form the infrastructure of the College's hostels in Cambridge and a small amount of farmland on the outskirts.

4.6.2 Comparison with Other Cambridge Colleges

Keynes's revolutionary allocation to equities was, in general, not emu-lated by other Cambridge Colleges until long after his death. Traditionally, their assets were largely invested in real estate (Acharya and Dimson 2007). For example, Trinity, the wealthiest College, had 83 percent of its capital invested in real estate and only 8 percent in equities in 1957 (Neild 2008, 125). Today, King's allocation to equities is still substantially larger than the average Cambridge College allocation. In 2012, the ten largest Cambridge College endowments,[8] excluding King's, allocated 35 percent to equities and 38 percent to property, compared with King's 64 percent in equities and 26 percent in property.

How should we view the relative impact of Keynes's stewardship of the King's endowment in a long-run context? In the absence of reliable total return figures, we draw on the findings of Neild (2008) and compare the endowment income of the other two of the three largest Colleges of the late nineteenth century, namely, Trinity and St John's. Combining the income of the three Colleges in 1871, Trinity's income was approximately 41 percent of the total with the remainder split evenly between St John's and King's. At the start of Keynes's tenure as bursar, Trinity's share had increased to 48 percent with St John's maintaining its 30 percent share compared to the 22 percent share of King's. However, King's income, benefitting from the substantial allocation to equities, had nearly drawn level with Trinity in the years immediately after Keynes's death (Trinity and King's commanded shares of 40 percent and 38 percent, respectively). Since the mid-twentieth century, Trinity has surged ahead, largely thanks to two successful real estate investments (Neild 2008). In 2012, its investment income was approximately three times that of St John's and eleven times that of King's.

4.7 Keynes's Legacy

Under Keynes's stewardship—a period that encompassed the Great Depres-sion and the Second World War—the Discretionary Portfolio of the King's

---

8. Data from published accounts of the following ten Colleges: Christ's, Clare, Corpus Christi, Emmanuel, Gonville and Caius, Jesus, Peterhouse, St John's, Trinity, and Trinity Hall.

endowment grew, including cash inflows, from just over £20,000 at the start of his tenure to £820,000 upon his death twenty-five years later in 1946. His investment record at his College was all the more remarkable considering his many achievements both as an academic and in public service. In contrast, Sir John Bradfield, who also achieved remarkable success as senior bursar of Trinity College between 1956 and 1992, was fully engaged with the responsibilities of managing his College's finances (Neild 2008, 131).

On his death, Keynes left his personal fortune amounting to £440,000,[9] approximately £15 million at 2012 prices, to King's. The bequest included financial investments, art, and valuable books and manuscripts. The art collection was valued at £30,000 in 1946 upon his death (Keynes Picture Bequest 273, 387), increasing to an estimated £17 million in 1988, and worth far more today (see Chambers, Dimson, and Spaenjers 2014).

Keynes himself reflected on his period in charge of the King's endowment in a memorandum to the Estates Committee in 1938 and in other writings (see Holder and Kent 2011). Keynes's revealing document provides four salutatory and lasting lessons for modern-day investors with a long-term horizon on how to think about managing their portfolios.

4.7.1 The Dangers of Market Timing

As discussed above, Keynes radically moved away from a top-down, market-timing approach in the early 1930s. Later on in 1938, Keynes reflected on the reasons for this shift:

> [Earlier] I believed that profits could be made by . . . holding shares in slumps and disposing of them in booms. [But] there have been two occasions when the whole body of our holding of such investments has depreciated by 20 to 25 percent within a few months and we have not been able to escape the movement . . . .
>
> As a result of these experiences I am clear that the idea of wholesale shifts is for various reasons impractical and indeed undesirable. Most of those who attempt it sell too late and buy too late, and do both too often, incurring heavy expenses and developing too unsettled and speculative a state of mind. (Moggridge 1983, 106)

Keynes had appreciated that market timing involves taking big bets on asset-class exposure. In contrast, bets on individual securities can, to a greater extent, benefit from diversification. While researchers such as Bollerslev, Tauchen, and Zhou (2009) provide some justification for market timing based on variance risk, this is short term and would have been expensive to implement. The Shiller (2005) view that markets overreact and are subject to persistent mispricing is closer to Keynes approach, but could not have been

---

9. According to Skidelsky (2005), Keynes was worth just under £480,000 and bequeathed £40,000 to friends and relatives. The balance of this capital sum reverted to King's upon the death of his widow.

verified empirically during the period of Keynes's bursarship, since long-term stock market data was unavailable to him. Keynes's judgment on the dangers of market timing anticipated a consensus that was to emerge decades later among academicians and investment professionals.

4.7.2 The Need for a Long View

Having decided to change his investment method, in 1938 Keynes explained that he considered a patient buy-and-hold approach to be the best way to invest but that this approach was challenging for most investment organizations to follow:

> I believe now that successful investment depends on . . . a steadfast holding of these in fairly large units through thick and thin, perhaps for several years, until either they have fulfilled their promise or it is evident that they were purchased on a mistake.
>
> But it is true, unfortunately, that the modern organization of the capital market requires from the holder of quoted equities much more nerve, patience and fortitude than from the holder of wealth in other forms. (Moggridge 1983, 106–7, 109)

As Chambers, Dimson, and Ilmanen (2012) emphasize, a large, perpetual endowment has a comparative advantage in buying for the long term and in providing liquidity to the market by avoiding procyclical behavior. Such investors should be able to exploit their comparative advantage in sticking to a well-considered investment strategy around which a prior consensus in the investment committee and within the investment organization has emerged.

As such, they can avoid the need to react precipitously during market crises by taking decisions "on the hoof," which run counter to their long-term strategy. Keynes eventually recognized the sense of this approach, but not until he had had time to reflect upon the events of 1929 and its aftermath. Along with most other investors, he had failed to foresee the sharp falls in stocks in October 1929. For the next two years he rotated in and out of UK equities and bonds in an attempt to protect the King's portfolio during the ensuing economic downturn. This experience caused him to reflect as follows:

> I do not think it is the business, far less the duty, of an institutional or other serious investor to be constantly considering whether he should cut and run on a falling market, or to feel himself open to blame if shares depreciate on his hands. I would go much further than that. I should say that it is the duty of a serious investor to accept the depreciation of his holdings with equanimity and without reproaching himself. Any other policy is antisocial, destructive of confidence, and incompatible with the workings of the economic system. (Keynes 1938, 38)

Hence, when the UK and US markets again fell sharply in 1937–1938, he stuck with King's equity positions. In the financial year ended August

1938, King's Discretionary Portfolio had underperformed the UK market by 13.9 percent. Keynes reduced the turnover of the King's equity portfolio from 26 percent to 9 percent. Similarly, having introduced US common stocks into King's portfolio in the early 1930s, he maintained his commitment to US stocks through the market sell-off in 1937–1938. Keynes was unable to pursue the same course at the insurer National Mutual, where he resigned as chairman in 1938 following considerable disagreement over his investment policy.

Unfortunately, these were lessons that King's subsequently failed to heed. Having invested the proceeds from the disposal of their stake in the Blackfriars real estate development into US equities just before the Wall Street crash of October 1987, they sold them again immediately after the market fell sharply and missed the subsequent recovery (Barter 1995).

4.7.3 The Importance of Liquidity

Keynes expressed a clear view about the need to understand the true illiquid nature of some assets. In his day, real estate was the main illiquid asset class and Keynes (1938, 108) warned that:

> Some Bursars will buy without a tremor unquoted and unmarketable investments in real estate which, if they had a selling quotation for immediate cash available at each audit, would turn their hair grey. The fact that you do not [know] how much its ready money quotation fluctuates does not, as is commonly supposed, make an investment a safe one.

Keynes was warning his peers that the apparent low volatility of real estate returns was not a true reflection of underlying returns when a genuine attempt is made to mark these investments to market. Today, private equity is somewhat analogous to real estate in that investors need to be wary of receiving adequate compensation for the illiquidity risk they take on. Hence, even investors with long horizons need to be wary of an overallocation to such illiquid assets, which can compromise any shorter-term liquidity requirements (Ang, Papanikolaou, and Westerfield, forthcoming).

4.7.4 Active-Passive Asset Management

Finally, Keynes was an extremely active investor who constructed equity portfolios that exhibited high double-digit tracking error compared to the UK market. Hence, he wrote:

> [My] theory of risk is that it is better to take a substantial holding of what one believes in than scatter holdings in fields where he has not the same assurance. But perhaps that is based on the delusion of possessing a worthwhile opinion on the matter. (Keynes 1945)

However, he also acknowledged that a fully diversified approach may be more suitable for investors who did not possess skill in equity investing, saying that:

The theory of scattering one's investments over as many fields as possible might be the wisest plan on the assumption of comprehensive ignorance. Very likely that would be the safer assumption to make. (Keynes 1945)

Hence, the alternative for many endowments and foundations with limited time and resources to devote to asset management is to think hard about minimizing management costs and to move toward a passive approach. As we saw when he explained the reasons for his abandoning his top-down investment approach, even Keynes had accepted that excessive transaction costs can eat into investment returns.

4.8 Conclusion

Keynes was an innovative investor with an unconventional investment approach. He had a substantial beneficial impact on King's endowment. He shifted King's asset allocation away from an undiversified reliance upon UK real estate to a diversified portfolio in which equities played a substantial role, despite the restrictions of the Trustee Acts. In so doing, he enabled King's to earn the risk premium on equities available to investors with a long-term horizon and pointed the way forward for subsequent bursars to follow. His stock selection also tilted the portfolio toward value and small-capitalization firms, which gave further opportunity for King's to earn the risk premia associated with these two systematic risk factors.

Furthermore, his experiences managing the King's endowment during the economic turbulence of the 1930s illustrate lessons still relevant to endowments and foundations today. Keynes's observations on investment spoke of the need to understand illiquid assets and the need to tailor investment policy to reflect the organization's investment skills and resources. He pursued unconventional strategies such as investments in commodities and currencies, again foreshadowing his twenty-first-century counterparts. Most relevant to the subject of this volume, he had to learn how to invest during financial crises. In 1929–1930, he confronted the challenges in pursuing a market-timing approach to investment. Thereafter, his switch to an investment approach reflective of the natural advantages accruing to investors with a long horizon allowed him to maintain his commitment to equities in 1937–1938 when prices fell sharply once more.

References

Accominotti, O., and D. Chambers. 2014. "Out-of-Sample Evidence on the Returns to Currency Trading." Centre for Economic Policy Research Discussion Paper no. 9852. http://ssrn.com/abstract=2293684.

Acharya, S., and E. Dimson. 2007. *Endowment Asset Management*. Oxford: Oxford University Press.

Ahearne, A. G., W. L. Griever, and F. E. Warnock. 2004. "Information Costs and Home Bias: An Analysis of US Holdings of Foreign Equities." *Journal of International Economics* 62 (2): 313–36.

Ang, A., D. Papanikolaou, and M. M. Westerfield. Forthcoming. "Portfolio Choice with Illiquid Assets." *Management Science*.

Baker, M., and M. Collins. 2003. "The Asset Portfolio Composition of British Life Insurance Firms, 1900–65." *Financial History Review* 10:137–64.

Banz, R. 1981. "The Relationship between Return and Market Value of Common Stocks." *Journal of Financial Economics* 9 (1): 3–18.

Barter, I. 1995. Bursar's Speech to the Annual Congregation, Kings College Cambridge, November 21. King's Archive KCAR/3/1/4, 1–4.

Bollerslev, T., G. Tauchen, and H. Zhou. 2009. "Expected Stock Returns and Variance Risk Premia." *Review of Financial Studies* 22 (11): 4463–92.

Brown, J., S. Dimmock, J.-K. Kang, and S. Weisbenner. 2014. "How University Endowments Respond to Financial Market Shocks: Evidence and Implications." *American Economic Review* 104 (3): 931–62.

Burton, H., and D. C. Corner. 1968. *Investment and Unit Trusts in Britain and America*. London: Elek.

Cain, J. H. 1942. *College and University Investments and Income, 1925–1941*. Washington, DC: American Council on Education Studies.

Campbell, J., and L. Viceira. 2002. *Strategic Asset Allocation: Portfolio Choice for Long-Term Investors*. Oxford: Oxford University Press.

Cavalli, N., and C. Cristiano. 2012. "Keynes' Speculation in the London Tin Market, 1921–30." In *Speculation and Regulation in Commodity Markets: The Keynesian Approach in Theory and Practice*, edited by M. C. Marcuzzo, 57–78. Rapporto tecnico, Dipartimento Scienze Statistiche, Sapienza, 21.

Chambers, D., and E. Dimson. 2013. "John Maynard Keynes, Investment Innovator." *Journal of Economic Perspectives* 27 (3): 213–28.

Chambers, D., E. Dimson, and J. Foo. Forthcoming. "Keynes the Stock Market Investor: A Quantitative Approach." *Journal of Financial and Quantitative Analysis*.

Chambers, D., E. Dimson, and A. Ilmanen. 2012. "The Norway Model." *Journal of Portfolio Management* 38 (2): 67–81.

Chambers, D., E. Dimson, and C. Spaenjers. 2014. "The Art Collection of John Maynard Keynes." Paper presented at the Art, Minds and Market conference, New Haven, CT, Yale School of Management, March.

Cristiano, C., and N. Naldi. 2012. "Keynes' Activity on the Cotton Market and the Theory of the 'Normal Backwardation': 1921–1929." In *Speculation and Regulation in Commodity Markets: The Keynesian Approach in Theory and Practice*, edited by M. C. Marcuzzo, 25–56. Rapporto tecnico, Dipartimento Scienze Statistiche, Sapienza, 21.

Davenport, N. 1975. "Keynes in the City." In *Essays on John Maynard Keynes*, edited by M. Keynes. Cambridge: Cambridge University Press.

Dimson, E., P. R. Marsh, and M. Staunton. 2002. *Triumph of the Optimists: 101 Years of Global Investment Returns*. Princeton, NJ: Princeton University Press.

———. 2014. *Global Investment Returns Sourcebook 2014*. Zurich: Credit Suisse Research Institute.

Dimson, E., S. Nagel, and G. Quigley. 2003. "Capturing the Value Premium in the UK." *Financial Analysts Journal* 59 (6): 35–45.

Dunbabin, J. 1975. "Oxford and Cambridge College Finances, 1871–1913." *Economic History Review* 28:631–47.

Fama, E., and K. French. 1992. "The Cross-Section of Expected Returns." *Journal of Finance* 47 (2): 426–65.

Fantacci, L., M. C. Marcuzzo, and E. Sanfilippo. 2010. "Speculation in Commodities: Keynes' Practical Acquaintance with Future Markets." *Journal for the History of Economic Thought* 32:1–22.

Foo, J. 2014. "Essays on Long Term Investing." PhD diss., Cambridge University.

Foresti, T., and E. Sanfilippo. 2012. "An Analysis of Keynes' Investments in the Wheat Futures Markets: 1925–1935." In *Speculation and Regulation in Commodity Markets: The Keynesian Approach in Theory and Practice*, edited by M. C. Marcuzzo, 79–105. Rapporto tecnico, Dipartimento Scienze Statistiche, Sapienza, 21.

French, K., and J. Poterba. 1991. "Investor Diversification and International Equity Markets." *American Economic Review* 81 (2): 222–6.

Goetzmann, W. N., J. Griswold, and A. Tseng. 2010. "Educational Endowments in Crises." *Journal of Portfolio Management* 36 (4): 112–23.

Hannah, L. 1986. *Inventing Retirement: The Development of Occupational Pensions in Britain*. Cambridge: Cambridge University Press.

Holder, M. E., and R. J. Kent. 2011. "On the Art of Investing According to Keynes." *Journal of Portfolio Management* 37 (3): 4–6.

Kent, R. J. 2012. "Keynes's Investment Activities While in the Treasury during World War I." *History of Economics Review* 56:1–13.

King's College Archive Centre, Cambridge, Administrative Records, KCAR.

King's College Archive Centre, Cambridge, Governing Records, KCGB.

King's College Archive Centre, Cambridge, The Papers of Richard Ferdinand Kahn, RFK.

Keynes, J. M. 1925. "An American Study of Shares versus Bonds as Permanent Investments." In *The Collected Writings of John Maynard Keynes*, vol. 12, edited by Elizabeth Johnson and D. E. Moggridge, 247–52. Cambridge: Cambridge University Press.

———. 1936. *The General Theory of Employment, Interest and Money*. London: Macmillan.

———. 1938. "Post Mortem on Investment Policy." King's College Cambridge, May 8, King's Archive, PP/JMK/KC/5/7.

———. 1945. Letter to F. C. Scott, February. King's Archive, JMK/PC/1/9/366.

Keynes Picture Bequest, King's College Cambridge, King's Archive PP/RFK/3/53, 273 and 387.

Lewis, K. K. 1999. "Trying to Explain Home Bias in Equities and Consumption." *Journal of Economic Literature* 37 (2): 571–608.

Moggridge, D. E. 1992. *Maynard Keynes: An Economist's Biography*. London: Routledge.

———, ed. 1983. *The Collected Writings of John Maynard Keynes*, vol. XII. Cambridge: Cambridge University Press.

Neild, R. 2008. *Riches and Responsibility: The Financial History of Trinity College, Cambridge*. Cambridge: Granta Editions.

Pierce, T. 1993. "Keynes' Personal Investing: Activities and Beliefs." *Social Science Journal* 30 (1): 13–22.

Saltmarsh, J. 1958. *King's College: A Short History*. Cambridge: Cambridge University Press.

Scott, P. 1996. *The Property Masters*. London: E. & F. N. Spon.

Sharpe, W. F. 1992. "Asset Allocation: Management Style and Performance Measurement." *Journal of Portfolio Management* Winter:7–19.

Shiller, R. J. 2005. *Irrational Exuberance*, 2nd ed. Princeton, NJ: Princeton University Press.

Skidelsky, R. 2005. *John Maynard Keynes, 1883–1946: Economist, Philosopher, Statesman.* New York: Penguin Books.

Smith, E. L. 1924. *Common Stocks as Long Term Investments.* New York: Ferris Printing Company.

Tobin, J. 1974. "What is Permanent Endowment Income?" *American Economic Review* 64 (2): 427–32.

Turner, M. E., J. V. Beckett, and B. Afton. 1997. *Agricultural Rent in England 1690–1914.* Cambridge: Cambridge University Press.

Wilkinson, L. P. 1980. *A Century of King's, 1873–1972.* Cambridge: King's College.

Woods, J. E. 2013. "On Keynes as an Investor." *Cambridge Journal of Economics* 37 (2): 423–42.

5

The Supply of and Demand for Charitable Donations to Higher Education

Jeffrey R. Brown, Stephen G. Dimmock, and
Scott Weisbenner

Charitable donations are an important source of funding for higher education, equaling 6.5 percent of total university and college spending in 2011.[1] For research/doctoral institutions, donations are even more important, equaling 10.5 percent of total spending. Roughly speaking, these donations are split between current-use gifts, which can be spent immediately, and capital gifts, which are used for buildings or added to the university's endowment fund. Payouts from these endowments, which are themselves the result of past donations, are also an important source of funding, equaling an additional 5.2 percent of research/doctoral universities' total spending (see Brown et al. 2012).

Given the importance of donations to university budgets, effective financial management of a university requires understanding the expected size of donations *and* how donations are correlated with other revenues and with expenditure needs. When universities are exposed to a broad economic downturn—such as the recent financial crisis and Great Recession—many of their revenue sources suffer simultaneous shocks. For example, during an economic downturn, endowment-dependent universities suffer reductions

Jeffrey R. Brown is the William G. Karnes Professor of Finance at the University of Illinois at Urbana-Champaign and a research associate of the National Bureau of Economic Research. Stephen G. Dimmock is an assistant professor at Nanyang Technological University. Scott Weisbenner is professor of finance and a James F. Towey Faculty Fellow at the University of Illinois at Urbana-Champaign and a research associate of the National Bureau of Economic Research.

The authors are grateful to the participants in the NBER preconference "Financial Crisis and Higher Education" for helpful comments and suggestions. We are grateful to Matt Hamill and Ken Redd of NACUBO and John Griswold of the Commonfund for assistance with data and for helpful discussions. For acknowledgments, sources of research support, and disclosure of the authors' material financial relationships, if any, please see http://www.nber.org/chapters/c12859.ack.

1. http://www.cae.org/content/pdf/VSE_2011_Press_Release.pdf.

in endowment payouts, state universities may need to absorb a reduction in appropriations due to fiscal pressure on the state, and there may also be public pressure to keep tuition low. Thus, the relation between charitable donations and economic shocks is important for understanding whether donations help to hedge, or, in contrast, exacerbate, the volatility of a university's revenues.

Of course, the same economic forces that affect other revenue sources to a university may also have a direct effect on donations. Indeed, we posit that there are two potentially offsetting effects that are important to disentangle. On the supply side, potential donors (e.g., alumni, corporations, etc.) may suffer a reduced capacity to give during bad economic times. Assuming that donations to a university are a normal good for donors, we would expect donations to fall when donors' incomes and asset values decline. On the other hand, the demand for donations increases during an economic downturn, as universities seek to maintain their operations in the face of declining resources from other sources. In essence, the marginal value of a donated dollar—especially a dollar that can be used for current spending—increases during bad economic times.

It is quite difficult to disentangle these two offsetting effects using only cross-sectional or aggregate time-series data. In this chapter, we attempt to separately identify these effects in panel data by using plausibly exogenous sources of variation on both the supply and demand side of the donations market, while controlling for university fixed effects. On the supply side, we proxy for potential donors' resources by using state-level measures of average income, house values, and the equity returns of firms headquartered in the same state as the university. On the demand side, we use shocks to a university's endowment as a measure of a university's demand for donations. Specifically, we construct a measure of endowment shocks that weights endowment returns by the size of the endowment relative to total university costs. In addition to university fixed effects, we also use region-by-Carnegie classification fixed effects to control for a wide range of both observable and unobservable characteristics that might otherwise lead to spurious correlations.

Our results indicate that both supply- and demand-side factors are important determinants of charitable giving to higher education. On the supply side we find that overall giving to higher education institutions is positively and significantly correlated with per capita income, the returns of local stocks, and house values. Put simply, when donors are doing better financially they donate more to higher education. On the demand side we find that when a university suffers an endowment shock donors respond by increasing donations to the school. Importantly, we show that it is not endowment returns that matter, as returns might be correlated with donors' economic well-being in a way that may not be controlled for by our supply-side variables. Rather, consistent with a measure of a university's demand for donations, it is the return weighted by the size of the endowment shock relative to the university's total costs that has a significant effect.

Additional supporting evidence comes from separately examining capital donations versus current-use donations. We find that capital donations—for which use of the funds is long term and typically more restricted—are more responsive to our proxies for donor ability (i.e., income and house prices). In contrast, current-use donations (which are more highly valued by universities during an economic downturn as a substitute for other declining resources) are much more responsive to endowment shocks. In other words, when a university suffers a negative endowment shock, which in turn leads to a decline in contemporaneous endowment payouts to the university (see Brown et al. 2012), donors respond to the need for immediate resources by directing gifts toward current use. Interestingly, these gifts do not appear to come at the expense of capital donations, at least after conditioning on the same set of covariates.

This chapter proceeds as follows. Section 5.1 provides background on donations to universities and reviews the literature. Section 5.2 introduces the data and explains the empirical strategy. Section 5.3 presents and discusses the empirical results. Section 5.4 concludes.

5.1 Background and Literature Review

Educational institutions are the second largest recipients of charitable donations in the United States, second only to religious institutions. In 2011, it is estimated that individuals and corporations donated $39 billion to educational institutions, which is about 13 percent of all charitable donations to any cause.[2] As with other charitable giving, donations to higher education are generally tax deductible,[3] and thus gifts to colleges and universities represent a significant "tax expenditure" for the federal treasury.

Charitable donations to a university can take the form of current-use gifts or capital gifts. Current-use gifts can be fully spent in the year received or according to the schedule provided by the donor. Capital gifts are for the university's long-term use, and come in two major types: gifts for buildings and gifts to the university's endowment funds. In the latter case, the investment income generated by the endowment provides support for the university in perpetuity. As discussed in Brown et al. (2012), endowments have grown enormously in importance for universities over the past few decades, although there is substantial heterogeneity in the extent to which universities

---

2. See http://www.voanews.com/content/us-charitable-donations-near-300-billion/1212970 .html.

3. In general, donations to colleges and universities are deductible from income for those itemizing expenses on their tax returns at the federal level. However, only 80 percent of donations made to athletic departments are deductible: this is Congress' way of approximating the noncharitable portion of such gifts (e.g., access to better football tickets).

rely on endowment income. According to our data (which we will discuss in more detail below), about 48 percent of donations to universities in the 2008/9 academic year ($12.4 billion total) were capital gifts, whereas the remaining 52 percent ($13.2 billion total) were current-use gifts. We will show below that these two types of gifts exhibit differential sensitivities to the economic environment, a factor that is important for universities to consider when planning and managing financial risks.

A number of papers have analyzed the determinants of charitable contributions in general, and contributions to higher education specifically. Due to the tax deductibility of charitable contributions, a large literature in public finance has examined how marginal tax rates affect charitable giving (e.g., Auten, Cilke, and Randolph 1992; Auten, Sieg, and Clotfelter 2002; Clotfelter 2012). Specific to higher education, a number of papers have examined the determinants of overall giving as well as of alumni giving.[4] These papers tend to find that educational quality and student involvement in campus activities are associated with greater alumni donations. Further, alumni donations are higher at universities that spend more on fundraising and at universities that admit students from wealthier families. Other researchers have focused on carefully identifying the impact on donations of specific factors such as financial aid granted to alumni when they were students (e.g., Dugan, Mullin, and Siegfried 2000; Cunningham and Cochi-Ficano 2002; Meer and Rosen 2012), the school's recent athletic performance (e.g., Rhoads and Gerking [2000], and cites therein; Meer and Rosen [2009b]), and self-interested giving (e.g., Butcher, Kearns, and McEwan 2011; Meer and Rosen 2009a).

The strand of the literature that is most relevant to ours is that examining whether donations are crowded out by other university resources. Oster (2001) uses the Voluntary Support of Education (VSE) data to examine whether endowment growth crowds out donations. She finds evidence of crowding out in the 1999 cross section, although there are concerns about identification due to unobserved differences across universities. When she controls for fixed effects, using panel data from the early 1980s through 1997, she finds no evidence of crowding out in the early years of her sample, although she continues to find some evidence of crowding out in later years. Earlier papers (e.g., Roberts 1984; Kingma 1989; Steinberg 1993) also report small crowding-out effects. Segal and Weisbrod (1998) examine whether donations are crowded out by commercial revenues, and find the opposite: the two revenue sources tend to positively covary.

Our results also relate to the literature on university endowment funds. There is also a small theoretical literature that considers (among other

---

4. Examples include Steinberg (1987); Baade and Sundberg (1996); Harrison, Mitchell, and Peterson (1995); Shulman and Bowen (2000); Cunningham and Cochi-Ficano (2002); Clotfelter (2003); and Ehrenberg and Smith (2003).

things) the joint relation of donation risk and endowment fund risk. Tobin (1974) argues that universities should ignore donation risk when making endowment decisions. In contrast, Black (1976) and Merton (1992) argue that universities should hedge donation risk through their portfolio allocations of endowment assets. Consistent with this hedging argument, Dimmock (2012) shows that universities with greater volatility of revenues (which include revenues from current-use donations) hold less volatile endowment portfolios. However, Brown et al. (2012) show that universities do not alter endowment fund payout rates to smooth out fluctuations in other revenues. Although several studies have shown that at least some endowments appear able to generate alpha (Lerner, Schoar, and Wang 2008; Brown, Garlappi, and Tiu 2010; Barber and Wang 2011), a factor that could influence a donor's decision of whether and when to give, these studies suggest that alpha is generated by allocations to risky alternative asset classes such as hedge funds, private equity, and venture capital. As shown by Dimmock (2012), the ability of universities to invest in these alternative asset classes depends, in turn, on the riskiness of the universities' nonendowment revenues, such as from donations.

In this chapter, we provide new evidence on how broader economic and financial market shocks affect donations to colleges and universities, taking into account both supply and demand effects. An important advance over the existing literature on donations is that we are able to separately identify these supply and demand effects by using plausibly exogenous variation in the size of the budget shocks faced by universities that result from endowment investment and payout decisions. Additionally, we use state-level measures of income, house values, and equity returns to identify the response of donations to economic shocks to likely donors.

5.2 Data and Empirical Strategy

5.2.1 Data and Sample

We combine data from multiple sources in this study, so as to create a data set with information on university finances, donations, and endowment funds, as well as on economic shocks. Our data source for university finances is the Integrated Postsecondary Education Data System[5] (IPEDS), collected by the National Center for Educational Statistics, a division of the US Department of Education. The IPEDS includes information from each university's financial statements, as well as university characteristics such as whether the university is public or private. Providing information through IPEDS is mandatory for all US postsecondary institutions, and institutions

---

5. For more information about this data set, see: http://nces.ed.gov/ipeds/.

that fail to provide information are barred from accessing federal funding and their students are ineligible for federally guaranteed student loans.

Our sources for university endowment fund data are a series of annual surveys produced by the National Association of College and University Business Officers (NACUBO) and by the Commonfund.[6] For the period 1997–2008, our endowment data come from the NACUBO Endowment Survey. Beginning in 2009, NACUBO joined forces with the Commonfund to produce the NACUBO-Commonfund Endowment Survey, which is our source of endowment data for the 2008/9 academic year.

Our source for data on university donations is the Voluntary Support of Education (VSE) data set produced by the Council for Aid to Education.[7] The VSE contains detailed information on charitable contributions to universities, including donation amounts, the purpose of gifts, and donor type. We merge the IPEDS data, endowment data, and VSE data by hand, matching on university name.

We use data from two additional sources for some of our measures of economic shocks. We use state-level economic variables from the Federal Reserve Economic Data (FRED) produced by the St. Louis Federal Reserve Bank.[8] We also create state-level stock return portfolios using data from the Center for Research in Securities Prices (CRSP) and Compustat databases.

5.2.2 Variables and Summary Statistics

From the data sources just described, we create the variables summarized in table 5.1 (See appendix table 5A.1 for variable definitions.) The summary statistics are pooled over the period 1997–2009, where year indicates the academic year end, that is, 2009 indicates either values for the period July 2008 through June 2009 (for flow variables), or values as of June 2009 (for stock variables). The average university in our sample has total costs of $288.6 million, while the average endowment fund is $451.9 million. On average, the endowment-to-university cost ratio is 1.83 across universities during the sample.

The average university in our sample receives donations of $31.2 million per year, equal to 15 percent of total costs.[9] Both the time-series and

6. For more information on this data set, see: http://www.nacubo.org/Research/NACUBO-Commonfund_Study_of_Endowments.html.

7. For more information about the VSE and the Council for Aid to Education, see: http://www.cae.org/content/pro_data_trends.htm.

8. See http://research.stlouisfed.org/fred2/.

9. In the introduction, we cited figures from the Council for Aid to Education stating that in 2011 aggregate donations to universities totaled 6.5 percent of aggregate university costs. The ratio of 15 percent, reported in table 5.1, is equal weighted across all universities in our sample, over the full sample period. The value-weighted average donation-to-cost ratio for the universities in our sample is 8.7 percent as of 2009 (our most recent data). Thus, the universities in our sample appear to be slightly more dependent on donations than the overall population of universities.

Table 5.1   Summary statistics of universities, donations to universities, and state economic conditions, 1997–2009

	Mean	Std. Dev.	10th	25th	Median	75th	90th
University size and donation-to-university measures							
Total university costs ($M)	288.6	531.6	24.1	40.7	86.1	266.0	765.5
Endowment assets (market value, $M)	451.9	1,758.8	17.5	36.5	91.6	280.0	840.9
Endowment-to-university cost ratio	1.83	2.51	0.15	0.40	1.02	2.18	4.26
Total donations to university ($M)	31.2	66.0	2.5	4.5	9.4	24.0	76.5
Total donations-to-university cost ratio	0.15	0.14	0.03	0.06	0.11	0.20	0.31
Capital donations to university ($M)	14.9	32.5	0.9	2.0	5.1	12.9	34.2
Current-use donations to university ($M)	16.3	36.4	1.1	1.9	4.0	10.4	43.0
Ratio of capital donations to total donations	0.51	0.20	0.24	0.37	0.52	0.66	0.76
Number of individual donors	12,372	17,323	1,823	3,475	6,268	13,214	30,791
Number of individuals solicited	61,724	81,600	9,821	16,183	29,949	70,507	159,019
Supply and demand factors for donations to university							
Annual change in income per capita in the state (%)	0.036	0.027	0.003	0.022	0.037	0.055	0.070
Annual change in house price index in the state (%)	0.046	0.065	−0.030	0.022	0.046	0.075	0.120
Stock return of firms in state (equal weight)	0.094	0.208	−0.193	−0.037	0.114	0.207	0.340
Stock return of firms in state (value weight)	0.057	0.218	−0.243	−0.095	0.084	0.208	0.298
Return of university endowment	0.062	0.122	−0.101	−0.019	0.084	0.156	0.195
Shock to university endowment	0.123	0.505	−0.122	−0.008	0.041	0.179	0.457
State government appropriations to university ($M)	45.3	91.6	0.0	0.0	0.0	51.7	160.8
Ratio of state appropriations to university costs	0.12	0.18	0.0	0.0	0.0	0.27	0.40
Annual change in University Costs (%)	0.053	0.101	−0.014	0.029	0.058	0.086	0.118
University is private institution?	0.65	0.48	0.0	0.0	1.0	1.0	1.0
University is doctoral institution?	0.29	0.46	0.0	0.0	0.0	1.0	1.0

Source: IPEDS.

Notes: Year represents academic year (e.g., 2009 represents the 2008/9 academic year). "Shock to university endowment" represents the product of the return on the endowment and the lagged endowment-to-university cost ratio (i.e, the fall in endowment value attributed to returns normalized by last year's university budget).

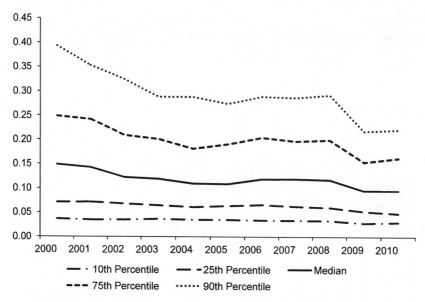

Fig. 5.1 Total donations to total costs

cross-sectional variation in the donations-to-costs ratio are summarized in figure 5.1. This figure shows a small overall decline in this ratio over time; although donations rose over this period, this was more than offset by the increase in university costs. The cross-sectional dispersion in the 2007–2008 period shows that the proportional decline in giving was greater for universities with higher ratios of donations-to-total costs. These donations are nearly evenly divided between capital gifts to current-use gifts. Capital gifts include all gifts that cannot be immediately spent, but instead are intended to provide ongoing support for the university.[10] Current-use gifts include all gifts that can be immediately spent by the university. From the VSE data we are also able to see the number of individual donors that the university solicited for a donation, as well as the number of individuals who made a donation to the university.

In the lower half of table 5.1, we summarize the variables that measure shocks to the supply of and demand for donations. Changes in per capita income and the housing price index for the states are both calculated using data from the FRED data set. The housing price index is based on data provided by the Federal Housing Finance Agency, and is calculated following the method proposed by Case and Shiller (1989) as described by Calhoun (1996).

---

10. During our sample period, approximately one-third of capital gifts were gifts for the construction or renovation of buildings. The remaining gifts were for endowment funds.

Using state headquarter locations from the Compustat database and stock returns from the CRSP database, we calculate equal and value-weighted returns for portfolios composed of all firms headquartered in each state. Following Brown et al. (2012), we define endowment shocks as follows:

$$(1) \qquad \text{Shock}_{i,t} = \text{Return}_{i,t} \times \frac{\text{Endowment Fund Size}_{i,t-1}}{\text{Total University Costs}_{i,t-1}}$$

where subscript i denotes the university and subscript t denotes the academic year. This variable captures the idea that a university with a large endowment-to-cost ratio may be more responsive to endowment returns than a university with a small endowment-to-cost ratio. For intuition, consider the extremes: a university that relies on endowment income to cover the majority of its expenses would likely respond to a given percentage return differently than a university whose endowment is a trivial share of its expenses. In essence, this means that there is variation in the "shock" variable arising from both the rate of return realized by the endowment and the size of the endowment relative to university costs. One can also think of the "shock" variable as the ratio of the change in the dollar value of the endowment attributable to its performance to the dollar flow of university expenditures.

5.2.3 Empirical Strategy

Our primary dependent variable is the log of total donations, although in some specifications we also separately examine current-use donations and capital donations. In our analysis we include measures of both supply- and demand-side determinants of donations, and we make use of the panel structure of the data to control for both university and year-by-Carnegie classification fixed effects.

Our basic empirical specification is as follows:

$$(2) \quad \ln\left(Donations_{i,t}\right) = \beta_1 \cdot \ln\left(Avg\ Income_{s,t}\right) + \beta_2 \cdot \ln\left(House\ Price_{s,t}\right)$$

$$+ \beta_3 \cdot Stock\ Return_{s,t} + \beta_4 \cdot Endowment\ Shock_{i,t}$$

$$+ \beta_5 \cdot X_{i,t} + \mu_i + \delta_{c,t} + \varepsilon_{i,t}$$

The dependent variable is the log of donation to university i in year t. The first set of explanatory variables are meant to proxy for the impact of the economy on a donor's ability to contribute, and includes the log of average state income, log average state house price, and average in-state stock return for state s in year t. The endowment shock variable measures the size of the endowment's return shock relative to the size of the university's operating budget. The X is a vector of other control variables, μ_i represents university fixed effects, and $\delta_{c,t}$ represents Carnegie classification-by-year fixed effects.[11]

---

11. For more information on Carnegie classifications, see http://classifications.carnegie foundation.org/.

The $\varepsilon_{i,t}$ is a mean-zero error term. Because we use a log-log specification for most variables, we can interpret the coefficients as elasticities.

5.3 Results

5.3.1 Baseline Results

We begin our analysis in table 5.2 by implementing the above specification. Looking first at the factors affecting the supply of donations, the significant coefficient of 0.52 on average state income implies that a 10 percent increase in average income in the university's home state increases donations to the university by about 5.2 percent. We also find that a 10 percent increase in home values in the state is associated with a 1.3 percent increase in donations to the university. Additionally, we also test the relation between donations and the returns of in-state companies. Our inclusion of this variable is motivated by the large literature indicating the prevalence of a local geographic "home bias" in individual investor portfolios (e.g., Ivković and Weisbenner 2005).[12] We find that donations respond to the equally weighted average return of stocks that are headquartered in the state: a 10 percentage point increase in the return of in-state companies increases giving by 0.7 percent, a small but statistically significant effect. Taken together, these results support the intuitive hypothesis that university donations rise and fall with the economic well-being of their likely contributors (i.e., home-state residents).

We then turn to an analysis of the demand side by focusing on the endowment shock variable. We find that when a university suffers a negative shock that is equivalent to losing 10 percent of one year's operating budget (i.e., Shock = –0.10), donors respond by increasing donations by 0.2 percent. This effect is significant at the 10 percent level, although its economic magnitude is relatively small. Our preferred interpretation of this finding is that donors respond to the increased need of the university, either on their own or through targeted efforts on the part of the university. We will explore these ideas in more detail below. The results in table 5.2 also show that donations to the university are unrelated to the level of state appropriations to the university.

Column (2) repeats the specification from column (1), but replaces the equal-weighted in-state stock returns with value-weighted in-state stock returns. The results are virtually the same as column (1). In column (3), we also add a control for the state's population; the coefficient for this variable

---

12. We have also constructed alternative measures of average income, home values, and local equity returns that account for the variation in students' state-of-origin. In these alternative measures, each university's shock variable is a weighted average of state shocks, where the weights are equal to the percentage of the university's alumni who were originally from that state. We find extremely similar results for all specifications, and thus we report only the state-level results in the interest of space.

Table 5.2   Determinants of donations to universities

	Ln(donations to university in $), 1997–2009				
	(1)	(2)	(3)	(4)	(5)
Ln(income per capita in state)	0.52**	0.54**	0.51**	0.53**	0.51*
	(0.23)	(0.23)	(0.24)	(0.23)	(0.31)
Ln(house price index in state)	0.13**	0.13**	0.14**	0.11*	0.16**
	(0.06)	(0.06)	(0.06)	(0.06)	(0.08)
Stock return in state (equal weighted)	0.07*		0.07*	0.06*	0.07
	(0.04)		(0.04)	(0.04)	(0.05)
Stock return in state (value weighted)		0.05*			
		(0.03)			
Shock to university endowment	−0.020*	−0.019*	−0.020*		−0.034*
	(0.012)	(0.012)	(0.012)		(0.019)
Ln(state population)			−0.07		
			(0.20)		
Return to university endowment				0.02	
				(0.09)	
Ln(1 + state appropriations to university)	0.002	0.002	0.002	0.003	0.007
	(0.003)	(0.003)	(0.003)	(0.003)	(0.005)
Type of universities included in regression	All	All	All	All	Doctoral
University fixed effects	Yes	Yes	Yes	Yes	Yes
University type-by-year-by-private fixed effects	Yes	Yes	Yes	Yes	Yes
R-squared (within a university)	0.21	0.21	0.21	0.21	0.36
Number of observations	6,661	6,661	6,661	6,869	2,108

Notes: See the appendix for variable definitions. Standard errors, shown in parentheses, allow for correlations among observations of a given university over time as well as cross-sectional correlations.

***Significant at the 1 percent level.

**Significant at the 5 percent level.

*Significant at the 10 percent level.

is insignificant. This is, perhaps, not surprising given that we include university fixed effects, which effectively function as state fixed effects because universities do not move across state lines. This, combined with year fixed effects, means that the log of population would only control for differential population growth trends across states, but the results suggest that any such differential trends are uncorrelated with donations.

The coefficient on the endowment shock variable is quite stable in columns (1), (2), and (3), with significance just above the 10 percent level. As discussed above, we believe that this shock variable—which weights endowment returns by the importance of the endowment to university operations—is a useful proxy for the relative need of a university for additional resources (see Brown et al. [2012], for evidence that endowment shocks have real effects on university operations). To ensure that endowment returns only matter insofar as they affect the university's budget, in column (4) we replace our shock variable with a simple measure of endowment returns. The coefficient on endowment returns is quite small and statistically insignificant. This is comforting, as it confirms that it is our return-measure that accounts for the endowment's importance to the university that is significantly correlated with donations to the university.

Although our specifications above control for an institution's Carnegie classification (and, indeed, interact this classification of the university with year effects), in column (5) we restrict the sample to the subset of doctoral institutions, a group for which endowments and donations play a particularly important role. The effects are, again, nearly identical to those from columns (1) through (3). If anything, the coefficient on the endowment shock variable is slightly larger than before (although, statistically different from zero, it is not statistically different from the prior specifications).

Overall, the results from table 5.2 suggest that donations rise with the economic well-being of the individuals in the state where the university is located (or, alternatively, the states from which many students likely originated). In addition, donations also rise with university need, as proxied by the endowment shock variable. This suggests that macroeconomic shocks affect university donations through both supply and demand channels, although our estimates suggest that the supply channel is quantitatively more important.

5.3.2 Capital Donations versus Current-Use Donations

As noted earlier, donations to universities can be designated for current use or for capital purposes (buildings or the endowment fund), and it is natural to expect that these types of donations may respond differently to economic shocks. Specifically, we expect that during a financial crisis universities' prefer current-use donations. Current-use gifts are particularly valuable during financial crises, because they can be entirely spent in the current period, when the marginal utility of spending is very high. Capital gifts, in contrast, must be consumed over many future periods, in which the marginal utility of spending is likely to be lower.

In table 5.3, we explore these differences. The first column is for comparison purposes only—it is simply a replication of column (1) from table 5.2, and shows the effect on total donations. In column (2), we add the logarithm of lagged university costs as an additional control variable. We add a control for lagged university costs because if donors are sensitive to the university's need, they might increase giving in response to higher costs. There is, however, a potential endogeneity concern in that universities might increase their budgets in anticipation of higher donations. Because of this concern, we show results both with and without this additional control variable. The results in column (2) are similar, although the significance of the coefficient on endowment shocks falls just below the 10 percent level.

In columns (3) and (4), the dependent variable is the log of donations that are specifically designated for capital purposes. The effects of average income, house prices, and stock returns are still significant, and in fact have slightly larger coefficients than in the regression of total donations. The coefficient on the endowment shock variable is of similar size as in the regression of total donations, but due to the larger standard error, it is no longer significant (the p-value drops from approximately 0.1 to 0.3). Thus, it appears that supply-side considerations (i.e., the resources of donors) are quite relevant for capital gifts and we cannot rule out the possibility that endowment shocks have no effect on donation levels.

When we turn to donations for current use, in columns (5) and (6), we find that current-use donations are less responsive to the economic characteristics of the donors, but are significantly responsive to endowment shocks. A negative endowment shock equal to 10 percent of a university's operating budget increases donations for current use by 0.24 percent. It is worth noting, however, that the magnitudes of the coefficients across the "capital" and "current-use" donations are not significantly different, although the extent to which each is statistically different from zero does vary across the specifications.

We are unable to distinguish to what extent the differential responsiveness of capital gifts and current-use gifts to endowment shocks is driven by donor perceptions of needs versus the university's own efforts to guide donations into certain categories. In all likelihood, both effects probably matter: the university may try to steer donors toward current-use donations, and donors may be more responsive to the need for current-use funds following an exogenous negative shock to the university's finances.

The results in columns (3) through (6) suggest that supply-side factors have a stronger effect on capital donations than on current-use donations. This may reflect a preference among donors for "legacy" gifts, which allow the donor to attach her name to a building or professorship in perpetuity. Thus, without the active guidance of the university, donors may naturally

Table 5.3   Regressions of various components of donations to universities, 1997–2009 (all dependent variables are in logarithms)

	Total donations to university		Capital donations		Current–use donations		Number of individual donors		Number of individuals solicited	
	(1)	(2)	(3)	(4)	(5)	(6)	(7)	(8)	(9)	(10)
Ln(income per capita in state)	0.52**	0.52**	0.66*	0.65*	0.37*	0.38*	0.17	0.17	0.04	0.06
	(0.23)	(0.23)	(0.38)	(0.38)	(0.22)	(0.22)	(0.18)	(0.18)	(0.23)	(0.22)
Ln(house price index in state)	0.13**	0.13**	0.21**	0.20**	0.07	0.07	0.16***	0.16***	0.08	0.05
	(0.06)	(0.06)	(0.10)	(0.10)	(0.06)	(0.06)	(0.04)	(0.04)	(0.06)	(0.06)
Stock return in state (equal weighted)	0.07*	0.07*	0.10*	0.10*	0.04	0.04	0.05*	0.05*	0.01	0.01
	(0.04)	(0.04)	(0.06)	(0.06)	(0.03)	(0.03)	(0.03)	(0.03)	(0.04)	(0.04)
Shock to university endowment	−0.020*	−0.018	−0.021	−0.012	−0.024**	−0.024**	−0.001	−0.003	−0.007	0.016
	(0.012)	(0.012)	(0.020)	(0.020)	(0.011)	(0.012)	(0.009)	(0.009)	(0.012)	(0.011)
Ln(1 + state approp. to university)	0.002	0.002	0.004	0.003	0.000	0.000	−0.004	−0.004	−0.003	−0.004
	(0.003)	(0.003)	(0.005)	(0.005)	(0.003)	(0.003)	(0.002)	(0.002)	(0.003)	(0.003)
Ln(lagged university costs)		0.02		0.10**		−0.00		−0.02		0.36**
		(0.03)		(0.04)		(0.02)		(0.02)		(0.03)
University fixed effects	Yes	Yes	Yes	Yes	Yes	Yes	Yes	Yes	Yes	Yes
Type-by-year-by-private fixed effects	Yes	Yes	Yes	Yes	Yes	Yes	Yes	Yes	Yes	Yes
R–squared (within a university)	0.21	0.21	0.13	0.13	0.26	0.26	0.18	0.18	0.23	0.25
Number of observations	6,661	6,661	6,646	6,646	6,660	6,660	6,592	6,592	6,534	6,534

Notes: See the appendix for variable definitions. Standard errors, shown in parentheses, allow for correlations among observations of a given university over time as well as cross-sectional correlations.

***Significant at the 1 percent level.

**Significant at the 5 percent level.

*Significant at the 10 percent level.

gravitate toward capital donations. The greater effect of supply-side factors on capital donations may be related to one of the key differences between current-use and capital donations. Capital donations tend to be significantly larger and come from fewer donors. Thus, economic shocks may primarily affect large gifts, rather than smaller donations.

There are two ways in which donations can increase: either the number of donors can increase or the average amount given per donor can increase. In the remaining columns, we explore how each of these factors is affected by our explanatory variables. In columns (7) and (8), the dependent variable is the number of individuals who make a donation, rather than the aggregate amount given to the university. The results show that increases in local house prices and state stock returns lead to a significant increase in the number of donors. In these specifications, however, the effect of per capita income is not significant.

In columns (9) and (10), we regress the number of individuals solicited for gifts on the economic shock variables. None of the results are significant; we fail to find support for the idea that universities change their solicitation efforts in response to either university need or donors' ability to give. There are several possible reasons for this finding. First, in all periods, the university should set the marginal cost of soliciting donations equal to the marginal benefits. During a financial crisis, the marginal benefit of donations is greater to the university, but the marginal cost of diverting resources toward fundraising is also greater. These effects may offset one another. Second, university financial need usually coincides with financial shocks to donors, and so the marginal benefits to fundraising may be lower because donors are less receptive. Finally, as readers who are alumni of US institutions may know from personal experience, many universities solicit virtually all alumni every year.[13] The number of individuals solicited variable does not reflect the intensity of solicitations (i.e., someone receiving ten solicitations is counted the same as someone receiving one solicitation), and it may be the intensity of solicitation, rather than the simple number of individuals contacted, that varies with economic conditions of the university and its likely donors.

5.3.3 Allowing for Lagged Effects

There are numerous reasons to think that donation responses to both supply- and demand-side factors may operate with a partial lag. For example, donors may plan their charitable contributions in advance, and universities, in turn, may take time to adjust their solicitation efforts. Thus, in table 5.4, we augment our basic specifications with a lagged version of all of the independent variables. For example, in column (1) we use the log of total donations as the dependent variable, and regress it against contemporaneous

---

13. The median ratio of solicited alumni to total alumni is 0.90, with 36 percent of universities soliciting greater than 95 percent of their alumni each year.

Table 5.4   Regressions of components of donations to universities allowing for response to lagged conditions, 1997–2009

	Total donations to university (1)	Capital donations (2)	Current-use donations (3)	Number of individual donors (4)	Number of individuals solicited (5)
Ln(income per capita in state)	0.00	−0.28	0.18	−0.16	0.23
	(0.39)	(0.64)	(0.37)	(0.29)	(0.37)
Ln(income per capita in state lagged)	0.67*	1.10*	0.35	0.36	−0.33
	(0.39)	(0.64)	(0.37)	(0.30)	(0.38)
Ln(house price index in state)	0.22*	0.29	0.06	0.06	0.04
	(0.13)	(0.21)	(0.12)	(0.10)	(0.12)
Ln(house price index in state lagged)	−0.10	−0.12	−0.01	0.13	0.06
	(0.12)	(0.20)	(0.12)	(0.09)	(0.12)
Stock return in state (equal weighted)	0.08**	0.13**	0.04	0.07**	0.00
	(0.04)	(0.06)	(0.04)	(0.03)	(0.04)
Stock return in state lagged	−0.03	0.03	−0.04	0.02	0.03
	(0.04)	(0.06)	(0.04)	(0.03)	(0.04)
Shock to university endowment	−0.015	−0.021	−0.017	0.004	−0.004
	(0.012)	(0.021)	(0.012)	(0.009)	(0.012)
Shock to univ. endowment lagged	−0.034**	−0.018	−0.031**	−0.014	−0.022
	(0.015)	(0.024)	(0.014)	(0.011)	(0.014)
Ln(1 + state approp. to university)	0.005	0.008	0.003	−0.004	−0.002
	(0.004)	(0.007)	(0.004)	(0.003)	(0.004)
Ln(1 + state approp. to univ. lagged)	−0.004	−0.007	−0.004	0.001	−0.002
	(0.004)	(0.006)	(0.004)	(0.003)	(0.004)

p-value of joint test for:					
Income and income lagged	0.009***	0.049**	0.029**	0.302	0.687
House price and house lagged	0.061*	0.082*	0.332	0.000***	0.072*
Stock return and return lagged	0.432	0.095*	0.951	0.034**	0.593
Shock and shock lagged	0.005***	0.173	0.004***	0.453	0.119
Approp. and approp. lagged	0.812	0.907	0.740	0.298	0.291
University fixed effects	Yes	Yes	Yes	Yes	Yes
Type-by-year-by-private fixed effects	Yes	Yes	Yes	Yes	Yes
R–squared (within a university)	0.22	0.13	0.27	0.19	0.24
Number of observations	6,455	6,440	6,454	6,390	6,334

Notes: See the appendix for variable definitions. All dependent variables are in logarithms. Standard errors, shown in parentheses, allow for correlations among observations of a given university over time as well as cross-sectional correlations.

***Significant at the 1 percent level.

**Significant at the 5 percent level.

*Significant at the 10 percent level.

and lagged income, contemporaneous and lagged house values, and so forth. Because the lagged values of the variables are often correlated with the contemporaneous measures, we examine the F-tests of the joint significance of each contemporaneous/lagged pair of controls in addition to the statistical significance of the individual variables. In general, we find that our earlier results hold, and often have slightly larger cumulative effects. For example, a 10 percent increase in average income increases donations in the following year by 6.7 percent, and the contemporaneous and lagged income variable are jointly highly significant (p-value of .009). The effect of changes in house prices remains significant, but the return of the state stock portfolio is no longer significant.

As discussed in Brown et al. (2012), it is especially important to control for lagged values when analyzing the effect of endowment shocks because university endowments typically follow payout policies that calculate payouts based upon lagged asset values. Thus, endowment shocks can have lasting effects. Consistent with this, we find a significant relation between lagged endowment shocks and donations to the university, with the contemporaneous and lagged effects jointly being highly significant.

As before, when we separate donations into capital gifts (column [2]) versus current-use gifts (column [3]), we find that income, housing, and the stock returns of in-state companies are significant predictors of capital gifts, whereas the combined effect of contemporaneous and lagged endowment shocks is not significant. In contrast, when we focus on current-use gifts, the income variables remain jointly significant, but the effect of house prices and stock returns are not significant. As before, a large endowment shock affects the level of current-use donations. Specifically, a negative endowment shock equal to 10 percent of a university's budget increases current-use donations by 0.17percent in the current year, and by an additional 0.31 percent in the subsequent year.

5.3.4 Asymmetric Effects of Endowment Shocks

In our prior work (Brown et al. 2012), we documented important asymmetries in how university endowment funds adjust payouts in response to positive versus negative endowment shocks. Specifically, we found that universities tend to closely follow their spending guidelines following positive shocks, but actively reduce their payouts below the level specified in their own payout guidelines following a negative shock.

In table 5.5, we explore whether donations also respond asymmetrically to positive versus negative endowment shocks. In column (1), we do not find a significant effect between contemporaneous endowment shocks and total donations. However, when we control for lags in column (2), we find that lagged negative endowment shocks have a significant effect on university donations. Specifically, in the year after a university experiences a negative shock equal to 10 percent of one year's university budget, donations

Table 5.5   Relation between donations to university and financial shocks to the endowment (broken into positive and negative shocks), 1997–2009

	Total donations to university		Capital donations		Current-use donations	
	(1)	(2)	(3)	(4)	(5)	(6)
Shock positive = max(shock, 0)	−0.016	−0.012	−0.038	−0.041	−0.013	−0.003
	(0.019)	(0.020)	(0.032)	(0.034)	(0.018)	(0.019)
Shock positive lagged		−0.011		−0.011		−0.018
		(0.020)		(0.033)		(0.019)
Shock negative = min(shock, 0)	−0.025	−0.019	0.007	0.013	−0.040	−0.039
	(0.028)	(0.030)	(0.045)	(0.049)	(0.026)	(0.029)
Shock negative lagged		−0.098**		−0.030		−0.073*
		(0.041)		(0.068)		(0.039)
p–value of test						
Shock positive + shock positive lagged = 0		0.358		0.216		0.386
p–value of test						
Shock negative + shock negative lag = 0		0.015**		0.827		0.015**
Other contemporaneous RHS controls?	Yes	Yes	Yes	Yes	Yes	Yes
Other lagged RHS controls?	No	Yes	No	Yes	No	Yes
University fixed effects	Yes	Yes	Yes	Yes	Yes	Yes
Type-by-year-by-private fixed effects	Yes	Yes	Yes	Yes	Yes	Yes
R–squared (within a university)	0.21	0.22	0.13	0.13	0.26	0.27
Number of observations	6,661	6,455	6,646	6,440	6,660	6,454

Notes: See the appendix for variable definitions. Dependent variables are in logarithms. "Shock" represents the product of the return on the endowment and the lagged endowment-to-university cost ratio (i.e., the fall in endowment value attributed to returns normalized by last year's university costs). Standard errors, shown in parentheses, allow for correlations among observations of a given university over time as well as cross-sectional correlations.

***Significant at the 1 percent level.

**Significant at the 5 percent level.

*Significant at the 10 percent level.

increase by nearly 1 percent. In contrast, donations do not respond to positive shocks, even with a lag, suggesting that individuals do not stop giving when the university experiences positive shocks, but that they do "step up" and assist following negative shocks. This finding has important implications for the question of whether endowment shocks "crowd out" endowment giving (e.g., Oster 2001). We find no evidence to suggest that positive shocks reduce giving, but there is some evidence that donors help to smooth the results of negative endowment shocks.

In columns (3) through (6), we again separately analyze capital gifts and current-use gifts (both with and without lags). Summarizing these four columns, we find that the effect of lagged negative endowment shocks on donations is concentrated in current-use gifts. It is not difficult to imagine the "sales pitch" that a university would make to donors in this case: "Last year, through no fault of our own, we suffered a large loss in our endowment. The endowment will be fine in the long run (after markets recover), but in the meantime we have an urgent and immediate need for current-use donations so that we can continue to serve our students." This result suggests that donors provide a form of revenue insurance for universities.

5.4 Conclusions

The evidence presented in this chapter suggests that donations to universities are strongly affected by macroeconomic factors through both supply and demand channels. On the supply side, donations increase when the economic resources available to donors—personal income, house values, and equity values—are higher. On the demand side, current-use donations respond to need: when a university suffers a negative endowment shock, donors respond by opening up their checkbooks and providing additional funds. Thus, when the economy as a whole suffers a negative shock (such as the global financial crisis or the Great Recession), these factors partially offset one another. As donors see their own resources dwindle, they are less likely to donate, consistent with charitable donations being a normal good. However, this effect is partially mitigated by the fact that donors appear to respond to the perceived need of the university.

Our findings have implications for the overall financial risk management of a university. Donations, payouts from endowments, tuition, state appropriations, and other income are all part of an overall revenue portfolio for the typical university. As with any portfolio management decision, it is important to consider the covariances of the different components of the portfolio. Donations positively covary with in-state income, home prices, and equity returns, and these same factors likely affect a university's ability to raise tuition revenue, obtain public funding, and so forth. As such, all else equal, a university that seeks to effectively manage the risk of its endowment portfolio would invest in such a way as to limit further correlations. This would involve, for example, underweighting the stocks of in-state companies (and companies in other states from which their student body comes). Of course, it is unclear whether universities think of their endowments in this way. Dimmock (2012) shows that endowment asset allocation is significantly related to the standard deviations of revenues, but fails to find support for the hypothesis that endowment funds consider the correlations between endowment returns and other revenue sources. Our prior work (Brown et al. 2012) suggests that universities manage endowment payout rates so as to maintain the size of the endowment for its own sake, rather than changing payout rates to provide a form of insurance against bad economic outcomes.

Although the endowments themselves are not invested to provide revenue insurance, our evidence suggests that donors are willing to play that role. That is, they are willing to donate more for current use when the university is suffering from economic hard times. Unfortunately, the effectiveness of donors as a form of insurance is severely limited by the fact that the donors are themselves subject to the same macroeconomic shocks. For the sake of illustration, consider the coefficients estimated in column (1) of table 5.2 combined with the median values for the 2008/9 academic year. The direct effect of the median endowment shock in that year implies an increase in donations of 0.4 percent. However, this is more than offset by the decrease in personal income and housing prices as well as the negative returns to the state-stock portfolios, for a net decrease to donations of 2.6 percent.

Appendix

Table 5A.1   Variable definitions

Variables	Data source	Definition
Total university costs	IPEDS	Total costs from the income statement
Endowment assets	NACUBO/Commonfund	$ value of the endowment fund
Endowment-to-university cost ratio		
Total donations to university	VSE	$ donations to university
Total donations-to-university cost ratio		
Capital donations to university	VSE	$ capital donations to the university
Current-use donations to university	VSE	$ donations for current operations of university
Ratio of capital donations to total donations		

(continued)

Table 5A.1   (continued)

Variables	Data source	Definition
Number of individual donors	VSE	no. of alumni, parents, faculty, students, and other individuals who donated
Number of individuals solicited	VSE	no. of alumni, parents, faculty, students, and other individuals who were solicited for a donation
Annual change in income per capita in the state (%)	FRED	Total personal income divided by population
Annual change in House Price Index in the state (%)	FRED	House price index for state
Stock return of firms in state (equal weight)	CRSP/COMPUSTAT	Equal-weighted portfolio returns for the companies headquartered in the state
Stock return of firms in state (value weight)	CRSP/COMPUSTAT	Value-weighted portfolio returns for the companies headquartered in the state
Return of university endowment	NACUBO/Commonfund	Return of the endowment portfolio
Shock to university endowment	IPEDS/NACUBO	Endowment return multiplied by the lagged endowment-to-university cost ratio
State government appropriations to university	IPEDS	$ government appropriations to the university
Ratio of state appropriations to university costs	IPEDS	
Annual change in university costs (%)	IPEDS	
University is private institution?	IPEDS	Indicates if the university is public or private
University is doctoral institution?	IPEDS	Carnegie classification is doctoral

References

Auten, Gerald E., James M. Cilke, and William C. Randolph. 1992. "The Effects of Tax Reform on Charitable Contributions." *National Tax Journal* 45:267–90.

Auten, Gerald E., Holger Sieg, and Charles T. Clotfelter. 2002. "Charitable Giving, Income, and Taxes: An Analysis of Panel Data." *American Economic Review* 92:371–82.

Baade, Robert A., and Jeffrey O. Sundberg. 1996. "What Determines Alumni Generosity?" *Economics of Education Review* 15:75–81.

Barber, Brad M., and Guojun Wang. 2011. "Do (Some) University Endowments Earn Alpha?" Working Paper, Graduate School of Management, University of California, Davis.

Black, Fisher. 1976. "The Investment Policy Spectrum: Individuals, Endowment Funds and Pension Funds." *Financial Analysts Journal* 32:23–31.

Brown, Jeffrey R., Stephen G. Dimmock, Jun-Koo Kang, and Scott Weisbenner. 2012. "How University Endowments Respond to Financial Market Shocks: Evidence and Implications." Working Paper, University of Illinois.

Brown, Keith C., Lorenzo Garlappi, and Cristian Tiu. 2010. "Asset Allocation and Portfolio Performance: Evidence from University Endowment Funds." *Journal of Financial Markets* 13:268–94.

Butcher, Kristen F., Caitlan Kearns, and Patrick J. McEwan. 2011. "Giving Till it Helps? Alumnae Giving and Children's College Options." Working Paper, Wellesley College.

Calhoun, Charles A. 1996. "OFHEO House Price Indexes: HPI Technical Description." Working Paper, Office of Federal Housing Enterprise Oversight.

Case, Karl E., and Robert J. Shiller. 1989. "The Efficiency of the Market for Single-Family Homes." *American Economic Review* 79:125–37.

Clotfelter, Charles T. 2003. "Alumni Giving to Private Colleges and Universities." *Economics of Education Review* 22:109–20.

———. 2012. "Charitable Giving and Tax Policy in the US" Working Paper, Duke University.

Cunningham, Brendan M., and Carlena K. Cochi-Ficano. 2002. "The Determinants of Donative Flows from Alumni of Higher Education: An Empirical Inquiry." *Journal of Human Resources* 37:540–69.

Dimmock, Stephen G. 2012. "Background Risk and University Endowment Funds." *Review of Economics and Statistics* 94:789–99.

Dugan, K., C. Mullin, and J. Siegfried. 2000. "Undergraduate Financial Aid and Subsequent Giving Behavior." Williams Project on the Economics of Higher Education Discussion Papers no. (DP-57). Department of Economics, Williams College.

Ehrenberg, Ronald G., and Christopher L. Smith. 2003. "The Sources and Uses of Annual Giving at Selective Private Research Universities and Liberal Arts Colleges." *Economics of Education Review* 22:223–35.

Harrison, William B., Shannon K. Mitchell, and Steven P. Peterson. 1995. "Alumni Donations and Colleges' Development Expenditures: Does Spending Matter?" *American Journal of Economics and Sociology* 54:397–412.

Ivković, Zoran, and Scott Weisbenner. 2005. "Local Does as Local Is: Information Content of the Geography of Individual Investors' Common Stock Investments." *Journal of Finance* 60:267–306.

Kingma, Bruce. 1989. "An Accurate Measure of the Crowd-Out Effect, Income Effect and Price Effect for Charitable Contributions." *Journal of Political Economy* 97:1197–207.

Lerner, Josh, Antoinette Schoar, and Jialan Wang. 2008. "Secrets of the Academy: The Drivers of University Endowment Success." *Journal of Economic Perspectives* 22:207–22.

Meer, Jonathan, and Harvey S. Rosen. 2009a. "Altruism and the Child-Cycle of Alumni Donations." *American Economic Journal: Economic Policy* 1 (1): 258–86.

———. 2009b. "The Impact of Athletic Performance on Alumni Giving: An Analysis of Micro Data." *Economics of Education Review* 28 (3): 287–94.

———. 2012. "Does Generosity Beget Generosity? Alumni Giving and Undergraduate Financial Aid." *Economics of Education Review* 31 (6): 890–907.

Merton, Robert C. 1992. "Optimal Investment Strategies for University Endowment Funds." In *Continuous Time Finance*, rev. ed., edited by Robert C. Merton, chapter 21. Malden, MA: Blackwell.

Oster, Sharon M. 2001. "The Effect of University Endowment Growth on Giving: Is There Evidence of Crowding Out?" Working Paper no. ES-10, Yale University.

Rhoads, Thomas, and Shelby Gerking. 2000. "Educational Contributions, Academic Quality and Athletic Success." *Contemporary Economic Policy* 18:248–58.

Roberts, Russell D. 1984. "A Positive Model of Private Charity and Public Transfers." *Journal of Political Economy* 92:136–48.

Segal, Lewis, and Burton Weisbrod. 1998. "Interdependence of Commercial and Donate Revenues." In *To Profit or Not to Profit*, edited by Burton Weisbrod, 105–28. Cambridge: Cambridge University Press.

Shulman, J., and W. Bowen. 2000. *The Game of Life: College Sports and Educational Values*. Princeton, NJ: Princeton University Press.

Steinberg, Richard. 1987. "Voluntary Contributions and Public Expenditures in a Federalist System." *American Economic Review* 77:24–36.

Steinberg, Richard. 1993. "Does Government Spending Crowd out Donations?" In *The Nonprofit Sector is a Mixed Economy*, edited by Avner Ben-Ner and Benedetto Gui. Ann Arbor, MI: University of Michigan Press.

Tobin, James. 1974. "What is Permanent Endowment Income?" *American Economic Review* 64:427–32.

6

The Impact of the Financial Crisis on Faculty Labor Markets

Sarah E. Turner

What impact has the Great Recession had on the faculty labor market in the United States?[1] In the initial stage of the financial crisis, the relatively widespread announcement of hiring freezes, salary freezes, and work furloughs—particularly at public universities—suggested a nontrivial potential impact of macroeconomic conditions on employment and wages. Because faculty are an "input" in the higher education market, financial shocks to universities affecting hiring and compensation potentially impact student outcomes such as degree attainment, research flows, and the distribution of faculty among colleges and universities.

Unlike demand for other goods and services, which commonly decline in an economic downturn, demand for college and university education tends to increase. As evidence, total enrollment increased from 18.2 million to 20.4 million between fall 2007 and fall 2009. Yet, with substantial declines in state appropriations combined with endowment losses early in the financial crisis, instructional staffing has not adjusted commensurately and there is evidence of a substantial increase in student-faculty ratios, particularly at public colleges and universities.

Sarah E. Turner is University Professor of Economics and Education and chair of the Department of Economics at the University of Virginia and a research associate of the National Bureau of Economic Research.

For acknowledgments, sources of research support, and disclosure of the author's material financial relationships, if any, please see http://www.nber.org/chapters/c12863.ack.

1. The NBER dates the most recent recession as the eighteen-month period from December 2007 to June 2009. In this analysis, we refer more generally to the financial crisis taking hold on a global scale in September 2008. Because the financial crisis hit college and university budgets with some lag, our focus in this chapter is on how faculty salaries and staffing have adjusted since 2008. In addition, the analysis concentrates on employment outcomes in the United States. One unanswered question is whether the financial crisis in the United States increased the flow of recent doctorates and faculty to universities abroad.

The adjustment of the faculty labor market to an economic downturn has potential effects on the "outputs" of higher education in terms of degree attainment and knowledge production. One point of consideration is the extent to which the impact of the Great Recession should be seen as a transitory event, with little long-term consequences, or as a structural change in the market conditions in US higher education.

A related observation is that the pace of adjustment of faculty labor markets is quite slow, particularly outside the most junior or "rookie" hires and nontenure-track appointments. Most fields operate on annual hiring cycles and senior hires generally take at least a year between initial posting and the commencement of a new hire. In all but the most opportunistic cases, movement of faculty in response to the financial crisis would not be initiated until the fall of 2009, with visible relocation not present until 2010. This process of long lags is not only a market characteristic, but places some notable limits on this analysis as much of the available data has yet to be released for years in which the effects of the recession are most likely to be seen.

Among colleges and universities in the United States there is considerable heterogeneity in sources of funds and how these resources have been affected by the fiscal crisis. Indeed, it is well established that US higher education is highly stratified in resources and student inputs, with this stratification increasing markedly in recent decades (Hoxby 2009). This analysis emphasizes the considerable heterogeneity across institutions in both the magnitude of the initial impact of the recent financial crisis and the duration of these effects. There are some indications that the financial crisis may widen stratification among institutions as resource differences determine an institution's capacity to hire at the junior and senior levels, as well as competing for top faculty in particular areas of expertise. A point of emphasis is that extended shocks are likely to have much larger impacts on a university's capacity to hire and retain faculty than even large shocks of short duration.

Perhaps the most significant distinction with lasting consequences for faculty labor markets and overall resources in higher education is the division between public and private colleges and universities. While there is no question that well-endowed institutions faced a significant hit to assets and liquidity at the start of the Great Recession, such shocks have proven to be relatively transitory. In contrast, those institutions receiving substantial state appropriations have faced more extended cuts in funding while also facing significant limitations in the capacity to raise alternative revenues through increased tuition charges. Institutions relying substantially on tuition revenues have also faced extended challenges: lagging incomes (and wealth loss) among families limits their capacity to pay for college and, in turn, the extent to which universities are able to cover (increasing) costs with tuition increases. Public institutions face a particularly difficult challenge as reductions in state support leave increasing tuition as one of the few channels of revenue available to avoid reductions in resources per student or student crowd-out.

The result is that the Great Recession has further widened differences between public and private universities in faculty staffing and, to some degree, salaries. In addition to the growing divergence between public and private institutions, differences among institutions within the private sector have also widened, as tuition-dependent private institutions face significant budgetary challenges.

This analysis begins with a brief discussion of the dynamics of faculty labor markets, outlining the importance of the tenure system, enrollment demand, and revenue structures in shaping faculty employment and wage responses to the Great Recession. In the second section, we provide an overview of employment and wage responses in the Great Recession, comparing the staffing responses in the Great Recession to prior cyclical downturns. This section distinguishes outcomes by faculty rank, focusing particular attention on the "rookie" market or recently minted PhDs, which is of particular significance in academia given the extent to which tenure limits the capacity to adjust employment of more experienced inputs.[2] The third section of the analysis turns to the presentation and testing of hypotheses about the determinants of adjustment of employment and salaries among institutions, examining how revenue sources and local economic conditions impact employment outcomes. In the final section, we consider whether there are discernible long-term implications and lessons from the observed evidence.

6.1 Why Are Faculty Labor Markets Different?
Expected Responses to the Great Recession

The impact of recessionary conditions on faculty labor markets is vastly different than in labor markets in goods-producing sectors. Among the points of contrast to emphasize are the differences in the nature of the employment relationship in faculty labor markets (notably tenure), countercyclical demand in enrollment, and the structure of revenues affected by cyclical shocks.

6.1.1 Faculty Employment Arrangements

First, with a substantial share of faculty at four-year colleges and universities appointed with tenure or in tenure-track appointments, university administrators have limited capacity to terminate employment or close

---

2. A particular area of interest explored in only the most limited way in this analysis is the extent to which the Great Recession changes faculty retirement decisions. One hypothesis is that faculty experiencing large declines in wealth associated with loss of housing value or loss of retirement equity may choose to postpone retirement. Two dimensions make the question of whether the response to the Great Recession differs from other fiscal downturns. First, with the end of mandatory retirement in 1994, many faculty are now unconstrained. In addition, as a higher fraction of faculty are now covered by defined contribution rather than defined-benefit pension plans, we would expect somewhat greater sensitivity to market conditions in retirement decisions.

departments where demand may be lagging or the mode of delivery may be obsolete. Data from the National Study of Postsecondary Faculty indicate that about 92 percent of all full-time faculty and instructional staff were employed at an institution with a tenure system.[3] In turn, of those faculty employed at an institution with tenure, 52 percent held tenure while 22 percent were in a tenure-track position. Thus, the capacity to make major changes in employment may be far more limited than in other sectors of the economy.

While it is possible for colleges and universities to eliminate tenured positions by closing entire departments or programs, the incidence of such restructuring is exceedingly limited (see Johnson and Turner 2009). One might also ask why small departments are not merged with each other to enhance efficiency.

6.1.2 Cyclical Enrollment Demand

Unlike many consumption goods, the student demand for higher education tends to increase during cyclical downturns as an empirical matter. While decreased capacity to finance college reduces enrollment demand or shifts students to relatively low cost institutions,[4] weak labor market conditions correspond to a relatively low opportunity cost of time and greater enrollment demand. Figure 6.1 shows the overall trend in college enrollment in relation to the unemployment rate. The top panel illustrates the secular increase in college enrollment in recent decades while the bottom panel shows the change in enrollment net of the secular trend.

As has been well documented, student enrollment demand is markedly countercyclical. In work conducted before the Great Recession, Fitzpatrick and Turner (2007) examined age-specific responses in college enrollment to state-level variation in the unemployment rate (1977–2003). They found that changes in local unemployment rates produce the largest relative changes in enrollment for those twenty-two and older, with a 1 percentage point change in the local unemployment rate producing about a 0.3 percentage point change in the enrollment for those between the ages of twenty-two and twenty-seven. More recently, Barr and Turner (2013) document considerable procyclicality in postsecondary enrollment for both recent high school graduates and older students in response to the most recent economic downturn.

The intuition is straightforward: as jobs become scarce, the opportunity cost of college falls. The change in enrollment tends to be concentrated among students who are at the margin of attending college, including nontraditional students (Turner 2003). Significantly, much of the increase in

3. US Department of Education, National Center for Education Statistics, 2004 National Study of Postsecondary Faculty, http://nces.ed.gov/das/library/tables_listings/showtable2004 .asp?popup=true&tableID=1313&rt=p.

4. For example, Lovenheim (2011) shows that, particularly for relatively low-income families, changes in housing wealth have a significant effect on enrollment.

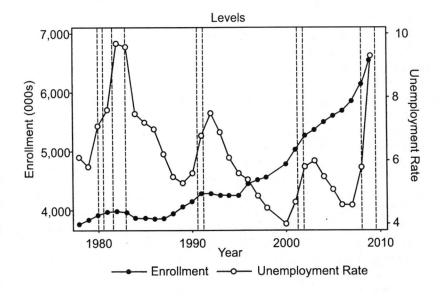

Levels

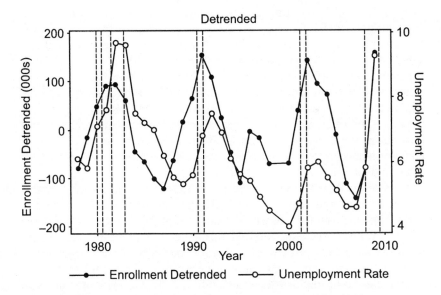

Detrended

Fig. 6.1 Trends in total enrollment and unemployment rates, 1980–2012

Sources: Figure from Barr and Turner (2013). Enrollment data are from NCES institution aggregate enrollment figures derived from HEGIS and IPEDS surveys.

Notes: "Detrended" enrollment removes a cubic trend from the series. Vertical lines indicate recessions as benchmarked by NBER.

college enrollment comes from students outside the pool of recent high school graduates (Betts and McFarland 1995; Christian 2006). There is far less research evidence to draw on with respect to the question of how recessions affect college choice. There is some evidence to suggest that fiscal downturns may lead moderate income students who are unlikely to be eligible for financial aid to shift from private colleges and universities to public colleges and universities, though such effects are not well established. (A point that we return to later in this chapter is that this enrollment response is disproportionately concentrated at open access, four-year institutions and community colleges.)

Increases in enrollment are most prominent at colleges and universities that are relatively elastic in supply, including open access four-year institutions. These institutions are generally nonresidential and focus degree and certificate programs in technical, professional, and vocational fields. In addition, there is some evidence that the enrollment response in the Great Recession has been somewhat greater than in prior cyclical downturns, resulting in part from a jump in the generosity of federal Title IV funding (including the increase in the maximum Pell grant). The Pell grant increased to a level of $5,500 in 2010, greater than the constant dollar value of the 1976 level of $5,345, which is an appreciable rise over the low of $3,430 in 1994 in constant dollars (Barr and Turner 2013). The increasing generosity of the Pell program and the rise in the number of recipients has contributed to a substantial increase in program expenditures over the last decade, with total expenditures rising from $7.9 billion in 2000 to $35.6 billion in 2010 (College Board 2011). The American Opportunity Tax Credit introduced under the American Recovery and Reinvestment Act of 2009 (ARRA) supplanted the Hope and Lifetime Learning credits with the rebranded tax credits, not only raising the annual credit from $1,800 to $2500, but also expanding the credit to higher- and lower-income taxpayers by expanding the phase-out range and adding a provision for refundability.

The College Board (2011) estimates that these tax-based expenditures for college education increased from $4.75 billion in 1998 to $14.83 billion in 2010. A distinguishing feature of the most recent recessionary period is the extent to which the generosity of federal financial aid programs such as Pell, but also tuition tax credits, increased at the start of the cyclical downturn.

When thinking about faculty staffing responses to the Great Recession, it is important to distinguish "new demand" and "replacement demand." To the extent that the increase in the enrollment demand in the Great Recession is purely transitory, one might think of it as imprudent for a university to respond to a short-term growth in student demand with a long-term hiring investment (such a tenure or tenure-track position). In this regard, we would expect those institutions with the largest cyclical increases in enrollment demand to respond in large part with increases in temporary staffing.

6.1.3 Revenue Streams in the Great Recession

While increased demand might be thought of as "good news" for faculty labor markets, substantial shocks to other college and university revenue sources during the financial crisis have had an adverse effect on tenure-track hiring and salaries in recent years. For most colleges and universities, tuition ("fee for service") covers only a portion of college and university operating expenditures. Students at many colleges and universities are the recipients of substantial subsidies from public appropriations and private endowment funds. Over the course of the last several decades, there is evidence that student subsidies have increased at the most selective institutions (particularly in the private sector), while declining somewhat in the public sector (see Hoxby 2009; Bound, Lovenheim, and Turner 2010).

A marked feature of the Great Recession is the extent to which both appropriations from public sources and private investment returns declined. Figure 6.2 shows state appropriations per full-time equivalent (FTE) at public institutions along with total state appropriations by year; figure 6.3 presents endowment returns. One point to note is that the timing of the decline in endowment returns actually modestly precedes the decline in state appropriations, suggesting that the impact of the fiscal crisis started somewhat earlier for endowment-dependent privates than for public institutions dependent on state appropriations. While 2007/8 is a "local peak" in appropriations, endowment income started its slide in this year only to fall dramatically in 2008/9.

Yet, while endowment returns have largely recovered in the two most recent years, state appropriations continue to slide on an aggregate level as well as a per-student basis. Moreover, while federal stimulus resources passing through the states may have moderated the impact of declining state resources in 2010 and 2011, this source of funding had largely disappeared by the 2011/12 academic year. For public universities, these funding cuts are layered on top of state funding mechanisms that were in disrepair prior to the recession (Kane, Orszag, and Gunter 2003). Kane, Orszag, and Gunter (2003) identify crowd out from Medicaid as one factor placing downward pressure on state higher-education funding while Rizzo (2004) identifies elementary- and secondary-education funding as another source of fiscal pressure on higher education. The evidence is clear that pressure to reduce state funding on higher education started well before the financial crisis (Bettinger and Williams 2012).

Examination of revenue streams by type of institution serves to illustrate how different types of colleges and universities are impacted by changes in the availability of funding for higher education. Table 6.1 shows the primary revenue sources for four-year colleges and research universities in the public and private sector for selected years from 1999–2009. In the public sector, a notable observation is that the ratio of net tuition (posted

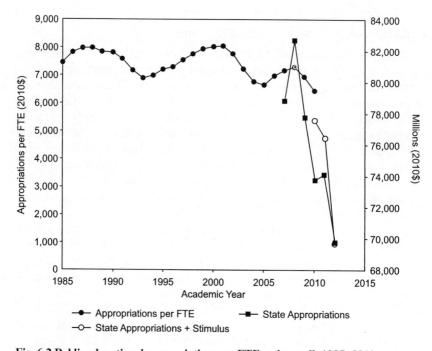

Fig. 6.2 Public educational appropriations per FTE and overall, 1985–2010

Source: State Higher Education Executive Offices and State Higher Education Finance (SHEF) project (http://www.sheeo.org/finance/shef-home.htm).

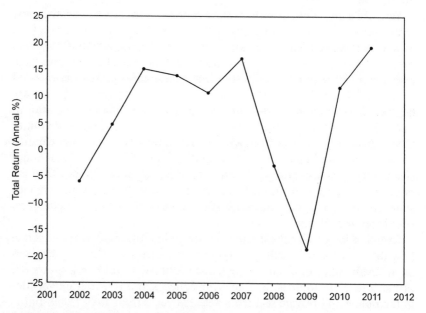

Fig. 6.3 Average annual endowment returns

Source: NACUBO endowment survey.

Table 6.1   Average revenues per FTE student, academic year 1999–2009

	Public			Private-nonprofit		
	Revenues per FTE (2009$)					
	1999	2007	2009	1999	2007	2009
Research institutions						
Net tuition	5,353	7,500	8,030	16,825	19,780	20,363
State and local appropriations	10,370	9,453	8,686	499	783	714
Federal appropriations + grants	4,940	7,908	8,098	9,105	11,431	11,273
Auxiliary enterprises	8,747	10,139	10,915	18,079	22,475	22,142
Operating revenues	29,410	34,752	35,736	43,777	53,661	53,617
Private gifts, investment, endowment return	2,204	3,351	−387	26,612	46,342	−30,256
Total operating revenue	31,614	38,103	35,350	70,389	100,004	23,361
MA institutions						
Net tuition	4,075	5,580	5,923	11,895	14,242	14,864
State and local appropriations	7,411	6,772	6,416	442	345	362
Federal appropriations + grants	1,493	1,990	1,968	1,046	906	892
Auxiliary enterprises	3,009	3,308	3,527	3,612	4,128	4,018
Operating revenues	15,956	17,591	17,778	16,458	19,255	19,762
Private gifts, investment, endowment return	407	614	273	5,096	5,778	−1,258
Total operating revenue	16,351	18,205	18,050	21,537	25,033	18,504

Source: Trends in College Spending 1999–2009. Delta Cost Project.

tuition-institutional aid) to operating revenues is about 0.22 among research universities and about 0.33 at master of arts (MA)-level institutions, implying the importance of subsidies from other sources. While the per-student subsidy from state sources declined between 2007 and 2009 (by 8 percent in the research sector and 5.2 percent in the MA sector), this decline followed secular declines of more than 8 percent between 1999 and 2007. As an accounting matter, the income statement records investment gains and losses along with private gifts on an annual basis that illustrate the large fluctuations in endowment returns. To this end, the magnitude of the 2009 market losses on a per-student basis are readily apparent for 2009 with per-student investment returns and private gifts declining by more than $30,000 among private research institutions. Because private institutions use spending-rule policies to smooth payouts over time, with typical spending rates about 5 percent of assets computed as a moving average over several years,[5] the realized

5. Brown et al. (2010) show that universities do not follow payout rules strictly, but actively reduce payouts when faced with negative (not positive) shocks to returns.

change in spending is appreciably more modest than the overall gains and losses from endowment and private gifts.

Over the course of the last decade, there has been quite a dramatic increase in net tuition revenues defined as the difference between the "sticker price" charges and institutional financial aid. At public institutions, net tuition revenues per FTE increased about 40 percent between 1999 and 2007, followed by increases of 6–7 percent between 2007 and 2009. In turn, net tuitions have also increased at private institutions, albeit from a higher base. For private institutions outside the research universities, tuition is the primary source of revenue and, as a result, changes in family financial conditions that impact capacity to pay for college may affect these institutions most markedly. Still, as "affordability" has become a buzzword in the political dialogue, there are strong limits on the further upward pressure in tuition that can realistically follow. While much of the political dialogue focuses on the increase in the "sticker" price increases,[6] net tuition revenue rises less than a dollar for dollar with increases in posted tuition as the financial need of aid-eligible students increases while the pool of aid-eligible students for whom expected family contribution is less than expected college costs may also increase.

In effect, funding shocks to appropriations from the states and declines in private funding sources effectively shift in the budget constraint to colleges and universities. Consider a simplified university budget constraint in which expenditures on faculty (F at wages w) and expenditures on capital and other inputs (K at price p) equal revenues from state appropriations, federal grants, and net tuition.

$$FW + pK = \text{Appropriations} + \text{Federal Support} + \text{Endowment Returns and Private Gifts} + \text{Net Tuition}.$$

In effect, funding shocks to appropriations from the state- and private-funding sources effectively shift in the budget constraint available to colleges and universities. Limited capacity to substitute capital for labor, combined with few degrees of freedom to reallocate workers, leaves few levers in the hands of university administrators. Moreover, colleges and universities will likely face limited capacity to raise tuition to produce additional revenues. The result is a tough choice between adding students at a "diluted," lower level of resources per student or raising tuition (Bound and Turner 2007).

So, when the financial crisis effectively cuts one or more of the sources of support in this budget constraint, how do universities adjust faculty

---

6. Bowen (2012) notes "The word 'affordability' has achieved iconic status and become a part of the ad wars in the 2012 presidential campaign." Such dialogue follows from attention to reference points such as the rise in the average price of a year at an in-state, public four-year college to $8,244 in 2011/12 from $2,242 (in 2011 dollars) thirty years earlier, which represents an annual growth rate of 4.4 percent beyond inflation (College Board 2011). As College Board data demonstrate, the charges net of financial aid by parents and students have increased much more modestly given the rise in the availability of federal financial aid and efforts by colleges and universities to increase need-based financial aid.

staffing?[7] In effect, the only options for adjustment are in compensation and hiring, with hiring latitude most likely constrained to junior-level appointments. Given the diversity of revenue sources across institutions as well as state-specific variation, we would expect to see considerable differences across universities in their response. Still, while revenue shocks may be local, faculty labor markets are largely integrated and national; the result is that the extent to which an institution can curtail compensation is effectively dictated by a competitive market.

In the next section, we present broad trends in hiring and compensation in the faculty labor market at the national level. In section 6.3, we turn to the measurement of how institutional characteristics and revenue composition explain changes in the faculty labor market in the Great Recession.

6.2 Broad Empirical Context

The sharp declines in revenues from state appropriations and private sources that became evident in 2008/9 brought an immediate response among some public administrators and university leaders. The most publicly visible manifestations of the financial crisis were the across-the-board personnel measures taken at some institutions including suspension of hiring, salary freezes, and furloughs, which amount to reductions in real earnings. In an informal analysis of university websites and student newspapers, we identified 24 of 100 research universities that instituted hiring freezes between the fall of 2008 and the spring of 2009, while an additional fourteen institutions instituted salary freezes. Table 6.2 provides examples of specific policies enacted at Association of American Universities (AAU) and National Association of Independent Colleges and Universities (NAICU) institutions. Especially hard-hit states include California, Maryland, and Illinois, which instituted across-the-board faculty furlough policies.

As is well known to university leaders, such across-the-board policies likely generate some inefficiency because they do not allow for the consideration of differential impacts and returns to staffing cuts. (Indeed, policies requiring cuts in core functions may actually increase costs as institutions must hire more expensive temporary staff or pay overtime in order to meet the needs of basic service provision.) Before turning to the examination of institutional microdata, this analysis charts the staffing and salary changes in the Great Recession in the context of other secular and cyclical trends over the last three decades.

6.2.1 Staffing Trends

Examined over the course of the last several decades, overall faculty-staffing levels have increased unambiguously across institution types. (Figure 6.4

---

7. Private institutions may have greater capacity than public institutions to adjust to temporary revenue shortfalls with intertemporal borrowing.

Table 6.2   **Faculty hiring and compensation policies in response to Great Recession**

A. AAU universities

Institution	Control	Hiring freeze	Salary freeze	Furlough
Indiana University	Public	2010/11 administrative pers.	2009/10 & 2010/11: 2 years of faculty and staff	
The Ohio State University	Public		2009/10	
The Pennsylvania State University	Public		2009/10 & announced March 25, 2011 faculty and salary freezes effective July 1, 2011	
Purdue University	Public		2008/9 & 2009/10: Oct 2010 merit-based increases returned system-wide FY2010 faculty and staff	
Rutgers, The State University of New Jersey	Public			
University of California, Davis	Public		Jan. 14, 2009 top admin. and senior management pay freeze through 2009/10	July 16th, 2009, a 2009/10 SYSTEM- WIDE furlough faculty and staff required 11–26 days
University of California, Berkeley	Public	Staff 2009/10 to present	Jan. 14, 2009, top admin. and senior management pay freeze 2009 through 2011	July 16th, 2009, a 2009/10 SYSTEM-WIDE furlough faculty and staff required 11–26 days
University of California, Irvine	Public		Jan. 14, 2009, top admin. and senior management pay freeze 2009 through 2012	July 16th, 2009, a 2009/10 SYSTEM -WIDE furlough faculty and staff required 11–26 days
University of California, Los Angeles	Public	Mar. 29, 2009, hiring reduction (faculty with EVC/provost approval/staff maintaining level of open positions on general funds; 354 FTE in 2009). (2013/14?)	Jan. 14, 2009, top admin. and senior management pay freeze 2009 through 2013	July 16th, 2009, a 2009/10 SYSTEM-WIDE furlough faculty and staff required 11–26 days
University of California, San Diego	Public		Jan. 14, 2009, top admin. and senior management pay freeze 2009 through 2014	July 16th, 2009, a 2009/10 SYSTEM-WIDE furlough faculty and staff required 11–26 days
University of California, Santa Barbara	Public		Jan. 14, 2009, top admin. and senior management pay freeze 2009 through 2015	July 16th, 2009, a 2009/10 SYSTEM-WIDE furlough faculty and staff required 11–26 days

Institution	Type		2009/10
University of Illinois at Urbana Champaign	Public		
University of Maryland at College Park	Public	Late 2008 system-wide "soft" hiring freeze with administrator review ends May 11, 2009. July 29th hiring freeze announced.	Sept 19, 2009, plan announced furloughs beginning FY2010 & 2011. State-funded faculty and staff
University of Michigan	Public		
University of Minnesota, Twin Cities	Public	November 11, 2008: System-wide hiring freeze of all nonessential positions.	
University of Missouri-Columbia	Public	November 18, 2008: Missouri system-wide hiring freeze for nongrant and noncontract-funded faculty and staff.	
The University of North Carolina at Chapel Hill	Public	January 3, 2011. State-funded positions hiring freeze for FY2011/12	
University of Virginia	Public	2008/9: External soft hiring freeze for admin/staff.	
The University of Wisconsin-Madison	Public		All employees Sept. 2010 results in 3% decrease
Brown University	Private	Nov. 1, 2008 (temporary for staff and admin)	
Carnegie Mellon University	Private	Dec. 9, 2007: Freeze July 1, 2009 through June 30, 2010. March 27, 2011, end planed before 2011/12 academic year.	
Harvard University	Private	November 25, 2008: Staff hiring frozen and dean of arts & sci. encourages canceling faculty searches	Dec. 9, 2008, faculty and nonunion staff
Johns Hopkins University	Private	Feb. 13, 2009	
New York University	Private	February 27, 2008: NYU admin. hiring freeze	

(continued)

Table 6.2   (continued)

B. NAICU institutions

Cost-cutting steps	2008 responses of independent colleges and universities to economic conditions		2009 responses of independent colleges and universities to economic conditions	
	Number	Percent	Number	Percent
Froze tuition levels	17	4.6	13	4.6
Froze new hiring	185	49.9	152	53.5
Froze salaries	82	22.1	133	46.8
Cut or froze institutional student aid budget	31	8.4	124	43.7
Slowed down current construction/renovation projects	180	48.5	107	37.7
Delayed maintenance	145	39.1	87	30.6
Laid off faculty	39	10.5	20	7
Laid off staff (nonfaculty)	58	15.6	54	19
Gave smaller than usual salary increases	154	41.5	78	27.5
Cut salaries/benefits	27	7.3	48	16.9
Cancelled planned construction/renovation projects	79	21.3	44	15.5
Cut student services	36	9.7	12	4.2
Cut academic programs	27	7.3	11	3.9

Sources: For panel A, author's compilation from university websites and press accounts. For panel B, "Survey on the Impact of the Economic Conditions on 2009 Enrollment, Financial Aid and Budgeting at Independent Colleges and Universities." NAICU, June 19, 2009. Available online at http://www.naicu.edu/news_room/full-results-naicu-fall-2009-economic-impact-survey. "Preliminary Results: Survey on the Impact of the Economic Conditions on Independent Colleges and Universities." NAICU, December 18, 2008. Available online at http://www.naicu.edu/docLib/200812181_naicueconsurveyprelim.pdf.

shows the increase from 1970 to 2010 using highly aggregated Department of Education data and combines staffing changes across a wide range of institutions.) Consistent with overall trends in enrollment growth, increases have been greatest in the two-year sector and among public institutions, with a marked shift to part-time staffing also evident in the data.

Beyond the broad secular trends in these data, there is also evident cyclical variation in faculty staffing. To see this variation, Figure 6.5 shows the changes in student-faculty ratios over the extended interval from 1990 to the present. Vertical lines on these graphs correspond to periods of documented recession and the unemployment rate is shown on the right axis. To quantify this change, we present a regression of the log of student-faculty measures on the log of national unemployment measures with the inclusion of a secular time trend. Over the whole interval, a 10 percent increase in the unemployment rate links to a 1.2 percent increase in the student-faculty ratios, with these adjustments particularly large at two-year institutions and in the public sector. Indeed, the largest adjustments are among part-time faculty and one would expect that such changes incorporate temporary adjustments to enrollment demand.

As will become evident in the next section, changes in staffing ratios in cyclical downturns are not simply limited adjustment to new demand. With sharp budget cuts, colleges and universities often address short-term budget constraints with suspensions in hiring.

6.2.2 Rookie Market Evidence

While federal and national data collections present only limited information on new hires, the effects of recessionary conditions on the market for junior faculty are evident in discipline-specific sources. Table 6.3 presents job postings by selected fields (economics, English, foreign languages, and sociology) as reported by professional associations. These data provide clear evidence of the sharp contraction in employment activity beginning with academic year 2008/9 and continuing to a steep drop in 2009/10.[8]

In the English field, assistant professor postings dropped 27 percent (from 990 to 714) between 2007 and 2008 and then declined a further 21 percent (to 562) between 2008 and 2009. Similarly, foreign language postings fell from 779 to 635, then to 452 between 2007 and 2009. While there was some modest recovery in these fields in 2010 and 2011, junior faculty postings in 2011 were 35 percent below the 2007 level in English and 34 percent below the 2007 level in foreign language fields. An interesting point of note is that postings at the nontenure-track instructor rank declined—but much more modestly—than those in the tenure-track category. There are some indica-

---

8. What is more, it is widely suspected that job postings in 2009/10 are an overestimate of the number of departments that engaged in full searches, as there is considerable evidence of canceled searches in the fall of 2008 and winter 2010.

A. Counts of Instructional Staff

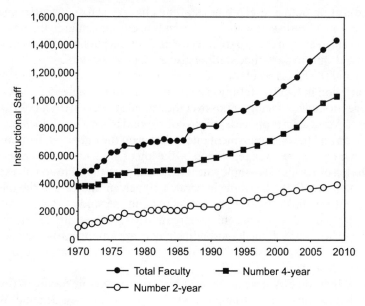

B. Share of Instructional Staff by Full-Time Status and Institutional Type

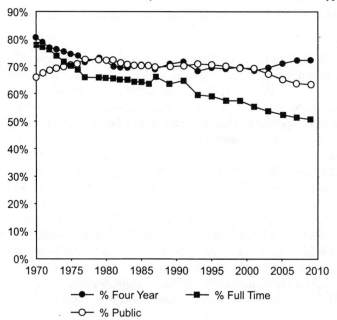

Fig. 6.4 Overall trends in instructional staff, 1970–2010

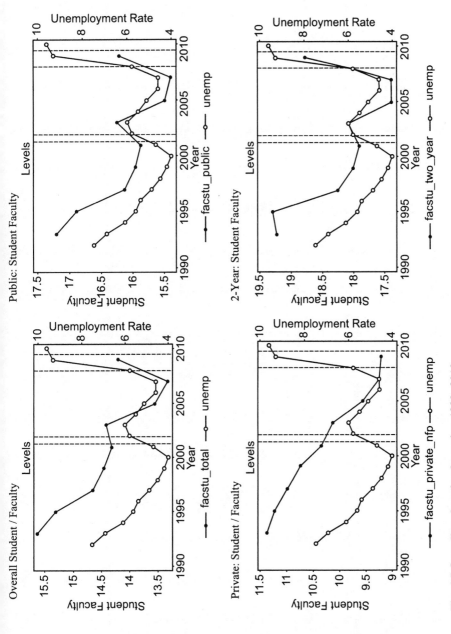

Fig. 6.5 Overall student-faculty ratios, 1990–2010

Table 6.3   Job postings by discipline, selected fields

Academic yr. beginning	Economics		English		Foreign language		Sociology	
	4-year	Univ. w/ grad. programs	Asst. professor	Instructor	Asst. professor	Instructor	All academic	Assistant professor
2000	277	650	1025	143	791	201		
2001	274	657	1006	123	739	183		
2002	266	632	963	113	765	171		
2003	218	635	865	103	667	192		
2004	229	643	956	136	689	210		
2005	301	720	914	125	686	219		
2006	264	770	1005	130	791	301	1,086	610
2007	315	959	990	178	779	320		
2008	287	1034	714	158	635	194	499	345
2009	198	949	562	157	452	220	351	214
2010	208	1112	643	120	503	218	482	303
2011	218	1199	640	138	509	251	551	354

Sources: Author's tabulations from professional societies including the American Economics Association, the MLA, and the American Sociology Association.

tions that institutions and departments have relied increasingly on instructors and other nontenure-track appointments when they are unable to gain authorization for permanent hires.

In economics, academic postings outside of research universities dropped from 315 in 2007 to 287 in 2008 and then further to 198 in 2009; by 2011 there was some rebound (to 218 postings), though this was nevertheless 31 percent below the 2007 level. Job postings at the research universities with graduate programs in economics exhibited a much more muted response to the fiscal crisis: they declined relatively modestly between 2008 and 2009 (from 1,034 to 949) and finished 2011 with a level of posting above that observed in 2007. These data suggest that the greatest sustained impact of the pull back in junior hiring has occurred outside the research sector.

6.2.3 Salaries

The measurement of how faculty wages and compensation respond to cyclical changes is dramatically complicated by the compositional changes in staffing associated with economic downturns. Averages—at the national level or even by type of institution—present a mix of changes in composition by rank, field of study, and institutional type. Delayed hiring combined with limited hiring at the junior level push average salaries up, even when changes in real wages to individuals have been minimal. While there is some evidence of increased stratification in salaries by type of institution and discipline over the long horizon (Johnson and Turner 2009), it is difficult to discern recession-induced changes in available data.

6.3 Modeling Stratification and Understanding
Changing Academic Employment Relations

Because colleges and universities differ markedly in revenue sources and student demand, we investigate the extent to which there are substantial differences in faculty labor-market adjustments in response to the Great Recession. We begin by documenting the sizable differences in employment changes by public-private status and by institutional type. We present these results both graphically and in a simple regression context to illustrate the magnitude of differences by sector.

For this analysis, we focus on four-year-degree-granting institutions in the public and private nonprofit sectors. While interesting in their own right, we set aside the analysis of for-profit institutions and community colleges as these institutions have few tenured faculty and are most likely to draw faculty from professionals in the local labor markets.

6.3.1 Evidence: Primary Data Sources

The data available for this inquiry come from two institutional surveys of colleges and universities. The annual administrative surveys of the Department of Education under the heading of the Integrated Postsecondary Data System (IPEDS) contain modules for the mandatory collection of data on staffing, enrollment, and finances. These data are collected on an annual basis, though the timing of data collection produces some unfortunate lags for this analysis; for example, fall 2010 is the most recent year of enrollment observed, while data on staffing is available only through academic year 2009/10.[9]

A second source of data is the annual surveys conducted by the American Association of University Professors (AAUP). This resource records full-time instructional staff. The data provide a full representation of the four-year institutions from the public and nonprofit sectors. The AAUP data have an advantage over the IPEDS data in that they provide coverage through 2011/12 in faculty counts, as well as distinguishing rank and salary by rank. Overall, one should view the data from IPEDS and AAUP data as complements not substitutes.

In addition, limited data on salaries and new hires by field among AAU institutions are also available for 2007–2011. These data afford a more detailed look at the hiring and compensation behavior among top research universities, though disclosure requirements do not permit the identification of specific private institutions to the researcher. As a result, while private-public aggregate comparisons are feasible within this interval, it is not possible to control in an econometric sense for fixed differences between the private institutions or for differences in the impact of the financial crisis.

The data available from these sources are somewhat short of the ideal data set that one would use to study many of the significant questions about academic labor markets. One shortcoming of both the AAUP and IPEDS data sets is that they do not record academic labor market outcomes by field of study. To the extent that faculty labor markets really operate at a disciplinary level (economists do not compete for the same jobs as engineers or English professors), it would be ideal to have counts for a wide range of institutions by discipline as well as rank and institution. What is more, systematic study of behaviors like retirement or attrition from the profession really requires access to unit-record data. While public institutions do place baseline salary information in the public domain as required by most state public information requirements, private institutions do not as a matter of practice share such information on a regular basis. There are surely large gains to be achieved for the research community and policymakers in higher education to making at least some of these data available to researchers in a restricted form.

6.3.2 Empirical Strategy

With more than a thousand four-year colleges and universities in the United States, the aim of this chapter is to identify the main labor market

---

9. In conducting the analysis we make use of the data assembled across surveys in the Delta Cost Project, allowing for institutionally consistent longitudinal analyses.

adjustments to the fiscal crisis and, in turn, the extent to which institutional fiscal circumstances contribute to the observed academic labor market outcomes. The analysis focuses on the period from 2006 to 2011, with years referring to the academic year beginning in the indicated fall (2006 is the 2006/7 academic year). As a starting point, we consider the basic empirical link between type of institution and faculty outcomes in a regression format:

$$Y_{it} = \alpha_i + \sum_{t=2007}^{2011} \delta_t + \sum_{t=2007}^{2011} \gamma_t D_i + \epsilon_{it},$$

where Y is an outcome such as faculty staffing in a given category (such as assistant professors) in year t for institution i. We are interested in, first, the evolution of the year-specific fixed effects and secondly, the extent to which these vary with institution categorization (D), which includes public-private control, Carnegie rank, and so forth. To make meaningful comparisons among institutions, we control for institutional fixed effects (α). Thus, the measured δ and γ parameters capture the average year-specific difference from the baseline year (2006). We focus on three primary outcome measures: counts of faculty by rank (available from 2006–2011), student-faculty ratios (available from 2006–2010),[10] and faculty salaries. (Faculty salary analysis using AAUP data are not reported in this draft. In the main, preliminary results indicate minimal real changes on the salary margin outside of research universities.)

6.3.3 Results

To begin, we present graphical results comparing faculty staffing by public-private control status for different rank levels—full professor, associate professor, assistant professor, and instructor. (In all cases, AAUP data are limited to full-time instructional personnel so these data do not record changes in the use of part-time staff; data from the IPEDS files provides some limited information on this staffing outcome.) Figure 6.6 illustrates the average trend in faculty by rank, with counts at public institutions shown on the left axis (black circles) and private institutions on the right axis (empty circles).[11] For all faculty categories, there is a broad upward trend in hiring from 2006–2008. After 2008, there is an unambiguous slowing of growth and—in some cases—decline in employment levels. For the "assistant professor" and "instructor" categories, the post-2008 decline is evident, likely reflecting institutional capacity to shift hiring in these headings relatively quickly. Examination of the full professor and assistant professor ranks

---

10. The most recent year of enrollment released by the Department of Education covers fall 2010.

11. Vertical lines indicate the "timing" of the recession recorded by NBER as the end of 2007 to mid 2009. What is clear from even the most basic consideration of the data is that the substantive impact of the financial crisis on the faculty labor market becomes apparent in these faculty counts somewhat later—with 2009 as the first year in which real effects are evident.

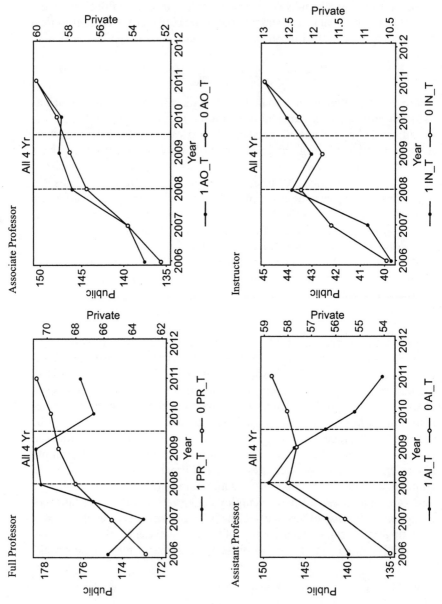

Fig. 6.6 Trends in average institutional full-time instructional faculty by rank, four-year institutions, 2006–2011

reveals a sharp divergence between public and private institutions in employment patterns. For public institutions we see an unambiguous decline, while for private institutions the height of the fiscal crisis is reflected in more of a plateau; the result is a relative widening of the staffing gap between public and private institutions, which is most evident at the junior faculty level.

Focusing on comparisons within broad Carnegie type, figures 6.7 and 6.8 illustrate hiring patterns at the full professor and assistant professor level. At the full professor level, private research universities demonstrate persistent increases in staffing while there is an unambiguous decline in senior appointments at public universities, with much of this decline taking hold in 2010 and 2011. At the junior level in figure 6.8, the persistent decline in hiring among public institutions from the peak in 2008 is clearly evident; the magnitude of these changes are also notable with declines from 9–11 percent in annual hiring.

While hiring levels tell part of the story, student-faculty measures provide a fuller indicator of the extent to which colleges and universities adjust to the pressures of the financial crisis by decreasing resources per student. Figure 6.9 shows the changes in student-faculty ratios, with increases indicating fewer resources per student; to ease comparison, the series for public (black circles) and private (empty circles) are indexed to the base of 2008. Across Carnegie classifications, the major "takeaway" is the divergence between public and private institutions in resources per student. Note that while we are only able to compute the student-faculty ratios to 2010, an expectation based on the hiring trends is that student-faculty ratios will continue on an upward trajectory.

Regression analysis presented in tables 6.4 through 6.7 serves to quantify these graphical presentations. A first question is whether there is an overall difference between the post-2008 years of observation and the pre-2008 years. In addition, we investigate whether there are differences between public and private institutions in these adjustments. First, in table 6.4, public institutions demonstrate a relative reduction of hiring at the full and assistant levels, with these differences particularly marked after 2010. These hiring trends are also evident across institution types and table 6.5 repeats this analysis, distinguishing research extensive (RS1) and research intensive (RS2) from other four-year, degree-granting institutions. Here, the private-public distinction is particularly evident at the senior and junior faculty levels, with relatively modest differences in the associate category. What is particularly noteworthy is that while private institutions appear to add senior faculty at a striking rate by 2011, public universities are actually shedding senior faculty. While we can make some inferences about junior hiring from the assistant professor category in table 6.6, a better source of information is the AAU Data Exchange, which records information on new hires. While new hires remain somewhat below levels in the 2007 base year, the decline in hiring (measured on a per-department basis) is more than

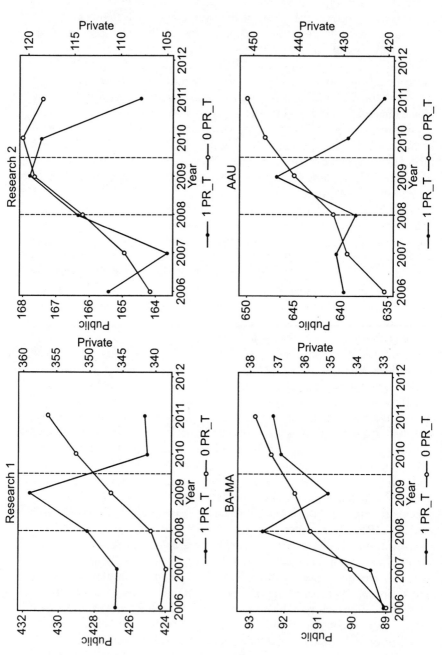

Fig. 6.7 Trends in average number of full professors by institution type, 2006–2011

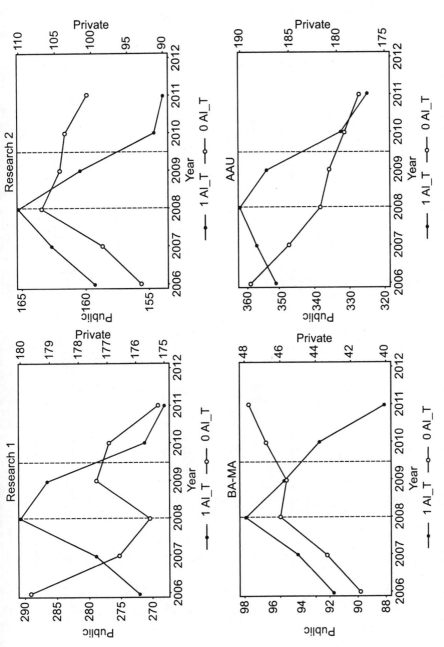

Fig. 6.8 Trends in average number of assistant professors by institution type, 2006–2011

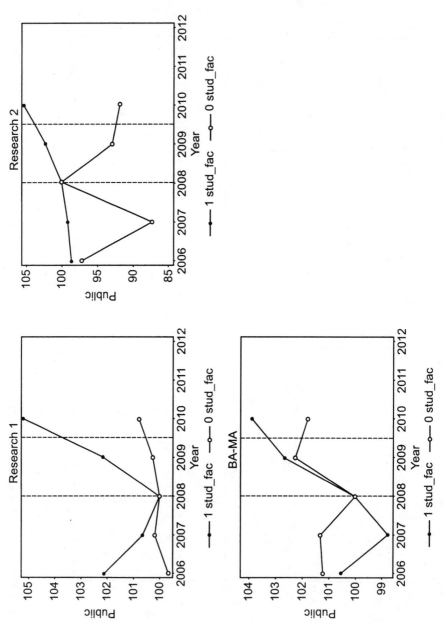

Fig. 6.9 Trends in average student-faculty ratios by institution type, 2006–2011 (indexed, base year = 2008)

Table 6.4   Fixed-effect regressions of log faculty counts on Great Recession indicators, 2006–2011

	ln (full prof.)		ln (assoc. prof.)		ln (asst. prof.)		ln (all faculty)	
Great R (2009–2010)	0.0275*** (0.00376)	0.0380*** (0.00485)	0.0283*** (0.00461)	0.0252*** (0.00642)	−0.00289 (0.00527)	0.0104 (0.00674)	0.0198*** (0.00249)	0.0249*** (0.00284)
Post-GR (2011)	0.0416*** (0.00547)	0.0668*** (0.00739)	0.0534*** (0.00665)	0.0503*** (0.00956)	−0.0174** (0.00795)	0.0180* (0.0101)	0.0332*** (0.00342)	0.0491*** (0.00424)
GR x public		−0.0213*** (0.00751)		0.00626 (0.00922)		−0.0269** (0.0105)		−0.0104** (0.00500)
Post GR x public		−0.0510*** (0.0109)		0.00629 (0.0133)		−0.0716*** (0.0158)		−0.0321*** (0.00680)
Constant	3.928*** (0.00246)	3.928*** (0.00245)	3.930*** (0.00299)	3.930*** (0.00299)	4.012*** (0.00349)	4.012*** (0.00347)	5.251*** (0.00162)	5.251*** (0.00161)
Observations	5,695	5,695	5,714	5,714	5,714	5,714	5,726	5,726
R-squared	0.028	0.037	0.030	0.030	0.002	0.012	0.042	0.051
Number of unitid.	1,291	1,291	1,295	1,295	1,296	1,296	1,300	1,300

Source: AAUP faculty salary survey, counts of full-time faculty. All regressions include institution fixed effects.

***Significant at the 1 percent level.

**Significant at the 5 percent level.

*Significant at the 10 percent level.

Table 6.5   Fixed-effect regressions of log faculty counts on Great Recession indicators by Carnegie type, 2006–2011

	ln (full professor)			ln (assoc. professor)			ln (asst. professor)		
	RS 1	RS 2	Oth. BA-MA	RS 1	RS 2	Oth. BA-MA	RS 1	RS 2	Oth. BA-MA
Great R (2009–2010)	0.0245*** (0.00660)	0.0225** (0.0109)	0.0490*** (0.00718)	0.0212 (0.0197)	0.0539*** (0.0163)	0.0114 (0.00885)	0.0141 (0.0143)	-0.0196 (0.0283)	0.0203** (0.00887)
Post-GR (2011)	0.0479*** (0.00819)	0.0244 (0.0224)	0.0918*** (0.0107)	0.0182 (0.0452)	0.0746*** (0.0212)	0.0420*** (0.0131)	-0.00457 (0.0233)	-0.0374 (0.0366)	0.0379*** (0.0135)
GR x public	-0.0201** (0.00993)	0.000686 (0.0139)	-0.0324*** (0.0103)	0.0110 (0.0212)	-0.0135 (0.0196)	0.0177 (0.0117)	-0.0424** (0.0184)	0.00190 (0.0335)	-0.0479*** (0.0135)
Post GR x public	-0.0528*** (0.0120)	-0.00366 (0.0255)	-0.0694*** (0.0146)	0.0335 (0.0463)	-0.00398 (0.0273)	0.00203 (0.0173)	-0.0663** (0.0289)	0.00107 (0.0489)	-0.112*** (0.0202)
Constant	5.844*** (0.00340)	4.863*** (0.00455)	3.657*** (0.00333)	5.473*** (0.00627)	4.857*** (0.00596)	3.780*** (0.00390)	5.406*** (0.00614)	4.820*** (0.0104)	3.918*** (0.00444)
Observations	735	433	3,078	735	433	3,079	735	433	3,079
R-squared	0.057	0.040	0.070	0.034	0.170	0.024	0.063	0.016	0.030
Number of unitid.	148	95	704	148	95	705	148	95	705

Source: AAUP faculty salary survey, counts of full-time faculty. All regressions include institution fixed effects.

***Significant at the 1 percent level.

**Significant at the 5 percent level.

*Significant at the 10 percent level.

Table 6.6   **Regression of new hires on Great Recession indicators, 2007–2011**

	New hires	
	(1)	(2)
Public	0.349***	0.349***
	(0.0244)	(0.0244)
Yr. dummy 2009	−0.0393	
	(0.0260)	
Yr. dummy 2010	−0.0693***	
	(0.0255)	
Yr. dummy 2011	−0.0302	
	(0.0255)	
Yr. d 2009 x public	−0.0722**	
	(0.0343)	
Yr. d 2010 x public	−0.122***	
	(0.0337)	
Yr. d 2011 x public	−0.146***	
	(0.0338)	
Post-2008		−0.0454**
		(0.0213)
Post-2008 x public		−0.114***
		(0.0279)
Department FE	X	X
Observations	5,743	5,743
R-squared	0.135	0.132

Source: AAU faculty salary survey.
***Significant at the 1 percent level.
**Significant at the 5 percent level.
*Significant at the 10 percent level.

twice as large for public institutions as private institutions. To this end, the data suggest that no sustained recovery has taken place in the junior faculty market.

To capture the effects of faculty staffing changes on resources per student, table 6.7 presents the parallel regressions of student-faculty ratios on period fixed-effects indicators. What is apparent is a sharp increase in student-faculty ratios (about 5.6 percent) for students at public institutions, with a more modest (less than 1 percent) change at private institutions. As such, these results provide quite robust evidence of the increased public-private stratification in faculty staffing associated with the financial crisis. What further analysis will explore is the extent to which this dynamic varies systematically with more detailed data on revenue structures (such as reliance on tuition, state appropriations, and endowment in advance of the fiscal crisis) as well as whether differences in state appropriations shocks impact hiring.

Table 6.7   Fixed-effect regressions of student-faculty ratios on Great Recession
             indicators by Carnegie type, 2006–2011

	ln (student/faculty)			
	Overall	RS 1	RS 2	Oth. BA-MA
Great Rec.	0.00322	0.00602	0.0245	0.0116**
(AY 2009/10)	(0.00406)	(0.00830)	(0.0200)	(0.00567)
GR x public	0.0537***	0.0292***	0.0171	0.0323***
	(0.00639)	(0.0109)	(0.0214)	(0.00752)
Constant	3.196***	3.058***	3.192***	3.224***
	(0.00151)	(0.00276)	(0.00425)	(0.00190)
Observations	4,582	588	347	2,464
R-squared	0.078	0.109	0.107	0.050
N of unitid	1,287	148	95	697

Source: AAUP faculty salary survey, counts of full-time faculty. All regressions include institution fixed effects. Student faculty ratios are calculated using data on "fall enrollment" from IPEDS.
***Significant at the 1 percent level.
**Significant at the 5 percent level.
*Significant at the 10 percent level.

While data on salaries are very limited, we are able to use limited data on salaries by field for AAU universities (essentially limiting this part of the analysis to research universities). The question at hand is whether salaries change differentially by public-private sector over the recession years, relative to the baseline of 2008. In table 6.8, we regress log salary (separately by rank) measured at the level of field and university on indicator variables for public control, year of observation, and the interaction of year and public status. Results show that, first, salaries are somewhat lower at public universities than private in the baseline, with the gap widening from 8.4 percent at the assistant level to about 17.8 percent at the full professor level. Moreover, while faculty at private universities see modest increases in salaries post-2008, salary growth at public universities lags appreciably, pointing to increased stratification in compensation as well as staffing levels.

6.4 Implications in the Short Term and the Long Term

Because faculty are an input to the educational production function, changes in staffing and the faculty labor market may be expected to impact student outcomes. There are good reasons to expect that the increased student-faculty ratios that have emerged from the Great Recession, particularly at public institutions outside the most research-intensive sectors, may have a direct impact on collegiate attainment and graduation rates, even as it is too early to measure these effects directly. While estimates of the direct effect of changes

Table 6.8   Regression of faculty salary levels on Great Recession indicators, 2007–2011

	Ln asst. salary		Ln assoc. salary		Ln full salary	
	(1)	(2)	(3)	(4)	(5)	(6)
Public	-0.0846***	-0.0846***	-0.116***	-0.116***	-0.178***	-0.178***
	(0.00662)	(0.00662)	(0.00785)	(0.00785)	(0.00925)	(0.00924)
Yr. dummy 2009	0.0419***		0.0325***		0.0444***	
	(0.00759)		(0.00925)		(0.0110)	
Yr. dummy 2010	0.0414***		0.0238**		0.0371***	
	(0.00803)		(0.00984)		(0.0118)	
Yr. dummy 2011	0.0476***		0.0287***		0.0437***	
	(0.00770)		(0.00943)		(0.0114)	
Yr. d 2009 x public	-0.0141		-0.0132		-0.0168	
	(0.00891)		(0.0110)		(0.0128)	
Yr. d 2010 x public	-0.0194**		-0.0168		-0.0246*	
	(0.00927)		(0.0114)		(0.0135)	
Yr. d 2011 x public	-0.0163*		-0.0160		-0.0146	
	(0.00907)		(0.0111)		(0.0132)	
Post-2008		0.0437***		0.0285***		0.0419***
		(0.00640)		(0.00769)		(0.00927)
Post-2008 x public		-0.0167**		-0.0155*		-0.0189*
		(0.00751)		(0.00907)		(0.0107)
Department FE	X	X	X	X	X	X
Observations	5,285	5,285	5,341	5,341	5,653	5,653
R-squared	0.720	0.720	0.572	0.571	0.512	0.511

Source: AAU faculty salary survey.
***Significant at the 1 percent level.
**Significant at the 5 percent level.
*Significant at the 10 percent level.

in academic resources on attainment are necessarily difficult, credible estimates from Bound, Lovenheim, and Turner (2010) point to the importance of resources per student in determining collegiate completion.[12]

Yet, evidence to date does not suggest that the cyclical downturn will be quickly reversed and, indeed, the evidence suggests that in the public sector many of the resource cuts that have impacted faculty hiring are likely to be permanent not transitory. How the faculty market adjusts to the continued period of fiscal retrenchment will ultimately affect the long-term prosperity of US higher education. While differentiation and stratification are predictable—and some would argue desirable—features of US higher education, the severe budget constraints in the market may limit the capacity of all but a few institutions to make the faculty investments needed to ensure long-term viability. Under present circumstances, the question of whether faculty who are able to generate credible outside offers (conditional on productivity) benefit disproportionately, resulting in widening salary differences tied to race and family circumstances.

Finally, with the employment effects of the Great Recession concentrated in the junior market and among new hires, the long-term "prospects for faculty in the arts and sciences" appear much dimmer than would be projected based on demographics and student demand. To the extent that the public not only shoulders some of the costs of graduate education, but also harvests some of the benefits in terms of research advances, there is a potentially large social cost to the persistence of an anemic job market. As Shirley Tilghman noted "The thing that will have the longest-term negative impact on colleges and universities is if we can't figure out how to continue the careers of young people just coming out of grad school" (Riley 2011).

References

Barr, Andrew, and Sarah E. Turner. 2013. "Expanding Enrollments and Contracting State Budgets: The Effects of the Great Recession on Higher Education." *Annals of the Amerian Academy of Political and Social Science* 650 (1): 168–93.

Betts, J., and L. McFarland. 1995. "Safe Port in a Storm: The Impact of Labor Market Conditions on Community College Enrollments." *Journal of Human Resources* 30:741–65.

Bound, John, Michael Lovenheim, and Sarah Turner. 2010. "Why Have College Completion Rates Declined? An Analysis of Changing Student Preparation and Collegiate Resources." *American Economic Journal: Applied Economics* 2 (3): 129–57.

Bound, J., and S. E. Turner. 2007. "Cohort Crowding: How Resources Affect Collegiate Attainment." *Journal of Public Economics* 91 (5–6): 877–99.

12. Of course, it will be several years before researchers are able to measure the link between the Great Recession and college completion and, even at this point, it will be difficult to untangle the extent to which any change in attainment reflects adjustments in selection or changes in student effort.

Bowen, William. 2012. "The 'Cost Disease' in Higher Education: Is Technology the Answer?" The Tanner Lectures, Stanford University, October.

Brown, J., Stephen G. Dimmock, Jun-Koo Kang, and Scott Weisbenner. 2010. "How University Endowments Respond to Financial Market Shocks: Evidence and Implications." NBER Working Paper no. 15861, Cambridge, MA.

Christian, M. 2006. "Liquidity Constraints and the Cyclicality of College Enrollment in the United States." *Oxford Economic Papers* 59 (1): 141–69.

College Board. 2011. *Trends in Student Aid.* Washington, DC: College Board Advocacy and Policy Center.

Fitzpatrick, Maria D., and Sarah E. Turner. 2007. "Blurring the Boundary: Changes in the Transition from College Participation to Adulthood." In *The Price of Independence: The Economics of Early Adulthood Initiatives,* edited by Sheldon Danziger and Cecilia Rouse, chap. 5. New York: Russell Sage Foundation.

Hoxby, Caroline. 2009. "The Changing Selectivity of American Colleges and Universities: Its Implications for Students, Resources, and Tuition." *Journal of Economic Perspectives* 23 (4): 95–118.

Johnson, William R., and Sarah Turner. 2009. "Faculty without Students: Resource Allocation in Higher Education." *Journal of Economic Perspectives* 23 (2): 169–89.

Kane, T., P. Orszag, and D. Gunter. 2003. "State Fiscal Constraints and Higher Education Spending." TPC Discussion Paper no. 11, Urban-Brookings Tax Policy Center.

Lovenheim, M. 2011. "The Effect of Liquid Housing Wealth on College Enrollment." *Journal of Labor Economics* 29 (4): 741–71.

Riley, Naomi. 2011. "The Economic Upside to Ending Tenure." *Chronicle of Higher Education,* June 19. http://chronicle.com/article/Smart-Ways-to-End-Tenure/127940/.

Rizzo, Michael 2004. "A (Less Than) Zero Sum Game? State Funding for Public Education: How Public Higher Education Institutions Have Lost." CHERI Working Paper no. 52, Cornell University.

Turner, S. 2003. "Pell Grants as Fiscal Stabilizers." Unpublished Manuscript, University of Virginia.

7

The Financial Crisis and College Enrollment
How Have Students and Their Families Responded?

Bridget Terry Long

7.1 Introduction

The Great Recession had far-reaching effects on both the supply and demand sides of higher education. On the supply side, postsecondary institutions experienced cuts to multiple revenue sources, including charitable giving and endowment returns, as detailed in other chapters of this volume. The level of government support was also impacted, especially in the form of state appropriations, which affect tuition prices. In terms of families, or the demand side of higher education, the downturn of the economy affected incomes and unemployment rates, thereby reducing economic well-being and stability. Moreover, home ownership and home equity levels have declined, reducing a major source of wealth and capital for many families. These changes likely impacted both the probability of enrolling in college and what a family can afford and is willing to pay for school.

This chapter explores the multiple ways college affordability was impacted by the Great Recession and the ways these changes affected college enrollment and expenditures. The central question is: How has the Great Recession affected family and student decisions regarding college enrollment, choice, and expenditures? The trends described above lend themselves to conflicting hypotheses. While reductions in family income and increases in tuition

Bridget Terry Long is academic dean and the Saris Professor of Education and Economics at the Harvard Graduate School of Education and a research associate of the National Bureau of Economic Research.

The author thanks Sarah Turner, Eric Bettinger, and participants at the NBER conference on the effects of the Great Recession on higher education for their comments and suggestions. Tolani Britton provided excellent research assistance. All opinions and mistakes are my own. For acknowledgments, sources of research support, and disclosure of the author's material financial relationships, if any, please see http://www.nber.org/chapters/c12862.ack.

prices could have negative effects on postsecondary enrollment, growing unemployment could have the opposite effect by reducing the foregone costs of attending school. Previous research has found that college enrollment rates often increase as the unemployment rate grows (Long 2004b), especially among sixteen- to twenty-four-year-olds due to lack of employment opportunities (Bell and Blanchflower 2011). Due to these negative and positive pressures, the predicted net effect of the recession on college enrollment rates is unclear and depends on the relative sizes of each effect.

The Great Recession is also distinctive from earlier recessions in several important ways. At the start of the Great Recession, college costs and student debt levels were at historic highs, suggesting that the role of loans in college enrollment was much more significant than during previous periods. In regard to the recession, it is important to highlight the substantially large, negative impact the economic downturn had on liquidity for many families. Additionally, the Great Recession coincided with the largest cohort of graduating high school students, thereby exacerbating the need for resources and pressure on institutional capacity. On the other hand, federal financial aid increased to an unprecedented level with the goal of enabling more individuals to access college. Therefore, although price increases and labor market effects may have largely determined the impact of past recessions on enrollment trends, the Great Recession occurred in a much more complex context, and the net effect of all of these changes in income, tuition prices, liquidity, demographics, and financial aid is not clear ex ante.

This chapter investigates the net effects of these multiple changes. Using the Integrated Postsecondary Education Data System (IPEDS), an annual survey of colleges, I investigate how families altered decisions about whether to attend and enrollment intensity (full- versus part-time attendance) after the start of the recession. Additionally, I examine possible changes in tuition costs and financial aid received, as measured by revenue received by postsecondary institutions. I exploit geographical differences in the severity of the recession to highlight how enrollment and expenditure trends changed for families in states that suffered more dramatically in terms of growth in unemployment and reductions in home values relative to families in other states.

The analysis suggests college attendance levels increased during the recession, especially in the states most affected by the recession. Part-time enrollment increased while full-time enrollment declined, and the gains in attendance were concentrated among students of color. The tuition revenue collected per student also grew, while grants did not offset the increase in cost and student loans increased.

The next section of the chapter details the effects of the recession on both the supply and demand sides of higher education. Then I describe the data sources and empirical framework. Section 7.4 discusses the results, and section 7.5 concludes.

7.2 The Effects of Recessions: Current Trends and Past Research

7.2.1 Trends in Tuition Pricing

Tuition prices at colleges and universities are influenced by multiple factors, with other revenue sources playing an important role due to the fact that the cost of educating a student is not fully covered by the price students pay. In the case of public institutions, the level of state appropriations is a strong determining factor of tuition levels. State appropriations allow the public colleges and universities to charge in-state students a discounted price and the level and distribution pattern of these state subsidies strongly influences student enrollment decisions (Long 2004a).

During the last several years, state appropriations to higher education have fallen significantly. According to the College Board (2012a), after accounting for inflation, state appropriations per full-time equivalent (FTE) student fell 25 percent from 2006/7 to 2011/12, including a 10 percent reduction from 2010/11 to 2011/12. Such reductions in state appropriations have had serious repercussions on tuition levels at public institutions. As shown in figure 7.1, the historical pattern is that when state appropriations per full-time equivalent (FTE) student fall, the list tuition and fees charged to students typically increase, and this has been the case during this most recent recession.[1] Because state constitutions generally require states to have balanced budgets each year, legislators have been cutting spending, and as with past recessions, appropriations to higher education have been a target. From 2007/8 to 2011/12, the mean list (published) tuition and fees at public four-year institutions increased 27 percent after accounting for inflation; they grew by 24 percent at public two-year institutions during the same period (College Board 2012a).[2]

The impact of declining state appropriation on tuition prices has been particularly large in some states. From 2008/9 to 2010/11, a difference of only two years, mean tuition and required fees at public four-year colleges and universities increased 32 percent in Florida and Georgia, 28 percent in Hawaii, 24 percent in Alabama, and 38 percent in California. Even community colleges, which tend to maintain low tuition growth in keeping with their mission of supporting access and affordability, have experienced increases

1. Often the downturn in state appropriations to higher education is delayed by a year or two after the start of a recession. This is because appropriations are funded out of tax revenue, which can often take a year to be affected by a recession. According to estimates by the National Governors Association during the beginning of the recession, states' combined budget shortfalls for FY2009 were expected to grow to $60 billion and then $80 billion during FY2010 (Chitty 2009). As such, even though this recession began in December 2007, the effect on tax revenue, and then in turn state appropriations and tuition prices, was not felt until the 2008/9 and 2009/10 school years.
2. Tuition means are weighted by full-time undergraduate enrollment. (College Board, *Annual Survey of Colleges*.)

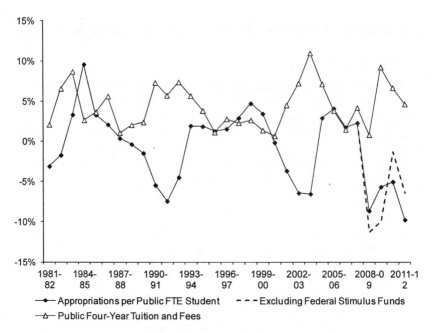

Fig. 7.1 Annual percentage change in state appropriations for higher education and real tuition and fees at public four-year institutions

Source: College Board (2012a, figure 12A).

Notes: State appropriations reported per full-time equivalent (FTE) student. Enrollment for fall 2011 was estimated based on preliminary IPEDS numbers. Appropriations are for institutional operating expenses, not for capital expenditures. Funding includes both tax revenues and other state funds allocated to higher education.

in their prices. During the same two years, mean tuition and required fees at public two-year colleges increased 33 percent in Georgia, 32 percentage in North Carolina, and 25 percent in Virginia.[3]

Fluctuating state appropriations not only affect list tuition prices at public institutions but also students' choices between public and private colleges, as well as the two-year versus four-year decision. When in-kind subsidies are large, students appear to choose public colleges even if the gap in resources between public and private options is substantial. Research also suggests that large levels of state appropriations, an in-kind subsidy, create incentives for students to favor public four-year colleges over two-year institutions (Long 2004b). The recent reductions in state appropriations may cause a shift in enrollment patterns.

During this same time period, the list tuition prices of private, nonprofit institutions have not grown as quickly as their public counterparts. From

3. Calculations by author using College Board (2011, table 6c). Tuition means are weighted by full-time undergraduate enrollment. (College Board, *Annual Survey of Colleges*.)

2007/8 to 2011/12, list tuition and fees at private, nonprofit, four-year institutions grew 13 percent, above the norm but about half of the growth rate at public colleges and universities (College Board 2012a).

7.2.2 Trends in Financial Aid

Underlying all of these increases in college prices is the government financial aid system. Although list price can have an effect on enrollment decisions, it is the net price after the application of financial aid that is the most influential. While tuition has increased in all sectors, government financial aid has, for now, remained robust.

The federal Pell grant is the largest need-based aid program and serves as the foundation for other aid, meaning that if students are eligible, the Pell grant is awarded first. The majority of Pell recipients come from families with incomes in the lowest economic quartile; according to Mahan (2011), about three-quarters of Pell grant recipients during 2008/9 had family incomes at or below $30,000. With the start of the recession, there was increased demand for the Pell grant. According to Chitty (2009), approximately 786,000 more students received a Pell grant in 2008/9 than the previous year. In fact, total expenditures in the Pell grant program doubled from 2007/8 ($15.9 billion) to 2009/10 ($31.5 billion), continuing to rise to $37.0 billion in 2010/11 (College Board 2012b). The growth in beneficiaries over multiple years has caused major financial shortfalls, which Congress has at times provided additional funding to cover. Most recently, to maintain the $5,550 maximum Pell grant award during 2011/12, the Department of Defense Full-Year Continuing Appropriations Act of 2011 (P.L. 112-10) provided $23 billion in discretionary appropriations to the program (Mahan 2011).

The federal student loan sector has also grown and changed to accommodate economic trends and increased need by families. After the recession had an effect on credit markets, causing many private student loan providers to stop or suspend lending, Congress passed the Ensuring Continued Access to Student Loans Act in 2008, which gave the US Department of Education the authority to make direct loans to students. Congress also increased the loan limits for students in the Federal Stafford Loan Program. Similar to the Pell Grant Program, the total amount of government loans has increased substantially during the recession. While the total given in federal loans was $74.6 billion in 2007/8, it rose to $110.4 billion in expenditures by 2010/11 (College Board 2012b).

There has also been increased pressure on institutional aid sources, financial aid given by colleges and universities. Institutional financial aid officers note that there has been a large increase in the number of financial aid applications they receive and requests for institutional aid. Given the growing economic instability caused by the recession, many families have contacted offices with revised aid requests due to changes in their circumstance, such as recent unemployment (Schachter 2009). According to the

College Board (2012b), total institutional grants have increased from $30.5 billion in 2007/8 to $42.1 billion in 2011/12. With the increases in financial aid from both the government and institutions, average net prices to families have not increased as dramatically as list prices during the recession. However, the number of families and students dependent on these aid resources has increased substantially. Although financial aid can dramatically reduce the overall cost of college, many students still have significant unmet needs (Long and Riley 2007; ACSFA 2010). Moreover, the receipt of financial aid is predicated on navigating a lengthy and complicated process, and this has been shown to be a deterrent to families accessing financial aid and attending college (Bettinger et al. 2012).

7.2.3 The Effects of the Great Recession on the Economic Conditions of Families

In the face of this recession, families have suffered lost income, greater debt, and more financial insecurity, factors that might negatively impact college outcomes. First, family incomes have fallen or remained stagnant, partly due to increasing unemployment. Nationally, the unemployment rates grew from 4.7 percent in September 2007 to 10.1 percent in October 2009.[4] For people under the age of twenty-five, unemployment increased from 11.5 percent during the first quarter of 2008 to 18.3 percent during the fourth quarter of 2010 (Bell and Blanchflower 2011).

This period of economic turmoil has also strongly affected the housing market by reducing the value of many families' homes, while others have lost their homes altogether. Glover et al. (2011, 1) conclude that "the average household experienced a decline in net worth of $177,000 between the middle of 2007 and the trough of the asset price decline in the first quarter of 2009." According to the Federal Reserve, American home owners lost more than $7 trillion in home equity. Previous research suggests that changes in home values can affect educational attainment (Johnson 2011), and other research has found that families rely on home equity as a way to finance college (Lovenheim 2011). Therefore, with reductions in home values and the ease of getting a home equity loan, there is some concern that the Great Recession may have reduced the likelihood of college attendance. Access to capital has also been reduced for many families as banks and financial institutions have been less willing to make loans or extend credit. Per household, ownership of credit cards declined 2.8 percent from November 2008 to April 2010. However, conditional on having some debt, credit card debt increased by nearly 25 percent (Hurd and Rohwedder 2010).

Overall, the effects of the recession have been widespread. According to Hurd and Rohwedder (2010, 1), "between November 2008 and April 2010 about 39 percent of households had either been unemployed, had negative

---

4. Bureau of Labor Statistics. Seasonally adjusted monthly data.

equity in their house, or had been in arrears in their house payments." Still, the severity of the recession has varied geographically. From the beginning of 2007 to the end of 2009, state unemployment rates grew by anywhere from 2.0 to 8.8 percentage points. Looking at changes in home values, another way to measure recession severity, eight states experienced gains in home prices while other states saw their homes lose on average 41.6 percent of their values.[5]

7.2.4 Recessions and the College Enrollment Decision

Under Becker's (1964) human capital model, when deciding whether to continue their educations, individuals compare the benefits of human capital to the costs of obtaining it. In terms of higher education decisions, an individual will weigh the costs and benefits, both monetary and otherwise, to decide whether to prepare for college, enroll in a postsecondary institution, and continue until completing a college degree. Theory suggests that college demand will depend upon the net benefit (benefits minus costs) of education, the prices of alternatives, and the preferences of the individual, subject to a lifetime budget constraint. Among the costs of education are tuition and foregone earnings, the income that an individual could have made had he or she decided to enter the labor market rather than attend school. On the other side, the benefits of higher education include increased earnings. Additional nonmonetary costs and benefits, such as the psychic costs of studying, the consumption value of college, and possible improved health outcomes due to education, may also be important. Numerous studies have confirmed the expected relationship between the factors detailed in the model and enrollment trends (Leslie and Brinkman 1987; Long 2007).

With regard to recessions and the business cycle, as earnings decrease and unemployment becomes more likely, theory suggests that individuals will be more likely to attend college. Such a pattern has been found during earlier recessions. For instance, Dellas and Sakellaris (2003) find that college enrollment decisions are countercyclical with the business cycle. Using the Current Population Survey from 1968 to 1988, which includes four US recessions, they find that a 1 percentage point increase in the unemployment rates is associated with a 2 percent increase in college enrollment. Other work has also found a positive relationship between unemployment rates and college enrollment (Card and Lemieux 2001; Long 2004b).

In some ways, the trends of the Great Recession mirror the economic changes of earlier recessions, and so one might expect to find the same pattern of increasing postsecondary enrollment. There were rampant increases in unemployment and reductions in income. It is also certainly not the first time that colleges and universities have suffered reductions in state appropriations. For instance, during the recession of the early 1990s,

---

5. See below for a more detailed discussion of these recession indicators.

state appropriations also fell substantially, and this led to substantial tuition increases at public institutions. More recently, during the recession of the early twenty-first century, reductions in state appropriates coupled with declining endowments resulted in significant tuition growth at both public and private colleges and universities (Breneman 2002).

However, while many of the changes brought on by the Great Recession have also been experienced during previous recessions, several factors make the current context very different. Even before the downturn, college prices were a much higher percentage of annual family income than any previous recession, making any marginal increase in tuition harder to overcome than ever before. The percentage of students taking out debt and the mean levels of student debt at baccalaureate graduation were also at historical highs and continuing to increase rapidly. The ability to get loans and willingness to take on debt to finance postsecondary attendance is a greater determinant of college enrollment than ever before, and this recession has had a direct effect on both of those factors. On the other hand, financial aid has increased substantially during this period, much more than any previous recessions. As noted above, total expenditures in the Pell Grant Program went from $15.9 billion in 2007/8 to $37.0 billion in 2010/11 (College Board 2012b).

Another thing that makes this recession different than most others is the demographic change that was also taking place at the same time. In 2008, the United States had the largest class of graduating high school seniors, about 3.2 million students. This exceeded the peak year of the baby boom, which was 1979, by more than 60,000. According to Breneman (2002), during the recessions of the early 1980s and 1990s, the lack of pressure from increased enrollments "served to cushion the economic blows somewhat." The same was not true during the early part of the twenty-first century, and so this helped to spur growth in student loans. The already important role of debt in college financing and the enormous enrollment pressure of the largest cohort of traditional-age college students has exacerbated the need for resources and capacity by institutions and families.

Therefore, unlike past recessions when changes in enrollment trends were largely a matter of price increases and labor market effects, the Great Recession has happened in a much more complex context with positive and negative pressures that might influence college enrollment, and this could have different effects on various subgroup populations. The growth in unemployment and financial aid could encourage many to enroll in college, but the decrease in family income, increase in the difficulty of securing private financing, increasing tuition prices, and strain on institutional capacity suggest that the propensity for college enrollment could decrease. The uncertainty and risk introduced by the recession could also affect college decisions as families may be less likely to take on more expensive, multiyear investments. Given the recession impacted the earning and job prospects of educated workers, some have even questioned whether the returns to college justify the cost, though employment conditions for individuals with only a high school degree were also adversely affected.

Early work confirms that the effects of the Great Recession have been distinctive from previous periods. Overall, Barr and Turner (2012) find that the enrollment response to the Great Recession has been larger, and they attribute the large growth in attendance to the unusual increase in the availability of financial aid (i.e., the Pell grant) as well as extensions in unemployment insurance benefits. Their research suggests that older students were proportionately more responsive to the recession. The largest shocks to enrollment occurred at community colleges and private baccalaureate (no research) colleges. To summarize, Barr and Turner conclude that while the reductions in state appropriations and increases in tuition prices might attenuate the overall enrollment response, these factors would not be strong enough to "undo" the increase in attendance. This analysis augments the previous work by bringing additional insight to the effects of the recession.

7.3 Data and Empirical Framework

7.3.1 Data Sources

My analysis uses data from the Integrated Postsecondary Education Data System (IPEDS), an annual survey of colleges that participate in the federal student financial aid programs. The IPEDS provides detailed information on multiple aspects of postsecondary institutions, including enrollment, revenue, and financial aid. Using this data set, I am able to measure student decisions and cost information at the institutional level. To capture the introduction to the recession, I use data from 2004/5 to 2009/10, with the postrecession time period being defined as 2007/8 and afterward, thereby allowing three years of observation both before and after the change. To be included in the sample, colleges needed to have at least five of the six possible years of data.

I use state-level variation in the severity of the recession to highlight trends most closely associated with the negative economic consequences of the downturn. The IPEDS data has the disadvantage of being organized by the state of residence of the institution, not the student. For the bulk of colleges, their enrollment and financial information is largely reflective of a population of students from within their state. According to the 2007/8 IPEDS, only 8 percent of students in a beginning cohort are from out of state, on average, though this variable is not collected for all institutions. However, to deal with the concern that institutional data may not be completely reflective of students from within the state, four-year colleges with less than one-third of their students from inside their state have been excluded from the sample.[6]

---

6. The results of the analysis do not change when lowering this threshold.

In addition, colleges in the most competitive category of the Barron's ratings have also been excluded due to the fact that they tend to respond to more national, rather than state, trends.

To gauge the severity of the recession, I measure how indicators changed from 2007Q1 to 2009Q4. This time frame begins and ends slightly before and after the official dates of the recession (December 2007 to June 2009) to fully capture changes that occurred during the downturn. I use two sets of economic measures. The first are quarterly unemployment rates available from the Bureau of Labor Statistics (BLS) as part of their Local Area Unemployment Statistics (LAUS). The rates are by state and seasonally adjusted. States have been put into two categories based on the size of the increase in the unemployment rate. While state unemployment rates grew by 2 to 8.8 percentage points from 2007Q1 to 2009Q4, states for which the rate grew by 6.5 percentage points or more are categorized as having a "large increase in the unemployment rate." Appendix table 7A.1 lists the states in this category.

The second economic indicator used to judge the severity of the recession focuses on home values. I use the Conventional Mortgage House Price Index (CMHPI), which is produced by the Federal Housing Finance Agency (FHFA). The index is based on Fannie Mae and Freddie Mac-eligible mortgages on single-family detached properties (with loan limits up to $729,750 for one-unit properties). I use the All-Transactions House Price Index, which includes both sales of property and appraisal values from refinance transactions. The CMHPI has been used in other studies on the impact of housing value and wealth on educational outcomes (Johnson 2011; Lovenheim 2011; Lovenheim and Reynolds 2012). From 2007Q1 to 2009Q4, the CMHPI fell in most states, from as little as 1.47 points up to 206 points; in seven states, the index increased during this time. I define states that had their CMHPI fall more than 80 points as having "large reductions in the CMHPI." Appendix table 7A.1 also lists the states in this category.

7.3.2 Empirical Framework

Following the basic human capital framework, college enrollment is modeled as a function of family background, income, and home ownership, which proxy for preparation levels and the ability to pay for college, and unemployment, which is a proxy for the foregone costs of attendance. I examine the effects of the Great Recession in two ways. First, I document differences in college enrollment trends by contrasting enrollment rates before and after the start of the recession, using a dummy variable $After_j$ that is equal to 1 if the school year is 2007/8, 2008/9, or 2009/10, which is equivalent to the fourth quarter of 2007 and afterward. However, because college enrollment rates have generally increased during the last several decades and would have likely continued to increase regardless of the recession, I must also control for this upward trend. I do so by also including a year trend, $Year_j$, in the model. To control for differences in state higher education systems and underlying propensities for enrollment, I also include state fixed effects (γ_i). The resulting equation is:

(1) $$y_j = \alpha_1 + \alpha_2 X_i + \alpha_3 \text{Year}_i + \alpha_4 \text{After}_i + \gamma_i + \varepsilon_{i,}$$

where i is postsecondary institution, y is the outcome of interest, and X is the vector of institutional characteristics that might also determine the outcome. In this equation, α_3 measures the annual growth in college enrollment rates over the entire period (the upward trend that would have happened regardless of the recession), and α_4 gives a sense of whether trends in college enrollment changed from the previous trajectory after the start of the Great Recession. If the Great Recession precipitated a jump in the percentage of individuals attending college *beyond* the already positive annual growth, one would expect α_4 to be positive.

The empirical analysis includes additional controls (X_i) found to be important determinants of an institution's enrollment, tuition costs, and financial aid receipt and amounts, the main outcomes of this analysis. These include: institutional level (dummy variables for two-year and less-than-two-year institutions, with the baseline category being a four-year institution); institutional sector (dummy variables for nonprofit, private, and for-profit institutions, with the baseline category being a public institution); the 2000 Carnegie classification (i.e., whether a research versus master's versus other type of institution); institutional type (dummy variable for being a public flagship, HBCU, HSI, having a medical school, and being affiliated with a hospital); total current operating expenditures; total expenditures squared; list in-state tuition and required fees; and Barron's competitiveness ratings (a series of dummy variables, from noncompetitive to highly competitive). In the regressions that use total enrollment as the dependent variable, I also control for a one-year lag in total enrollment. All other models control for present year total enrollment; for instance, to determine the impact of the recession on full-time enrollment, I control for the size of the institution. Because of persistent differences in the higher education systems of each state, I also include state fixed effects in all models. In the models, the standard errors have been adjusted by clustering at the institutional level.

To determine how the severity of the recession had differential effects on the outcomes, I use a differences-in-differences (DD) methodology. The first difference is before versus after the recession as captured by After_i. The second difference is between states adversely affected by the recession to a large degree versus a small degree. Using ordinary least squares estimation, the DD calculation can be made:

(2) $$y_j = \beta_1 + \beta_2 (\text{Recession\_High}_i * \text{After}_i) + \beta_3 \text{Recession\_High}_i + b_4 \text{After}_i + \varepsilon_{i.}$$

The parameter β_2 is the reduced-form effect of the recession in highly affected states relative to less-affected states—it measures whether institutions in states that experienced the largest adverse effects from the recession acted differently from institutions in states that were not as affected by the recession (though almost every state experienced the economic downturn to some extent). The variables "Recession_High" and "After" are dummy variables equal to 1 if the college or university's state suffered large increases in unemployment (or large reductions in the home price index) or the quarter was 2007Q4 or after; otherwise, the variables are equal to zero. As noted above, this is an imperfect measure of the impact of the recession because a college may draw some of its students from outside of its state. However, the most selective schools and schools that draw less than one-third of their students from inside their state have been excluded from the sample because they are less likely to respond to state trends.

7.4 The Estimated Effects of the Great Recession

Table 7.1 displays the summary statistics of the IPEDS sample. On the left is the sample of all families. The bulk of the institutions in the sample are four-year colleges and universities, and the sample is evenly split between public and nonprofit, private institutions, with another 19 percent being for-profit, proprietary schools. Most of these schools focus on associate, bachelor's, and master's degrees, though there are a number of specialized institutions, which include schools of engineering and technology, schools of art, music, or design, health profession schools, and schools of business and management. Most of the schools in the sample are noncompetitive or have an unranked competitiveness level, which suggests they are not selective. In terms of the severity of the Great Recession, the states of the colleges and universities experienced an average growth of 5.1 percentage points in the unemployment rate from the first quarter of 2007 to the fourth quarter of 2009. About 22 percent of institutions are designated as being in states that were hardest hit by the recession, defined as experiencing 6.5 percentage points or more growth in unemployment during the time period. In terms of home values, the home price index fell on average 48.6 points in the states of the institutions, of which 20.2 percent being in states that witnessed a reduction in home values of 80 points or more.

7.4.1 The Effects of the Recession on College Enrollment

Table 7.2 focuses on the impact of the recession on college enrollment levels measured at the institutional level. The first three models focus on total fall enrollment,[7] while the following three models examine the total fall full-time equivalent (FTE) enrollment, which adjusts part-time enrollment

---

7. Students reported are those enrolled in courses creditable toward a degree or other formal award; students enrolled in courses that are part of a vocational or occupational program, including those enrolled in off-campus centers; and high school students taking regular college courses for credit.

Table 7.1   **Summary statistics**

Institutional level/sector	
Four-year	0.6082
Two-year	0.3721
Less than two-year	0.0196
Public	0.4117
Private (nonprofit)	0.3996
Proprietary (for-profit)	0.1887
Carnegie classification (2000)	
Research/doctoral institutions	0.0648
Master's institutions	0.1635
Bachelor's institutions	0.1542
Associate institutions	0.3511
Specialized institutions	0.1164
Tribal institutions	0.0084
Unknown	0.1416
Institutional type	
Public flagship university	0.0132
Historically black college or university (HBCU)	0.0265
Hispanic-serving institution	0.0114
Has a medical school	0.0334
Affiliated with a hospital	0.0172
Institutional competitiveness (Barron's ranking)	
Noncompetitive	0.3391
Less competitive	0.0777
Competitive	0.1808
Very competitive	0.0601
Highly competitive	0.0185
Unknown competitiveness	0.3238
Other institutional characteristics	
Total student enrollment	5,205
	(10,758)
Total expenditures (per $1,000)	$95,728
	(322,717)
In-state tuition and required fees	$11,051
	(8,641)
Recession severity measures	
State unemployment rate change 2007Q1 to 2009Q4 (percentage points)	5.12
	(1.50)
Large unemp. growth (6.5+ percentage points)	0.2195
State home price index (CMHPI) change 2007Q1 to 2009Q4	−48.63
	(59.65)
Large HPI reduction (fell 80+ points)	0.2020
Observations	20,065
Number of colleges and universities	3,374

Source: IPEDS 2004/5 to 2009/10.

Notes: Four-year colleges with less than one-third of their students from inside their state have been excluded from the sample, along with colleges in the most competitive category of the Barron's ratings (a total of fifty institutions). To be included in the sample, colleges needed to have at least five of the six possible years of data. Standard deviations shown in parentheses.

Table 7.2   The effects on college enrollment by the severity of the recession

Dependent variable	Total enrollment			Full-time equivalent (FTE) count		
	(1)	(2)	(3)	(4)	(5)	(6)
After recession (2007Q4 and after)	23.64	4.29	4.26	19.99	7.21	8.19
	(19.16)	(15.93)	(16.15)	(19.45)	(15.55)	(16.12)
After recession * Large unemp. growth (6.5 pct. or more)		88.09*			58.17	
		(47.87)			(35.82)	
Large unemp. growth (6.5 pct. or more)		−159.05			−177.49	
		(144.09)			(153.66)	
After recession * Large HPI reduction (fell 80 pts. or more)			95.67**			58.23*
			(48.47)			(35.35)
Large HPI reduction (fell 80 pts. or more)			−357.20			−317.76
			(219.49)			(221.06)
Year trend	40.60***	40.61***	40.65***	30.97***	30.98***	31.00***
	(7.85)	(7.85)	(7.84)	(6.85)	(6.85)	(6.85)
Observations	19,987	19,987	19,987	19,992	19,992	19,992
R^2	0.99	0.99	0.99	0.99	0.99	0.99

Notes: All regressions include the following controls: institutional level (dummy variables for two-year and less-than-two-year institutions); institutional sector (dummy variables for nonprofit, private, and for-profit institutions); 2000 Carnegie classification; institutional type (dummy variable for being a public flagship, HBCU, HSI, having a medical school, and being affiliated with a hospital); total expenditures; total expenditures squared; list in-state tuition and required fees; Barron's competitiveness ratings (a series of dummy variables); and a one-year lag in total enrollment. All models also include state fixed effects. Standard errors are shown in parentheses and have been clustered by institutional ID. Four-year colleges with less than one-third of their students from inside their state have been excluded from the sample, along with colleges in the most competitive category of the Barron's ratings.

***Significant at the 1 percent level.

**Significant at the 5 percent level.

*Significant at the 10 percent level.

before adding it to the full-time enrollment number. [8] As shown by the year trend variable, enrollment has generally grown during this time period. Focusing on the effects of the Great Recession, as shown by the "after recession" dummy variable, college enrollment levels at each institution were even a little higher after the start of the recession, though the results are not statistically significant. However, focusing on the enrollment levels in states more severely affected by the recession, it is clear that enrollment increased at a faster rate at these institutions postrecession. In particular, total fall enrollment jumped in states that experienced large increases in unemployment or reductions in the home price index. The effect on the FTE count was also positive but smaller, hinting at the possibility that the growth in enrollment was not all full-time students.

Table 7.3 investigates the effects of the recession on enrollment intensity by separating out the effects of the changes on full-time versus part-time college enrollment. As shown by the first three models, full-time enrollment levels were generally lower after the start of the recession, though colleges and universities in the hardest hit states had a weak overall pattern of small growth in full-time enrollments (the results are not statistically significant). In contrast, part-time enrollment grew substantially after the start of the recession across all states, as shown in models 4 through 6. Similar results are found if one uses the percentage of enrollment that is full-time or part-time rather than enrollment counts. [9]

The impact of the recession on enrollment was not evenly distributed by race or ethnicity. As shown in table 7.4, the growth in enrollment levels favored minority students in states hit hardest by the recession, while the enrollment levels of white students grew slightly overall but declined at institutions in states that struggled the most with the economic effects of the recession. In models 2 and 3, the top row suggested the enrollment of white students grew by about 21 on average per institution, but there were large reductions at institutions in the states most severely affected. Meanwhile, these same states experienced large growth in the level of enrollment among minority students. As suggested by the complicated nature of the context and recession, the effects on college enrollment appear to differ by racial subgroup.

Table 7.5 examines how the completion of certificates and degrees changed after the start of the recession. For instance, models 1 and 2 focus

8. The full-time equivalent of an institution's part-time enrollment is estimated by multiplying part-time enrollment by factors that vary by control and level of institution and level of student. For instance, part-time undergraduate enrollment is multiplied by 0.40 at a public, four-year college. The estimated full-time equivalent of part-time enrollment is then added to the full-time enrollment of the institution.

9. Across all institutions, the percentage of enrollment that was full-time fell about 0.5 percentage points while the percentage of enrollment that was part-time grew about 0.35 percentage points, with small differences in the growth or reduction in states that experienced a huge decline in home values.

Table 7.3   The effects of the recession on college enrollment intensity (full- and part-time)

Dependent variable	Full-time enrollment			Part-time enrollment		
	(1)	(2)	(3)	(4)	(5)	(6)
After recession (2007Q4 and after)	−35.01	−37.53***	−38.23***	61.48***	48.99***	53.78***
	(22.24)	(11.15)	(12.85)	(9.94)	(10.04)	(10.01)
After recession * Large unemp. growth		11.47			55.67	
		(69.42)			(34.08)	
Large unemp. growth (6.5 pct. or more)		−38.22			−318.05	
		(493.02)			(472.24)	
After recession * Large HPI reduction			15.90			38.08
			(63.61)			(33.94)
Large HPI reduction (fell 80 pts. or more)			−97.99			−589.11
			(626.88)			(649.16)
Year trend	−4.89	−4.89	−4.88	−13.84*	−13.84*	−13.81*
	(13.71)	(13.71)	(13.69)	(7.38)	(7.38)	(7.38)
Observations	20,064	20,064	20,064	17,924	17,924	17,924
R^2	0.89	0.89	0.89	0.89	0.89	0.89

Notes: All regressions include the following controls: institutional level (dummy variables for two-year and less-than-two-year institutions); institutional sector (dummy variables for nonprofit, private, and for-profit institutions), 2000 Carnegie classification; institutional type (dummy variable for being a public flagship, HBCU, HSI, having a medical school, and being affiliated with a hospital); total expenditures; total expenditures squared; list in-state tuition and required fees; Barron's competitiveness ratings (a series of dummy variables); and total student enrollment. All models also include state fixed effects. Standard errors are shown in parentheses and have been clustered by institutional ID. Four-year colleges with less than one-third of their students from inside their state have been excluded from the sample, along with colleges in the most competitive category of the Barron's ratings. Similar results are found if one uses the percentage of enrollment that is full-time or part-time rather than enrollment counts.

***Significant at the 1 percent level.

**Significant at the 5 percent level.

*Significant at the 10 percent level.

Table 7.4   The effects of the recession on college enrollment by race/ethnicity

Dependent variable	White enrollment			Minority enrollment		
	(1)	(2)	(3)	(4)	(5)	(6)
After recession (2007Q4 and after)	-10.29 (7.50)	21.11** (9.78)	20.92** (10.18)	12.33 (10.50)	-3.05 (12.16)	-9.21 (13.16)
After recession * Large unemp. growth		-143.04*** (27.97)			70.09** (34.73)	
Large unemp. growth (more than 6.5 pct. pts.)		347.55 (461.37)			62.75 (379.12)	
After recession * Large HPI reduction			-154.19*** (29.71)			106.42*** (36.24)
Large HPI reduction (fell 80 pts. or more)			345.95 (428.09)			-595.59 (429.50)
Year trend	-29.23*** (8.01)	-29.23*** (8.01)	-29.29*** (8.02)	21.88* (11.23)	21.88* (11.23)	21.93* (11.24)
Observations	20,065	20,065	20,065	20,065	20,065	20,065
R^2	0.88	0.88	0.88	0.82	0.82	0.82

Notes: All regressions include the following controls: institutional level (dummy variables for two-year and less-than-two-year institutions); institutional sector (dummy variables for nonprofit, private, and for-profit institutions), 2000 Carnegie classification; institutional type (dummy variable for being a public flagship, HBCU, HSI, having a medical school, and being affiliated with a hospital); total expenditures; total expenditures squared; list in-state tuition and required fees; Barron's competitiveness ratings (a series of dummy variables); and total student enrollment. All models also include state fixed effects. Standard errors are shown in parentheses and have been clustered by institutional ID. Four-year colleges with less than one-third of their students from inside their state have been excluded from the sample, along with colleges in the most competitive category of the Barron's ratings.

***Significant at the 1 percent level.

**Significant at the 5 percent level.

*Significant at the 10 percent level.

Table 7.5 The effects of the recession on degrees and certificates completed

Dependent variable	Certificates less than one year		Certificates one to two years		Certificates two to four years		Associate degrees		Bachelor's degrees	
	(1)	(2)	(3)	(4)	(5)	(6)	(7)	(8)	(9)	(10)
After recession (2007Q4 and after)	51.57***	55.96***	16.47***	12.32***	22.21***	25.13***	16.02***	3.47	−9.37**	−36.50***
	(5.40)	(10.53)	(2.14)	(2.50)	(2.10)	(2.82)	(3.89)	(5.41)	(4.24)	(5.52)
After recession * Large unemp. growth		−17.36		18.74**		−9.98*		57.21***		119.38***
		(32.36)		(8.98)		(4.91)		(21.20)		(23.92)
Large unemp. growth (6.5 pct. pts. or more)		81.15**		14.76		5.49***		−55.73		46.64
		(35.08)		(16.31)		(1.74)		(52.92)		(196.78)
Year trend	2.26	2.26	1.91**	1.90**	0.34	0.33	−0.43	−0.46	10.57***	10.63***
	(1.93)	(1.93)	(0.78)	(0.78)	(0.23)	(0.23)	(1.29)	(1.29)	(2.12)	(2.12)
Observations	13,463	13,463	14,494	14,494	11,215	11,215	16,501	16,501	14,830	14,830
R^2	0.20	0.20	0.25	0.25	0.17	0.17	0.75	0.75	0.87	0.87

Notes: All regressions include the following controls: institutional level (dummy variables for two-year and less–than–two-year institutions); institutional sector (dummy variables for non-profit, private, and for-profit institutions); 2000 Carnegie classification; institutional type (dummy variable for being a public flagship, HBCU, HSI, having a medical school, and being affiliated with a hospital); total expenditures; total expenditures squared; list in-state tuition and required fees; Barron's competitiveness ratings (a series of dummy variables); and total student enrollment. All models also include state fixed effects. Standard errors are shown in parentheses and have been clustered by institutional ID. Four-year colleges with less than one-third of their students from inside their state have been excluded from the sample, along with colleges in the most competitive category of the Barron's ratings.

***Significant at the 1 percent level.

**Significant at the 5 percent level.

*Significant at the 10 percent level.

on the completion of certificates that take less than one year. [10] The results suggest that after the recession, the number of awards made by institutions in the form of certificates increased, with the largest growth in the number of less-than-one-year certificates. Certificates that take one to two years to complete also increased in states that had especially high growth in unemployment (similar results were found when using the CMHPI definition instead). The number of associate degrees awarded also increased after the recession, most notably in states with higher unemployment rates. In terms of bachelor's degrees, the number awarded fell after the recession in comparison to before, but again, in states that were hit hardest by the recession, the number of bachelor's degrees awarded increased on average. For all these models, similar results were found when looking at the differential effects in states with large reductions in the CMHPI. While this analysis does not include a long enough time frame to suggest that the recession affected initial student pathways and longer-term degree attainment, it may suggest that after the recession, upper-level students were more likely to stay in school to complete their degrees, especially in states where unemployment rates were particularly high.

7.4.2 The Effects of the Recession on What Families Pay: Tuition Costs and Financial Aid

To understand how the recession affected college affordability for families, table 7.6 focuses on the tuition revenue collected by institutions. The outcomes are all adjusted to be reported per FTE student. Models 1 through 3 focus on the gross tuition and required fees revenues collected by colleges, which includes student aid applied to tuition and fees. Models 4 through 6 instead use net tuition and required fees as the dependent variable, which is defined as the amount of money the institution takes in from students after institutional grant aid is provided. Finally, models 7 through 9 isolate the tuition revenue that comes directly from students—it does not count any financial aid, including federal, state, and institutional grants.

From all of the models, it is clear that families paid on average more after the recession than before. This is on top of a general increasing trend in the tuition revenue per FTE that happened throughout the analysis window. Most notably, the amount directly from students and their families increased $360 on average. The growth in costs to families were especially large in the states that experienced the recession more severely, with the increase being far more than double regardless of whether looking at states with large increases in unemployment or reductions in home values. While the Pell grant did increase during this time period, such increases appear to have

10. The outcome is defined as the total number of awards granted that require completion of an organized program of study in less than one academic year (two semesters or three quarters), or designed for completion in less than thirty semester or trimester credit hours by a student enrolled full-time.

Table 7.6   The effects of the recession on college tuition revenue

Dependent variable	Gross tuition and fees revenue per FTE			Net tuition and fees revenue per FTE (includes government aid to students)			Net tuition directly from students per FTE (does not include aid)		
	(1)	(2)	(3)	(4)	(5)	(6)	(7)	(8)	(9)
After recession (2007Q4 and after)	165.26*	44.25	84.70	220.00**	78.67	119.14	360.14***	261.73**	286.27**
	(95.86)	(106.51)	(95.03)	(92.46)	(101.43)	(89.58)	(113.12)	(122.83)	(116.24)
After recession * Large unemp. growth		550.49**			643.58***			447.82**	
		(233.33)			(230.46)			(174.08)	
Large unemp. growth (more than 6.5 pct. pts.)		1,083.78			1,062.07			350.82	
		(710.62)			(743.35)			(614.67)	
After recession * Large HPI reduction			398.04**			498.93***			365.11**
			(195.09)			(188.17)			(159.08)
Large HPI reduction (fell 80 pts. or more)			2,336.30*			3,483.44**			3,311.11***
			(1,321.21)			(1,374.98)			(930.81)
Year trend	157.60***	157.61***	157.77***	122.65***	122.63***	122.83***	−127.12***	−127.12***	−126.97***
	(34.22)	(34.22)	(34.21)	(33.12)	(33.11)	(33.10)	(33.37)	(33.38)	(33.37)
Observations	20,039	20,039	20,039	20,036	20,036	20,036	20,045	20,045	20,045
R^2	0.65	0.65	0.65	0.52	0.52	0.52	0.53	0.53	0.53

Notes: All regressions include the following controls: institutional level (dummy variables for two-year and less-than-two-year institutions); institutional sector (dummy variables for nonprofit, private, and for-profit institutions); 2000 Carnegie classification; institutional type (dummy variable for being a public flagship, HBCU, HSI, having a medical school, and being affiliated with a hospital); total expenditures; total expenditures squared; list in-state tuition and required fees; Barron's competitiveness ratings (a series of dummy variables); and total student enrollment. All models also include state fixed effects. Standard errors are shown in parentheses and have been clustered by institutional ID. Four-year colleges with less than one-third of their students from inside their state have been excluded from the sample, along with colleges in the most competitive category of the Barron's ratings. The outcome is per full-time equivalent student (FTE). Net tuition and required fees is the amount the institution takes in from students after institutional grant aid is provided (it includes government financial aid contributed in the name of the students. Net tuition directly from students is the tuition revenue that comes directly from students and does not count any financial aid [federal, state, local, or institutional grants]).

***Significant at the 1 percent level.
**Significant at the 5 percent level.
*Significant at the 10 percent level.

been outweighed by growth in college tuition prices and reductions in other forms of financial aid.

Table 7.7 provides additional evidence to suggest that financial aid receipt declined after the recession. First, even with major changes to the Pell grant, models 1 and 2 suggest that the percentage of students at the institutions in the sample who received a federal grant did not change after the recession. Moreover, the students at those institutions received on average less in grant aid than before. This might not indicate a reduction in an aid program; instead, it may reflect a change in the types of students receiving aid, and the amount could have declined due to less intense attendance patterns (i.e., part-time students receive less financial aid than full-time students). Similar results were found examining states with large reductions in the CMHPI. Meanwhile, student loan amounts increased. While there was a positive, though statistically insignificant, increase in the percentage of students who took out a loan, the mean amount received increased. In separate analyses, I did not find a change in the percentage of students who received institutional grants or the mean amount received.

7.5 Conclusions

The Great Recession has had important effects on both the supply and demand sides of higher education. Families suffered from reduced college affordability in the form of decreasing family incomes and home values and rising college tuition prices. Meanwhile, growing unemployment reduced the foregone costs of attendance, suggesting some of the trends caused by the recession could have had positive effects on college enrollment and spending. Moreover, complications such as the strong reliance on debt to finance college expenditures, large cohorts of recent high school graduates, and changing federal aid policy made the conditions surrounding the Great Recession even more complicated. Taken together, it was unclear, ex ante, what the overall effect of the Great Recession would be on college enrollment and family expenditures.

Taken in sum, the results suggest that the net effect of the recession has been positive in terms of college enrollment levels. While college enrollment increases generally each year, after the start of the Great Recession, there was an additional increase in attendance, and the growth in enrollment levels was concentrated at colleges and universities in the states that were hardest hit by the recession. The growth was strongest in terms of part-time enrollment and among students of color, thereby suggesting that the effects of the recession were not evenly felt by type of potential student. The growth in short-term awards suggests that higher unemployment did reduce the foregone costs of attending college, but the largest growth was in shorter, perhaps more vocational, programs that award certificates that take less than two years to complete. However, there may have also been an effect on degree

Table 7.7   The effects of the recession on financial aid received

Dependent variable	Federal grants				College loans			
	Percentage received		Mean amount received		Percentage received		Mean amount received	
	(1)	(2)	(3)	(4)	(5)	(6)	(7)	(8)
After recession (2007Q4 and after)	-0.3397	-0.6178	-190.86***	-182.70***	0.1138	0.0860	475.98***	506.31***
	(0.3868)	(0.3974)	(20.39)	(21.50)	(0.3788)	(0.4006)	(45.90)	(47.93)
After recession * Large unemp. growth		1.2955		-37.74		0.1298		-138.91**
		(0.7930)		(29.04)		(0.7202)		(69.94)
Large unemp. growth (more than 6.5 pct. pts.)		15.5182***		-52.57		-8.7517**		-134.52
		(3.5566)		(194.31)		(4.4465)		(260.14)
Year trend	2.2664***	2.2664***	378.23***	378.24***	1.0312***	1.0312***	345.08***	345.11***
	(0.1244)	(0.1244)	(6.88)	(6.88)	(0.1263)	(0.1263)	(15.14)	(15.14)
Observations	18,964	18,964	19,059	19,059	18,964	18,964	17,614	17,614
R^2	0.33	0.33	0.41	0.41	0.52	0.52	0.47	0.47

Notes: All regressions include the following controls: institutional level (dummy variables for two-year and less-than-two-year institutions); institutional sector (dummy variables for nonprofit, private, and for-profit institutions); 2000 Carnegie classification; institutional type (dummy variable for being a public flagship, HBCU, HSI, having a medical school, and being affiliated with a hospital); total expenditures; total expenditures squared; list in-state tuition and required fees; Barron's competitiveness ratings (a series of dummy variables); and total student enrollment. All models also include state fixed effects. Standard errors are shown in parentheses and have been clustered by institutional ID. Four-year colleges with less than one-third of their students from inside their state have been excluded from the sample, along with colleges in the most competitive category of the Barron's ratings. The percentages and mean amounts are for full-time, first-time degree/certificate-seeking undergraduates.

***Significant at the 1 percent level.

**Significant at the 5 percent level.

*Significant at the 10 percent level.

completion among upper-level students, especially in states that experienced large increases in unemployment.

In terms of college affordability and financing, families paid more in tuition on average. Gross tuition and required fees as well as tuition revenue, not including financial aid, both increased after the recession at a rate that outpaced the general, annual upward trend. These increases were focused at institutions in states most severely affected by the recession. Examining trends in federal grants and loans confirms the findings that college affordability declined during the recession, even with the policy expansion of the Pell grant.

The overall enrollment and cost effects are similar to those found with previous recessions, but given all the factors that changed during the Great Recession, it is not surprising that the impact varied along a number of dimensions, including enrollment intensity, race/ethnicity, and type of degree awarded. The relative strength of the positive and negative influences of the recession varied by type of student. Moreover, just as the severity of the recession differed by state, so did the impact on college enrollment and affordability. This suggests that the effects of the Great Recession were varied due to the complex context.

Appendix

Table 7A.1   **Geographic variation in the severity of the recession (large changes in state unemployment rate and home price index [CMHPI], 2007Q1– 2009Q4)**

Large absolute increase in unemployment rate (more than 6.5 percentage points)		Large absolute reduction in HPI (fell 80 points or more)	
Alabama	Illinois	Arizona	Massachusetts
Arizona	Michigan	California	Nevada
California	Nevada	Florida	New Jersey
Florida	Rhode Island	Hawaii	Rhode Island
		Maryland	

Source: Bureau of Labor Statistics (BLS), Local Area Unemployment Statistics (LAUS), Federal Housing Finance Agency (FHFA), housing price index (CMHPI) of conventional mortgages.

Notes: The CMHPI represents Fannie Mae and Freddie Mac-eligible mortgages on single-family detached properties (provided for loan limits up to $729,750 for one-unit properties). The All-Transactions House Price Index, which includes both sales of property and appraisal values from refinance transactions, is used here. The correlation between the two measures is 0.607. The correlation between the two measures is 0.5204.

References

Advisory Committee on Student Financial Assistance. 2010. *The Rising Price of Inequality: How Inadequate Grant Aid Limits College Access and Persistence.* Washington, DC: US Department of Education.

Barr, Andrew, and Sarah Turner. 2012. "Out of a Job and into School: Labor Market Policies and College Enrollment during the Great Recession." Working Paper, University of Virginia.

Becker, G. 1964. *Human Capital: A Theoretical and Empirical Analysis.* New York: Columbia University Press.

Bell, David N., and David G. Blanchflower. 2011. "Young People and the Great Recession." *Oxford Review of Economic Policy* 27 (2): 241–67.

Bettinger, Eric, B. T. Long, Philip Oreopoulos, and Lisa Sanbonmatsu. 2012. "The Role of Application Assistance and Information in College Decisions: Results from the H&R Block FAFSA Experiment." *Quarterly Journal of Economics* 127 (3). doi: 10.1093/qje/qjs017.

Breneman, David W. 2002. "For Colleges, This Is Not Just Another Recession." *Chronicle of Higher Education, The Chronicle Review* B7. http://chronicle.com/weekly/v48/i40/40b00701.htm.

Card, David, and Thomas Lemieux. 2001. "Dropout and Enrollment Trends in the Postwar Period." In *Risky Behavior among Youths: An Economic Analysis*, edited by Jonathan Gruber, 439–82. Chicago: University of Chicago Press.

Chitty, Haley. 2009. "The Economy and Student Financial Aid: Troubling Trends—and the Silver Lining." *University Business*, January. Accessed August 25, 2012. http://www.universitybusiness.com/article/economy-and-student-financial-aid.

College Board. 2011. *Trends in College Pricing.* New York: The College Board Advocacy & Policy Center.

———. 2012a. *Trends in College Pricing.* New York: The College Board Advocacy & Policy Center.

———. 2012b. *Trends in Student Aid.* New York: The College Board Advocacy & Policy Center.

Dellas, Harris, and Plutarchos Sakellaris. 2003. "On the Cyclicality of Schooling: Theory and Evidence." *Oxford Economic Papers* 55 (1): 148–72.

Glover, Andrew, Jonathan Heathcote, Dirk Krueger, and José-Víctor Ríos-Rull. 2011. "Intergenerational Redistribution in the Great Recession." NBER Working Paper no. 16924, Cambridge, MA.

Hurd, Michael D., and Susann Rohwedder. 2010. "Effects of the Financial Crisis and Great Recession on American Households." NBER Working Paper no. 16407, Cambridge, MA.

Johnson, Rucker C. 2011. "The Impact of Parental Wealth on College Enrollment & Degree Attainment: Evidence from the Housing Boom & Bust." Working Paper, University of California, Berkeley.

Leslie, L., and P. Brinkman. 1987. "Student Price Response in Higher Education." *Journal of Higher Education* 58:181–204.

Long, Bridget T. 2004a. "Does the Format of an Aid Program Matter? The Effect of In-Kind Tuition Subsidies." *Review of Economics and Statistics* 86 (3): 767–82.

———. 2004b. "How Have College Decisions Changed Overtime? An Application of the Conditional Logistic Choice Model." *Journal of Econometrics* 121 (1–2): 271–96.

———. 2007. "The Contributions of Economics to the Study of College Access and Success." *Teachers College Record* 109 (10): 2367–2443.

Long, Bridget T., and Erin K. Riley. 2007. "Financial Aid: A Broken Bridge to College Access?" *Harvard Educational Review*. http://hepg.org/her/abstract/229.

Lovenheim, Michael F. 2011. "The Effect of Liquid Housing Wealth on College Enrollment." *Journal of Labor Economics* 29 (4): 741–71.

Lovenheim, Michael F., and C. Lockwood Reynolds. 2012. "The Effect of Housing Wealth on College Choice: Evidence from the Housing Boom." NBER Working Paper no. 18075, Cambridge, MA.

Mahan, Shannon M. 2011. "Federal Pell Grant Program of the Higher Education Act: Background, Recent Changes, and Current Legislative Issues." May 12. Washington, DC: Congressional Research Service.

Schachter, Ron. 2009. "The State of Student Aid." *University Business*, July/August. http://www.universitybusiness.com/article/state-student-aid.

8
Federal and State Financial Aid during the Great Recession

Eric Bettinger and Betsy Williams

8.1 Introduction

Shifts in need-based financial aid policies in the United States, particularly the Pell grant, have historically been sporadic and incremental. Lawmakers have been reluctant or unable to achieve consensus around steady growth, and so the Pell grant has often stagnated and failed to maintain pace with increases in college costs. The "corrections" to the Pell have come sporadically, and lawmakers have often needed an extra push to establish consensus behind large increases in the Pell. The Great Recession of 2008 provided such a push. In response to the recession, Congress passed the 2009 American Recovery and Reinvestment Act and the 2010 Student Aid and Fiscal Responsibility Act. Together these two acts set in motion increases in both the size of individual Pell grants and the overall Pell expenditure.

Even in historical perspective these changes are extreme. Consider that over the thirty-eight-year history of the Pell grant award, the maximum real Pell award has either been stagnant or slightly decreasing in fifteen years and had less than 5 percent growth in another seven of those years. Only in three periods has the Pell seen substantial growth: the Pell maximum increased over five years from $1,050 to $1,800 (between 1975 and 1980); the award steadily grew over eight years from $2,340 to $4,000 (from 1996 to 2004); and then it rose over these three years from $4,050 to $5,350 (between 2007 and 2010). Outside of the initial years of the Pell, this growth during the Great

Eric Bettinger is associate professor of education at Stanford University School of Education and a research associate of the National Bureau of Economic Research. Betsy Williams is a doctoral student in the economics of education at Stanford University.

For acknowledgments, sources of research support, and disclosure of the authors' material financial relationships, if any, please see http://www.nber.org/chapters/c12861.ack.

Recession was the most rapid growth over a three-year period in the history of the Pell grant, with the maximum Pell grant growing by over 32 percent. The growth in overall expenditure is also extreme in historical perspective. With the exception of its foundational years, the annual growth in overall Pell grant expenditure has exceeded 10 percent only a dozen times. The annual growth rate in overall expenditure has topped 20 percent just four times in its history, and two of those times occurred during the Great Recession; Pell expenditure grew by 15 percent, 25 percent, and then 64 percent going into 2008, 2009, and 2010, respectively. The three-year growth rate (134 percent) in overall expenditure over the Great Recession was over twice the maximum of the three-year growth rates over the life of the program.[1]

While advocates and supporters of the Pell have lauded this increase (e.g., Shireman 2007; Katsinas et al. 2012), it is unclear how this historic increase has actually affected student outcomes. In particular, this historic increase in federal financial aid comes at a time when states' investments in higher education have been declining, and for reasons we discuss below, states face unprecedented fiscal pressures in maintaining public services. Public economists often investigate the links between state and federal policies. Federal policy is never made in a vacuum, and state lawmakers often consider changes in federal policy when forming state policies. If state policymakers considered the federal increase in the Pell grant when deciding on their own state budget allocations, they might have altered their policies accordingly. If, for example, states decided to reduce their budget allocations in response to the increase in the Pell, then the overall impact on students might be far less than anticipated in the passing of the stimulus.

The response of states to the Pell program is precisely the focus of our study. We attempt to document the trends in state and federal policies during the Great Recession. Our study does not establish the causal relationship between state and federal policies during the Great Recession, but we show a pattern: as many as half of the states have reduced the generosity of their financial aid programs in response to the Great Recession. This pattern of reducing generosity in the wake of increases in the Federal Pell Grant Program is not new, and we document that this potential fiscal federalism has become more apparent since 2000.

To illustrate how state policies have changed, we provide examples from multiple states showing how their financial aid programs have changed over time. We use student-level data from Ohio to illustrate how students' net aid packages changed in response to the combined changes in federal and state aid policy. Using these student-level data, we provide one example of how this policy may have had disproportionate effects on the poorest of students.

---

1. The prior maximum was the three-year growth rate of 61 percent covering the period from 2001 to 2003. We have also excluded the earliest years of the program when the program was stabilizing.

Section 8.2 provides a brief overview of student aid programs in the United States. We document trends in both state and federal aid. In section 8.3 we document trends in state and federal policies, we show how the correlation between state and federal policies has changed over time, and we discuss more generally how the Great Recession only intensified fiscal pressures on state governments. We provide some examples of specific states that illustrate this trend. In section 8.4 we present evidence from Ohio. We demonstrate how student aid packages have changed during the Great Recession, and we show how these changes have differed across students. In section 8.5 we interpret these results, relating them to the theory of fiscal federalism.

8.2 Background on State and Federal Student Aid Programs

8.2.1 Federal and State Student Aid Programs

The idea of broadly targeted federal financial aid for higher education was publicly proposed halfway through the twentieth century, although not enacted for another quarter century. In its 1947 report, the Truman Commission imagined a larger role for the federal government in higher education; in particular, they suggested making the educational provisions of the Servicemen's Readjustment Act of 1944 (or the GI bill) into a larger public policy program (Thelin 2004).

These ideas resonated politically. At the beginning of 1960s several states took up the ideas presented in the Truman Commission report, developing their own various financial aid programs (Hansen and Stampen 1994). Twenty-eight states developed programs before the Pell grant was created by the Higher Education Amendments of 1972, and most of the other states came on board in its immediate wake (Gladieux, Hauptman, and Knapp 1994).

However, through the 1960s there was little federal political support for these recommendations, and research contracts instead were the predominant federal funding mechanism for higher education, spurred by federal policy for competitive scientific research and development. The unequal distribution of research funds was not politically savvy; in 1960 a majority of these federal dollars went to only six schools, and to only a handful of departments at each of those schools. This funding arrangement further suffered from the growing distrust of awarding federal contracts to campuses with civil unrest (Thelin 2004).

In 1968 the financial aid ideas from the Truman Commission were revived in the Carnegie Commission for Higher Education's report, *Quality and Equality: New Levels of Federal Responsibility for Higher Education*. In particular, the report recommended that generous federal funds for college be given as "opportunity grants" directly to students to attend colleges of their choice. The report, revised in 1970, was popularly seen as the basis of the Basic Educational Opportunity Grants created in 1972 (Lagemann 1989).

By this time political support had gathered for these portable student grants for full-time undergraduate study, soon called Pell grants. Student lobbying groups, the Carnegie Commission, and the Rivlin Commission championed it, over objections from the academic establishment. Legislators saw great direct benefits to their constituents, especially if their state colleges and universities did not get exclusive federal research grants. Making money available to all accredited colleges, the program brought low-income students many more choices while carrying funding to a broad array of institutions (Thelin 2004). The federal bill also encouraged the growth of state-level aid with a State Student Incentive Grant that would match states' need-based grant dollars (Gladieux, Hauptman, and Knapp 1994).

8.2.2 Other Forms of Financial Aid

State and federal need-based grant programs are certainly not students' only source of funding. The College Board estimates that students in the 2009/10 school year received $154.5 billion in financial aid (College Board 2010). Of this, 18 percent, or about $28.2 billion, came through the Federal Pell Grant Program. States provided an additional $8.6 billion in grants to students, and to institutions, an additional $26.0 billion. The largest component of aid is the Federal Student Loan Program, which makes up $65.8 billion, or about 43 percent, of all federal aid. Until recently, the federal government did not award merit-based financial aid. The Federal Academic Competitiveness Grant is the first federal award to include a merit component. Other federal grant programs, including the Academic Competitiveness Grant and National Science and Mathematics Access to Retain Talent (SMART) grants, made up an additional $12.0 billion in aid. Pell grants and state need-based grants make up about one-quarter of the overall financial aid awarded to students.

States' need- and merit-based aid programs have existed alongside each other in many states for decades. The College Board, relying on data from the National Association of State Student Grant and Aid Programs (NASSGAP), show that non-need-based grants increased sharply throughout the 1990s. In the 1989/90 school year, non-need-based grants made up about 11 percent of states' total expenditure on student grants for college. Need-based grants made up the other 89 percent. By 2000, non-need-based grants rose to 22 percent, and the average expenditure in such programs per student tripled. Non-need-based grants continued to rise through the early part of the twenty-first century, although like need-based grant aid, their generosity has decreased in the last few years.

State appropriations are another way in which states support public and private institutions. In the 2010/11 academic year, excluding the federal stimulus dollars, states gave about 76.1 billion dollars to higher education (College Board 2011). This is a considerable decline from the peak in appropriations of 84.7 billion in the 2007/8 academic year. During the 2010/11 school year, the College Board estimates an increase in appropriations of about 2.8 billion as a result of the federal stimulus. The overall size of the appropriations budget is nine to ten times the size of student grant programs. These often cover operating expenses and other regular budget items.

8.2.3 State Budget Crunch

There is a substantial literature and set of media reports that document the ongoing fiscal crises that many states face in their budgets (see Steinhauer 2008; Johnson, Oliff, and Williams 2011). While declining revenues during the Great Recession have intensified the fiscal pressures states face, a growing amount of fiscal pressure, particularly with respect to the funding in higher education, has been building since even before the recession.

Kane and Orszag (2003) discuss these fiscal pressures. They focus on the expansion of Medicaid and its growing costs during the 1990s. They show that Medicaid expenditures depleted state budgets, and states decreased their investments in higher education as a result of these growing costs. Rizzo (2004) builds on Kane and Orszag by investigating how primary and secondary school spending might also have increased the fiscal pressure on states' higher education budgets. Rizzo argues that equalization of funding forced states to make greater financial commitments to K-12 education. As states struggled to increase spending in low-income districts, they reduced the funding of higher education. As much as 25 percent of the increase in funding for K-12 came from decreasing investments in higher education. This reduction in state appropriations affected tuition costs and explains part of the rise in college tuitions during the 1990s and early twenty-first century.

8.2.4 Theories of How States and Institutions Respond

Quite a few studies investigate how higher education institutions adjust tuition levels in relation to federal financial aid. The Bennett hypothesis, suggested by secretary of education William Bennett in 1987, is that colleges and universities appropriate Pell grants via tuition increases. Empirical evidence is mixed. Singell and Stone (2007) find that tuition at private institutions and out-of-state tuition at public institutions increases dollar for dollar with the Pell, but in-state tuition does not respond. Rizzo and Ehrenberg (2004) find that higher in-state tuition is associated with increased federal and state need-based grants and subsidized loan access, but states raise need-based aid at the same time. Long (2004) finds only weak increases in tuitions after the HOPE Tax Credit and Lifelong Learning Tax Credit: public two-year colleges charging $1,000 to $2,000 with large numbers of students eligible for the credits increased tuition 18 percent more than other colleges, but there was no such change for public four-year colleges.

Recent working papers suggest evidence of capture in certain contexts. Cellini and Goldin (2012) find evidence for higher tuition at for-profit Title

IV schools (eligible for federal funding) relative to non-Title IV schools. They use for-profit schools that offer certificates, associate degrees, and non-degree programs and control for school quality (for instance, passage rates on state cosmetology exams) where possible. Turner (2012) uses a combination of regression discontinuity and regression kink designs to identify changes, finding that 16 percent of Pell grant aid is captured by schools in prices, with patterns varying by institution type.

As Hoxby (1997) mentions, federal financial aid may not be salient enough to many higher education institutions to have a large effect on their tuition policies; in contrast to health care payments, the federal government is a fairly minor payer for most schools. This would largely depend on how many students are eligible for aid and how high tuition levels are relative to grant levels. Federal aid policy may be more salient to large public schools, but they face opposing political considerations when setting tuition. However, an entire state will certainly have a large number of needy students, so the level of Pell grant funding should be salient to any state offering its own portable need-based financial aid packages.

8.3 Relationships between State and Federal Programs

8.3.1 Historical Aggregate Relationships

Historically, states have had the largest responsibility in funding higher education. As we discussed above, states have a variety of ways in which they invest in higher education. The two largest programs are the direct operating and capital subsidies offered to public universities and student-level subsidies, including both need- and merit-based awards. As we discussed above, our focus is on student-level, need-based portable subsidies.

We focus on these need-based subsidies since these are the programs that run most parallel to the Pell grant program. Changes in the availability of Pell grant funds directly affect the funds available for the students eligible for these state need-based awards. Additionally, these state need-based aid programs have high visibility as media and students' direct reports from financial aid offices are likely to mention these programs.

Figure 8.1 shows the generosity of the Pell grant and state need-based awards over time. The data for this come from the College Board. The College Board estimated these data by combining data from the NASSGAP survey with data from the Integrated Postsecondary Education Data System (IPEDS). The College Board adjusted these to be in current dollars. As the figure shows, the general trend over time is for increased levels of state need-based aid over time. The peak was in 2007/8 when per-student spending was nearly $500. Once the recession began, need-based aid declined in 2008/9 and again in 2009/10.

We have also plotted in figure 8.1 how the Pell grant, in real dollars, has changed over time. The two have similar trend lines in that both have

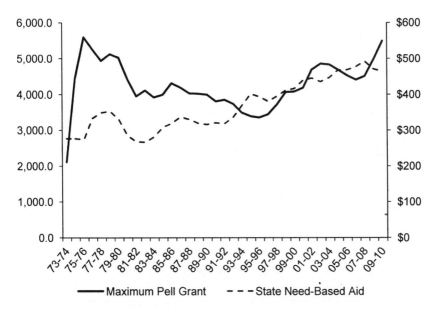

Fig. 8.1 Real maximum value of the Pell and state need-based aid over time
Source: College Board (2011).

increased in generosity over time. This increase in generosity is small relative to the corresponding trend in tuition costs (College Board 2011).

There are a few interesting patterns when we compare these series. In the long period leading up to 1990, Pell funding and state aid seemed to move in unison. When the Pell grant increased, states expanded state aid as well. In fact, the correlation between the Pell and state need-based grants was about 0.37 between 1974 and 1990. For each five-year period, we computed the correlation. In each year, we cycled the oldest observation out of the computation and added the new year's observation. This set of correlations is always positive, and it exceeds 0.5 for more than half of the sample. Interestingly, as figure 8.2 shows, the Pell grant maintained a negative correlation with unemployment rates throughout the 1970s and 1980s: real Pell grant aid went up when unemployment rates were low and vice versa.

These patterns changed in 1990. First, starting around the recession of 1990, the real value of the Pell grant began falling. The Pell's real value continued to decline until around 1996. Starting in 1996, the Pell began a sustained increase, which lasted through 2004. State grants followed a different pattern. Throughout the 1990s and early into the twenty-first century, state need-based aid had a period of sustained growth. What is interesting is that this growth seemed to accelerate when the Pell's growth was slow (early 1990s, 2004–2008) and decelerated or even dropped when the Pell's growth was large (2001–2003, post-2008). Aside from the late 1990s, where the Pell

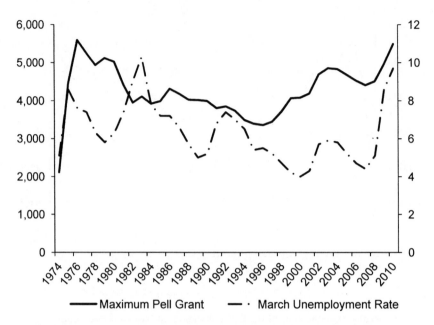

Maximum Pell Grant — **· March Unemployment Rate**

Fig. 8.2 Real maximum value of Pell grants and the March unemployment rate, 1974–2010

Source: Number of Pell recipients from the US Department of Education "2009–2010 Federal Pell Grant End-of-Year Report." March unemployment rate from the Current Population Survey. Real dollars inflated to March 2011 dollars using March consumer price index (CPI) figures from BLS.

Note: Number of Pell recipients is measured for the school year ending in the stated year; for example, the figure for 1974 is for the school year 1973/74.

and state awards seemed to have a positive correlation, the correlation in every other period since 1990 has been negative. This is a dramatic change from the pattern prior to 1990.

The pattern between the business cycle and Pell grant expenditure seemed to change as well after 1990. While unemployment rates and the real Pell grant maintained a negative correlation (i.e., unemployment rates increased and Pell decreased) throughout the 1990s, the correlation was considerably lower in its absolute value in the 1990s (−.141) versus the 1980s (−.320). After 2000, the correlation changes dramatically, turning from negative to positive (.726). Unlike any other period in the history of the Pell, policymakers started to increase the Pell during economic downturns while letting it stagnate (in real terms) during economic upswings. Conversely, state policymakers maintained a negative relationship with the business cycle. When unemployment rates increased after 2000, states decreased (or at least slowed the growth) of state need-based aid programs.

Why did this change occur? There are a number of plausible explanations for this pattern. First, as we discussed in the prior section, states

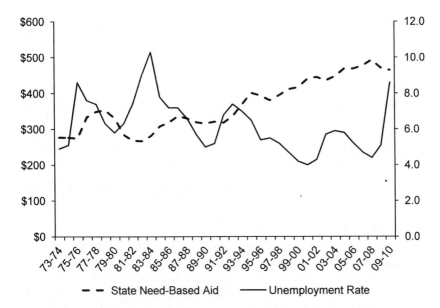

Fig. 8.3 Real average state aid and the March unemployment rates over time
Source: College Board (2011). March unemployment rate from CPS.

faced unprecedented fiscal pressures during the early twenty-first century. The decline in state revenues during the 2000 and 2008 recessions, and the increased pressure on maintaining state fiscal programs might have forced states to cut other state programs.

A potentially complimentary story involves fiscal federalism. States face a dilemma anytime that they consider budget cuts. The story of fiscal federalism in a period where budget cuts are happening is about strategically coordinating federal budget changes to state spending cuts. If the federal government takes on a more significant role in funding a particular program, the state, regardless of the fiscal pressure they face, can strategically make decisions in response.

The underlying phenomenon here is a shift in the way that Pell grant increases occur rather than a change in state policies. As figure 8.3 illustrates, the relationship between real state need-based grants and the business cycle has been fairly constant over time. With only a few exceptions, states' commitments to need-based student aid have been procyclical over time. As unemployment rates have risen, states have generally decreased their overall expenditure on state-based financial aid. Pell grant generosity followed a similar pattern prior to 2000. After 2000, the federal government began using the Pell as a countercyclical measure.

We discuss this further below. However, the newly found countercyclicality of the Pell creates a policy hedge for states. Prior to 2000, students could face "triple" cuts. An economic downturn could impact their family's finances directly, could reduce their Pell grants, and could reduce their state need-based grants. With a countercyclical Pell, the last two effects could offset each other.

Additionally, a goal of this chapter is to document the relationship between state and federal spending during the Great Recession. A key point in examining the correlations between the business cycle and state and federal need-based aid is that the structural change in these correlations likely began around 2000 and predates the Great Recession. The magnitude of the increase during the Great Recession might have been historic, but the increase itself was consistent with the early twenty-first century. We will return to this discussion in the final section of the chapter.

8.3.2 Heterogeneity in States' Responses

While thus far we have described overall trends across states, we now turn our attention to understanding the heterogeneity in state policies. For this exercise, we rely on data from the National Association of State Student Grant and Aid Programs (NASSGAP 1972–2012). The NASSGAP has annually collected and published data on state financial aid for higher education since 1969. It collects information on programs and spending directly from its members, the state agencies that administer state-funded financial aid. It is commonly used as a data source by organizations such as the College Board and the National Center for Education Statistics. The NASSGAP is one of the few sources of state need-based aid data. Sources like IPEDS and the National Postsecondary Student Aid Survey (NPSAS) often conflate receipt of state need-based aid with institutional aid. Even so, the state data vary in their quality. The NASSGAP surveys state representatives, and there are some inconsistencies in the data.[2] The data consistently report the overall expenditure of grant aid categorized by level (undergraduate or graduate) and whether awards are need based. Other measures reported vary by year. From 1973 through 1994 NASSGAP directly reports the number of students per state receiving grants. From 1995 through 2002 we construct this from NASSGAP estimates of the percentage of students receiving need-based aid. From 2003 through 2010 we use the count of recipients in the state's primary need-based aid program. Thus, the number data change over time in how they are measured, but they are consistent across states within any year.

There is substantial variation across states and time in state need-based aid programs. Most states have had an active state need-based program every year since at least 1982. There are a few exceptions, when states are between

2. For instance, the classification of the large DC TAG program differs across years, leading to substantial variation across years. As a federally funded program, DC TAG is excluded from the NASSGAP report in some years. With a means test of one million dollars, the program is classified as non-need-aid in some years and need-based aid in others.

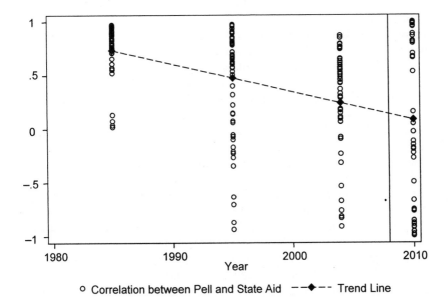

○ Correlation between Pell and State Aid   − −◆− − Trend Line

Fig. 8.4 State correlations between average state need-based grant and the Pell grant
Source: Authors' computations using NASSGAP data.

programs (e.g., Wyoming 2001) or when states have opted out of programs for a few years (e.g., South Dakota 1998–2009). In most years, there might be a single state without a program. The only exception was between 1999 and 2003 when in any year two to four states were without a program.

Our concern is on how state programs relate to federal programs. To get at this, we examine the correlation by decade[3] between federal and state programs. We define our measure of state need-based aid to be the average aid per student receiving aid. We do this in figure 8.4. In the first decade (pre-1990), the average correlation between each state's need-based program and the Pell grant is 0.76. Without exception, the correlations between state need-based programs and the Pell grant are positive in this period.

When we examine the 1990s, we see movement among multiple states. The average correlation remains positive but drops by almost half (to 0.40). About 25 percent of states have a negative correlation between Pell and their programs. From 2000 to 2008, the average correlation fell again (falling to 0.31); however, only 20 percent of states had negative correlations. While there are fewer states with a negative correlation, the negative correlations are stronger than in the prior period, causing the average correlation to drop. Finally, we compute the correlation for the period after 2008. This is the

3. The "decades" are only roughly approximated. They go from 1982–1990, 1991–2000, 2001–2007, and 2008–2011.

period after the start of the Great Recession. Over this period, the average correlation between state and federal policies becomes even more negative, and half of the states have a negative correlation with the level of the Pell.

The exercise of examining the relationship between state and federal policies raises two additional observations. First, there is substantial heterogeneity across states. Many states have maintained a positive correlation with Pell grants, even through the Great Recession. However, some of the positive relationships might overstate the correlation. Oregon, for example, uses a biennial budget. In the first year, they had excess demand and hence a large surge in overall expenditure; however, this has depleted the available funds for the second year. In 2009, $97.1 million was approved for the Oregon Opportunity Grant over two years (Oregon University System 2010); however, spending for the 2009/10 school year drastically increased to $76.5 million as "huge numbers of recently unemployed, high-need students return to postsecondary education, resulting in an explosion in demand for financial aid" (Oregon Student Access Commission 2012) with a large state share as defined by the new shared responsibility model. This left only $20 million for the 2010/11 school year. While Oregon might be an exception, many states have maintained the generosity of their programs for the average student receiving grant aid.

Second, in light of the change in the cyclicality of the Pell, the correlation between Pell and state grants might have different meanings over time. Pell grant aid shifted from a procyclical program to a countercyclical program. On average, states' responses were more muted. They continued to behave procyclically, and on average, their relationship became increasingly negatively correlated to the Pell grant schedule. However, these average changes in states' programs hide substantial heterogeneity. Over time more and more states have gravitated, whether consciously or not, toward having their respective programs counterbalance changes in the Pell program. During the Great Recession, states were almost equally divided between expanding and contracting. There is suggestive evidence that changes in the relationship between the Pell and some state programs began occurring as early as 2000.

8.3.3 Examples of Specific State Policy Shifts

Another way to detect how the relationships between state and federal programs have changed over time is to examine the specific rules of the programs to see whether the rules of these programs have influenced the correlation. In some cases, states have actively altered their programs to account for the Pell and its subsequent changes. We provide two examples (Oregon and Minnesota) of these changes in this section. In the next section of the chapter, we analyze primary student-level data from Ohio to illustrate both the relationship between Ohio's program and the Pell and the distributional consequences of state and federal policy changes on students' aid packages.

Minnesota

Minnesota had an early assigned student responsibility model, lauded by the Carnegie Council on Policy Studies in Higher Education in 1979, which turned into a design for shared responsibility (Misukanis 2008b). The Minnesota State Grant program first determines how much students at each institution should contribute from their own work, savings, and borrowing; this is set as a percentage of the recognized price of attendance (the student contribution was 46 percent of price, in 2008). Price of attendance includes both tuition and fees (capped for private programs, if tuition exceeds the allotted amount) and living and miscellaneous expenses (LME). After subtracting out the assigned student responsibility, the family portion is subtracted (expected family contribution [EFC]-adjusted to not double count student resources), leaving the taxpayer responsibility. First the Pell grant is charged, and then Minnesota grants are set to cover the remainder. This last point is important in that Pell, students' contributions, and family contributions are accounted for prior to any consideration of Minnesota grants. Thus, holding costs and incomes constant, a one-dollar increase in the Pell grant leads to a one-dollar decrease in state aid. Additionally, if appropriations are too low, then students and families must make up the difference (Misukanis 2008a).

When the Pell grant increased in 2009, Minnesota lowered its state grants, redistributing some of the savings within the aid program. "Money made available by the Pell Grant increase was used to increase LME (Living and Miscellaneous Expense Allowance) and the four-year tuition maximum, which contributed to an increase in the number of recipients" (Grimes 2010, 11). This shared model led to a negative correlation between state and federal aid programs.

Finally, as we discussed above, it is important to recall that need-based aid is just one component of states' overall aid to schools. For example, in 2009, Minnesota public institutions awarded $144 million in institutional aid. This is substantial relative to the $264 million Minnesotans received in Pell grant funding and $156 million from Minnesota state grants in the same year (Grimes 2010).

Oregon

Oregon began to look for a new financial aid model in 2005, spurred to change by a "financial aid wall" that abruptly cut off all assistance to students when family incomes exceeded a cutoff (Mills 2007). Looking to end this sharp discontinuity, Oregon adopted its shared responsibility model in 2007. It requires students to submit their Free Application for Federal Student Aid (FAFSA) and then calculates state grant awards based on cost, demonstrated need, and federal aid. Specifically, the state subtracts from its calculated cost of education (including cost of living) the student share, the expected family contribution, Pell grant, and an assumed federal tax credit. What remains is the state award amount, though it may be reduced by about a fifth of the EFC in tough financial times. The student share is calculated based on working fifteen hours a week all year at minimum wage, plus $3,000 in loans for students at four-year institutions (Oregon Student Assistance Commission 2010).

In 2007, the program was funded for up to $106 million over two years. As mentioned above, a similar biennial amount was approved in 2009. Although the Oregon Student Access Commission put into place several policies meant to limit costs, large numbers of needy students received awards, using most of this during the 2009/10 school year, leaving only $20 million for awards in 2010/11 (Oregon Student Access Commission 2012).

8.4 Case Study of Ohio

Ohio is a good example of how some states altered their need-based aid programs during the Great Recession. Ohio's need-based grant program in higher education is the Ohio College Opportunity Grant (OCOG). Prior to the 2009/10 school year, OCOG was awarded based on families' EFC. Similar to the Pell grant, OCOG was a fixed amount based on the EFC of the family. While the Pell grant in 2008/9 was available to families whose EFC was less than $4,040, OCOG was available only to families whose EFC was at or below $2,190. In the 2008/9 school year, OCOG ranged from $2,496 to $300 in the public sector. Awards in private colleges were twice as high while awards in career colleges were 60 percent higher. The OCOG imposed an additional constraint in that families had to have an income below $75,000 regardless of EFC (Ohio Association of Student Financial Aid Administrators 2008).

In the wake of the Great Recession and the passage of the stimulus package in February 2009, Ohio dramatically altered the OCOG schedule in July 2009. The OCOG became a flat award of $1,008 for any family with EFC at or below $2,190 and with an income less than $75,000. Students at private colleges continued to receive higher awards, and their award was $2,256. Students at for-profit colleges were excluded from the grant. The biggest change came for students attending community colleges or branch campuses. These students were also excluded from the grant (Foust 2009, 1).

Figure 8.5 illustrates the change in the OCOG from 2009 to 2010. The figure only holds true for students attending four-year colleges at the main university campuses. For students attending two-year colleges or branch campuses, the OCOG in 2010 would have been zero.[4] For most EFC ranges

---

4. The OCOG awards for students attending university regional branch campuses and Central State University were also reduced to $0 in 2010, while students at Shawnee State University saw a reduction to a flat $480. For convenience, in the following discussion we exclude Shawnee State, Central State, and the branch campuses. We include technical colleges and two-year state colleges in the category of community colleges.

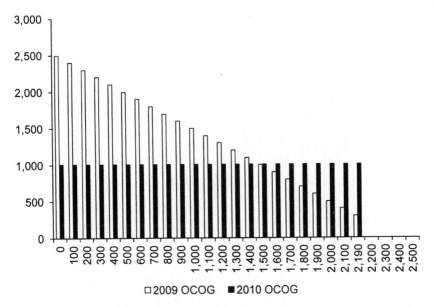

Fig. 8.5 OCOG amounts in 2009 and 2010 by family EFC for attendees at four-year main campuses
Source: Authors' calculations based on schedules published by the Ohio Board of Regents.

covered in the figure, there is a downward adjustment in students' state need-based aid awards. The most needy students (i.e., EFC = 0) experience a decline in aid of 60 percent.

Not every student was worse off with the policy change. While an EFC of $2,100 represents a low-income student (the highest EFC to maintain Pell eligibility was $4,041 in 2009), the student's family still has more resources than a student with an EFC of $0. Students with an EFC of $2,100 experienced more than a threefold increase in their OCOG award from 2009 to 2010.

Figure 8.6 shows the total Pell and OCOG awards to students who attended four-year university main campuses in 2009 and 2010. For low values of EFC, these total awards were higher in 2009. The decline in OCOG was even more than the increase in the Pell. At an EFC of about $1,000, the total awards are roughly equivalent, and at higher EFCs the increases in OCOG and the Pell make it so the total award increases from year to year. The Student Aid and Fiscal Responsibility Act in 2010 expanded eligibility for the Pell from EFCs of $4,041 to EFCs of $4,617—increases in these ranges are entirely due to the new Pell eligibility. It is important to note that awards in figure 8.6 only cover students attending the main university campuses. Students at regional campuses and Central State did not receive OCOG awards in 2010, while students at Shawnee State received a reduced award in 2010.

Figure 8.7 shows how the award schedules for the community colleges and regional branch campuses changed from 2009 and 2010. In these colleges,

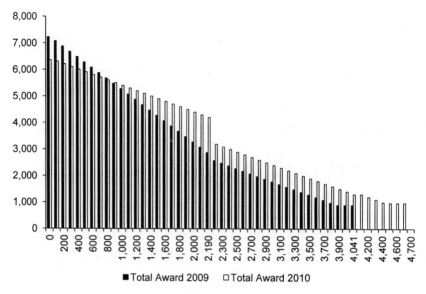

Fig. 8.6 Total Pell and OCOG awards by family EFC for attendees at four-year main campuses

Source: Authors' calculations based on schedules published by the Ohio Board of Regents.

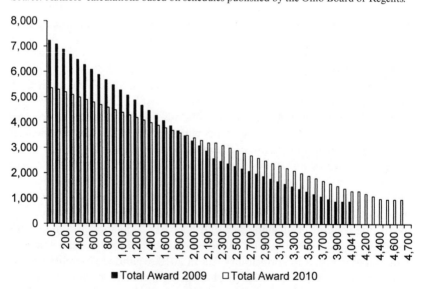

Fig. 8.7 Total Pell and OCOG awards by family EFC for attendees at community colleges (and Central State and regional campuses)

Source: Authors' calculations based on schedules published by the Ohio Board of Regents.

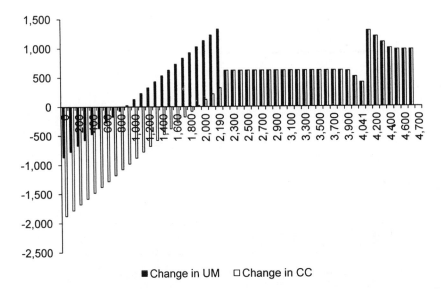

Fig. 8.8 Change in total award for community college and university main students by family EFC
Source: Authors' computations based on schedules published by the Ohio Board of Regents.

total awards were much lower in 2010 than in 2009 for EFCs below $2,000. For EFCs over $2,000, the total awards improved from 2009 to 2010. Figure 8.8 sums up the changes for both community colleges and university main campuses. The plots show how awards changed relative to the prior year for each EFC.

One final way to describe the change in the policies is to measure the "recapture" rate of the federal subsidy. While Ohio might well have reduced OCOG even without the stimulus package, suppose that Ohio's intent was to reduce the burden of OCOG while maintaining the same affordability. We have already shown that at some EFC levels the loss from OCOG was much larger than the $620 increase in the Pell grant. In these cases, Ohio more than fully captured the federal subsidy. Figure 8.9 shows our estimates of the recapture rate. We limit these to be between 0 and 100 percent since we are not considering redistribution yet. For community colleges or branch campuses, the recapture rate is almost full across the full range of EFCs, which had previously been eligible for financial aid. Above about a $2,000 EFC, the recapture rate falls below 100 percent. In the range where the recapture rate is full, the state captures the entire increase in the Pell, and students see no improvement in their affordability. When the recapture rate falls below 100 percent, students start to see benefit relative to the preexisting state policy, but this is often split between the state and the student. For students at the university main campuses, the recapture rate is

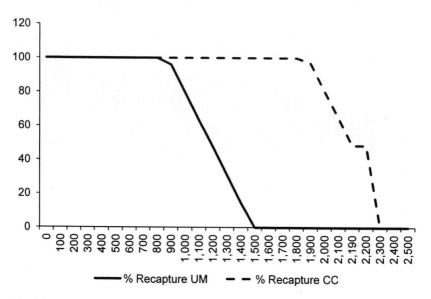

Fig. 8.9 Percent of Pell increase recaptured by decrease in state aid by EFC and sector
Source: Authors' computations based on schedules published by the Ohio Board of Regents.
Notes: Recapture represents the amount of the increase in the Pell that was offset by state reductions. Recapture rate is constrained to be between 100 percent and 0 percent.

full for EFCs up to about $1,000 and then it slowly fades out until an EFC of about $1,500. After $1,500, the state has no recapture of the federal subsidy.

So far, we have only examined the state policy in the abstract. The overall impact of the policy in terms of redistribution across students and in terms of overall state budget relief depends on the distribution of students across EFC categories.

We have data on specific students and their Pell and OCOG awards for the 2009 and 2010 fiscal years. We only observe the students if they completed a FAFSA, and many students who file FAFSAs in one year do not do so in subsequent years (Bettinger 2004). Additionally, many universities require students to complete FAFSAs even if they are not eligible for Pell aid. The FAFSA is used to determine subsidized and unsubsidized loan eligibility, work study, and other institution-level financial aid programs. We do not observe aid given through these channels. Our focus is on students who are Pell eligible, including its extension to individuals with an EFC of $4,617 in 2010. About 47.6 percent of FAFSA filers in 2009 had EFCs below this threshold, while 51.8 percent of FAFSA filers in 2010 had EFCs below this threshold.

Any analysis comparing students in different years faces a series of obstacles. Given the recession, incomes may have fallen (which might explain

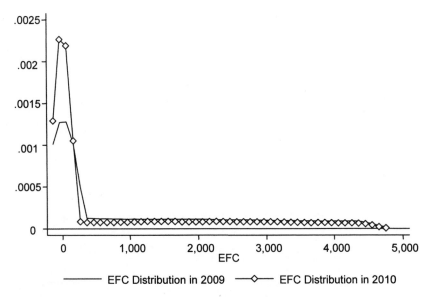

——————— EFC Distribution in 2009   ——◇—— EFC Distribution in 2010

Fig. 8.10 Distribution of EFCs among Ohio students in 2009 and 2010
Source: Authors' calculations based on data from the Ohio Board of Regents.

why more FAFSA filers had EFCs below $4,617 in 2010). Students may have chosen different colleges (given that the relative price of two-year versus four-year college changed). More students may have attended (or not) as a result of a change in their financial status. We will discuss these possibilities below in greater detail. For the first round of analysis, we will assume that the distributions of students who file FAFSAs, across EFCs, and across sectors of higher education are comparable across time.

Figure 8.10 shows the distribution of EFCs across 2009 and 2010. In 2009, about 50 percent of students whose EFC was below the Pell threshold had an EFC of 0. The 2009 distribution was much more uniform above this floor effect at the EFC of 0. In 2010, just over 60 percent of students whose EFC was below the Pell threshold had an EFC of 0.

Figures 8.11 and 8.12 show the breakdown in each year by university main campuses[5] and other campuses (branch campuses and community colleges). In both 2009 and 2010, students not attending the university main campuses have significantly lower EFCs. In both 2009 and 2010, students who are Pell eligible at university main campuses have EFCs that are about $380 higher than students at other campuses. Similarly, students at university main campuses are 17 percentage points less likely to report an EFC of zero than students at other campuses. To put this in context, across both years only about 37 percent of students attended university main campuses, and

5. We include Shawnee State and Central State in these computations.

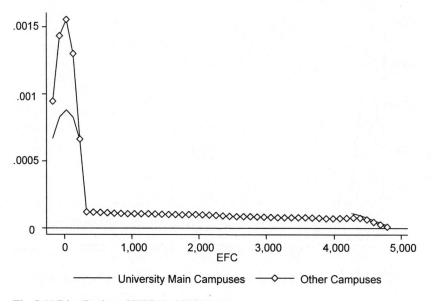

Fig. 8.11 Distribution of EFCs in 2009 by campus

Source: Authors' calculations based on data from the Ohio Board of Regents.

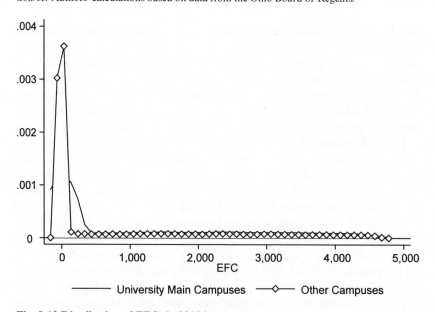

Fig. 8.12 Distribution of EFCs in 2010 by campus

Source: Authors' calculations based on data from the Ohio Board of Regents.

the percent in university main campuses actually fell by almost 3 percentage points between 2009 and 2010.

The shifts in the Pell and OCOG schedules suggest a dramatic reduction in the overall amount of state financial aid awarded in 2010. This is not uniformly the case because the underlying population shifted. In fact, in our sample, we see an increase in the number of FAFSAs being filed by Pell eligible individuals in 2010. The increase in the sample and the shift to the left in the underlying distribution of EFC from 2009 to 2010 is consistent with economic times becoming considerably worse. Nonetheless, given that students with an EFC of zero were a plurality and that the change in OCOG most dramatically affected them, the policy change led to significant decreases in most students' total aid awards, even after controlling for the increase in the historic increase in the Pell. About 74.5 percent of students had a lower total aid award in 2010 than they would have had with the same EFC in 2009 despite the increase in the Pell.

As the OCOG schedules implied, the losers in the policy changes in Ohio were most definitely the individuals with the lowest incomes. For these individuals whose awards were lower due to the new policy, the average family income was $17,190. As we noted above, however, there were some "winners" in the policy changes. There were ranges of EFCs where the increase in Pell aid was more than the reduction in the OCOG. Among these individuals, the average family income was around $46,004. Hence, there were two simultaneous effects going on. Aid awards were dropping for the poorest students (average income of $17,190) and some redistribution was happening to actually increase the aid for families who earned roughly Ohio's median household income.[6]

One can already see that Ohio's reduction in financial aid was dramatic, and figure 8.13 confirms this. Figure 8.13 comes from the annual NASSGAP survey used in the prior section. Ohio's spending on financial aid fell off a cliff in 2010. Ohio's spending on need-based financial aid fell by 66 percent. Given our data, we project that the increase in Pell expenditure to students in Ohio public higher education under the stimulus was about $68 million in 2010 relative to prior years. This is a conservative estimate in that we are only considering students who first entered college in 2005. In figure 8.14 we replicate figure 8.13, while including the extra Pell that we estimate came to Ohio as a result of the historic increase in the Pell grant funding. Even with this extra funding, Ohio's overall spending on student need-based aid dropped dramatically.

In sum, Ohio's change in financial aid policy completely dwarfed the historic changes in the Pell grant. Families at the bottom of the income distribution were disproportionately affected by the policy. The drop in their OCOG

---

6. From 2006 to 2010, the census measures Ohio's median family income as $47,358 (US Census Bureau 2006–2010).

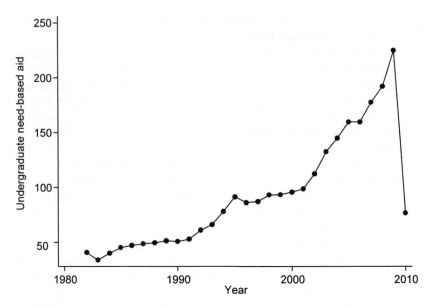

Fig. 8.13 Aggregate state need-based spending in Ohio in millions of nominal dollars, 1982–2010

Source: NASSGAP surveys.

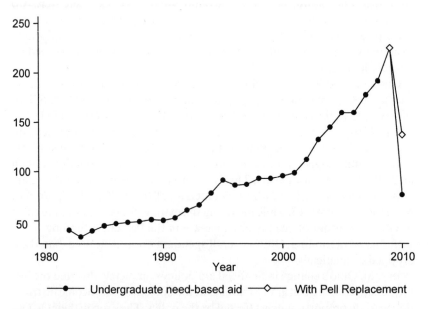

Undergraduate need-based aid ⎯⎯◇⎯⎯ With Pell Replacement

Fig. 8.14 Aggregate state need-based spending in Ohio with estimated capture from Pell, in millions of nominal dollars

Source: NASSGAP surveys and authors' calculations based on data from the Ohio Board of Regents.

awards was far greater than the increase in their Pell awards. By contrast, individuals who attended university main campuses and students from more affluent families experienced increases in their overall awards. The Pell grant and often the OCOG award increased for these families.

Of course, there are some caveats in our analysis. As we mentioned above, the underlying population of students within Ohio public higher education who filed FAFSAs changed from year to year. Incomes in Ohio declined; the relative prices of two-year and four-year colleges changed (i.e.. students at four-year colleges could potentially receive more aid than students at two-year colleges); some students may have entered (or not entered) college as a result of economic difficulty; and newly Pell-eligible students may have filed FAFSAs at different rates than previous students. We do not analyze these changes in the observed population; however, in most cases, these circumstances, coupled with the policy change, would not have made a large difference in the analysis. For example, income declines should lower families' EFCs. On average, recorded EFCs for Ohio public college students declined by $250 between 2009 and 2010. Among students who filed FAFSAs in both 2009 and 2010, the median change was zero while the mean change was a reduction of $698. The reduction of about $700 in EFC would have been offset by an increase of Pell of $700. The key question is how the reduction in EFC would have affected students' OCOG awards. In this group, the mean OCOG award declined by $800 and the median award by nearly $500. Again, the Pell might have offset some of the increased need, but the OCOG reductions still made potential awards lower in the aftermath of the policy changes in Ohio.

As we discuss in the next section, a key limitation is the identification of the counterfactual. Would Ohio have imposed such draconian measures in the absence of the Pell reform? In the absence of the reform, would the cuts have been more modest? Is this a case of fiscal federalism, where Ohio reacted to the federal policy? Or is this a case where Ohio and other states faced dramatic cuts and the federal government attempted to mitigate the impact on students?

In trying to understand if a scaled-back program was related to the change in the Pell, we interviewed a senior state administrator who explained, "You're absolutely right about the Pell increases. Here in Ohio, we call that budgeting. . . . As Pell goes up, state aid goes down." The administrator cited Minnesota and Oregon as having similar procedures.

This trade-off between federal and state is built into OCOG policy. While the federal definition of need includes cost of living, Ohio's defined cost of attendance includes only tuition and fees, and Pell funding and EFC are subtracted from this cost before the state is charged. Thus, students with the lowest EFCs who attend the cheapest institutions may have unmet need by the federal definition, but under Ohio's revised policy they receive no aid from Ohio as long as the tuition and fees are covered by a combination of the Pell and the family contribution, and they are treated identically to some students with lower unmet federal need.

A series of guidance memos from the Ohio Board of Regents explains the changes for the 2009/10 school year. "The flattened OCOG scale is a direct result of the Pell/EFC first concept. In essence, the OCOG formula takes a fixed number (tuition/general fees), subtracts a fixed number (Pell/EFC combo of $5,350), and results in a fixed number (OCOG eligibility capped at the appropriate maximum award)" (Foust 2009a). The reason community colleges and several other campuses have OCOG schedules of 0 in 2010 is because tuition and general fees are below the Pell/EFC combination of $5,350 (Foust 2009b). Ohio community and technical colleges averaged $4,734 for tuition, fees, and books in the 2009/10 school year (authors' calculations based on IPEDS data). While the Pell grant takes into account students' living expenses, Ohio's fixed number starting point only accounts for tuition and general fees. Since Pell grants represent the "first dollar" in Ohio's formula, Pell, while allowable for living expenses, is used for tuition and fees, and the OCOG, which does not have a living allowance, is left to pay whatever portion of tuition and fees Pell and EFC do not cover.

Regardless of intent or cause, the cuts in Ohio completely overshadowed any increase in the Pell, and the majority (75 percent) of families on financial aid were worse off. These families were also the poorest of the need-based eligible families.

Is Ohio's experience representative of other states? This is an open question. As we mentioned, 45 percent of states reduced need-based grant aid expenditure in the aggregate between 2009 and 2010. Ohio was an extreme case, and only one state cut aggregate spending by a larger percent. However, throughout the United States there was a surge of students who were eligible for financial aid awards, and so even among the states that increased their aggregate expenditure, increasing numbers of recipients lowered the average spending on any individual student in almost a third of these states.

8.5 Conclusion

Our analysis explores how states adjusted their need-based aid programs in response to the Great Recession and the corresponding federal policy. Our findings are mixed. Many states maintained the generosity of their programs, but about half of states reduced their per-student spending. Given the budgetary pressures facing states, this is not surprising.

Additionally, we have shown that since at least 2000, many states have altered their financial aid programs. Prior to 2000, their financial aid programs generally had a positive relationship with the generosity of the Pell. After 2000, state programs have increasingly had a negative correlation with the Pell grant. There appear to be two driving forces for this shift. First, the federal government is increasing the real value of the Pell in a countercyclical rather than procyclical way. States tend to respond procyclically. Second, many states have aggressively pursued shared models of student funding. Under the shared model, states consider a set of costs including tuition, fees, and in some cases, living expenses. In this model, state aid pays for the remainder of students' expenses (up to a limit) after EFC and Pell are incorporated into students' aid packages. Holding costs constant, a one-dollar increase in the Pell results in a one-dollar reduction in students' state need-based grants. The only time that Pell and state aid would increase is if an increase in Pell aid is less than the increase in college tuition plus previous unmet need, as recognized by the state. For a fixed EFC, both Pell and state grant aid would increase with tuition. However, if the growth in the Pell grant was large, such as we saw with the historic increases in the Pell program during the Great Recession, the growth in the Pell might exceed the growth rate of tuition and fees. In this case, the "surplus" would automatically reduce the size of state need-based aid programs. As such the state program would show a negative correlation with the Pell.

We do not attempt to disentangle whether the historic increases in the Pell caused more stringent state need-based aid policies than would have been attempted in the absence of the federal increase. However, in the one in-depth case study we present, the timing of the announcement of the revised program was such that lawmakers and policymakers already knew the size of the Pell grants and could have incorporated it into their decision making. Through the minutes of meetings and an interview with a state leader, we have at least suggestive evidence that Ohio took advantage of the generosity in the Pell and further scaled back state aid. However, in the process of scaling back their program, Ohio's policy change had redistributive consequences. The poorest families saw their college awards decline for a given EFC while families near the median income experienced increases in their overall aid packages.

The evolution of state and federal need-based grant programs has some interesting relationships with the academic literature in public finance. Developing a negative relationship between state and federal need-based aid might create more stability in students' overall need-based aid. State policy becomes a hedge against federal policy while federal policy might provide a stimulus in recessionary times when states' budgets are strained. Additionally, as state officials incorporate information on federal policymaking in their decision making, they can exercise fiscal federalism by giving themselves the last say in the size of need-based aid programs. The shared model of need-based aid establishes states as the final decision maker in the overall public subsidy to needy students.

A key implication of this shift in policymaking is that the political rhetoric around Pell grant increases may be largely hollow. If states hedge against increases by altering their generosity, then students are not likely to see the promised increases in aid generosity. As we showed, some states do capture the federal aid.

An important observation is that the trends we see during the Great Recession were already appearing as early as 2000. While more states have altered their programs, the federal government and a large percentage of states were already adjusting their student finance models to this new modality during the 2001 recession. Their reaction during the Great Recession has thus been consistent with this "new" model of student financing.

Finally, while we have focused on need-based aid, our study is limited. States support students in many other ways, most notably state appropriations for public institutions. We have not examined how these have changed over the Great Recession. We have avoided this purposefully in that we are focused on the highly visible programs that actively redistribute to low-income families. Similarly, we cannot observe institutional aid or the role that institutions might play in strategically altering prices. These institutional policies can alter the affordability options and may be an additional hedge against changes in federal or state policy changes. We have little information about how these aid policies changed during the Great Recession.

References

Bettinger, E. P. 2004. "How Financial Aid Affects Persistence." In *College Choices: The Economics of Where to Go, When to Go, and How to Pay For It*, edited by C. M. Hoxby, 207–38. Chicago: University of Chicago Press.

Cellini, S. R., and C. Goldin. 2012. "Does Federal Student Aid Raise Tuition? New Evidence on For-Profit Colleges." NBER Working Paper no. 17827, Cambridge, MA.

College Board. 2010. *Trends in Student Aid, 2010*. Washington, DC: College Board.

———. 2011. *Trends in Student Aid, 2011*. Washington, DC: College Board.

Foust, C. 2009a. State Grants and Scholarships (SGS) Guidance Memo: Addendum to SGS 10-006, Ohio Board of Regents.

Foust, C. 2009b. State Grants and Scholarships (SGS) Guidance Memo: Ohio College Opportunity Grant (OCOG), Ohio Board of Regents.

Gladieux, L. E., A. M. Hauptman, and L. G. Knapp. 1994. "The Federal Government and Higher Education." In *Higher Education in American Society*, edited by P. G. Altbach, R. O. Berdahl, and P. J. Gumport. Amherst, NY: Prometheus Books.

Grimes, T. 2010. "Highlights of Financial Aid Awarded 2009." St. Paul, MN: Minnesota Office of Higher Education. http://www.ohe.state.mn.us/pdf/highlights 2009.pdf.

Hansen, W. L., and J. O. Stampen. 1994. "Economics and Financing of Higher Education: The Tension between Quality and Equity." In *Higher Education in American Society*, edited by P. G. Altbach, R. O. Berdahl, and P. J. Gumport, 101–25. Amherst, NY: Prometheus Books.

Hoxby, C. M. 1997. "How the Changing Market Structure of US Higher Education Explains College Tuition." NBER Working Paper no. 6323, Cambridge, MA.

Johnson, N., P. Oliff, and E. Williams. 2011. "An Update on State Budget Cuts." Washington, DC: Center on Budget and Policy Priorities. http://www.cbpp.org/cms/?fa=view&id=1214.

Kane, T. J., and P. R. Orszag. 2003. "Higher Education Spending: The Role of Medicaid and the Business Cycle." In *The Brookings Institution Policy Brief*. Washington, DC: The Brookings Institution.

Katsinas, S. G., R. F. Mensel, L. Hagedorn, J. Friedel, and M. D'Amico. 2012. "Pell Grants and the Lifting of Rural America's Future." The Education Policy Center, University of Alabama. http://www.uaedpolicy.ua.edu/pell.html.

Lagemann, E. C. 1989. *The Politics of Knowledge: The Carnegie Corporation, Philanthropy, and Public Policy*. Middletown, CT: Wesleyan University Press.

Long, B. T. 2004. "The Impact of Federal Tax Credits for Higher Education Expenses." In *College Choices: The Economics of Where to Go, When to Go, and How to Pay For It*, edited by C. M. Hoxby. Chicago: University of Chicago Press.

Mills, J. 2007. [OSU Supporters] Rainy Days and Revenue Forecasts. *Office of Government Relations Collection, Scholars Archive at OSU*. Archived electronic mail.

Misukanis, M. 2008a. Overview of the Minnesota State Grant Program, Minnesota State Grant Review. St. Paul, MN: Minnesota Office of Higher Education.

Misukanis, M. 2008b. Overview of the Prior Model, Minnesota State Grant Review. St. Paul, MN: Minnesota Office of Higher Education.

National Association of State Student Grant and Aid Programs (NASSGAP). 1972–2012. Annual Surveys, 3rd through 42nd. https://www.nassgap.org/view repository.aspx?categoryID=3.

Ohio Association of Student Financial Aid Administrators. 2008. Ohio College Opportunity Grant (OCOG) Award Table 2008–2009. http://www.oasfaa.org/docs/outreach/OCOG-Pell_08-09.pdf.

Oregon Student Access Commission. 2012. "History of the Oregon Opportunity Grant." http://oregonstudentaid.gov/oog-history.aspx.

Oregon Student Assistance Commission. 2010. "Oregon Opportunity Grant Program Policies and Procedures, 2010–11." Eugene, OR.

Oregon University System. 2010. "OUS 2009–2011 Budget Summary." http://www.ous.edu/sites/default/files/dept/communications/FactSheetOUS_Budget09-11_FINAL4_revFeb2010.pdf.

Rizzo, M. J. 2004. "A (Less Than) Zero Sum Game? State Funding for Public Education: How Public Higher Education Institutions Have Lost." Cornell Higher Education Research Institute Working Paper no. 52, ILR School, Cornell University.

Rizzo, M. J., and R. G. Ehrenberg. 2004. "Resident and Nonresident Tuition and Enrollment at Flagship State Universities." In *College Choices: The Economics of Where to Go, When to Go, and How to Pay For It*, edited by C. M. Hoxby. Chicago: University of Chicago Press.

Shireman, R. 2007. "National Expert on Student Loans Praises Key Reforms in Senate Higher Education Measures, Urges Rapid Passage." June 20. http://ticas.org/files/pub/Senate_HEA_6_20_07.pdf.

Singell, Jr., Larry D., and J. A. Stone. 2007. "For Whom the Pell Tolls: The Response of University Tuition to Federal Grants-in-Aid." *Economics of Education Review* 26 (3): 285–95.

Steinhauer, J. 2008. "Facing Deficits, States Get Out Sharper Knives." *New York Times*, Nov. 16.

Thelin, J. R. 2004. *A History of American Higher Education*. Baltimore, MD: Johns Hopkins University Press.

Turner, L. J. 2012. "The Incidence of Student Financial Aid: Evidence from the Pell Grant Program." Working Paper, Department of Economics, Columbia University.

US Census Bureau. 2006–2010. American Community Survey. https://www.census.gov/acs/www/.

9

Did the Fiscal Stimulus Work for Universities?

Michael F. Dinerstein, Caroline M. Hoxby,
Jonathan Meer, and Pablo Villanueva

9.1 Introduction

The American Recovery and Reinvestment Act (ARRA) was enacted in February 2009 with the objective of "saving and creating jobs" in the immediate future—that is, 2009 and 2010. The ARRA's 831 billion dollars were intended to offset at least some of the decrease in aggregate demand associated with the financial crisis and Great Recession. Other key parts of this essentially Keynesian policy were the federal budget signed by President Obama in March 2009, which contained 400 billion dollars in spending beyond what had been proposed by the G. W. Bush administration for the 2009 fiscal year (October 2008–September 2009), and the unusually high budget (3.72 trillion) enacted for fiscal year 2010 (October 2009–September 2010).

Michael F. Dinerstein is a PhD candidate in economics at Stanford University. Caroline M. Hoxby is the Scott and Donya Bommer Professor in Economics at Stanford University, a senior fellow of the Hoover Institution, and a research associate and director of the Economics of Education Program of the National Bureau of Economic Research. Jonathan Meer is the Private Enterprise Research Center Professor and associate professor of economics at Texas A&M University and a faculty research fellow of the National Bureau of Economic Research. Pablo Villanueva is a PhD candidate in economics at Stanford University.

We thank John Griswold of the Commonfund Institute for his generous help with NACUBO-Commonfund data. We thank Rachel Croson, David Croson, and Nancy Lutz for explaining the complexities of the databases that record federal research grants. We thank Eric Bettinger, Jeffrey Brown, Keith Brown, David Chambers, Raj Chetty, Stephen Dimmock, Elroy Dimson, John Etchemendy, Amy Finkelstein, John Friedman, William Goetzmann, Bridget Long, Michael McPherson, Sharon Oster, James Poterba, Cristian Tiu, Sarah Turner, and Scott Weisbenner for providing us with data and very helpful comments. We acknowledge support from NSF Grant SES-0922005 for access to the Quarterly Workforce Indicators data. The authors are solely responsible for the content of the paper. For acknowledgments, sources of research support, and disclosure of the authors' material financial relationships, if any, please see http://www.nber.org/chapters/c12864.ack.

Postsecondary institutions were important recipients of stimulus funds—both funds officially designated as ARRA and funds contained in the unusually large budgets for fiscal years 2009 and 2010. Federal revenue received by postsecondary institutions comes mainly in two forms: research-related funds (in the form of grants and contracts) and student aid (most of which is directed to low-income students). Between the 2007/8 and 2009/10 school years, federal research-related revenues rose, in real dollars, by 14 percent and federal spending on student aid rose by 80 percent. These funding increases were a stark departure from the 2002/3 to 2007/8 period, when real federal revenues received by postsecondary institutions were approximately flat.

There are a few key criticisms of stimulus policies in general as an antirecessionary tool. First, because budgeting, legislating, disbursing funds, and creating jobs all take time, the revenues may not reach the intended recipients fast enough. Second, the United States is not a closed economy, so some of the intended effect of the stimulus may "leak" out. That is, a recipient of funds may purchase goods produced overseas or hire foreign workers—lessening the effect on domestic aggregate demand. Third, the recipients of the funds may "save" them rather than spend them immediately on employees' wages or purchasing goods. We do not mean to suggest that the recipients might *literally* save the stimulus funds. Rather, they might increase their spending relative to the counterfactual (in which they received no stimulus funds) by only a fraction of the funds they receive. In many expectations scenarios, this is a logical response to explicitly temporary funds. For instance, recipients may expect that stimulus funds they receive now will translate into higher taxes or lower funding in the future, in which case they may save for those eventualities. Or, the stimulus funds may be large relative to what the recipient thinks he can spend productively and quickly on the intended use—a research project, say. In that case, he may withdraw nonfederal funds that he would have spent on the project and save those funds for future projects. Or, the recipient may not wish to hire a person he will be committed to after the stimulus funds disappear. Instead, he may hire only a fraction of the intended employees and save some other funds to keep those employees on when the stimulus funds are gone. It is important to note that "saving" may take the form of a recipient dissaving *less*—that is, borrowing less—than he would have in the absence of stimulus funds.

(Henceforth, we use the word "save" to refer to any change in a postsecondary institution's finances that had the effect of increasing total spending by less than a dollar for dollar of its stimulus-motivated federal funds. It is important to understand this locution because it rarely refers to literal saving. Another phrase that is useful is a "full flypaper effect." This is the phenomenon in which federal funds increase spending in the intended area dollar for dollar.[1]

---

1. The "flypaper effect" is so named because it describes the phenomenon in which money "sticks where it hits"—that is, spending in the intended area increases by the full amount of the transfer from the government.

If the advent of stimulus-motivated federal funds does not cause a full fly-paper effect, then it means that the institution has moved some of its other funds away from the relevant activity—but not necessarily to the future, which would be saving. In this case, we will say that the institution has "reallocated" some of the federal funding. This locution does not refer to literal reallocation that would violate the terms of the federal funding.)

Interestingly, some of the criticisms of stimulus policies likely apply less to postsecondary institutions than to typical contractors. As an administrative matter, postsecondary institutions are well equipped to receive and spend federal funds quickly. Undergraduate students can receive increased aid almost immediately, and revenue can quickly fund graduate and postdoctoral students to work on research projects. Student assistants, postdoctoral students, and non-tenure-track instructors can be hired without the creation of "permanent" positions. Some postsecondary institutions have a queue of research projects in the funding pipeline (already proposed but not yet funded), and the timing of such queued projects can possibly be accelerated with little or no loss of productivity. Although some stimulus funds could be used to purchase equipment that is produced overseas, both instruction and research tend to occur through interpersonal interactions so that leakage to foreign countries is minimal. Commentators have even argued that leakage outside of the institutions' immediate neighborhood is limited so that stimulus funding could buoy up the economy of a "college town" or county dominated by a university.[2]

On the other hand, some criticisms of stimulus policies may be particularly applicable to postsecondary institutions. Colleges and universities may save some of the stimulus funds by reducing (relative to the counterfactual in which they received no funds) their borrowing or their rates of spending from their endowments. Public colleges and universities may receive smaller appropriations from their state legislatures when they receive stimulus funds—that is, it may be the state government that ultimately receives some of the funds. Indeed, some states' financial aid formulas are such that the state automatically reduces the aid it gives students when the Pell grant increases.[3] Both private and public universities may hesitate to create long-term positions and may find it difficult to accelerate the timing of projects because they do not want to invest in capital (labs, equipment, offices) that will be excessive in normal times.

In short, postsecondary institutions provide an important environment for investigating the effects of stimulus funds. They give us a window on how stimulus policies work, and they provide a testing environment that is likely more favorable to stimulus policies than the rest of the economy. Moreover, the question of how the stimulus affected postsecondary insti-

2. See, for instance, Belkin 2012.
3. See Bettinger's chapter 8 in this volume.

tutions is interesting for its own sake because it reveals a great deal about their objectives and constraints. We are especially interested in how federal stimulus spending—whether classified as ARRA or not—affected universities' expenditures (on research, student aid, on other activities), universities' employment, universities' endowment spending, state governments' appropriations to their public universities, and economic activity in the counties containing universities.

It is crucial to understand that we will not argue that postsecondary institutions did something wrong if they saved or reallocated some stimulus dollars by whatever means. To the extent that universities contribute to the economy by producing useful human capital, inventions, and other public goods (as opposed to merely generating make-work jobs and incomes to prop up aggregate demand), society would prefer that universities allocate funds to their most productive use. Such allocation is probably not consistent with a full flypaper effect. We return to this topic in our conclusions.

The main empirical obstacle to our investigation is establishing what would have occurred if little or no stimulus was enacted. Specifically, we face endogeneity and omitted variables problems. The endogeneity problem is particularly obvious in the case of student aid, which—like unemployment insurance—is something of an automatic stabilizer. When a recession hits, family incomes fall and students become more needy. Given the way federal financial aid formulas work, student aid automatically increases—even if Congress enacts no increase in the Pell grant or other aid formulas. Colleges whose local economies are harder hit will experience a larger increase in student need and, thus, a larger increase in federal aid. Thus, with a naive empirical strategy, reverse causality would likely confound the causal effects of increased federal student aid. Such reverse causality may affect research funding as well. If a legislator's local college or university was particularly hard hit by the recession or financial crisis, he may have made greater effort to obtain federal research money for it. A naive strategy would then *understate* the causal effect of stimulus spending. However, there is an omitted variables problem that would likely cause *overstatement*: a university that is particularly "up and coming" in research may have more projects in the pipeline that get funded quickly when stimulus funds arise. Such a university would likely have enjoyed increased spending and employment (relative to other universities) even without the stimulus.

To overcome these empirical challenges, we employ two instrumental variables: (a) a Bartik-style instrument (Bartik 1991) that applies nationwide rates of increase in research funding by agency to universities whose initial dependence on these agencies differs; and (b) a simulated instrument that applies the change in the maximum Pell grant to institutions with varying initial numbers of students eligible for the maximum grant.

To see how the first instrument works, consider two universities, the first of which had most of its federal research funding through the National Aeronautics and Space Administration (NASA) before the recession, and the second of which had most of its federal research funding through the National Institutes of Health (NIH) before the recession. Nationally, NASA research funding grew by 29 percent from the 2007/8 school year to the 2009/10 school year. Over the same period, national NIH research funding grew by 16 percent. If each university simply got its preexisting share of the national increases in funding, then the first university would receive more stimulus spending than the second university. This difference between the two universities' receipt of stimulus spending would *not* be a function of their need for money or of their upward trajectory since it is not plausible that the national spending increases were set with a mind to the impact on these two universities. Indeed, we definitively eliminate this possibility by excluding each university from the calculation of the nationwide increase applied to its initial conditions. Thus, we have a credible instrument for the increases in federal research funding that were experienced by otherwise similar universities.

To see how the second instrument works, consider two universities, the first with numerous students eligible for the maximum Pell grant prior to the recession and the second with few students eligible for the Pell grant prior to the recession. We compute the change in funding that each university would have experienced had each of its students who were initially eligible for the maximum grant received the change in the maximum grant that was enacted between 2006/7 ($4,050) and 2009/10 ($5,350). This increase is solely a function of each university's initial conditions and the national policy change in the maximum Pell grant. It is *not* a function of the change in the neediness of each school's students. This formula-and-initial-conditions change in federal student aid is a plausible instrument—especially for universities that recruit students from the nation or a fairly large region. Below, we elaborate on this and other issues regarding the instruments.

The remainder of the chapter is organized as follows. In section 9.2, we describe federal funding directed to postsecondary institutions before and during the stimulus period. We briefly review what economics predicts that universities should do with stimulus funds in section 9.3. We describe our data in section 9.4 and our empirical strategy in section 9.5. We show results for university outcomes (revenues, expenditures, employment, and so on) in sections 9.6 and 9.7. Results for local economy outcomes are presented in section 9.8. Finally, in section 9.9, we discuss our findings and draw conclusions.

9.2 Federal Funding for Postsecondary Institutions, before and during the Stimulus

The three key events in stimulus spending are the ARRA itself, the much-augmented budget for the 2009 fiscal year, and the large budget for the 2010 fiscal year. Hereafter, we refer to all federal spending for fiscal years 2009 and 2010, not just official ARRA spending, as "stimulus motivated." Given the timing of federal disbursements, we expect most stimulus-motivated funding to affect postsecondary institutions' revenues in the 2009/10 school year, although a small fraction may show up as early as the 2008/9 school year. Of course, institutions may have begun to anticipate increased federal funding as early as midway through the 2008/9 school year.

Federal funds directed to postsecondary institutions come in three basic forms: (a) grants and contracts, (b) student aid, and (c) appropriations. Federal grant and contract funds are revenues intended to support specific research projects or similar activities.[4] Federal student aid is primarily directed toward low-income students, and its most important component by far is the Pell grant.[5] Appropriations are funds received by an institution through an act of Congress, except grants and contracts. Institutions are meant to use appropriations to meet their normal operating expenses, not to conduct specific projects. The most important examples are federal appropriations to land grant institutions, tribal colleges, and historically black colleges and universities. State Fiscal Stabilization Funds, temporary revenues received by universities under ARRA, are also appropriations.

Most federal funds directed to postsecondary institutions fund activities that are closely related to the primary missions of the institutions—undergraduate and/or doctoral instruction and research. We expect closely related funding to be at least somewhat fungible with other streams of revenue—thus allowing at least some of the saving and reallocation described above. For instance, a private institution could presumably use federal revenue to fund research that it would otherwise have funded with income from its endowment. Or, a public institution might be able to use federal revenue to aid students whom it would otherwise have aided with revenue from the state government. However, we recognize that some federal revenue has low fungibility. Most obviously, a small share (slightly less than 10 percent) of grants and contracts fund "independent operations"—federally funded programs directed by postsecondary institutions.[6]

For the purposes of this study, the key distinction is between federal student aid funds (hereafter "federal aid funds") and all other federal funds,

---

4. In our study, we consistently exclude Pell and all other student aid funds from grants and contracts, even if they are included as nonoperating grants by the institution. In this way, we avoid double-counting Pell and other aid revenue.

5. In terms of federal expenditures, other important forms of aid are Supplemental Educational Opportunity Grants (SEOG) and State Student Incentive Grants (SSIG). However, the Pell program alone made up 87 percent of federal grant aid in 2009/10. There are also a number of federal tax breaks related to higher education—most importantly, the tuition tax credits. These "tax expenditures" are important to the federal budget but they do not flow to postsecondary institutions in a direct way and they were largely unaffected by the recession or urge for stimulus spending.

6. Examples include Argonne National Laboratory at the University of Chicago, the Jet Propulsion Lab at California Institute of Technology, SLAC National Accelerator Laboratory at Stanford University, and the Lawrence Livermore National Laboratory of the University of California.

including appropriations, directed to postsecondary institutions. This distinction is key because (a) the latter type of funds is more likely to be intended for research; (b) the latter type of funds is inherently institution-specific, not driven by a formula that applies to all institutions; and (c) both types of funds can be increased as a stimulus measure, but only the former type of funds automatically increases as the incomes of an institution's students fall (the automatic stabilizer property).

9.2.1 Federal Funding for Postsecondary Institutions in a "Base" Year: 2006/7

Table 9.1 shows how federal funds were distributed among postsecondary institutions in 2006/7, the last school year before the financial crisis and Great Recession hit.[7] The table shows amounts in 2010 dollars, adjusted using the GDP deflator.[8] The first column of the table classifies institutions by their Carnegie classification and their control (private or public).[9] The only classifications that are not fairly intuitive are the two types of research universities. Both types offer a wide range of baccalaureate programs and are "committed to graduate education through the doctorate." However, the "extensive" ones award fifty or more doctoral degrees per year across at least fifteen disciplines, while the "intensive" ones need to award only ten doctoral degrees per year across three or more disciplines, or at least twenty doctoral degrees per year overall.

The second column of table 9.1 shows the number of institutions in each category. For reasons that will become clear in section 9.4, we have omitted for-profit schools, nearly all of which would fit into either the associate or baccalaureate/master's category. The third through fifth columns show the federal funding—grants and contracts, appropriations, student aid—for each category of institution. The next three columns show federal funding *per institution*, and the final three columns show federal funding as a share of the institutions' stable operating revenue. (Appendix table 9A.1 shows alternative versions of the final three columns, with institutions' total revenue defined more broadly than stable operating revenue is defined. The magnitudes differ, but the pattern is similar.)

The first thing to observe in table 9.1 is that the vast majority (86 percent) of federal grant and contract funding goes to research universities and medical schools. There are a fairly small number (302) of such institutions,

---

7. The 2007/8 school year actually looks very similar because most spending was determined before the financial crisis was recognized. The key data for table 9.1 are from the Delta Cost Project database (US Department of Education 2012), which we describe in section 9.3.

8. Revenue and expenditure patterns are very similar when deflated using the Consumer Price Index (CPI-U). These results are available from the authors.

9. We use the year 2000 Carnegie classifications to exclude the possibility that the impact of the financial crisis or recession might influence a classification. For a detailed description and justification of the Carnegie classifications, see Carnegie Foundation for the Advancement of Teaching (2001).

Table 9.1   Federal funds directed to postsecondary institutions by category of funds and type of institution, 2006/7

Institution type:	Number of institutions	Grants & contracts (millions)	Appropriations (millions)	Aid (millions)	Grants & contracts per institution (millions)	Appropriations per institution (millions)	Aid per institution (millions)	Grants & contracts as % of stable operating revenue	Appropriations as % of stable operating revenue	Aid as % of stable operating revenue
Private ext. research	49	11,803.8	280.8	554.4	240.9	5.7	11.3	21.32	0.51	1.00
Public ext. research	102	18,079.8	191.1	2,259.0	177.3	1.9	22.1	15.61	0.16	1.95
Private int. research	42	816.7	0.7	201.2	19.4	0.0	4.8	9.28	0.01	2.29
Public int. research	64	3,060.3	27.0	675.0	47.8	0.4	10.5	13.57	0.12	2.99
Private medical	18	880.4	14.9	7.0	48.9	0.8	0.4	17.34	0.29	0.14
Public medical	27	1,071.6	0.0	14.2	39.7	0.0	0.5	10.69	0.00	0.14
Private engineering	1	0.0	0.0	0.0	0.0	0.0	0.0	0.00	0.00	0.00
Public engineering	2	33.2	0.0	3.7	16.6	0.0	1.8	20.24	0.00	2.25
Private other health	21	10.8	0.0	11.1	0.5	0.0	0.5	2.23	0.00	2.29
Public other health	2	24.8	0.0	0.1	12.4	0.0	0.1	12.87	0.00	0.07
Private BA/MA	781	1,161.3	162.1	1,901.9	1.5	0.2	2.4	3.29	0.46	5.39
Public BA/MA	346	2,228.1	10.6	2,528.9	6.4	0.0	7.3	5.60	0.03	6.36
Private associate	82	18.7	1.3	61.8	0.2	0.0	0.8	4.45	0.32	14.67
Public associate	962	2,348.2	106.1	4,266.5	2.4	0.1	4.4	5.63	0.25	10.23

Notes: The table shows federal funds directed to postsecondary institutions in the 2006/7 school year. Federal funds come in three basic forms: (a) grants and contracts, (b) appropriations, and (c) student aid. These categories are defined further in the text. Institutions are grouped by their 2000 Carnegie classification (Carnegie Foundation for the Advancement of Teaching 2001).

so their per-institution amounts of federal grant and contract funding dwarf the per-institution amounts received by any other category of schools. Federal grant and contract funding represents between 9 and 21 percent of these institutions' stable operating revenue.[10]

Although research universities and medical schools also receive a large share (65 percent) of federal appropriations funding, the per-institution amounts are very small relative to grants and contracts, and appropriations funding never reaches even 1 percent of their stable operating revenues. These institutions receive 30 percent of all federal student aid, and such aid funding represents as much as 3 percent (public intensive research universities) of stable operating revenue.

Summing up, research universities and medical schools play the dominant role in federal grant and contract funding *and* federal grant and contract funding plays an important role in the finances of these schools. Federal student aid also plays a nontrivial role in research universities' finances. Thus, we should expect these institutions to be affected by stimulus-motivated federal funding.

The picture is fairly different for associate and baccalaureate/master's institutions, which are shown toward the bottom of table 9.1. Although they receive 14 percent of federal grant and contract funding, the per-institution amounts are small and such funding represents only 3 to 6 percent of their stable operating revenues. In contrast, they receive 70 percent of all federal aid funds, and such funds represent between 5 and 15 percent of their stable operating revenues. (Appropriations funding plays only a very small role). In short, associate and baccalaureate/master's institutions—of which there are many—have finances in which federal aid funds play an important role and in which federal grants and contracts play a much smaller role.[11]

The remaining categories of institutions are so thinly populated that it is not useful to discuss them here, although we analyze some of them later.

9.2.2 Stimulus Period Increases in Federal Funding for Postsecondary Institutions

Did postsecondary institutions actually receive notable increases in federal funding during the stimulus period—especially in the 2009/10 school year? In this section, we show that they did.[12]

10. Even when their total revenue is most broadly defined (see appendix table 9A.1), federal grant and contract funding represents between 6 and 14 percent of the total revenue of research universities and medical schools.

11. We suspect that the federal grant and contract numbers are overstated for associate and baccalaureate/master's institutions. This is because Pell grants often appear as nonoperating federal grants in their accounts. The Delta Cost Project database attempts to remove Pell and other aid from "grants and contracts," but we believe—based on cross-validation with other data sources—that some share of federal aid is not removed from nonoperating grants.

12. The key data for these figures are from the Delta Cost Project database (2012), which we describe in section 9.4.

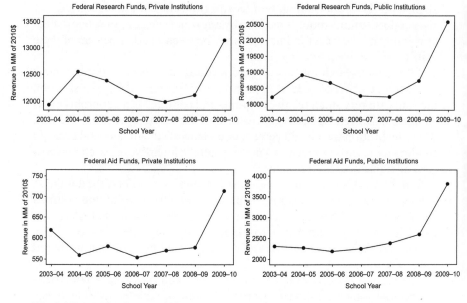

Fig. 9.1 Federal funds received by extensive research universities from 2003/4 to 2009/10

Figures 9.1 through 9.5 show federal funds, by category of institution, from the 2003/4 school year through the 2009/10 school year.[13] All amounts are in 2010 dollars, adjusted using the GDP deflator. Each figure has four subfigures: (a) federal grants, contracts, and appropriations for private institutions; (b) federal grants, contracts, and appropriations for public institutions; (c) federal student aid funds for private institutions; and (d) federal student aid funds for public institutions. We consolidate appropriations with grants and contracts because of their nature (see above) and their small magnitude (table 9.1).

Consider figure 9.1, which focuses on extensive research universities. Between 2006/7 (the base year we employed in table 9.1) and 2009/10, real federal research funds jumped by 16 percent for private extensive research universities and 20 percent for public extensive research universities. Over the same period, federal aid funds jumped by 37 percent for private extensive research universities and by 79 percent for public extensive research universities. (Keep in mind that the larger percentage increases in aid add up to fewer total dollars than the substantial but more modest percentage

13. We select 2003/4 as the first school year in the figures because, prior to that, some institutions were reporting their finances using a form that can be hard to reconcile with the form used from 2003/4 onward (GASB 34/35). To avoid apparent but spurious changes in revenues due solely to reporting, we do not show prior years. However, the period from 2000/1 through 2003/4 was fairly stable for most federal funding streams, and this can be seen for institutions that reported in the same manner throughout.

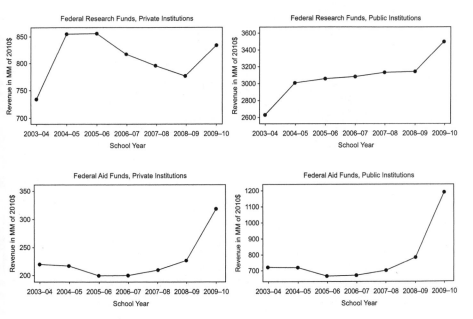

Fig. 9.2 Federal funds received by intensive research universities from 2003/4 to 2009/10

increases in research-related funding. This is because federal aid funds make up much less of extensive research universities' total revenue than do federal research-type funds. This is evident if one looks at the scale of the subfigures' vertical axes.) In any case, the key conclusion from figure 9.1 is that extensive research universities experienced a full dose of the federal stimulus.

The picture is slightly more mixed for intensive research universities, shown in figure 9.2. On the one hand, federal student aid grew between 2006/7 and 2009/10 by a massive 68 percent at private intensive research universities and by an even greater 82 percent at public intensive research universities. Note though that these growth rates were from smaller per-institution bases than those of the extensive research universities. Over the same period, the public intensive research universities saw their federal research-type funding rise by 20 percent. Private intensive research universities also experienced a rise of 8 percent in federal research-type funding in 2009/10, owing to the stimulus. This rise, however, only reversed a fall in such funding from a peak amount in 2005/6. In short, all of the intensive research universities experienced stimulus funding, but the research funding pattern is slightly less consistent than that of extensive research universities. This is probably because the per-institution amounts of research-type funding are sufficiently small in the base year that each year's federal research-type funding represents a fairly small number of grants. Thus, these funding streams are inherently less stable than the parallel streams for extensive research uni-

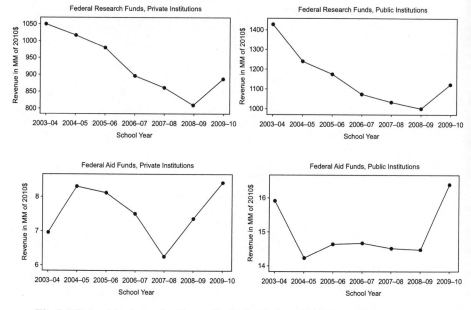

Fig. 9.3 Federal funds received by medical schools from 2003/4 to 2009/10

versities, whose base-year funding per institution is as much as ten times larger.

The story for medical schools (figure 9.3) is also one in which stimulus funding reversed a decline in federal funding rather than caused fairly flat federal funding to peak. Both private and public medical schools experienced falling federal research-type funding from 2003/4 onward—right up until stimulus motives increased their federal funding in 2009/10 (by 11 percent for privates and 13 percent for publics). Their federal student aid also grew substantially in the stimulus period, but it started from such a small base that it is not important to their finances.

The time patterns for baccalaureate/master's and associate schools (figures 9.4 and 9.5) are fairly similar—albeit on a much smaller scale—to those for intensive research universities. Stimulus motives generate massive percentage increases in federal aid funds. The baccalaureate/master's and the public associate schools also see large percentage increases in federal research-type funding.[14] However, for baccalaureate/master's and associate schools, the per-institution amounts of research-type funding are an order of magnitude smaller than those of intensive research universities and as much as two orders of magnitude smaller than those of extensive research universities. Thus, even large percentage increases in research-type funding translate into small per-

14. For private baccalaureate/master's schools, this stimulus-driven increase in research-type funding reverses a previous decline.

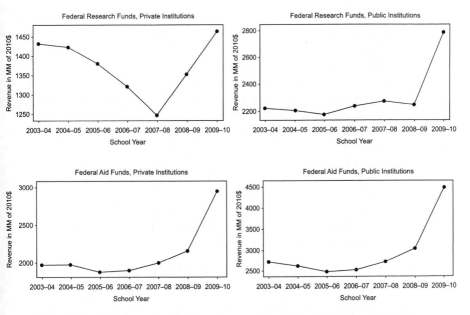

Fig. 9.4 Federal funds received by baccalaureate/master's colleges from 2003/4 to 2009/10

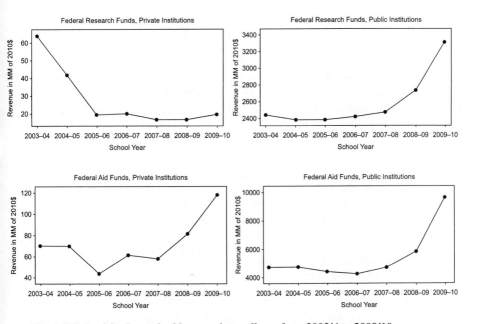

Fig. 9.5 Federal funds received by associate colleges from 2003/4 to 2009/10

centage increases in these schools' total revenues. Thus, it is the increases in federal aid funds that are potentially important for their finances.

Overall, we conclude from figures 9.1 through 9.5 that stimulus motives generated substantial increases in all federal funds directed to postsecondary institutions. Extensive research universities and public intensive research universities are the easiest to analyze because (a) the increases in funding that they experienced were substantial relative to their total revenues, both for research-type and aid funding and (b) their federal funding was fairly flat in the prestimulus period so that it is not difficult to predict what they would have experienced if stimulus funding had not occurred. Other institutions are somewhat harder to analyze because their prestimulus federal funding was falling *or* their federal research-type funding was too small to be important to their finances *or* their federal student aid increased greatly but presents us with an endogeneity problem that we hinted at in the introduction and take up in detail in section 9.5.

9.2.3 Federal Research and Development Funding by Source

As mentioned above, our first instrument exploits the fact that various sources of federal research funding—NIH, NASA, the National Science Foundation (NSF), Defense, Energy, Agriculture, and so on—did not all enjoy the same stimulus-driven increase in federal funding.

We turn to a different database (National Science Foundation 2012) to construct figure 9.6, which shows federal research funding for each of the main agencies or departments that directs funds to postsecondary institutions, from 2003/4 to 2009/10. These are: Agriculture, Defense, Energy, Health and Human Services (HHS, the vast majority of which is NIH), NASA, and the NSF. In each figure, the amount for each year (in real dollars) is shown relative to the amount in 2006/7, the base year. Thus, the value of 1.16 for HHS in 2009/10 shows that federal research funding from HHS increased by 16 percent in real terms between 2006/7 and 2009/10.

Among all the major agencies/departments, only Agriculture shows no stimulus-motivated boost in research funding. The others have quite widely differing percentage increases. The lowest is that of HHS at 16 percent and the highest is Defense at 58 percent. NSF funding jumped by 23 percent, Energy by 28 percent, and NASA by 29 percent.[15]

9.3 What Economic Theory Predicts about Universities' Use of Stimulus Funds

In this section, we briefly review what economic theory predicts about how universities should use federal stimulus funds. This theory is related to fiscal federalist theory regarding the manner in which lower-level govern-

---

15. We were unable to allocate about 3 percent of ARRA research funding because its agency or department information was unavailable.

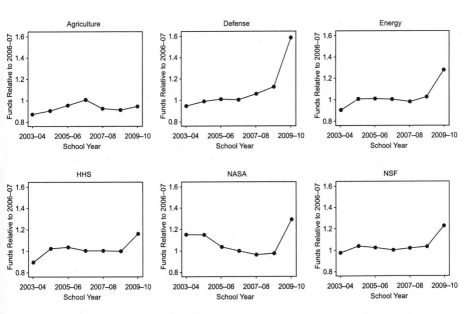

Fig. 9.6 Real federal research funds received by postsecondary institutions relative to the 2006/7 school year

ments, like states or municipalities, should react to grants from higher-level governments, like the federal government.

Consider a federal research grant that arrives at a university owing to the stimulus. It is a windfall that is formally intended to be spent on research. Suppose that the university normally allocates funds among numerous uses of which research spending is only one. Other key uses of funds would typically include instruction, student aid, public service, maintenance and operation of plant and equipment, construction, and saving money for the future through an endowment. In its last prerecession base year, the university might be allocating funds according to figure 9.7, which shows a division of funds between research expenses and all other activities. If the university is allocating money to maximize its objectives, the division of funds will be such that an indifference curve representing those objectives is just tangent to the budget constraint that represents the trade-off between research and all other activities.

The stimulus-motivated federal research funds shift the university's budget constraint out by the amount of the windfall. If the windfall is smaller than what the university planned to spend on research from fairly unrestricted sources, the shift in the budget constraint does not affect its slope: an extra dollar for research might as well be an extra dollar that is unrestricted.[16] This is shown in panel B of figure 9.8. If the windfall is so large that it exceeds

16. By "fairly unrestricted," we do not only mean funds that are classified as "unrestricted," but all funds that can be shifted forward in time to another fiscal year or shifted to a somewhat different research or instructional use.

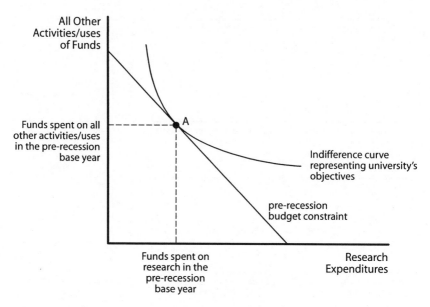

Fig. 9.7 A university maximizing its objectives via spending on research and nonresearch activities

what the university planned to spend from fairly unrestricted sources, it may make a dollar of research effectively less expensive than a dollar allocated to any other activity. As a result, the windfall would not only shift the budget constraint but affect its slope as well, as shown in panel C of figure 9.8.

If the university were to spend every dollar of the windfall on research *and* leave all its other funding allocations unchanged, it would arrive at a point like B in panel A of figure 9.8. This represents a full flypaper effect: every federal research dollar "sticks where it hits" not only because it is itself spent on research (which is legally necessary) but because it does not trigger any reallocation of other revenue. Except under extraordinary conditions, a full flypaper effect is not consistent with a university previously maximizing its objectives. This is shown in panels B and C of figure 9.8, where the university's postwindfall, objectives-maximizing allocations are illustrated by the points marked C. At points like these, the university spends some of each windfall dollar on research but reallocates or saves some of it for other activities. We expect the postwindfall budget to be more skewed toward research when the restrictions on the university's funds are greater.

We have used federal research funds as an example, but the analysis goes through for federal aid funds as well. The main difference is that there are quite different restrictions that constrain institutions' use of aid funds. In particular, an institution that initially has low tuition might be constrained to raise its tuition if it wants to reallocate or save federal aid funds for other activities. See Turner (2012) for an analysis of how an institution might achieve this.

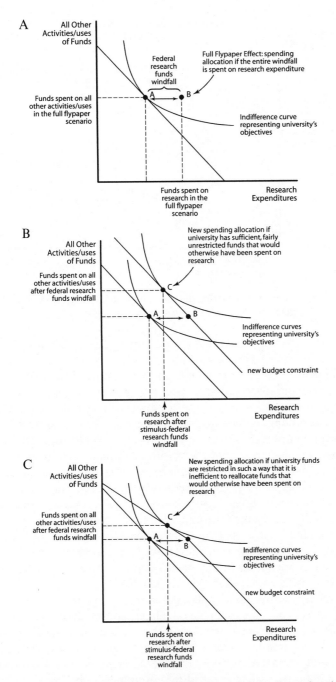

Fig. 9.8 *A*, a university's spending in a full flypaper scenario; *B*, a university maximizing its objectives with sufficient prior research spending to make stimulus funds unrestricted; *C*, a university maximizing its objectives with insufficient prior research spending to make stimulus funds unrestricted

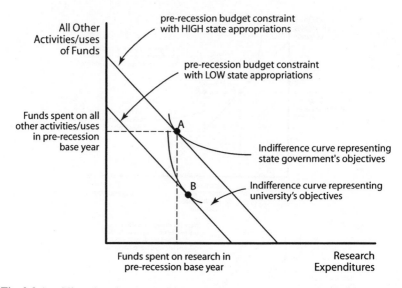

Fig. 9.9 A public university maximizing the state government's objectives rather than suffer a reduced budget in order to maximize its own

Later in this chapter, we discuss the possibility that public universities were not maximizing their objectives prior to the arrival of the windfall. While even private universities might fail to maximize their objectives— owing to restrictions placed on their spending by governments or donors— there is a much more obvious struggle that affects public universities. These universities' decisions can be highly constrained by the state governments that control an important source of their revenues (state appropriations) and that also regulate their admissions (often limiting the number of out-of-state students), tuition, aid programs, public service programs, salaries, and even line-item spending. The degree to which state governments control their public universities differs greatly from state to state and sometimes differs substantially among the institutions within a state.[17]

Consider a public university that, prerecession, had objectives represented by the indifference curve marked "university" in figure 9.9. Its state government's objectives are represented by the indifference curve marked "state" in the same figure. (The objectives shown are such that the university has a stronger preference for research than the state government, but this is not necessarily the case.) Prerecession, the state might offer high appropriations if the university complies with the state government's objectives, creating the possibility of point A, or low appropriations if the university pursues its own objectives, creating point B. The figure is set up so that the university chooses point A, with high appropriations and acceptance of the government's objectives.

17. See Aghion et al. (2009).

Now consider what occurs if the university receives a windfall in the form of federal research funds at the same time that the state government's tax revenue falls. If the state government did nothing, then the university's budget constraint would shift, just as it did in panel C of figure 9.8, and the university might choose a point like that labeled C in panel A of figure 9.10. But, appropriations to the university are more difficult for the state government to fund at just the same time that federal research funds arrive, so it is quite possible that the state's high appropriations offer will become less generous, causing the university to choose the low appropriations state in which it is allowed to pursue its own objectives. This is illustrated by point D in panel B of figure 9.10. Observe that the university has now allocated more money toward research—and not just because of the direct effect of the federal research funds. The federal funds allow the university to switch from the state government's objectives to its own. This switch may have consequences that reach far beyond allocating dollars to research. The university may shift toward *all* activities and policies that it prefers more than the state does. This could include admitting different students, charging different tuition, or allocating aid funds differently.

The theory we have presented is overly simple. Negotiations between universities and state governments are not only complex but repeated over time. Similarly, all universities (private and public) interact with the federal government repeatedly. The repeated nature of the interactions color how universities respond to federal funding. Also, universities' nongovernment sources of revenue are constrained in numerous ways, not only by formal restrictions on how funds are spent but also by fundamental elasticities. A university cannot, for instance, raise tuition without affecting which students enroll. Nevertheless, the theory we have presented brings out some key predictions:

1. Universities will spend more of the stimulus-motivated federal funds on the purposes for which it is statutorily intended when restrictions effectively reduce the cost of intended-area spending relative to spending on all other uses.

2. We should not expect a full flypaper effect unless universities' budget allocations are *highly* restricted.

3. Universities that allocate stimulus-motivated federal funds in a manner that is fairly similar to how they allocated a marginal dollar of funds prerecession are probably demonstrating that they were maximizing their objectives prior to the recession and that they have sufficient fairly unrestricted funds to keep doing this.[18]

---

18. The alternative interpretation would be that, prerecession, universities were already constrained to spend more on the intended uses for windfall federal funds than they have liked. In this case, if the restrictions imposed by the windfall were very similar to those that constrained the universities prerecession, they would spend the windfall similarly but be maximizing their objectives in neither situation.

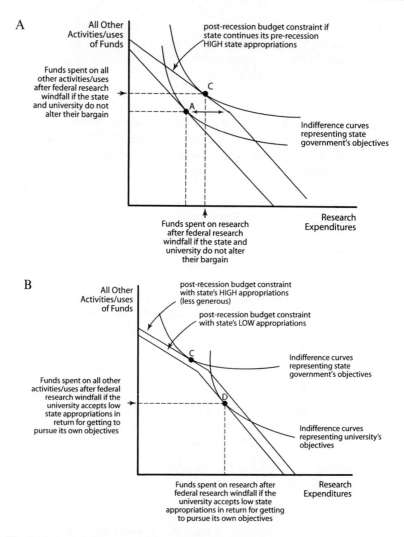

Fig. 9.10 *A*, a public university maximizing the state government's objectives even after the receipt of stimulus funds; *B*, a public university maximizing its own objectives after state government appropriations fall in response to the availability of stimulus funds

4. Universities that were not maximizing their own objectives prerecession (possibly public universities) may be triggered to choose a different bargain with their state governments or other sources of nonfederal funds.

9.4 Data

We use three main types of data: (a) data based on postsecondary institutions' reports of their finances and employment; (b) data based on the federal government's records of its transfers to postsecondary institutions, and (c) data based on states' reports of their workforces.

9.4.1 Data Based on Postsecondary Institutions' Reports of Their Finances and Employment

The "backbone" of our data is the Integrated Postsecondary Education Data System ([IPEDS] US Department of Education 2012), which is based on mandatory self-reporting by institutions. IPEDS contains many elements that we use: institutional characteristics, financial reports, and employment reports. The IPEDS variables relevant to this study are available on an annual basis and cover a specific school year or, in the case of financial variables, an institution's fiscal year. All postsecondary institutions relevant to this study have fiscal years that begin and end in a summer month. For instance, 2006/7 is the school/fiscal year that contains September 2006 through May 2007, plus some combination of summer months.[19]

By combining data from the annual IPEDS surveys, we can construct a fairly complete history for each institution. In the case of financial variables, however, such construction is tricky because the reporting procedures have changed over time, and public and private institutions use somewhat different accounting traditions. Fortunately, the Delta Cost Project Database (US Department of Education 2012) contains IPEDS data that have been translated into consistent measures so that we can confidently conduct longitudinal analyses of trends. We use this version of the IPEDS data for financial variables whenever it is more consistent than the normal IPEDS data.

Because its endowment survey is much more detailed than the IPEDS survey, we use the NACUBO-Commonfund Study of Endowments ([NCSE]; National Association of College and University Business Officers and Commonfund Institute 2009–2010) for outcomes related to endowments.[20] In particular, we take the spending rate on the endowment from this source. This data set has an extraordinarily useful combination of objective data on what universities *do* with their business officers' explanations of *why* they do them.

As of the time of writing, the most recent financial data that are available cover 2009/10.

9.4.2 Data on the Federal Government's Transfers to Postsecondary Institutions

We constructed a history of federal government funds received by the research universities, medical schools, and other health professional schools

19. Among the research universities and medical schools on which we focus our analysis in sections 9.5 and 9.6, 85 percent have a fiscal year that ends on June 30, 10 percent have a fiscal year that ends on August 31, 4 percent have a fiscal year that ends on May 31, and 1 percent have some other fiscal year end date.

20. For years prior to 2009, we use the Commonfund Study of Endowments (see Commonfund Institute 2003–2008).

that received at least one million dollars in 2005/6.[21] Constructing this history is a painstaking process, as described in the data appendix, owing to the fact that federal agencies' records are designed for tracking the history of specific grants, not for constructing time series of federal revenues. These data have important benefits, however. They allow us to identify the exact source and timing of each stream of federal revenue. Since stimulus funding is predicated on the idea that federal spending will affect economic outcomes *soon*, we want to know when federal funds are actually received.

Although not all federal agencies have funding data available, especially for the prestimulus period, we obtained detailed administrative data from the sources that generate the vast majority of transfers to postsecondary institutions: NIH, NSF, NASA, and the Pell grant program. These sources generate 99 percent of all federal transfers to postsecondary institutions and 75 percent of all research-type transfers. Our NIH data come from the Research Portfolio Online Reporting Tool ([RePORT] National Institutes of Health 2013); our NSF and NASA data come from research.gov (National Science Foundation 2013); and our Pell data come from the Federal Student Aid Data Center (US Department of Education 2013). We take other agencies' data (Defense, Energy, and Agriculture are the key ones) from the National Science Foundation (2013).

In the data appendix, we describe these sources and our exact procedures for recording the recipient and timing of each transfer in detail. However, our basic procedure is as follows: data on the number of Pell grant recipients and total aid is matched to the postsecondary institution to which the funds are disbursed and to the quarter when the funds are disbursed.[22] For grants and contracts, we identify each project that has a university as a recipient, taking care to include grants received by university-affiliated hospitals and independent operations. We allocate funding to the relevant university uniformly by month starting with the project's budget start date and ending with the budget end date.[23] We can thus aggregate the disbursements by year or by quarter, as needed. Grants hosted by the National Bureau of Economic Research are matched to the university(ies) of the principal investigator(s).

9.4.3 Data Based on States' Reports of Their Workforce

We obtain accurate, up-to-date data on local economic activity from the Quarterly Workforce Indicators Database ([QWI] US Department of Com-

---

21. The million dollar threshold is in terms of fiscal year 2010 dollars. We have NSF, NIH, and NASA data on 263 institutions but have data on federal funding for Agriculture, Energy, and Defense for only 206 of these institutions. We include the University of California-Merced despite the fact that it did not have a Carnegie classification in the year 2000.

22. Prior to fiscal year 2007, we can only match disbursements to the year, not the quarter. Therefore, we use the quarterly pattern from fiscal year 2007 to backcast disbursement by quarters in prior years.

23. We use the project start and end dates if budget start and end dates are unavailable.

merce 2013).[24] The QWI contains very current data because it is largely based on administrative data that the US Bureau of the Census gathers from unemployment wage records and from businesses. The key suppliers of these data are the state labor market agencies. The census merges these administrative data with demographic information from the US Census and other surveys.

We obtain the QWI information at the county-by-quarter level—associating each university with the county in which it is located.[25] Our key outcomes from the QWI are employment and payroll variables. Massachusetts is, unfortunately, not included in the QWI.

9.5 Empirical Strategy

If all the variation in federal funds directed to postsecondary institutions were exogenous, we would estimate the following simple regression that is standard for exercises of this sort (for instance, estimating a local government's response to a grant from the federal government):

$$(1) \qquad Exp_{it} = \beta_0 + \beta_1 Federal\ Funds_{it} + \mathbf{X}_{it}\beta_2 + \gamma_i + \varepsilon_{it}$$

or its first-differenced version:

$$(2) \quad Exp_{it} - Exp_{i,t-1} = \beta_1(Federal\ Funds_{it} - Federal\ Funds_{i,t-1}) + (\mathbf{X}_{it} - \mathbf{X}_{it-1})\beta_2 \\ + (\varepsilon_{it} - \varepsilon_{i,t-1}),$$

where i indexes the postsecondary institution, t indexes time, a t-1 subscript indicates a variable lagged one period, Exp_{it} is the institution's expenditure or some other outcome likely to be affected (revenue, research expenditures, the payroll, employment, the spending rate from the endowment), $Federal\text{-}Funds_{it}$ is federal funding received by institution i in period t, $\mathbf{X}_{it}$ is a vector of control variables, γ_i is an institution-specific intercept, and ε_{it} is a white noise error term.

If the outcome is total expenditure, we would interpret an estimated coefficient on $FederalFunds_{it}$ that is not statistically significantly different from one as "no saving." If the outcome and federal funding are aligned—for instance, research spending regressed on federal research funds—then an estimated coefficient that is not statistically significantly different from one is a full flypaper effect. Coefficients less than 1 are generally indicators of the institution reallocating or saving federal funds. An estimated coefficient greater than 1 would suggest that the federal funding induced the institution to match the federal funds with some funds from its other sources.

In practice, we make a few modifications to equation (2), which is the basis of our preferred specification. First, because we observe that different insti-

---

24. For a useful description of the QWI, see Abowd et al. 2009.
25. There are a few cases in which an institution is located in more than one county. In such cases, we assign an institution to the county in which it primarily operates.

tutions had different typical growth in expenditures (and other outcomes), prior to the base year, we compute each institution's average preexisting growth in each outcome variable using 2003/4 to 2006/7 as the "pre" period. We subtract these preexisting growth estimates from our outcome variables. This ensures that we start from a realistic counterfactual for each institution. We also allow for a nonzero intercept in the estimating equation.[26]

Second, we do not necessarily expect private and public institutions to respond similarly to federal funding, owing to the differences in their governance, alternative funding, and objectives. Thus, we estimate the above equation separately by an institution's control.

Third, we do not expect institutions to respond identically to funds from different sources. Most obviously, responses to research-type funds and aid funds are likely to differ because they are differentially fungible, they are intended for very different uses, and—most obviously—they flow to the institution in somewhat different ways. Unlike research funds, aid funds are intended to flow to students, so an institution can reallocate them only by changing its tuition or changing its institutional grant aid to students.

In short, we estimate regressions of the form:

$$(3)\ Exp_{it} - Exp_{i,t-1} - PreGrowth_i$$
$$= \alpha_0 + \alpha_1(Federal\ Research\ Funds_{it} - Federal\ Research\ Funds_{i,t-1})$$
$$+ \alpha_2(Federal\ Aid\ Funds_{it} - Federal\ Aid\ Funds_{i,t-1})$$
$$+ (\mathbf{X}_{it} - \mathbf{X}_{i,t-1})\alpha_3 + (\upsilon_{it} - \upsilon_{i,t-1}),$$

separately for private and public institutions.[27] $PreGrowth_i$ is the average value of $Exp_{it} - Exp_{i,t-1}$ for institution i during the period from 2003/4 to 2006/7.[28] We estimate equation (3) using data from our base year (2006/7) onward.

Finally, we slightly modify equation (3) for use with the QWI data in which county employment and payroll are the outcomes. We can do better than estimate a preexisting growth rate because there are many counties that do not contain a relevant postsecondary institution but that are otherwise economically similar to a county that does. We therefore construct a synthetic control county for each county with a relevant institution.[29] We subtract the outcome for the synthetic control county from the dependent variable rather than subtract the preexisting growth rate:

---

26. We get similar results if we impose a zero intercept.

27. We would like to be able estimate separate effects for each source of research-type funds—the NSF versus the NIH, for instance. We do not believe that we can do this credibly, however. See footnote 30.

28. We do not remove institution-specific preexisting growth in federal funds because, as will be seen, such institutional differences are excluded automatically by our instrumental variable, by construction.

29. Synthetic control methods are described by Abadie, Diamond, and Hainmueller (2010, 2011). We construct a synthetic control county for each county that contains a relevant postsecondary institution.

(4) $(Exp_{it} - Exp_{i,t-1})^{university\ county} - (Exp_{it} - Exp_{i,t-1})^{synthetic\ control\ county}$

$= \mu_0 + \mu_1 (Federal\ Research\ Funds_{it} - Federal\ Research\ Funds_{i,t-1})$

$\quad + \mu_2 (Federal\ Aid\ Funds_{it} - Federal\ Aid\ Funds_{i,t-1})$

$\quad + (\mathbf{X}_{it} - \mathbf{X}_{i,t-1})\mu_3 + (\xi_{it} - \xi_{i,t-1}).$

9.5.1 The Potential Endogeneity of Federal Research-Type Stimulus Funding

There are two main reasons why federal research-type stimulus funding may not be exogenous. First, institutions whose revenues are particularly hard hit by the crisis or recession may be more aggressive about obtaining federal research funds, perhaps with the assistance of congressmen and senators from their state. Such reverse causality would cause equations (3) and (4) to understate the stimulative effect of transfers. Second, institutions that are going to have especially fast future growth anyway (regardless of the stimulus) may have a disproportionate share of projects that are "in the pipeline"—with the consequence that their federal funding would increase disproportionately in the stimulus period. This would cause overstatement of the stimulative effect. Overstatement would also occur if the institutions best able to generate research projects that receive stimulus funds happen to be institutions that are unusually *unaffected* by the crisis and recession, perhaps because of their location or their nonfederal sources of funding.

We need an instrument that contains credibly exogenous variation in the stimulus-driven increase in federal research-type funds that institutions experience. We propose an instrument based on (a) an institution's prestimulus funding from each federal source, and (b) the stimulus-period percentage increase in funding from each of these sources that is directed to all institutions other than the institution in question. Specifically, if year $t = 0$ is the base year, our instrument for $(FederalResearchFunds_{it} - FederalResearchFunds_{i,t-1})$ is:

(5) $[NIHFunds_{i0} \cdot (1 + p_{-i,0\ to\ t}^{NIH}) + NSFFunds_{i0} \cdot (1 + p_{-i,0\ to\ t}^{NSF})$

$\quad + NASAFunds_{i0} \cdot (1 + p_{-i,0\ to\ t}^{NASA}) + AgricFunds_{i0} \cdot (1 + p_{-i,0\ to\ t}^{Agric}) +$

$\quad DefenseFunds_{i0} \cdot (1 + p_{-i,0\ to\ t}^{Defense}) + EnergyFunds_{i0} \cdot (1 + p_{-i,0\ to\ t}^{Energy})]$

$\quad -[NIHFunds_{i0} \cdot (1 + p_{-i,0\ to\ t-1}^{NIH}) + NSFFunds_{i0} \cdot (1 + p_{-i,0\ to\ t-1}^{NSF}) +$

$\quad NASAFunds_{i0} \cdot (1 + p_{-i,0\ to\ t-1}^{NASA}) + AgricFunds_{i0} \cdot$

$\quad (1 + p_{-i,0\ to\ t-1}^{Agric}) + DefenseFunds_{i0} \cdot (1 + p_{-i,0\ to\ t-1}^{Defense}) +$

$\quad EnergyFunds_{i0} \cdot (1 + p_{-i,0\ to\ t-1}^{Energy})]$

where $p_{-i,0\ to\ t}^{Source}$ is the percentage increase from year 0 to year t in federal research-type funding from source, *Source* directed to all postsecondary institutions except institution i. By excluding institution i's own funding from the percentage increase calculation, we eliminate the possibility that an intention to affect institution i motivated the percentage increases in the federal funding it received.

Our proposed instrument fulfils the exclusion restriction if (a) the percentage increases in each source of federal funding (excluding the relevant institution) were not motivated by the potential effect on the relevant institution, and (b) institutions with different initial federal funding-by-source allocations were not going to diverge *differentially* from their past behavior anyway (that is, in a world with no stimulus-motivated funding). The latter restriction is a bit complex, so an intuitive example might help. Suppose that there are two types of research universities—(a) those in which NIH accounts for two-thirds of federal funding and NASA accounts for one-third, and (b) those in which NIH accounts for one-third of federal funding and NASA accounts for two-thirds. Then our instrument would indicate that the latter group of universities gets a substantially larger boost in federal research funding in the stimulus period (because NASA's percentage increase was much bigger than NIH's). Since equation (3) is in first-differences—that is, comparing every university to its own previous year—our instrument would only be problematic if the NIH-dominated universities were going to change their behavior anyway (in a world with no stimulus) in a manner that was systemically different from the way the NASA-dominated universities were going to change their behavior anyway (in a world with no stimulus). We are not aware of a narrative that suggests that this problem exists— always remembering that the narrative must be about systematic differences in changes, not systematic differences in levels. Our identifying assumptions are standard for a Bartik-type instrument based on the *interaction* between an entity's initial conditions and policy-driven changes over which the entity itself has no control.[30]

9.5.2 The Endogeneity of Federal Student Aid to Local Family Incomes

In figures 9.1 through 9.5, we demonstrated that postsecondary institutions of all types experienced substantial, stimulus-driven increases in federal aid funds. A key reason was that the aid formulas themselves became more generous. In fact, the formula changes were touted as being one of the best channels for the stimulus because they could take effect quickly and were intended to put money into the hands of young, low-income people who might be especially likely to spend it. The main change in the formula was an increase in the maximum Pell grant from $4,050 in 2006/7 to $5,350 in 2009/10. Thus, a postsecondary institution could expect to receive increased

---

30. The reader may observe that we could construct an instrument for each separate funding source and thereby estimate a version of equation (3) in which NIH, NSF, NASA, and other federal research-type funding all enter separately. However, the coefficients would then be identified by functional form (specifically, the assumption that all the effects are linear in the scale of federal funding), and we would not argue for the credibility of such estimates. Our proposed instrument is much more credible because it exploits idiosyncratic variation in the federal funding mix among institutions of comparable scale.

federal aid funds roughly in proportion to the number of students it enrolled who already received the maximum Pell grant. Our empirical strategy uses this policy-driven variation in the federal aid revenue that institutions received, and we take steps to ensure that it is exogenous.

Not all of the increases in federal aid funds were driven by stimulus policy. Aid funds also increased because family incomes and liquid assets fell with the crisis and recession, and this creates an endogeneity problem. A student's aid is a function of his expected family contribution (EFC), which is determined by applying the current federal formula to his family's income, liquid assets, and other dependents' needs. The lower are a family's income and assets, the greater is the federal aid for the student—*unless* the student's EFC is such that he already receives the maximum Pell grant.[31]

The relationship between family income and federal aid funds generates an endogeneity problem. Suppose that a postsecondary institution's students suffer owing to the financial crisis or Great Recession. Their families might lose employment, income, or assets. Then, even if the institution were to enroll precisely the same students and the aid formulas did not change, it would likely find that its federal aid funds increased because its students had grown more needy. Such a change in the institution's finances would be caused by the crisis and recession—not by stimulus-motivated changes in federal aid. Thus, a naive correlation between federal aid and a university's outcomes would partly reflect causality that runs from crisis/recession to outcomes, not just from stimulus funding to outcomes.

Our empirical strategy breaks apart the two strands of causality by exploiting the nationwide change in the maximum Pell grant. Recall that a student at the maximum Pell grant does not receive more aid if his family income falls. He only receives more aid if the maximum Pell grant rises—a policy over which he has no control. To form our proposed instrument, we take the prestimulus (2006/7) number of students at each institution who are at the maximum Pell and compute the increase in federal aid funds that the institution would see if every prestimulus student at the maximum got the new maximum *and* there were no change in the students enrolled *and* there were no changes in the incomes of the students already enrolled. That is, our proposed instrument for $(FederalAidFunds_{it} - FederalAidFunds_{i,t-1})$ is:

(6) $(NumberAtMaxPell_{i0} \cdot MaxPellGrant_t) -$
$\qquad\qquad (NumberAtMaxPell_{i0} \cdot MaxPellGrant_{t-1})$,

---

31. The formula for a student's EFC is complicated because it takes account of a wide array of possible family circumstances. However, the relationship between a student's family income and his federal aid is strong (R-squared of 0.93) if he is not at the maximum Pell grant and does not come from an above-median income family. The R-squared statistic is based on authors' calculations based on the National Postsecondary Student Aid Survey 2008 (US Department of Education 2009).

where year $t = 0$ is the base year. This is an example of a simulated instrument, the distinctive feature of which is applying a policy change to an unchanging group of actors.[32]

A restriction necessary for validity of this instrument is that schools with different initial conditions (in this case, different numbers of students eligible for the maximum Pell grant) were not going to diverge *differentially* from their past behavior anyway (that is, in a world with no stimulus-motivated boost in the Pell grant). More precisely, the part of a school's counterfactual change in behavior that cannot be predicted by the covariates in X should not be systemically related to its value of the instrument. This assumption will be problematic in the case of schools that recruit their students almost entirely from their local labor market. It should not be problematic in the case of schools that recruit their students on a national or large regional market.

To see this, consider two research universities that both recruit their students nationally. Suppose that although they are otherwise quite similar, the first places more emphasis on fields of study that appeal to high aptitude low-income students (engineering, medicine) and therefore enrolls more students eligible for the maximum Pell grant. When the maximum Pell grant increases, the first research university will receive a bigger increase in its federal aid funds than the second, but there is little reason to think that the two universities' behavior would have diverged differentially anyway at this same time. Even if part of the reason that the first research university recruits more low-income students is that it is located in a low-income neighborhood, the low-income neighborhood is unlikely to determine the school's outcomes in the crisis and recession. For instance, Yale's being located in a low-income neighborhood probably has very little effect on year-over-year changes in its student body, alumni donations, ability to attract research funds, or earnings from its endowment. In the short term, all of these Yale outcomes are determined at a far more national level—on national financial markets, for example. In fact, we can and do control for the initial employment and wages in Yale's and all other research universities' and medical schools' local labor markets and find that our instrument still has ample statistical power. This

---

32. In practice, constructing our instrument is slightly more complicated because we have to estimate each institution's number of students at the maximum Pell grant in the base year. We estimate it because, unfortunately, this number is not reported in the federal student aid database. We perform the estimation by analyzing how prior (to the stimulus period) changes in the maximum Pell grant affected schools' aid funds. On these prior occasions, the schools' aid funds should have changed only because of students who were at the maximum—at least so long as the economy was not falling into a recession at the same time. Thus, we can back out how many students were at the maximum. Details are in the data appendix. We are not terribly concerned about estimation error in this procedure because (a) the resulting measurement error is likely to be classical and classical measurement error in an instrument is not a problem for estimation, and (b) the stimulus-motivated change in the maximum Pell grant is so large that its change dwarfs minor errors that come from estimating the number of students eligible for the maximum grant.

is evidence that much of these institutions' variation in Pell-eligible students comes from their idiosyncratic recruiting, not their neighborhood.

To see why the instrument is less credible among schools that recruit students very locally, consider two public associate (community) colleges, each of which draws its students almost exclusively from the county whose government supports it. Suppose that the first county is blue collar and the second is white collar. The first community college is initially likely to have more students who are eligible for the maximum Pell grant because its local families have lower incomes. In the counterfactual where no stimulus-motivated change in the Pell grant occurred, the first community college would probably suffer more in the recession than the second. This is because, in the recession, blue-collar employees systemically suffered greater losses in employment and income than white-collar employees.[33] Thus, our proposed instrument would be correlated with the error term—the change in the school's counterfactual behavior that cannot be predicted by the covariates in X. Of course, we could add numerous indicators of the counties' initial labor market conditions (the share of workers in each occupation and so on) to the vector X in an attempt to make our instrument more credible. However, since the differences in the schools' Pell-eligible population came from precisely those labor market conditions, our instrument would then have no statistical power.

Summing up, we have a powerful and, we believe, credible simulated instrument for the stimulus-motivated change in federal aid funds—but only for institutions that do not draw most of their students from a local labor market. This eliminates virtually all the associate institutions and a good share of the baccalaureate/master's institutions as well. Since these two categories of institution could only have been much affected by stimulus-motivated changes in federal aid (federal research funding is unimportant to them), we hereafter focus our analysis on research universities, medical schools, and a few other health institutions that receive very substantial federal funding.[34]

9.6 Informal, Graphical Illustrations of the Effect of Stimulus Funding

Before proceeding to the formal econometric analysis, we illustrate some of our basic results using figures that are the graphical analog of the estimating equations. The advantage of the figures is that they provide solid intuition. The disadvantages, relative to the econometric analysis, are twofold.

33. This fact is shown by numerous studies—for instance, Hoynes, H., Miller, D. L., and Schaller, J. (2012) or US Bureau of Labor Statistics (2012).

34. See below for our exact selection criteria. A small number of very selective liberal arts colleges do, in fact, recruit students from the entire nation. The Pell-based instrument should be credible and have statistical power for them. They should therefore be susceptible to analysis—although not for the effects of federal research funds, of which they have only a small amount. Medical and other health schools are interesting to us because they account for such a large amount of federal research funding.

First, in order to show the results clearly, we focus on the schools that were most or least affected by stimulus-driven funding, omitting the schools in intermediate situations. Thus, although the main graphical findings carry over to the full set of universities, minor aspects of the graphs are probably best ignored because they are insufficiently representative. Second, the figures do not deal with the endogeneity problems that the instrumental variables remedy.[35] Thus, we focus the figures on federal research funding, which is less likely to be endogenous than aid funding.

Figure 9.11 shows sources of revenue (panels A and B) and categories of expenditure (panels C and D) for private institutions from 2003/4 through 2009/10. The left-hand panels (A and C) are based on the twelve institutions that were *most* affected by federal stimulus-driven research funding: each of them experienced at least a 25 percent increase in funding relative to 2006/7. The right-hand panels (B and D) are based on the five institutions that were *least* affected by stimulus-driven research funding: each of them experienced only a minor (inflation-adjusted) increase in funding relative to 2006/7. (There are no private institutions that experienced a zero increase or a decrease in funding.)

Importantly, each revenue or expenditure line in the figure is based on the *residual* of that variable from its 2003/4 through 2006/7 time trend. This allows us to focus on the changes in each variable from its preexisting trend. It is the use of these residuals that makes the figures the analog of the estimating equation. A consequence of using the residuals is that all the lines are centered around zero in the prestimulus period.

Panel A of figure 9.11 shows that, for the most affected schools, revenue from all federal sources rose dramatically in 2009/10 relative to the preexisting trend. There is a smaller increase in 2008/9. This is not surprising because the schools were selected based on the increase in their federal research funding, but it does show that other federal funding did not simultaneously fall to offset the increase in research funding. What is noteworthy is that, during the same period, all other sources of revenue either fell or stayed on trend. Most strikingly, revenue from tuition payments and the sales of educational activities fell substantially.[36]

Panel B of figure 9.11 shows the same revenue streams for the least affected private schools. Of course, their federal revenue rises by a much smaller amount than it does for the most affected schools. What is note-

35. We can construct figures that are the analog of the reduced-form of our instrumental variables procedure. In practice, these figures—which are available from the authors—simply look like muted versions of figures 9.14 and 9.15. This appearance is to be expected since the research instrument and actual research funding are not perfectly correlated. See the results of the first stage regression, below.

36. Revenues from educational activities are revenues from the sales of goods or services that are "incidental to the conduct of instruction, research or public service." For research universities, common examples include the rental of university-owned buildings and equipment, sales of publications, and sales of analytic services.

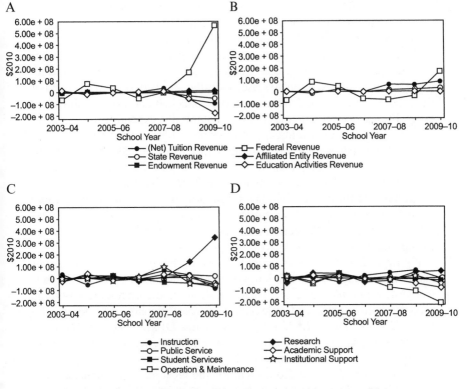

Fig. 9.11 Revenues and expenditures of the private universities most and least affected by stimulus-driven federal research funding

Notes: Panel A, revenues of private universities most affected by stimulus-driven research funding; panel B, revenues of private universities least affected by stimulus-driven research funding; panel C, expenditures of private universities most affected by stimulus-driven research funding; and panel D, expenditures of private universities least affected by stimulus-driven research funding.

worthy, however, is that their revenue from tuition *rises*, and their revenues from other sources also rise modestly or stay on trend. Comparing panels A and B, we surmise that increased federal research funds may have allowed schools to maintain their financial aid promises and otherwise keep tuition down during the recession.

Panel C of figure 9.11 shows the expenditures of the private institutions most affected by stimulus-driven research funding. The first thing to observe is that their research expenditures rise, but not by the full amount of the increase in federal funding (the vast majority of which is research funding for the schools in question). This is because, as we noted in panel A, the schools' other sources of revenue fell when their federal funding rose—making it impossible for them to increase research expenditures by the full amount of the federal funding increase unless they were to cut other categories of expenditure sufficiently to balance the books. The institutions' expenditures on other categories (instruction, academic support, student support, and so on) do fall, but they fall too modestly to balance the books.

Panel D of figure 9.11 shows the same expenditure categories for the private institutions least affected by stimulus-driven federal research funding. Their research expenditures rise modestly—and not by the full extent of their increase in federal funding (compare panels B and D). Notably, their expenditures in some other areas fall substantially: expenditures on operations and maintenance and expenditures on academic support. This fits a narrative in which schools defer maintenance when their budgets are tight.

Considered together, panels A through D suggest that not all of the federal research funding sticks where it hits. Private universities appear to reallocate some of the money that they would otherwise have spent on research to goals such as holding down tuition and keeping up expenditures in areas other than research. We can assess these relationships in a more rigorous, causal manner in the econometric analysis.

Figure 9.12 is the same as figure 9.11 except that it shows data for *public* research universities. The left-hand panels (A and C) are based on the thirteen institutions *most* affected by federal stimulus-driven research funding: each of them experienced at least a 25 percent increase in funding relative to 2006/7. The right-hand panels (B and D) are based on the fourteen institutions that were *least* affected. Each experienced only a modest inflation-adjusted increase in federal research funding

Panel A of figure 9.12 shows that, for the most affected public schools, revenue from federal sources rose dramatically in 2009/10 relative to the preexisting trend. This is to be expected given the selection of schools, so what is striking is that revenue from state sources fell by approximately the same amount as the increase in federal revenue. However, revenue from tuition and from education activities *rose* very substantially in 2009/10. Even with the decrease in state revenue, the public schools that experienced the greatest increases in stimulus-driven federal research funding ended up with *greater* revenue in 2009/10 than we would have expected based on their preexisting trends.

Panel B of figure 9.12 shows the same revenue streams for the least affected public schools. Their federal revenue rises modestly compared to the increases for the most affected schools. Interestingly, though, their revenue from tuition and educational activities rises modestly as well. This pattern is a muted version of what we see for the most affected public schools. Moreover, their state revenue falls by more than their federal revenue rises. Overall, their 2009/10 revenues are above what we would expect based on their preexisting trend, but they only achieve these higher revenues through the *combination* of higher tuition revenue, higher educational activity revenue, and higher federal revenue.

Panel C of figure 9.12 shows the expenditures of the public institutions most affected by stimulus-driven research funding. The first thing to observe

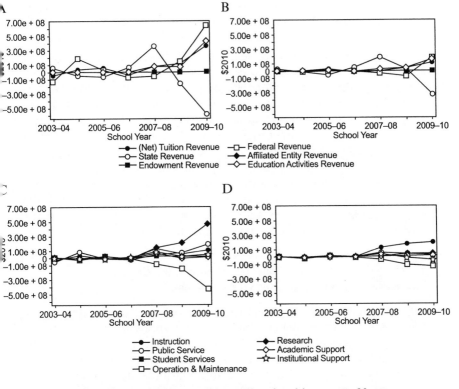

Fig. 9.12 Revenues and expenditures of the public universities most and least affected by stimulus-driven federal research funding

Notes: Panel A, revenues of public universities most affected by stimulus-driven research funding; panel B, revenues of public universities least affected by stimulus-driven research funding; panel C, expenditures of public universities most affected by stimulus-driven research funding; and panel D, expenditures of public universities least affected by stimulus-driven research funding.

is that their research expenditures rise very substantially—not by the full amount of the increase in federal funding but by an amount quite close to it (especially when we recall that not all of their federal revenue is for research). Their expenditures on instruction and public service rise modestly. Their expenditures on operations and maintenance fall very substantially. Overall, their expenditures in 2009/10 are above the preexisting trend. This, recall, is made possible by the fact that their revenue in 2009/10 is also above the preexisting trend, owing to increases in federal, tuition, and educational activity revenue.

Panel D of figure 9.12 shows the same expenditure categories for the public institutions least affected by stimulus-driven federal research funding. Their research expenditures rise just slightly—not by the full extent of their increase in federal funding (compare panels B and D). Interestingly, their expenditures on instruction rise. Their expenditures on operations and maintenance fall.

Analyzed simultaneously, panels A through D of figure 9.12 indicate a fascinating narrative (one that we confirm below). A public institution that was able to get substantial federal research funding during the stimulus period may have made a bargain with its state government in which it lost state appropriations (of an amount equal to its increase in federal revenue), but gained the ability to raise its tuition and to sell more educational activities. Since the public universities in question were setting their tuition and other prices well below what the market would bear previous to 2009/10 (especially if one looks at the tuition of competing private universities), this is plausible. Put another way, the public institutions used the crisis to move closer to the private institutions on key dimensions: market-based tuition, market-driven sales of educational activities, and the like. Of course, we need econometric analysis to confirm that these relationships are causal.

9.7 The Effect of Stimulus Funding on Universities' Revenues, Expenditures, Employment, and Other Outcomes

In this section, we use econometric analysis to show plausibly causal effects of stimulus funding on postsecondary institutions' revenues, expenditures, employment, and institutional aid to students. We also show the effects on other outcomes that the institutions themselves only influence or partially control: their endowment spending and state appropriations.

9.7.1 The First Stage of the Instrumental Variables Estimations

Before showing the effects that are our main interest, it is useful to demonstrate that our instrumental variables have considerable explanatory power and have coefficients that are in the range of what we expect, given how they are constructed. Table 9.2 shows these results. The two instruments are the Bartik-type instrument for federal research funds and the simulated instrument based on the Pell grant formula and the institution's prerecession number of students at the maximum grant. Columns (1) and (3) show the first-stage estimates for private institutions; columns (2) and (4) show the first-stage estimates for public institutions. The standard errors in the table are robust and clustered at the institution level.

Table 9.2 shows estimates from our preferred specification, in which we do not include controls for the prerecession economic characteristics of the county in which the institution is located. We prefer this specification because the prerecession economic characteristics of small counties are not published so that we must fill them in using less precise state economic characteristics. However, appendix table 9A.2 shows exactly parallel estimates based on equations in which we do include the controls, all measured in the year 2006 unless otherwise specified: the unemployment rate, per capita

Table 9.2 First-stage estimates: Regressions of federal funding variables on instruments

Dependent variable:	Dependent variable: Year-over-year change in federal research funds		Dependent variable: Year-over-year change in federal Pell funds	
Type of postsecondary institution:	Private research universities and medical schools (1)	Public research universities and medical schools (2)	Private research universities and medical schools (3)	Public research universities and medical schools (4)
Explanatory variable:				
Bartik-type instrument based on change in federal research funds	1.004*** (0.183)	1.103*** (0.146)	0.010* (0.005)	0.092*** (0.019)
Simulated instrument based on change in maximum Pell grant	7.421 (6.555)	0.067 (0.751)	4.134*** (0.750)	5.043*** (0.639)
Observations	300	524	300	524
R-squared	0.403	0.483	0.219	0.464

Notes: The table shows estimates of the first-stage equations described in the text. Each column represents a regression. Robust standard errors clustered at the institution level are shown in parentheses. An observation is a postsecondary research university or medical school in a year between the 2006/7 and 2009/10 school years, inclusive. All amounts are in real dollars, adjusted for inflation using the GDP deflator. The dependent variables are the year-over-year change, in dollars, of federal research funds (columns [1] and [2]) and federal Pell grant funds (columns [3] and [4]). The Bartik instrument is constructed by applying the national rate of growth in a given federal agency's funding (national *excluding* the institution itself) to the institution's base year funding from that agency and then summing over all agencies. See equation (4) in the text. The Pell-based simulated instrument is constructed by applying the change in the maximum Pell grant to each institution's estimated number of students eligible for the maximum grant in the base year. See equation (5) in the text. Asterisks indicate *p*-value.

***Significant at the 1 percent level.

**Significant at the 5 percent level.

*Significant at the 10 percent level.

income, a house price index, the change in the house price index from 2000 to 2006, the number of stable jobs, the number of stable hires, the average earnings in stable jobs, farm income as a share of all personal income, and population. These controls help to ensure that the Pell-based instrument is not correlated with omitted economic characteristics that might predict how the area fares in the recession.

Recall that the Bartik-type instrument for federal research funds is constructed so that no institution's own needs or research trajectory can affect the instrument. This construction should produce first-stage coefficients on the instrument that are fairly close to 1.[37] In columns (1) and (2) in table 9.2, we see coefficients of the expected magnitude: 1.0 for private institutions and 1.1 for public institutions. The relevant instrument is statistically powerful: the t-statistics on the coefficients are 5.5 for private institutions and 7.6 for public institutions (of which there are about twice as many as there are private institutions).

Similarly, the Pell formula-based instrument is highly statistically significant, with the relevant t-statistics being 5.5 for private institutions and 7.9 for public institutions. The relevant coefficients are constructed in such a way that their coefficients should be greater than 1.[38] The relevant coefficients are 4.1 for private institutions and 5.0 for public institutions—within the range that we expect.

9.7.2 How the Stimulus Affected *Private* Universities' Expenditures, Employment, and Other Outcomes

Table 9.3 presents estimates based on *private* research universities and medical schools. For these institutions, endowments are a potentially important source of income and a means of saving federal research funds. On the other hand, state appropriations are not important to these institutions. Thus, table 9.3 shows key outcomes like expenditures, employment, tuition revenue, institutional student aid, and the spending rate from endowments, but it does not show state appropriations.

---

37. The coefficient should not be equal to 1 because the institutions are not all of the same size.

38. The construction of the instrument merely affects the scale of the coefficient in the first stage equation: the magnitude of this coefficient does not affect the instrumental variables results. Nevertheless, to see why we expect the coefficient to be greater than 1, recall that the instrument is the number of students estimated to be eligible for the maximum Pell grant times the change in the maximum Pell grant. The first reason why the coefficient on the instrument should be greater than 1 is that we estimated the number of students at the maximum grant using prerecession changes in the maximum grant, and these changes took place several years ago when institutions enrolled fewer students. The second reason why the coefficient on the instrument should be greater than 1 is that institutions with more students at the maximum grant also have students who are Pell-eligible but below the maximum grant. These students may become eligible for additional Pell aid either because (a) the institution responds to the change in the maximum Pell grant by raising tuition, or (b) because their families become poorer as a result of the recession. We show evidence below that phenomenon (a) does occur.

Table 9.3   The effect of stimulus-motivated federal funds on *private* research universities and medical schools

	Dependent variable is year-over-year change (minus prerecession trend) in:							
	Total expenditure (1)	Research expenditure (2)	Instructional expenditure (3)	Number of employees (per $1,000 of funds) (4)	Total payroll (5)	Net tuition revenue (6)	Institutional grant aid (7)	Scaled spending rate from endowment (8)
Year-over-year change in federal research funds	0.094 (0.451)	0.231* (0.136)	−0.474* (0.275)	0.031 (0.041)	0.123 (0.186)	−0.032* (0.017)	0.017* (0.009)	−0.102* (0.057)
Year-over-year change in federal Pell funds	3.683 (3.580)	2.941 (1.976)	1.090 (1.839)	0.020 (0.406)	10.892 (9.957)	−0.518 (1.197)	0.677* (0.374)	−0.010 (0.463)
Dependent variable controls for the prerecession trend (per equation [3])	yes	yes	yes	yes	yes	yes	yes	yes
Prerecession economic characteristics	no	no	no	no	no	no	no	no
Instrumental variables estimates	yes	yes	yes	yes	yes	yes	yes	yes
Observations	300	300	300	300	300	255	255	296

Notes: The table shows estimates of equation (3) described in the text. Each column represents a regression. Robust standard errors clustered at the institution level are shown in parentheses. An observation is a private postsecondary research university or medical school in a year between the 2006/7 and 2009/10 school years, inclusive. All amounts are in real dollars, adjusted for inflation using the GDP deflator. The dependent variables are the year-over-year change in various expenditures and other outcomes. The units are dollars unless otherwise specified. See text and equations (4) and (5) for a description of the instrumental variables. In regressions with fewer observations, some institution did not report data. Asterisks indicate *p*-value.

***Significant at the 1 percent level.

**Significant at the 5 percent level.

*Significant at the 10 percent level.

Private universities' research expenditures rose by about twenty-three cents for every dollar of stimulus-motivated federal research funds. This suggests that they reallocated or saved some funds they would otherwise have spent on research for other purposes, and the other outcomes shown in table 9.3 give us some idea what those other purposes were. Their net tuition revenue fell by three cents and their institutional grant aid rose by two cents for every dollar of stimulus-motivated federal research funds they received. This suggests that they reallocated some funds to keep tuition down and aid up for their students. The point estimates for their total employees and payroll are positive but statistically insignificant—more because of large standard errors than because the point estimates are small. Thus, it is possible that some of the reallocated funds were used to protect jobs.

The spending rate variable requires a bit of explanation. We want to focus as much as possible on policy variables that the institution can control, and the spending *rate* is much more under an institution's control than total spending from the endowment (the spending rate times the base used by the institution). A typical base is something like "a running average of the last three years' market value of the endowment," and institutions change the definitions of their bases infrequently. Most of the change in the base from year to year is driven by past market performance, over which the university has no control at the time it makes spending decisions. In short, we want to focus on the spending rate and not spending from the endowment, but we must scale the spending rate in such a way that it could logically have the same relationship with a dollar of federal funds if the rate is applied to a massive base like Harvard's or a smaller base like Pace University's. Therefore, we multiply each spending rate by its base in the base year and use this "scaled spending rate." This makes the coefficient easy to interpret: a dollar increase in federal funding generates a change of X dollars in endowment spending, purely through the change in the spending rate, which is under the institution's control.

We find that spending rates from private universities' endowment fell such that endowment spending fell by ten cents for every dollar of stimulus-motivated federal research funds. This result is not surprising given the clear tension in the 2008/9 fiscal year when many private universities felt constrained to maintain spending rates that were difficult when many of their funds were underwater.[39] Thus, when stimulus-motivated funds arrived—mainly in the 2009/10 fiscal year—schools that could use them to relieve a little of the tension appear to have done so.

Interestingly, instructional spending fell by about forty-seven cents for every dollar of stimulus-motivated federal research funds. At first this result seems surprising, but at least part of it is explained by the fact that private research universities have quite a large number of people on their payroll

---

39. This is the authors' interpretation of comments in the NCSE surveys of 2009 and 2010.

who divide their time between instruction and research. These people appear to have shifted toward doing more research when stimulus-motivated federal funds were available but the universities' budgets were otherwise very tight. For instance, using IPEDS data, we found that stimulus-motivated federal research funds were associated with a substantial shift of graduate assistants from teaching duties (instructional spending) to research duties (research spending).[40] We found a similar shift from instruction to research among employees with faculty status who are not part of tenure system. (Many such employees are found in laboratories and medical schools.) These are only two of the fairly obvious ways in which such shifts can take place. For instance, faculty who remain primarily instructors can buy out a course or an undergraduate student who would have done an independent project (using instructional funds) can work on a research project headed by a faculty member. In short, we believe that at least some of the fall in instructional spending was a reallocation of the universities' resources toward research, and this reallocation may have enabled the universities to protect jobs and student support.

We estimated the effects of stimulus-motivated federal funds on several categories of expenditures not shown in table 9.3. These suggest that money reallocated from federal research funds was broadly distributed as small percentage increases across all other areas (student services, academic support, public service, and so on).[41] This is consistent with the highly imprecise point estimate suggesting that total expenses rose by 9.4 cents for every stimulus-motivated federal research dollar. In other words, part of the windfall research dollar was allocated to research (including the shifting of people from instruction to research), but much of the windfall dollar was probably allocated in much the same way that an unrestricted, additional dollar of revenue would be at the university in question.[42] This is what economic theory predicts would occur in a university whose prerecession allocation of revenue was approximately optimal and whose funds were somewhat but not wholly restricted.

At private universities, stimulus-motivated Pell grant receipts had no statistically significant effects except on institutional grant aid, which rose by sixty-seven cents for every dollar of Pell funds. This result is probably not a strictly causal effect but a reflection of the tendencies of private universities that have an unusually large number of Pell grant-eligible students. These universities increased their own institutional aid to students as the maximum Pell grant increased. Since the students were made better off by the increase in the maximum grant, these schools must have either given such students an even bigger increase in aid than they received through the increase in the

40. These calculations are available from the authors.
41. These results are available from the authors.
42. That is, if every institution spends the additional funds in a broad manner that is idiosyncratic, the overall estimates end up being imprecise.

302 M. F. Dinerstein, C. M. Hoxby, J. Meer, and P. Villanueva

grant or—more likely—given increased aid to other students whose incomes were modest but too high to qualify for the Pell grant.

The overall picture that emerges from private universities is as follows. They appear not to have reacted much to stimulus-motivated Pell funds, but they did react to stimulus-motivated federal research funds. When they received an extra dollar of such funds, they spent part of it on research but implicitly reallocated some of it to keep tuition down, keep student aid up, possibly protect some jobs, and relieve the pressure on their endowments (by allowing the spending rate to fall relative to the counterfactual).

We performed a variety of specification tests on our estimates for private universities. These are shown in appendix table 9A.3. When we add covariates for preexisting economic conditions in the county, the coefficient estimates generally exhibit the same pattern but the standard errors rise. For private universities, we consider this an important specification test only for the effect of stimulus-motivated Pell grant funds on institutional aid. This is the only effect likely to be biased by a correlation between the Pell-based instrument and preexisting economic conditions. This effect survives the addition of covariates. When we estimate the equation by ordinary least squares, the pattern of coefficients on stimulus-motivated federal research funds is very similar except that the change in instructional spending is substantially smaller. This suggests, if anything, that it was the universities that were *less* likely to shift instructors to research that received more stimulus-motivated funding for *non*exogenous reasons.

9.7.3 How the Stimulus Affected *Public* Universities' Expenditures, Employment, and Other Outcomes

The effects of stimulus-motivated federal funds turn out to be quite different for *public* research universities and medical schools. The estimates are shown in table 9.4.[43]

Public universities' research expenditure rose approximately dollar for dollar with stimulus-motivated federal research funds, and instructional spending rose by about sixty-two cents for every dollar. State appropriations fell by about twenty-nine cents for every dollar of stimulus-motivated federal research funds. The greater expenditure on instruction may have been paid for by increases in net tuition (thirty-six cents for every dollar of federal research funds) and small decreases in institutional grant aid (three cents for every dollar of federal research funds). The negative but statistically insignificant coefficients on total employees and payroll suggest that, if anything, public universities that received federal research funds cut jobs. Overall, a consistent and interesting picture arises. A public research university that

43. Table 9.4 shows state appropriations as an outcome because they are highly relevant to public universities. However, it does not show endowment-related outcomes, as these turned out to be largely irrelevant.

Table 9.4   **The effect of stimulus-motivated federal funds on *public* research universities and medical schools**

	Dependent variable is year-over-year change (minus pre-recession trend) in:							
	Total expenditure (1)	Research expenditure (2)	Instructional expenditure (3)	Number of employees (per $1,000 of funds) (4)	Total payroll (5)	Net tuition revenue (6)	Institutional grant aid (7)	State appropriations (8)
Year-over-year change in federal research funds	-0.238 (0.393)	1.238*** (0.159)	0.618** (0.247)	-0.039 (0.054)	-0.070 (0.195)	0.364*** (0.105)	-0.030*** (0.011)	-0.287* (0.171)
Year-over-year change in federal Pell funds	0.125 (1.121)	0.238 (0.275)	1.341*** (0.375)	0.082 (0.107)	-0.526 (0.538)	1.003*** (0.346)	0.079* (0.043)	-2.122*** (0.626)
Dependent variable controls for the prerecession trend (per equation [3])	yes	yes	yes	yes	yes	yes	yes	yes
Prerecession economic characteristics	no	no	no	no	no	no	no	no
Instrumental variables estimates	yes	yes	yes	yes	yes	yes	yes	yes
Observations	515	524	524	524	524	460	460	524

Notes: The table shows estimates of equation (3) described in the text. Each column represents a regression. Robust standard errors clustered at the institution level are shown in parentheses. An observation is a public postsecondary research university or medical school in a year between the 2006/7 and 2009/10 school years, inclusive. All amounts are in real dollars, adjusted for inflation using the GDP deflator. The dependent variables are the year-over-year change in various expenditures and other outcomes. The units are dollars unless otherwise specified. See text and equations (4) and (5) for a description of the instrumental variables. Asterisks indicate *p*-values.

***Significant at the 1 percent level.

**Significant at the 5 percent level.

*Significant at the 10 percent level.

enjoyed stimulus-motivated federal research funds reoriented itself toward research and instruction, raised tuition (by increasing in-state tuition, enrolling more out-of-state students who pay higher tuition, or both), and reduced institutional grant aid (perhaps by substituting out-of-state students for low-income in-state ones). These institutions may have been able to make these changes, which have a flavor of greater independence from state government, precisely because their ability to bring in federal research funds caused their state governments to think that they could reduce appropriations without generating chaos. Put another way, this quantitative evidence is in line with the theory in section 9.3 and with the graphical evidence of the previous section: prominent public research universities may gain independence from state governments during recessions by increasing their reliance on research funding and tuition and decreasing their reliance on state appropriations. In fact, we have heard several narratives from public university trustees who participated in making such "grand bargains." The public universities' greater independence has been (at least anecdotally) associated with greater emphasis on research and instruction, more out-of-state students, and prices that are closer to market-based pricing. We believe that our study provides the first systematic, as opposed to anecdotal, evidence of this phenomenon.

Stimulus-motivated Pell grant receipts had important effects on public universities. Their net tuition revenue rose dollar for dollar with Pell grant revenue generated by the increase in the maximum grant. Net tuition revenue excludes tuition paid by Pell grants, so this effect is *not* mechanical. Instead, this effect indicates that public universities responded logically to the incentives provided by the Pell grant formula. The formula is such that, when the maximum Pell grant rises, institutions with sufficiently low tuition have an incentive to raise their tuition to fully tap the change in the maximum grant, thereby maximizing revenue from the federal Pell program. Students who receive the maximum Pell grant before and after the tuition increase may be no worse off, but higher-income students pay (at least some of) the higher tuition from their own funds. Institutional grant aid also rose by eight cents for every dollar of stimulus-motivated Pell funds. This was probably not a strictly causal effect but—like the corresponding estimate for private universities—evidence that public universities with more Pell-eligible students also had more students with modest incomes who did not qualify for the increased grant but who needed greater aid because of the recession or the tuition increase.

Even more interesting, state governments appear to have taken *all* the increases in revenue from the stimulus-motivated changes in the maximum Pell grant and *all* the increases in revenue from the related tuition increases: state appropriations fell by about two dollars for every dollar of additional Pell funds generated by the increase in the maximum grant. State governments must have used the money they would otherwise have appropriated to universities for other programs or to prevent taxes from rising.

Finally, it is worth noting that instructional spending rose when a public university received more Pell revenue as a result of the increase in the maximum grant. We interpret this as further evidence of what public universities do when they can act more independently because they become more reliant on tuition revenue and less reliant on state appropriations.

In appendix table 9A.4, we show specification tests for our baseline public university results shown in table 9.4. Adding prerecession economic characteristics of the county does not change any of the coefficients in a meaningful way. This lack of change is especially important for the coefficients on stimulus-motivated Pell funds since it was the Pell-based instrument that we thought might be correlated with area's economic characteristics. Appendix table 9A.4 also shows that OLS results are generally very similar to the section 9.4 results.[44]

All in all, the picture that emerges from the public universities is as follows. Federal stimulus-motivated research and Pell funds made public universities less reliant on state appropriations and more reliant on tuition revenue (as well as on the federal funds themselves). The consequence was apparently a reorientation toward research and instruction. The reorientation toward research is not at all surprising given that many federal funds were intended for research. The reorientation toward instruction is probably a sign that public research universities were moving toward a tuition-dependent model of finance, in which attracting out-of-state students and other high-ability-to-pay students is important.

9.7.4 A Note on "Adding Up"

All revenue is either spent or saved, so one might expect that, when an additional dollar of federal funds arrived at a university, it would be easy to see how the changes in (a) spending, (b) saving, and (c) other sources of revenue sum to one. The numbers do sum to one for each institution, but it is difficult to present regression estimates that demonstrate this in a transparent way. The reason is twofold. First, outside of the major, generic categories like research and instructional, many spending categories are highly institution-specific. For instance, institutions with independent operations or medical schools have idiosyncratic spending patterns. Second, institutions have many ways to save and dissave: endowments; debt; additions to and subtractions from land, infrastructure, buildings, equipment, and art and library collections; changes in capital leases; and changes in construction schedules. We found that we had two alternatives, neither of which was informative. We could sum up all of the idiosyncratic categories into motley aggregates that would mechanically satisfy the sum-to-one rule, but

---

44. We examined the effects of more detailed categories of expenditure and employment. These enrich but do not change the picture that emerges from the results already described. In particular, stimulus-motivated federal research funds raised spending on research salaries (fifteen cents for every dollar), academic support services, and student services. We also examined the public universities' receipt of State Fiscal Stabilization Funds, which were part of ARRA. These appear as appropriations in section 9.2. As anticipated (see table 9.1), we found that these funds made such small contributions to the revenues of major public research universities that their effects, if any, could not be discerned.

these did not admit of coherent interpretation. Alternatively, we could show regressions for fairly disaggregated categories, but these required so much interpretation (for instance, knowing which institutions had independent operations) that they were far from transparent. These problems were aggravated by the fact that, when universities fall on temporary hard times, they often employ their budgetary ingenuity in exactly the areas that were most idiosyncratic in the first place. Suffice it to say that adding up does occur for each institution and that a good share of the reconciliation occurred in areas that are not highly salient.

9.8 The Effect of Stimulus Funding on Areas Where Universities Are Located

Some commentators on universities sanguinely predicted that stimulus funds would prop up the local economies surrounding universities. In this section, we investigate this possibility. However, our results in the previous section lead us to expect less than dramatic results, especially for public universities where a good share, if not the majority, of stimulus funds made their way into the hands of nonuniversity beneficiaries of state spending and possibly of state taxpayers. These people may have spent the stimulus money to prop up aggregate demand, but there is little reason to think that they spent it in the immediate vicinity of the universities themselves. Stimulus funds that found their way into students' hands would presumably be spent around the universities, but the federal funds provoked tuition increases at public universities so that many students would presumably feel poorer, not richer. Research spending rose, but the lack of increase in university employment suggests that employees were moved around within universities with little net increase in universities' local employment.

Table 9.5 shows estimates of how federal stimulus funding affected employment and payroll in counties in which universities are located. The outcomes are based on the QWI, and the estimates are from section 9.4 regressions. The left-hand side of the table shows results for counties in which private universities are located, and the right-hand side of the table shows results for counties in which public universities are located.

We observe no statistically significant effect of stimulus-motivated Pell funds on the employment or payrolls of counties in which private institutions are located. We also observe no statistically significant effect of stimulus-motivated federal aid funds on employment or payroll in counties where public universities are located. We observe a small but statistically significant *negative* effect of stimulus-motivated federal research funds on employment in counties where public universities are located: the estimates suggest that a dollar of stimulus-motivated research funds reduces employment in the county by 0.0001 jobs. When we examine more detailed subcategories of employment, the last of these results is not clarified. It is also

Table 9.5   The effect of stimulus-motivated federal funds on the economies of counties in which research universities and medical schools are located

	At least 1 private research university or medical school		Only public research universities or medical schools	
	Employment (1)	Total payroll (2)	Employment (3)	Total payroll (4)
	— Dependent variable is year-over-year change (minus prerecession trend in control counties) of counties containing:			
Year-over-year change in federal research funds	−0.0004	−51.209	−0.0001*	−5.993
	(0.0004)	(33.398)	(0.00005)	(4.377)
Year-over-year change in federal Pell funds	0.0002	−27.201	−0.0004	−31.121
	(0.0010)	(90.864)	(0.0004)	(24.672)
Dependent variable controls for the prerecession trend (per equation [3])	yes	yes	yes	yes
Synthetic control counties included to establish time effects (see text)	yes	yes	yes	yes
Prerecession economic characteristics of the county	yes	yes	yes	yes
Instrumental variables estimates	yes	yes	yes	yes
Observations				

Notes: The table shows estimates of equation (3) described in the text. Each column represents a regression. Robust standard errors clustered at the county level are shown in parentheses. An observation is a county in a year between the 2006/7 and 2009/10 school years, inclusive. All monetary amounts are in real dollars, adjusted for inflation using the GDP deflator. The dependent variables are the year-over-year change in employment and payroll. The units are dollars unless otherwise specified. See text and equations (4) and (5) for a description of the instrumental variables. Asterisks indicate *p*-values.

***Significant at the 1 percent level.

**Significant at the 5 percent level.

*Significant at the 10 percent level.

not sensitive to our including or excluding prerecession county economic characteristics. Since the result does not carry over to the payroll (jobs may have been lost but no payroll was), we are inclined to think that the negative effect on employment is spurious.

In any case, we find no evidence that federal stimulus funds directed to universities propped up employment or payroll in the counties immediately surrounding them.

Even the most generous interpretation of the QWI results suggests that there is no local multiplier.

9.9 Discussion and Conclusions

There are two ways to evaluate the stimulus provided to universities. First, we could evaluate whether universities served as an effective means to prop up aggregate demand quickly—by getting money into the hands of (university and individual) consumers who would spend it right away rather than save it, thereby creating a multiplier as envisioned by Keynesian logic. Second, we could evaluate whether universities spent stimulus funds in a manner that was likely to be productive for society, with a large share of the benefits likely arising in the mid- to long term owing to the fact that human capital and research investments do not pay off immediately even if they are superbly made. Ambivalence about the manner in which the stimulus for universities should be evaluated shows up clearly in commentators' and analysts' anecdotal reports. Some of them tout universities for creating jobs and propping up aggregate demand in "university towns." Others say that universities used stimulus funds to keep students in school (raising human capital in the mid- to long run), to invent technology that would ultimately increase economic growth, or to conduct research that would otherwise help society (through better medical care, for example).[45]

We conclude that there is little evidence in this chapter that universities

---

45. We found many examples of both types of arguments on the ScienceWorksForUs website, which features reports and commentary by numerous university leaders and researchers. As examples of the first type of argument, consider that the University of California claimed that $837 million in ARRA research funds created over 1,400 jobs at its schools. The University of Chicago claimed that its $75 million in ARRA funding "preserv[ed] and creat[ed], on average, close to 100 jobs." As an example of the other type of argument, consider Stanford's statement that "SLAC National Accelerator Laboratory, a facility that serves 3,000 visiting scientists and students each year, has received $90.2 million for infrastructure improvements, accelerator research support and cutting-edge instrumentation for advanced X-ray studies." This appears to be a claim about long-run benefits to research, not job creation. Some universities' statements contain a mixture of both arguments. For instance, the University of Vermont stated that "In Vermont to date, over $20 million in ARRA funds have advanced research and created or leveraged more than fifty paid positions at UVM and throughout the state." See http:// www.scienceworksforus.org/images/stories/PDFs/uc%20arra%20brochure.pdf; http://www .scienceworksforus.org/press-releases/universities-highlight-benefits-of-stimulus-research -funding; http://www.scienceworksforus.org/images/stories/PDFs/university%20leaders %20comment%20on%20benefits%20of%20recovery%20act%20final.pdf.

were an effective route for stimulus funds if the only goal was propping up local aggregate demand. While our estimates have standard errors that do not allow us to rule this out as a possibility, there are many pieces of evidence that run counter to this idea. Most obviously, there is at best very weak evidence that universities created jobs or increased their payrolls as a result of stimulus funding. There is certainly no evidence for a multiplier. Also, state governments essentially took all of the stimulus funding directed to public universities—albeit by indirect means. While the states might have allocated these funds in such a way that they stimulated the state's—as opposed to the local—economy, it would surely have been more in keeping with Keynesian logic to give state governments the funds in the first place and mandate that they spend them quickly. Giving the funds to universities and subsequently renegotiating the implicit bargain between state governments and universities must have slowed down stimulus spending. Similarly, it appears that some of the stimulus funds for private universities ended up in the hands of the families whose students were enrolled. While these families may well have consumed more in consequence, the Keynesian stimulus effect might have been greater if the money was simply sent to them in the first place (perhaps through a tax credit) rather than make its way to them in a roundabout and necessarily slow manner. Private universities appear to have saved a small share of their federal research funds for future use. This policy is not one that boosts aggregate demand immediately. Finally, public universities seem to have used the stimulus funds to set their tuition higher, as part of their gaining independence from state governments. The higher tuition probably depressed the consumption of middle- to upper-income students.

So far as we know, there is no plausibly causal evidence that contradicts our conclusion that federal stimulus funds did little to prop up aggregate demand. Universities' own claims about jobs created or preserved were purely formulaic. They simply divided their extra federal funds by their average salary or some similar number.[46] None, so far as we know, analyzed its payroll in a plausibly causal way. There is at least one simulation based on input-output tables: Ash and Palacio (2012). However, this method is also formulaic: it does not attempt to identify exogenous variation in federal funds or to construct credible counterfactuals.

In contrast to the lack of evidence for the stimulus funds propping up aggregate demand, an array of evidence indicates that universities used stimulus funds to increase their investments in research and instruction.

Private universities used the federal research funds to do additional research, presumably thereby complying with the terms of their research grants and contracts. They shifted some graduate students and other employees from teaching to research to fulfill their greater research needs, to support their students, and to protect jobs. They reallocated some funds that

46. See Kelderman (2009).

they would otherwise have spent on research and used them to keep tuition down, increase institutional grant aid, and—possibly—maintain jobs that they would otherwise have had to eliminate. They saved some funds for the future by slightly reducing the spending rate on the endowment. Private universities passed the entirety of the stimulus-motivated increase in the maximum Pell grant to students. This lack of reaction may have been due to their having such high initial tuition that the Pell formula contains no incentive to raise it. Their lack of reaction may also be because Pell grant funds are not terribly important to them, as shown in section 9.2.

In short, private research universities and medical schools undoubtedly care about research, but they also appear to feel impelled to maintain implicit or explicit commitments to keep tuition from accelerating quickly, to provide aid, to support graduate students, to maintain employment, and to protect their endowments for future use. In fact, private universities appear to have used stimulus-motivated federal funds as economic theory suggests they would if (a) they were attempting to maximize the same objectives both before and after receiving the federal windfall, (b) these objectives require them to spend on a broad array of activities, and (c) restrictions on the uses of funds made it efficient (cheaper) to use a disproportionate share of the windfall funds in the areas for which they were formally intended. That is, private universities are roughly described by panel C of figure 9.8.

Public universities apparently used the stimulus to gain independence from state legislatures, increase tuition for students who could afford it, and reorient their activities into greater alignment with the market. Both federal research and federal Pell grant funds induced substantial reductions in state appropriations that were offset by tuition increases. This suggests that some combination of the following is true:

1. During recessions, state governments have different priorities than maintaining their appropriations to postsecondary institutions.

2. State governments and/or public universities conclude that a sufficiently large number of prospective students can actually afford higher tuition that it can be raised during recessions without causing enrollments to fall so much that the universities' finances get worse instead of better. Some of this ability-to-afford is mechanical because low-income students receive increased Pell grants, but much of it is not mechanical.

3. State governments and/or public universities are willing to accept the trade-off of lower appropriations in return for greater independence (to set tuition, enroll out-of-state students, and allocate resources within the university).

4. When they are more reliant on tuition and federal funds and less on state appropriations, public research universities spend more on research and instruction and less on other categories of spending.

In short, if we evaluate the stimulus directed to universities based on the second criteria—Did they use it to benefit society?—our evidence is about as positive as could be expected for short-run evidence.[47] Only a longer-term study—something in the manner of Aghion et al. (2010)— could investigate whether the research and human capital investments made by universities during the stimulus period actually paid off by raising economic growth, patentable inventions, and the like.

Overall, we conclude that the stimulus for universities probably did not work well if the goal was quickly propping up aggregate demand, especially in the areas surrounding the schools. However, we also conclude that universities used stimulus funds in a manner that was consistent with an intention to benefit society in the mid- to long term. We must leave an evaluation of these benefits to future investigators.

---

47. Even raising public university tuition likely benefits society. This is because highly subsidized tuition at public universities can distort human capital investment choices in a manner that is likely to reduce social welfare relative to more individuated solutions to the human capital investment problem, such as student loans or individual-specific financial aid. Peltzman (1973) and Hansen and Weisbrod (1969) drew economists' attention to these distortions long ago.

Appendix

Table 9A.1   Federal funds directed to postsecondary institutions by category of funds and type of institution, 2006/7

Institution type:	Grants & contracts as % of total revenue excluding auxiliary, hospital, independent operations	Appropriations as % of total revenue excluding auxiliary, hospital, independent operations	Aid as % of total revenue excluding auxiliary, hospital, independent operations	Grants & contracts as % of total revenue including auxiliary, hospital, independent operations	Appropriations as % of total revenue including auxiliary, hospital, independent operations	Aid as % of total revenue including auxiliary, hospital, independent operations
Private ext. research	15.17	0.36	0.71	11.15	0.27	0.52
Public ext. research	20.04	0.21	2.50	13.93	0.15	1.74
Private int. research	7.39	0.01	1.82	6.14	0.00	1.51
Public int. research	17.65	0.16	3.89	12.91	0.11	2.85
Private medical	26.48	0.45	0.21	13.20	0.22	0.11
Public medical	20.92	0.00	0.28	10.22	0.00	0.14
Private engineering	0.00	0.00	0.00	0.00	0.00	0.00
Public engineering	20.74	0.00	2.30	18.57	0.00	2.06
Private other Health	2.39	0.00	2.45	1.86	0.00	1.91
Public other Health	15.63	0.00	0.09	12.26	0.00	0.07
Private BA/MA	2.45	0.34	4.01	2.07	0.29	3.39
Public BA/MA	6.46	0.03	7.33	5.41	0.03	6.14
Private associate	4.23	0.30	13.93	3.54	0.25	11.67
Public associate	5.98	0.27	10.86	5.47	0.25	9.93

Notes: The table shows federal funds directed to postsecondary institutions in the 2006/7 school year as a share of total revenue defined in two different ways. Related statistics are shown in table 9.1. Federal funds come in three basic forms: (a) grants and contracts, (b) appropriations, and (c) student aid. These categories are defined further in the text. Institutions are grouped by their 2000 Carnegie classification (Carnegie Foundation for the Advancement of Teaching 2001).

Table 9A.2 **First-stage estimates: Regressions of federal funding variables on instruments and prerecession economic characteristics of counties in which postsecondary institutions are located**

Dependent variable:	Dependent variable: Year-over-year change in federal research funds		Dependent variable: Year-over-year change in federal Pell funds	
Type of postsecondary institution:	Private research universities and medical schools (1)	Public research universities and medical schools (2)	Private research universities and medical schools (3)	Public research universities and medical schools (4)
Explanatory variable:				
Bartik-type instrument based on change in federal research funds	1.165*** (0.128)	1.112*** (0.163)	0.013* (0.006)	0.088*** (0.023)
Simulated instrument based on change in maximum Pell grant	6.717 (4.931)	0.359 (0.745)	4.103*** (0.616)	4.806*** (0.679)
Prerecession economic characteristics of county	yes, see notes	yes, see notes	yes, see notes	yes, see notes
Observations	264	496	264	496
R-squared	0.430	0.495	0.291	0.477

Notes: The table shows estimates of the first-stage equations described in the text. Each column represents a regression. Robust standard errors clustered at the institution level are shown in parentheses. An observation is a postsecondary research university or medical school in a year between the 2006/7 and 2009/10 school years, inclusive. All amounts are in real dollars, adjusted for inflation using the GDP deflator. The dependent variables are the year-over-year change, in dollars, of federal research funds (columns [1] and [2]) and federal Pell grant funds (columns [3] and [4]). The Bartik instrument is constructed by applying the national rate of growth in a given federal agency's funding (national *excluding* the institution itself) to the institution's base year funding from that agency and then summing over all agencies. See equation (4) in the text. The Pell-based simulated instrument is constructed by applying the change in the maximum Pell grant to each institution's estimated number of students eligible for the maximum grant in the base year. See equation (5) in the text. The prerecession economic characteristics of the county are the following, all for the 2006 year unless otherwise noted: the unemployment rate, per capita income, a house price index, the change in the house price index from 2000 to 2006, the number of stable jobs, the number of stable hires, the average earnings in stable jobs, farm income as a share of all personal income, and population. Asterisks indicate *p*-value.

***Significant at the 1 percent level.

**Significant at the 5 percent level.

*Significant at the 10 percent level.

Table 9A.3   **Specification checks for the effect of stimulus-motivated federal funds on *private* research universities and medical schools**

	Total expenditure	Research expenditure	Instructional expenditure	Number of employees (per $1,000 of funds)	Total payroll	Net tuition revenue	Institutional grant aid
Dependent variable is year-over-year change (minus prerecession trend) in:							
Instrumental variables estimates with prerecession economic characteristics							
Year-over-year change in federal research funds	0.407	0.098	−0.267	0.069	0.193	−0.063	0.016
	(0.466)	(0.162)	(0.243)	(0.048)	(0.213)	(0.087)	(0.014)
Year-over-year change in federal Pell funds	4.018	2.547	0.031	−0.310	12.291	−1.198	0.482*
	(3.663)	(1.877)	(2.955)	(0.268)	(10.107)	(1.049)	(0.290)
Ordinary least squares estimates							
Year-over-year change in federal research funds	0.166	0.268**	−0.151**	0.019	0.181	−0.073*	0.027***
	(0.129)	(0.107)	(0.069)	(0.013)	(0.137)	(0.041)	(0.008)
Year-over-year change in federal Pell funds	1.434	1.026	0.654	0.103	2.605	0.791	0.078
	(2.878)	(0.618)	(1.216)	(0.190)	(2.543)	(0.585)	(0.112)

Notes: The table shows estimates of equation (3) that are alternatives to the estimates shown in table 9.3. The notes for that table apply, except that the bottom panel of this table reports ordinary least squares estimates and the top panel reports regressions that include the prerecession economic characteristics of the county in which the institution is located. These are: the unemployment rate, per capita income, a house price index, the change in the house price index from 2000 to 2006, the number of stable jobs, the number of stable hires, the average earnings in stable jobs, farm income as a share of all personal income, and population.

***Significant at the 1 percent level.

**Significant at the 5 percent level.

*Significant at the 10 percent level.

Table 9A.4   **Specification checks for the effect of stimulus-motivated federal funds on *public* research universities and medical schools**

					Dependent variable is year-over-year change (minus prerecession trend) in:			
	Total expenditure	Research expenditure	Instructional expenditure	Number of employees (per $1,000 of funds)	Total payroll	Net tuition revenue	Institutional grant aid	State appropriations
Instrumental variables estimates with prerecession economic characteristics								
Year-over-year change in federal research funds	−0.385	1.205***	0.616**	−0.061	−0.180	0.381***	−0.026**	−0.318*
	(0.359)	(0.170)	(0.272)	(0.060)	(0.196)	(0.111)	(0.012)	(0.161)
Year-over-year change in federal Pell funds	−0.045	0.405	1.224***	0.153	−0.530	0.972***	0.085*	−2.326***
	(1.400)	(0.311)	(0.414)	(0.140)	(0.664)	(0.342)	(0.046)	(0.684)
Ordinary least squares estimates								
Year-over-year change in federal research funds	−0.335	0.852***	0.320**	−0.007	−0.121	0.220***	−0.005	−0.205*
	(0.283)	(0.084)	(0.127)	(0.026)	(0.130)	(0.056)	(0.008)	(0.120)
Year-over-year change in federal Pell funds	0.049	0.526**	1.374***	0.010	−0.618	0.950***	0.022	−1.617***
	(0.548)	(0.209)	(0.267)	(0.060)	(0.427)	(0.185)	(0.023)	(0.341)

Notes: The table shows estimates of equation (3) that are alternatives to the estimates shown in table 9.4. The notes for that table apply, except that the bottom panel of this table reports ordinary least squares estimates and the top panel reports regressions that include the prerecession economic characteristics of the county in which the institution is located. These are: the unemployment rate, per capita income, a house price index, the change in the house price index from 2000 to 2006, the number of stable jobs, the number of stable hires, the average earnings in stable jobs, farm income as a share of all personal income, and population.

***Significant at the 1 percent level.

**Significant at the 5 percent level.

*Significant at the 10 percent level.

Data Appendix

Data Sources

The NASA data was obtained from Research.gov. We use data where the recipient's name includes "Univ.," "College," "Polytech," or both "Institute" and "Tech."[48]

The data for NIH transfers to universities was obtained from the Research Portfolio Online Reporting Tool (RePORT). Since we have data on all transfers made by NIH (not only to universities), we only use data for which the recipient's name includes the words "Univ.," "College," "Polytech," both "Institute" and "Tech.," or both "School" and "Medicine." We keep university affiliated hospitals by looking for names with "Hospital," "Medical," "Health," or "Cancer."

Our main source of NSF data is the NSF itself. We use data where the recipient's name includes "Univ.," "College," "Polytech," or both "Institute" and "Tech." We use this data set for fiscal years 2000 to 2009 and supplement it with extracts from Research.gov. Regarding the latter, we only kept grants where the organization type was university or college.

We are confident that, in searching the aforementioned databases, we have not missed any research universities, medical schools, or important "other health" institutions. This is because we can compare the data we gather to that gathered by the NSF in its *Higher Education Research and Development Survey* (NSF 2013). What we gather is a superset of what is gathered in that survey, apparently because the survey respondents fail to report or aggregate some research funds we observe. We use that survey for data on federal research funds received by each postsecondary institution from agencies *other* than NASA, the NIH, and NSF. The most important such agencies are Agriculture, Defense, and Energy.

Financial aid data were downloaded from the Federal Student Aid Gateway. For years prior to 2006/7 we have yearly, not quarterly, data.

IPEDS Data were downloaded from the public Data Center at http://nces.ed.gov/ipeds/datacenter/DataFiles.aspx. Delta Cost Project data were downloaded from http://nces.ed.gov/ipeds/deltacostproject/. QWI data were downloaded from http://www.vrdc.cornell.edu/qwipu/.

Associating Grants and Contracts with the Universities That Received Them

Grants and contracts must be matched to the appropriate university. Standardized school codes are included in the Pell and IPEDS data. For other

---

48. Research.gov says data on NASA grants is really only reliable for fiscal year 2007 onward. However, we also use data from 2006 and before.

grants, we start by using the zip code associated with the grant to find a school with the same zip code. We verify all potential matches manually by comparing the grant's institution name to the school we have matched it to. Among remaining grants, we then look for schools with a zip code whose first three digits match the first three digits of the grant's zip code. Again, we verify all potential matches manually. Finally, for remaining grants we have not matched, we match them by examining the name of the school. Of our matched grants, 73 percent are matched by the zip code, 23 percent are matched by the zip code's first three digits, and 4 percent are matched only by name.

We take care to include research grants to university-affiliated hospitals and independent operations. Grants hosted by the National Bureau of Economic Research are matched to the university(ies) of the principal investigator(s).

Special Grants

Several types of grants might be prone to double counting, and thus we take measures to avoid accidentally including them twice. These grants are forward funding and grant transfers. Forward funding can occur if an agency doles out the full grant in annual increments (a "continuing grant"), but at some point in the grant's life the agency gives the institution the rest of the grant's balance all at once. This forward funding can appear in the data as a separate entry from the original grant. Grant transfers might occur if a principal investigator (PI) switches universities. The amount left on a continuing grant will then be forwarded to the new institution and appear as a new grant.

We identify forward funding as grants having the same PIs, title, and university but different grant numbers and amounts. If the earlier grant is for a larger amount, then we subtract the second grant amount from the first.

We identify grant transfers as grants having the same PIs, dates, and title but different universities, grant numbers, and amounts. If the earlier grant is for a larger amount, then we subtract the second grant amount from the first.

Grant Disbursement Timing

For Pell grants in fiscal year (FY) 2007 or later, our data are quarterly and thus identify which quarter the money was disbursed. Prior to FY2007, we only know yearly disbursements, so we need to spread the disbursement out across that fiscal year's quarters. To do so, we take the quarterly distribution of disbursements for FY2007 and assume the same distribution for previous years. Thus, if FY2007 Quarter (Q) 1 had 20 percent of the total disbursement in FY2007, we assign 20 percent of the FY2006 total to FY2006Q1.

For the NASA, NIH, and NSF grants, we allocate funding to the relevant university uniformly by month starting with the project's budget start date and ending with the budget end date. We use the project start and end dates if budget start and end dates are unavailable. We can thus aggregate the disbursements by year or by quarter, as necessary.

Outcome Variables

We use a number of variables from IPEDS. For number of employees, we used "all employees total'' in the "Employees by Assigned Position" form or—equivalently—"ftall1" + "ptall1" in the Delta Cost Project data.

For institutional grant aid, we used "IGRNT_T," the "total amount of institutional grant aid received by full-time, first-time undergraduates." This variable comes from the "Student Financial Aid and Net Price" form. It is the variable known as "institutional_grant_aid" in the Delta Cost Project data.

The rest of the variables come from the IPEDS "Finance" forms. Private institutions (as well as some public institutions) file the FASB form while other public institutions file the GASB form. Therefore, we combine variables from the two forms.

We get total expenditure from "F2B02" ("total expenses") in the FASB and "F1D02" ("total expenses and other deductions") in the GASB. This variable is "total01" in the Delta Cost Project data. We get research expenditure from "F2E021" ("research-total amount") in the FASB and "F1C021" ("research-current year total") in the GASB. This variable is "research01" in the Delta Cost Project data. We get instructional expenditure from "F2E011" ("instruction-total amount") in the FASB and "F1C011" ("instruction-current year total") in the GASB. This variable is "instruction01" in the Delta Cost Project data. We get state appropriations from "F2D03" ("state appropriations-total") in the FASB and "F1B11" ("state appropriations") in the GASB. This variable is "state03" in the Delta Cost Project data. We get total payroll from "F2E132" ("total expenses-salaries and wages") in the FASB and "F1C192" ("total expenses deductions-salaries and wages") in the GASB. This variable is "total02" in the Delta Cost Project data. Finally, we use the net tuition revenue from students not including Pell grants from the Delta Cost Project data: "net_student_tuition."

For the QWI data, we use two main variables: "emp" ("employment: counts") and "payroll" ("total quarterly payroll: sum").

Pell Grant Instrument

To construct our Pell grant instrument, we need to estimate the number of students at the maximum Pell grant in the base year, for each institution. This number is not reported in the Federal Student Aid Gateway database. Therefore, we estimate the number by analyzing how a prior change in the maximum Pell grant affected schools' aid funds.

For the prior change, we use the change between FY2007 and FY2008. The maximum Pell grant increased from $4,050 to $4,310. As a check, we also run our regressions using the change between FY2001 and FY2002 (maximum increased from \$3,330 to \$3,750). Results are very similar to the results using the FY2008 change.

For school i and year t, we estimate the percentage (p_{it}) of Pell recipients at a school who receive maximum funding. Let m_{2007} and m_{2008} be the maximum grants in the two years. Let a_{it} be the average amount received by students not at the maximum. Let $y_{i,2007}$ and $y_{i,2008}$ be the average Pell funding for all recipients.

We observe the yearly maximum amounts, m_{2007} and m_{2008}, and the total yearly disbursement for each school, $y_{i,2007}$ and $y_{i,2008}$. We do not observe the average amount received by students not at the maximum, but we assume that the amounts are the same in the two years. Thus, we assume $a_{i,2007} = a_{i,2008} = a_i$. We also assume that the percentage of Pell recipients at a school who receive maximum funding is stable across the two years: $p_{i,2007} = p_{i,2008} = p_i$.

For each year we have the following equation:

$$m_{2007}p_i + a_i(1 - p_i) = y_{i2007}$$

$$m_{2008}p_i + a_i(1 - p_i) = y_{i2008}.$$

Thus when we combine them we can estimate p:

$$\hat{p}_i = (y_{i2008} - y_{i2007})/(m_{2008} - m_{2007}).$$

We bound $\hat{p}_i$ between 0 and 1.

References

Abadie, Alberto, Alexis Diamond, and Jens Hainmueller. 2010. "Synthetic Control Methods for Comparative Case Studies of Aggregate Interventions: Estimating the Effect of California's Tobacco Control Program." *Journal of the American Statistical Association* 105 (490): 493–505.

———. 2011. "Synth: An R Package for Synthetic Control Methods in Comparative Case Studies." *Journal of Statistical Software* 42 (13): 1–17.

Abowd, John M., Bryce E. Stephens, Lars Vilhuber, Fredrik Andersson, Kevin L. McKinney, Marc Roemer, and Simon Woodcock. 2009. "The LEHD Infrastructure Files and the Creation of the Quarterly Workforce Indicators." In *Producer Dynamics: New Evidence from Micro Data*, edited by Timothy Dunne, J. Bradford Jensen, and Mark J. Roberts, 149–230. Chicago: University of Chicago Press.

Aghion, Philippe, Matthias Dewatripont, Caroline Hoxby, Andreu Mas-Colell, and Andre Sapir. 2009. "The Governance and Performance of Research Universities: Evidence from Europe and the US" *Economic Policy* 25 (61): 7–59.

Ash, Michael, and Shantal Palacio. 2012. "Economic Impact of Investment in Public Higher Education in Massachusetts: Short-Run Employment Stimulus, Long-Run Public Returns." Unpublished Report, University of Massachusetts.

Bartik, Timothy J. 1991. "The Effects of Metropolitan Job Growth on the Size Distribution of Family Income." Upjohn Working Paper no. 91-06, W. E. Upjohn Institute for Employment Research.

Belkin, Douglas. 2012. "Tough Times for Colleges—and College Towns." *Wall Street Journal*, July 23, A2.

Carnegie Foundation for the Advancement of Teaching. 2001. *The Carnegie Classification of Institutions of Higher Education*. 2000 edition with a foreword by Lee S. Shulman. Menlo Park, CA: Carnegie Foundation for the Advancement of Teaching.

Commonfund Institute. 2003–2008. *Commonfund Benchmarks Study*. http://www.commonfund.org/ei/2012%20EI%20Level%20I%20Prereading%20Material/zDiscretionary%20Readings-Reference%20Materials/Commonfund%20Benchmarks%20Studies/2011%20Commonfund%20Benchmarks%20Study%20of%20Foundations.pdf.

Hansen, W. Lee, and Burton A. Weisbrod. 1969. "The Distribution of Costs and Direct Benefits of Public Higher Education: The Case of California." *Journal of Human Resources* 4 (2): 176–91.

Hoynes, H., D. L. Miller, and J. Schaller. 2012. "Who Suffers during Recessions?" *Journal of Economic Perspectives* 26 (3): 27–48.

Kelderman, Eric. 2009. "How Many Higher-Education Jobs Stimulus Saved Remains Unclear." *The Chronicle of Higher Education*, November 2. http://chronicle.com/article/How-Many-Higher-Education-Jobs/49025/.

National Association of College and University Business Officers and Commonfund Institute. 2009–2010. *NCSE: NACUBO–Commonfund Study of Endowments*. http://www.nacubo.org/Research/NACUBO-Commonfund_Study_of_Endowments.html.

National Institutes of Health. 2013. *Research Portfolio Online Reporting Tools (RePORT)*, 2004 to 2012. http://projectreporter.nih.gov/reporter.cfm.

National Science Foundation, National Center for Science and Engineering Statistics. 2012. *Higher Education Research and Development Survey*. 2003 to 2010. http://caspar.nsf.gov.

National Science Foundation, National Center for Science and Engineering Statistics. 2013. *Research.gov*, 2005 to 2012. http://www.research.gov.

Peltzman, Sam. 1973. "The Effect of Government Subsidies-in-Kind on Private Expenditures: The Case of Higher Education." *Journal of Political Economy* 81 (1): 1–27.

ScienceWorksForUS. 2010. "American Recovery and Reinvestment Act One Year Later: Recovery Act-Funded Research Advancing Science, Aiding the Economy and Contributing to America's Prosperous Future." http://www.scienceworksforus.org.

Turner, Leslie. 2012. "The Incidence of Student Financial Aid: Evidence from the Pell Grant Program." Working Paper, Department of Economics, Columbia University.

US Bureau of Labor Statistics. 2012. *The Employment Situation: July 2012*. Monthly News Release. http://www.bls.gov/news.release/archives/empsit_08032012.pdf.

US Department of Commerce. Bureau of the Census. Longitudinal Employer-Household Dynamics Program. 2013. *Quarterly Workforce Indicators*, 2003 to 2012. http://www.vrdc.cornell.edu/qwipu/.

US Department of Education, Institute of Education Sciences, National Center for Education Statistics. 2009. *2007–08 National Postsecondary Student Aid Study (NPSAS:08) Restricted-Use Data File*. Electronic data. November 2009 edition.

———. 2012. *Delta Cost Project Database 1987–2010*, 2000/1 to 2009/10 School Years. nces.ed.gov.

———. 2012. *Integrated Postsecondary Education Data System (IPEDS)*, 2000/1 to 2010/11 School Years. nces.ed.gov.

US Department of Education, Office of Federal Student Aid. 2013. *Federal Student Aid Data Center*, 2003/4 to 2011/12 School Years. http://studentaid.ed.gov/data-center.

Contributors

Eric Bettinger
Stanford School of Education
CERAS 522, 520 Galvez Mall
Stanford, CA 94305

Jeffrey R. Brown
Department of Finance
University of Illinois, Urbana-
Champaign
515 East Gregory Drive
Champaign, IL 61820

Keith C. Brown
Department of Finance, #B6600
McCombs School of Business
The University of Texas at Austin
Austin, TX 78712-1179

David Chambers
Cambridge Judge Business School
Trumpington Street
Cambridge CB2 1AG, United
   Kingdom

Stephen G. Dimmock
Division of Finance and Banking
Nanyang Technological University
Singapore 639798

Elroy Dimson
Cambridge Judge Business School
Trumpington Street
Cambridge CB2 1AG, United
   Kingdom

Michael F. Dinerstein
Department of Economics
Stanford University
579 Serra Mall
Stanford, CA 94305

Justin Foo
Cambridge Judge Business School
Trumpington Street
Cambridge CB2 1AG, United
   Kingdom

William N. Goetzmann
School of Management
Yale University
Box 208200
New Haven, CT 06520-8200

Caroline M. Hoxby
Department of Economics
Stanford University
Stanford, CA 94305

Bridget Terry Long
Harvard University
Graduate School of Education
Gutman Library 465
6 Appian Way
Cambridge, MA 02138

Jonathan Meer
Department of Economics
Texas A&M University
TAMU 4228
College Station, TX 77843

Sharon Oster
School of Management
Yale University
135 Prospect St.
New Haven, CT 06520

Cristian Ioan Tiu
366 Jacobs Management Center
Department of Finance and
    Managerial Economics
School of Management
University at Buffalo
Buffalo, NY 14260

Sarah E. Turner
Department of Economics
University of Virginia
249 Ruffner Hall
Charlottesville, VA 22903-2495

Pablo Villanueva
Department of Economics
Stanford University
579 Serra Mall
Stanford, CA 94305

Scott Weisbenner
Department of Finance
University of Illinois, Urbana-
    Champaign
340 Wohlers Hall, MC-706
1206 South Sixth Street
Champaign, IL 61820

Betsy Williams
Stanford School of Education
CERAS 520, 520 Galvez Mall
Stanford, CA 94305

Author Index

Subject Index